Daughters of the Nile

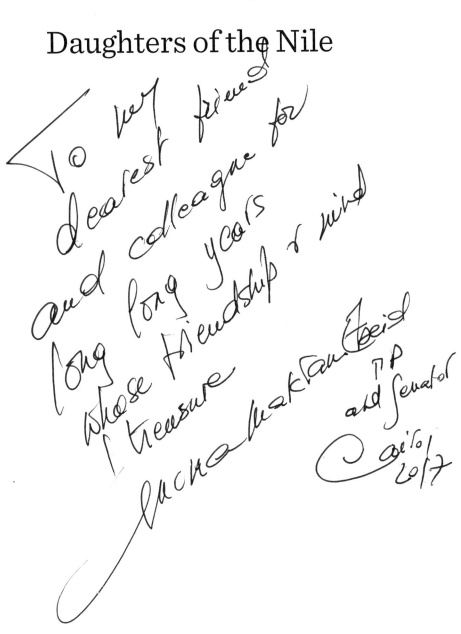

To my dearest friend
and colleague for
long long years
whose friendship I mind
I treasure

Mona Makram Ebeid
M P
and Senator

Cairo
2017

Daughters of the Nile:

Egyptian Women Changing Their World

Edited by

Samia I. Spencer

Preface by Melanne Verveer

Cambridge
Scholars
Publishing

Daughters of the Nile: Egyptian Women Changing Their World

Edited by Samia I. Spencer

This book first published 2016

Cambridge Scholars Publishing

Lady Stephenson Library, Newcastle upon Tyne, NE6 2PA, UK

British Library Cataloguing in Publication Data
A catalogue record for this book is available from the British Library

ISBN (10): 1-4438-9457-5
ISBN (13): 978-1-4438-9457-9

TABLE OF CONTENTS

ACKNOWLEDGMENT

SAMIA I. SPENCER

After two years of close collaboration with 37 outstanding compatriots, it is with great anticipation that all of us look forward to seeing in print the fruit of our amicable yet intensive labor. This book is the collective undertaking of many friends and acquaintances whose enthusiasm, imagination, and connections allowed the project to develop and come to life. Azza Heikal in Paris was first among those who encouraged me to pursue an idea that I casually mentioned to her in spring 2014. In fact, her book *Immeubles Heikal* was, no doubt, a source of inspiration. It related the childhood memories of neighbors of different backgrounds who grew up in Alexandria in buildings owned by her family and are now scattered around the world.

Having spent most of my academic life studying French women in the Enlightenment and beyond, it occurred to me to bring together women who share a common experience as Egyptians and now live in different parts of the globe, or who spent part of their lives beyond their country's borders before returning to settle in their native land. Azza encouraged me to invite mutual friends who would in turn recommend other acquaintances. Among the early supporters who expanded the circle are Magda El-Nokaly, Safaa Fouda, Mahassen Ghobrial, Ioanna Mavrides, Nermine Mitry, Faiza Shereen, and Abla Sherif. They made sure that the pioneers they introduced to me would respond positively to my invitation and follow through with their commitment. I owe them much appreciation for their eagerness and assistance.

An early contributor who must be singled out is Seheir Kansouh. From the start, she has been a firm believer in the importance of the project and has continued to provide staunch and unwavering commitment for more than two years. Through her prominent position at UNDP Cairo and her frequent travels around the globe, she has acquired an amazing professional network. Alone, she recruited nearly half the contributors, put me in touch with them, and convinced them to take part in a venture whose leader they did not know. Throughout the process, she remained steady and confident in its successful outcome, even when I had serious doubts. She stayed in close contact with me, sending frequent messages to check on daily progress and offering help to secure missing or delinquent materials. Her unparalleled care and warm friendship were matched only by her boundless generosity and hospitality. She came twice to visit me in Paris, and in June 2015, she opened her heart and her home in Cairo to more than a dozen contributors with whom I met, and who had the opportunity to get acquainted with each other. This book owes Seheir its depth, breadth, and much of its life.

I would also like to express my profound gratitude to the contributors without whom the book would not exist. They took precious time away from their demanding responsibilities to respond to my call and concentrate on an unexpected task, unrelated to their professional and family obligations. They had to focus carefully on the past and analyze their journeys in light of the present. They shared their life experiences openly and honestly, some actually revealing very personal and very intimate details. For many authors writing in English was a challenge because it is neither their native language nor one they handle with ease. Even among those who are fluent in English or were educated in English schools, the task was complicated because they may be skilled at drafting financial reports or scientific papers, but not at writing in a narrative style. I am grateful to all for agreeing to share their fascinating stories with a larger readership, and for allowing me to edit their submissions and rework their chapters.

Behind the scene, several friends and acquaintances provided substantial support and assistance. They include Mari and Terry Ley of Auburn University, who carefully read and provided insightful comments on part of the manuscript; Moez Doraid, Director of the Coordination Division at UN Women in New York, and Ahmad H. Fawzi, Director of UN Information Service in Geneva, for suggesting important contacts; Mona Makram Ebeid for putting me in touch with Melanne Verveer; Hedayat Islam and Fatenn Kanafani for recommending an illustration by Alaa Awad for the cover; and Jocelyn Mims of Hilton Head Island, South Carolina, and my son Sam Spencer of Champaign, Illinois, for finding a most unusual and creative way to deliver a hard copy of the full manuscript to Jack G. Shaheen.

At Cambridge Scholars Publishing, it was a real treat to work with Anthony Wright, Courtney Blades, Sophie Edminson and Amanda Millar. Their gentle cooperation, understanding, and advice were crucial in bringing to a happy conclusion a long and complicated project.

Last but not least, although the name of my husband, William A. Spencer, does not appear in the Table of Contents, his participation and technical skills were invaluable. He spent countless hours formatting texts and pages, embedding and touching up photos, checking proofs, preparing zip files, and communicating with the typesetter and the publisher: he can legitimately claim parenthood of the book.

Special thanks are also extended to readers who purchase the book. In addition to discovering the lives of extraordinary Egyptian women, they contribute to two critical charities. Profits from sale of the volume will be donated in equal parts to Marie Assaad's Association for the Protection of the Environment and Hanna Aboulghar's *Banati* ("my daughers" in Arabic)—an NGO that cares for girls in street situations. On behalf of those whose lives will be touched by the proceeds, heartfelt appreciation is hereby expressed to the generous benefactors.

Paris, August 2016

PREFACE

MELANNE VERVEER
FORMER US AMBASSADOR FOR GLOBAL WOMEN'S ISSUES

Daughters of the Nile: Egyptian Women Changing the World is a collection of autobiographical presentations by a cross-generational group of Egyptian professional women that provides an important example of the history of achievement of women in the Middle East—all the more important because of the negative stereotypes and ignorance that often color today's discourse. It also provides many inspiring lessons for life for women the world over. From time to time, I have had the privilege to get to know and work with women in Egypt, and I count among them many personal friends, including a few in this book. In my contacts with them, I was impressed with their indomitable spirit, their remarkable leadership in government, international organizations and civil society, and their deep desire to improve the quality of life in their country and beyond.

The women depicted in this book—from nonagenarians to Millennials—have strived to develop professionally, to balance work and family, not without difficulties, and to make a difference, often against pushback and adversity, including patriarchy and discrimination. As one determined author wrote: "I owe it to my gender to demonstrate that women can aspire to any profession and perform eminently." Some contributors have played key roles in advancing women's progress by overcoming barriers in the professions, and in society more broadly. Although a diverse group from different religious and social backgrounds and circumstances, they were, for the most part, privileged to attend good schools, and supported by families that valued education and had a profound influence on their development. One recounts that her father believed that it was more important to educate girls than boys because if a woman ever found herself in a difficult situation, she would be able to leave it and take care of herself. Another father urged his daughter to pursue challenging positions.

The autobiographies come from women who have succeeded in a range of professions, from engineering, medicine, diplomacy and banking, to politics, business, aerospace and academe. At a time when society recognizes the importance of attracting women to the STEM field (science, technology, engineering and math), it is crucial to note that many Egyptian women were engaged in pioneering work in these areas long before women in most other parts of the world. Their stories include their work as trailblazers in marketing, as the first women deans of engineering schools in the US and Canada, as central bankers, and as the first woman to sit on the board of the Egyptian Stock Exchange. They also include the story of two young sisters who with no previous experience in business established one of the most innovative independent bookstore chains in Egypt.

Success did not come easily for most. Some were widowed at a young age, lost a child, or were confronted with corruption, favoritism and bribery that not only curtailed their prospects but their country's as well. For example, one was ranked third worldwide in Taekwondo but not selected for the country's Olympic team because of favoritism in the sports federation. Later, she went on to become a Senator. An Egyptologist was told she could not do field work as a woman archeologist, living away from family and mingling with men. Discrimination, of course, was not confined to Egypt. When she moved to the United Kingdom, her professor told her: "I don't take girls on my team." Others described the bias in politics, but did not give up and remained committed to their goals. Those working to advance women's opportunities were aware that a large portion of breadwinners in their country are women, yet they are often discriminated against and marginalized—not unlike their sisters in many other nations. A mother of two small children whose husband had died at the age of forty was asked by a future employer in Europe how she would "manage with two young boys." Shocked by his query, she asked if he would ask the same question of a single dad, and turned down his offer.

Many contributors were personally affected by the political upheavals and conflicts in Egypt—whether the 1952 Revolution that brought Nasser to power, the 1956 Suez crisis, the 2011 Revolution, or the 2013 popular uprising that toppled the Muslim Brotherhood. In the 1960s, some were uprooted and left Egypt in order to escape the strife and destabilization. In these cases, their stories are written from Canada, the US and other places they call home today, but the influence of their Egyptian heritage remains profound. They also struggled, as women still do everywhere, to balance their professional lives with their family obligations. A few authors wrote about careers that seemed doomed, others had to put their plans on hold as they followed their husbands to new assignments, and others yet wrote about the challenges of being new moms. This is a theme that recurs in their personal recollections—a struggle well recognized by women in similar circumstances throughout the world.

As someone who has written about the way that women are increasingly using their growing power for purpose, I was inspired by the stories about commitment and the desire to change the world for the better. One contributor wrote: "The meaning of one's life is determined by the contribution one makes." Even in retirement, she felt that she still had a great deal to give. Another talked about the importance of paying back to one's country the debt one owes. There are countless examples of women engaged in mentoring, helping young Egyptians, assisting entrepreneurs, working across the religious divide to promote interfaith understanding and tolerance, creating and building women's organizations, developing a national strategy for micro-finance that could transform the lives of the poorest of the poor, working to end female genital mutilation, advocating for progressive legislation and gender equality—feminists who understood that feminism is liberation for all. I was taken by the example of those who were working to help the garbage collectors of Cairo, the Zabbaleen, enhance their skills and enable them to have a better life. Thanks to a contributor living overseas that community found a market abroad for the products that the women had learned to make.

It is also noteworthy that women were on the frontlines of the 2011 Revolution—Christians and Muslims side by side aspiring for a new Egypt. They were also active in working to end the rule of the Muslim Brotherhood shortly thereafter. Although the situation in Egypt and the region remains challenging, it is women like those whose stories are told in this book who will be responsible for building a better future for all.

Daughters of the Nile offers the wisdom derived from a purpose-filled life overcoming adversity and striving to reach one's potential. In the words of a successful Egyptian woman: "Set your goals high and work hard to follow your dream. You can make a difference. You can improve the world around you." This is great advice for readers everywhere—in Egypt, in the Middle East and beyond.

Washington, DC, August 2016

INTRODUCTION

SAMIA I. SPENCER

Egypt fascinates, perhaps more so than many other countries. Children in schools around the world learn about the pharaohs and fantasize about them. Visiting the pyramids, the Sphinx, Luxor, or admiring the innumerable Egyptian monuments scattered around the globe, Nefertiti in Berlin, Rosetta Stone in London, or King Tutankhamun in Cairo or in a roving exhibit are on many wishlists. The largest and most famous museums in the world, even modest ones, proudly flaunt and display their ancient Egyptian holdings. Fascination with Egypt is not limited to individuals and museums, it extends to entire countries, France is a case in point.[1] One needs to look no farther than Paris to see the evidence: an Egyptian obelisk standing in Place de la Concorde, a metro station entirely decorated in ancient Egyptian style, amazing collections exquisitely arranged in the Louvre, annual exhibits devoted to Egyptian art, history, culture, or new discoveries; not to mention invaluable collections of Egyptian artifacts at the Bibliothèque nationale, hundreds of publications celebrating Franco-Egyptian relations, and many associations promoting friendship between the two nations.[2]

The fascinating history, culture and mythology of ancient Egypt highlights its kings and queens, women and men portrayed full size side by side, as equal partners, each playing a different role and assuming distinct responsibilities. What about their descendants: contemporary Egyptian women? Who are they? What do we know about them? What is their status in society? What have they contributed to the development of their nation and the world? Other than Nefertiti or Cleopatra, most people would be hard pressed to mention an Egyptian woman by name, much less to speak of accomplishments, although Egypt's female artists, singers, and movie stars are celebrities in the Arab world. Where could one go for responses to the questions above? A Google search produced much material on women in ancient Egypt, with names and functions of its queens and goddesses, but little on modern times. Wikipedia, the popular source of information today, acknowledged the inadequacy of its two-part entry on Egyptian women, one titled "Women in Ancient Society," the other "Modern Status." The first ended with the rise to power of ancient queens, the second leaped forward a few millennia to open with statements on veiling and gender segregation, and quoted two dozen articles and reports detailing their regressive condition.

What happened to Egyptian women during the thousands of years separating these two parts? Wikipedia readers remain uninformed. Academic sources on Egyptian women were somewhat more fruitful, referencing publications on such topics as attitudes toward emancipation of women resulting from changing political situations (Gran 1977), the segregated patriarchal systems in the 18th and 19th centuries (Hatem 1986), the early twentieth-century feminist movement (Badran 1988), or contraception and fertility rates among different social classes (Mahler 1996). Once again, none addressed the professional achievements of women in contemporary society.[3]

Perhaps this is because in recent decades the media paid little or no attention to Egypt. Readers old enough may remember Sadat's historic visit to Israel in 1977 and the signing of the Camp David Peace Accords between the two countries; but then, women were not an issue. However, since 2011 and the ill-named "Arab Spring," images of Egyptian women have flooded TV screens and print media showing them among crowds of shouting demonstrators. Reporters have focused on their trials and tribulations, depicting them as victims of police violence, gang rape, virginity tests, honor killings, and female genital mutilation (FGM). No wonder people outside the region could only deplore their lot and pity their fate!

Listening to the news and reading the papers, I felt like Jack G. Shaheen who, for years, watched "hordes of TV Arabs parade across the screen. It was a disturbing experience, similar to walking into those mirrored rooms at amusement parks where all you see is distorted self-images."[4] The unflattering portrayal, and the biased and truncated reports are one of the main reasons for the undertaking of the present volume. Looking around me and speaking with friends, I saw different Egyptian women, unlike those shown in newspapers and on TV—a group the media clearly overlooks and ignores, intentionally or unintentionally. They are extraordinary pioneers and achievers whose successes and accomplishments have been recognized and honored by some of the highest national and international institutions and governments. Why are they not in the limelight? Why have the media—one of the most important sources of information, education, and enlightenment—disregarded these outstanding innovators and groundbreakers? Why has the news focused exclusively on a segment of the population that perpetuates arrogant colonialist attitudes, outdated stereotypes, and obsolete Orientalist clichés? I could not begin to comprehend their motives, nor did I try to analyze their intentions.[5]

Instead, it occurred to me that it was time to take a positive step to try to correct the flawed images, and remedy the grave omissions. When I started to discuss the idea with a handful of close friends, their response was not only enthusiastic, it was overwhelming. The project was born, and it would be simple. I would ask a few successful Egyptians to write their stories, in which they would recall their upbringing, the values instilled in them, and the principles that guided them throughout their lives. They would also speak of the difficulties they encountered as they rose to the top of their professions and mention the honors they received. The objective was three-pronged. The first aimed at attempting to break the monolithic stereotype of Egyptian women as loud, uneducated and uncivilized, dressed in loose unattractive garb, submissive, and dominated by men. The second sought to make the world aware of modern Egyptian champions who are improving the quality of life in the societies and broader environments in which they live and work. The third purpose, just as important as the first two, was to provide positive role models for new generations of women in Egypt and beyond, inspire them to set their goals very high despite the obstacles they may encounter along the way, and show them that the sky is not the limit.

These goals would be achieved by including a broad sample of women born in different parts of the country, raised in distinct family settings, currently at various stages of their careers, and practicing in diverse fields and occupations, both within and outside Egypt. Every effort was made by the friends who joined me in this initiative to identify professionals who had broken glass ceilings and paved the way for other women to follow. Initially, a sample of about 15 to 20 contributors was anticipated, but as the word spread and other achievers and pioneers were identified, the book ended with nearly twice as many chapters—a number both large and small. While it is greater than planned, it is also very small considering that the 38 achievers featured in this book represent only a fraction of the outstanding Egyptian women who are making the world a better place.

As chapters arrived and I began to edit them, I found many surprises and unanticipated results, including some similar and opposite experiences. The combined effort of the friends who helped to identify the contributors allowed diversity to be achieved on the geographical, educational, and professional levels. The book includes stories of Egyptian women of various national origins and religious backgrounds; some grew up in Egypt, while others were raised abroad where their diplomat fathers were posted. Nearly half the contributors currently live in Egypt; the other half reside in Canada, France, Switzerland, the UK, and the US. Some readers may wonder why these women and countries were selected. Simply because it is where we had friends and acquaintances who were able and willing to take part in the project.

Regarding the participants' education, it was expected and confirmed that all would be well educated, recipients of Bachelors, Masters, or PhD degrees. The proportion of doctorates—half the authors—was much higher than anticipated (20/38), but the findings revealed astonishing results that need to be emphasized and highlighted. Egyptians were the very first women to receive PhDs in Engineering in Canada, and to serve as Deans of Colleges of Engineering. They were among the first to obtain graduate degrees in Engineering in the US as well, where an Egyptian was the first woman to chair a Department of Aerospace Engineering—all having received the Bachelor of Engineering degree from Egyptian universities. Another Egyptian engineer broke more than one glass ceiling when she was elected President of the American Society of Mechanical Engineers (ASME). As an Egyptian-Canadian, she was the first person from outside the US to be elected to the top post of that international professional organization of more than 130 000 mostly male members, and the first from the Middle East. Evidently, Egyptian women were studying Engineering in Egypt in the late1960s and early1970s, far ahead of women in some of the most developed nations in the world.

It is not only in engineering that our compatriots broke glass ceilings and achieved records. For example, one contributor was the first woman to serve as Deputy Secretary General at the World Council of Churches in Geneva; another was the first African inducted into the Taekwondo Hall of Fame and the youngest ever appointed to the Egyptian Senate; and yet another was the youngest in the world to reach the position of sub-governor of the central bank of her nation at age 36, before being recruited by the International Monetary Fund (IMF) in Washington, DC. The only person to have concluded the sale of a Greek bank during the recent Greek financial crisis through a subsidiary in Egypt is one of our authors. "The most beautiful voice on New York radio" belongs to an Egyptian lady, and the first Chair of the International Committee on the Right of the Child at the Center for Human Rights in Geneva is a contributor to this book. The 2014 Stars Award for Child Protection in the Middle East and North Africa—selected from 277 competitors and awarded in London by President Bill Clinton—went to an NGO founded by a fellow citizen. Likewise, the first person to obtain a US Department of Defense contract for her employer to refurbish the equipment of military laboratories in

Belarus was an Egyptian woman. Indeed, our contemporaries are worthy of their predecessors, the brilliant queens and goddesses of ancient Egypt.

The authors' professional accomplishments and successes were achieved in nearly all professions: academe, the arts, banking, development, diplomacy, economics, engineering, entrepreneurship, finance, government, medicine, public relations, science and technology, social services, sports, international relations, and international organizations, all reaching the zenith in their respective fields. Five in the group were recognized in 2016 among "the 50 Most Influential Women in the Egyptian Economy." Despite the differences in personalities, conditions, and circumstances, all share certain values: they are committed and passionate about their professions, have an unflinching belief in the importance of education and hard work, and are armed with staunch determination to overcome the obstacles that stand between them and their dreams.

For many, reaching their goals was excruciatingly difficult, whether for tragic family reasons or strict professional rules. Some lost their fathers or spouses along the way and unexpectedly found themselves assuming responsibility for younger siblings or children. A contributor who became a widow at a very young age still vividly remembered the extent of her distress more than twenty years after the passing of her partner. She used powerful words to describe her grief: "I wished I were Indian to be cremated with my husband." Several cases also stand out as exceptionally hard, for other reasons. How could a woman diplomat married to a career diplomat achieve her professional goals and preserve their family life, while her husband is posted abroad and Egypt prohibits the employment of husband and wife in the same embassy? For this determined lady, it took tenacity and resolve to reach the top of her profession. These were also the qualities that allowed two contributors to overcome various family and personal circumstances, and pursue doctoral studies despite obstacles and interruptions. A photo shows one of them in cap and gown surrounded by her grown-up children, the other received the PhD the same day her daughter graduated from high school. Another case relates to the strict weight regulations of a young athlete's sport. She had to starve herself and go to bed crying out of hunger—the price to pay to achieve her dream.

Because of the large age spread among the contributors—the oldest, in her mid-90s, was assisted by her granddaughter in the drafting of her chapter, and the youngest is in her late 20s—the changing history and culture of Egypt since the mid-twentieth century appears in the background between the lines, although one author sought to provide a clearer and more elaborate backdrop. Several participants, who came of age in the 1960s, during the dark socialist regime and dire economic conditions under President Nasser, left their native land in search of a brighter future elsewhere. On the other hand, those among a younger generation, who started their careers under President Sadat's "open door" policies, found greater potential in their own nation. Several authors spent part of their early years in Alexandria, a cosmopolitan town unlike any other until the late 1950s/early 1960s. Readers will no doubt notice some overlap in their chapters, as they all long for a liberal, tolerant, broadminded, and urbane society, and a charming and elegant city, both of which exist only in our memories today.

Forgotten or unknown habits, practices, and historical events occurring in the mid/late twentieth century, in both Egypt and other parts of the globe, are also discussed in the 37 stories. For example, many readers may not know that European women went to Egypt to seek employment as nannies in upper-class Egyptian families, or that a Marxist Revolution overthrew the Emperor of Ethiopia. Discrimination and affirmative action were addressed in astonishing ways in the US Deep South, while Switzerland did not allow foreign students to be accompanied by their spouses and children. A Canadian scientific research center was built with no ladies' restrooms because no women were ever expected to work there. There was a time before cell phones when international calls required advance reservation for specific time and duration, with no guarantee they would go through.

For more than half the participants who made their careers either entirely or partially outside Egypt, the question of identity was crucial. For some, the transition to another country and culture was fairly smooth, as they were welcomed in the new homeland. Others endured discrimination, loneliness, and conditions to which it was hard to adapt. After 9/11, with increased hostility toward Arabs and Muslims, some among those who were well integrated in distant countries were disquieted and shamed, although they could not be blamed for the heinous crime. They felt compelled to act, to break the stereotype of the Arab and Muslim as a terrorist, and built bridges between the different cultures and religions, in order to create a better informed and more tolerant environment. For their efforts to improve the quality of life in their community, they were later recognized and honored.

Although Egyptian women are the main focus of this book, Egyptian men also came out as winners, breaking the stereotype of the Middle-Eastern sexist macho male. Many successful women credited their achievements to their loving and supporting fathers or husbands who inspired them, encouraged them, and stood by them as they reached their full potential. In some cases, the exceptional attitudes of these Egyptians were far more progressive than those of most males, whether in the East or the West. For example, an Egyptian husband in the late 1960s offered to keep and care for a six-month-old baby so that his wife could complete medical training in a different part of the country. Another sacrificed his own career so that his partner could pursue her own educational and professional goals. These extraordinary Egyptian men deserve to be applauded and recognized, even as they rest in their graves today.

For all the daughters of the Nile in this sample, Egypt is deeply rooted in their hearts. A few who made their career in a different country have chosen to spend their golden years in their birthplace; those who live abroad are committed to serve their native land in one way or another; and those who continue to sip from the Nile are devoted to improving the quality of life for their fellow citizens. This overview of their accomplishments aims to whet the curiosity of readers as they begin to explore the fascinating stories of some extraordinary women. It is my hope that this modest initiative will inspire other writers, researchers, and scholars to pursue the path it has opened, for there are many more treasures to unearth, many more issues to investigate, and many more pioneers to spotlight.

Paris, May 2016

Notes

[1] Among the many books on Franco-Egyptian relations, Robert Solé's *L'Egypte passion française* (Paris: Éditions du Seuil, 1997) remains one of the most comprehensive and best documented.

[2] For more information on Egyptian artifacts held by various French institutions, see Azza Heikal's chapter (193-202).

[3] References for the articles cited above are the following: Judith Gran, "Impact of World Market on Egyptian Women," *Middle East Research and Information Project* 58 (June 1977): 3-7; Mervat Hatem, "The Politics of Sexuality and Gender in Segregated Patriarchal Sytems," *Feminist Studies* 12.2 (1986): 256-74; Margot Badran, "The Feminist Vision in the Writing of Three Turn-of-the-Century Egyptian Women," *Bulletin (British Society for Middle-Eastern Studies)* 15.1-2 (1988): 11-20; K. Mahler, "Lower Egyptian Fertility Linked to Later Marriage, Increased Method Use," *International Family Planning Perspectives* 22.4 (1996): 179-81.

[4] Jack G. Shaheen, *The TV Arab* (Bowling Green, Ohio: Bowling Green University Popular Press, 1984), 4. In his outstanding analysis of Arabs in the media, Shaheen's attention is focused on Arab men, there is not much on women; in fact, "women" is not even an entry in the Index.

[5] For studies on the biased stereotypical representation of Arabs in US popular culture, see also Jack G. Shaheen's *Reel Bad Arabs. How Hollywood Vilifies a People* (New York: The Olive Branch Press, 2001), and *Guilty. Hollywood's Verdict on Arabs after 9/11* (New York: The Olive Branch Press, 2008). Noha Mellor has written extensively on Arab media and Arab identity. Among others, see *The Making of Arab News* (Lanham, PA: Rowman & Littlefield, 2005); *Modern Arab Journalism* (Edinburgh: Edinburgh University Press, 2007); or *The Egyptian Dream: Egyptian National Identity and Uprising* (Edinburgh: Edinburgh University Press, 2015).

BETWEEN EGYPT AND SWEDEN: A PASSION FOR IMPROVING THE LIVES OF EGYPTIAN CHILDREN

HANNA ABOULGHAR

I was born in 1968, in the small town of Alvesta in southern Sweden, to a Swedish mother and an Egyptian father. Egypt had just lost the 1967 war against Israel, and my parents thought it would be safer for my mother to give birth in her hometown. At six-months, she took me to Egypt where I have lived ever since.

The older child, Hanna, with her parents Kristina and Dr. Mohamed Aboulghar, and her younger sister Mona, in the garden of their Alvesta Home, summer 1971

Growing up in Egypt, in a home with two very different cultures greatly affected my perspective and world views. The Swedish model of social justice that seeks to achieve equality and fair chance for all makes me particularly sensitive to social injustice and inequality in Egypt. At the same time, I identify myself as Egyptian, and appreciate the warmth of Egyptian culture and its close social networks that bond people together. This makes it hard to be angry or unaccepting of my country's flaws; rather, it has the effect of making me hold tighter to my Egyptianess.

I was educated in a British-Egyptian school that caters mostly to upper middle-class children. At that time, it was one of the best in Egypt, but in retrospect its curriculum appears limited and outdated. I went on to get my General Certificate of Education (GCE), which offered a taste of a more vibrant educational model, and it was also a way to avoid the rigid Egyptian high school examination. In 1986, I entered medical school at Cairo University, my dream since I was 8-years old. There, too, the system was archaic, based mostly on knowledge by rote, with little emphasis on practice or clinical skills. The student body was polarized, divided into groups defined by religion and socio-economic status. The general atmosphere exuded competitiveness and tension. Except for the Muslim Brothers and a few Socialists, politics had limited place on campus.

Upon graduating five years later, I was offered a three-year residency in the Department of Pediatrics at the Cairo University Hospital. The first year was excruciating, as newcomers were in charge of 40 patients as well as management of the departmental personnel, with minimal input from their seniors. The daunting task was frustrating, in light of our limited experience and skills. At the end of the residency, Master's degree in hand, I joined the Neonatology Department at the Faculty of Medicine. By then, I was married and the mother of two beautiful daughters, and also pursuing doctoral studies that were successfully completed in 2000. Deeply involved in motherhood with kids in kindergarten, having started a private practice, I should have been comfortably ensconced in uneventful routine—but that was not going to be.

The Middle East was in turmoil. Israeli forces had attacked the West Bank, surrounded Yasser Arafat's headquarters, and cut off his power. The Arab world was raging from yet another humiliating slap on the face, felt by many as a personal affront. It took then-President Hosni Mubarak over a week to come out with a meek response. The University was storming with infuriated students, and I attended my first ever demonstration. Anger at the international injustice toward the Palestinians was mixed with resentment at the corrupt Egyptian regime. I believe that the first spark that led to Egypt's 2011 Revolution may have been ignited in 2001.

It is around that time that I began to notice the many children who lived on the streets of Cairo, with or without parents. The difference between their situations and the privileged lives of my daughters started to make me feel uncomfortable, even guilty. That sentiment intensified when I read about a young boy who went to sleep under a truck, seeking warmth on a cold winter night; the next morning he was ran over when the driver moved the vehicle. I had the urge to do something to help, and looked for people or organizations that could support my efforts. There was only one non-government organization (NGO) that worked with children in street situations (CSS); it was founded by an Englishman and run by an Egyptian Board. Together, we established the first shelter for girls in street situations, in the poor Cairo neighborhood of Imbaba.

In 2005, I was elected to the Board of the NGO, and served for three years until it split. The Executive Manager sought to control the NGO and, through her powerful connections at the Ministry of Social Affairs, toppled the Board and took charge with some of her allies. For me, it was a moment of personal defeat to see the Center that I had toiled untiringly to develop, and in which my family had strongly believed to the extent of buying the building, taken over by people I did not trust. Simultaneously, similar situations were unfolding at both the University and the private hospital where I worked. A new generation of young and energetic people, hoping to change a stifled system that had no room for reform or innovation, was blocked by rigid and recalcitrant elders. The political landscape was turbulent as well, insurgency was ignited by *Kefaya* (an Arabic word meaning "enough")—a resistance movement seeking to counter Mubarak's plan to hand over Egypt to his son and his business friends. On campus, the "9th of March" was a group of faculty defending academic freedom. These were only two among many that opposed the Mubarak regime. Police and security used all means at their disposal to subdue the protestors, and, to a great extent, they succeeded. For the first time in my life, I felt as though Egypt was turning its back on me.

In the meantime, I had connected with Samih Sawiris, a prominent businessman who offered to build a large shelter for girls in the Cairo suburb "6th of October" (so named after the date of Egypt's triumph in the 1973 war against Israel). He asked me to see the project through in collaboration with his mother, Yousriya Loza Sawiris, a longstanding philanthropist who presided over another charitable organization. Within a year, *Banati* Foundation was established in 2010 as an independent entity ("Banati" is an Arabic word meaning "my daughters"). We laid out the plans for the building and management, and developed a method to deal with girls in street situation by working with the few people who had experience in that field. Among the 40,000 or so active Egyptian NGOs, only ten worked with CSS, and only two had shelters for girls.

One of my closest and most reliable associates is Hind Samy, the bravest woman I know. She has dedicated her life to street girls, doing whatever it takes to save them: visiting and talking with them, supporting them emotionally, mediating between them and their parents, taking them to the hospital, and acting as the mothers they never had. Hind has also cared for some who were wounded from assault or rape; identified bodies of girls killed on the street; helped teenage mothers to deliver their babies; and, on some of these occasions, she was interrogated by the police. Although she comes from a traditional family, Hind is open-minded and compassionate, and treats these girls who are generally scorned by Egyptian society at large with respect, neither condemning nor judging their decisions or promiscuity. A creative person, she always manages to find solutions for their problems; fortunately, her family firmly believes in her mission, often lending a helping hand.

Another person who has dedicated his life to the cause is Abdelsamie Labib, the shelter manager and the father figure for the girls. Contrary to Hind, he is traditional and conservative, even authoritarian at time; yet, he manages to inspire safety and security. Abdelsamie is loved and respected by the girls and their families. Over the years, he and I have developed a bond of trust and understanding that bypasses our different backgrounds and mentalities.

At Banati, there are three types of intervention. One is the Reception Center where Hind and her outreach team are based. It is located in an old part of the city, and open weekdays 9 AM to 5 PM. The mobile unit of the Center is equipped with a fridge for food storage, an examination bed for the nurse, and foldable tables and chairs to be used in parks and recreation areas for children's activities. When Hind and her team go out in the mobile unit, they target populous areas, and circulate in groups of two, always mixed gender for safety. They have maps showing where they are likely to encounter children in street situations (CSS). They approach the girls, talk with them, and offer them a sandwich or a cup of tea. Generally, the youngsters accept, but reveal very little information about themselves. It takes many visits and long conversations before they open up and trust the social worker enough to agree to go to the Banati Reception Center. There, they meet the rest of the team, and receive hot meals, clothes, bath, and medical care when needed; but more importantly, they are surrounded with love and affection.

Over the past five years, a Psychological Awareness and Intervention Protocol has been developed by our psychologists and psychiatrists in collaboration with UNICEF. Banati is proud to have achieved this project, which serves as a blueprint for other NGOs invested with similar missions. The process starts with social workers discreetly investigating how the girls ended up on the street. Once authorized by the girls, social workers visit the parents or guardians, an undertaking usually requiring travel to distant places or dangerous areas of Cairo, Alexandria, or beyond. The attempted visits are often in vain since girls sometimes provide incorrect information, even after lengthy sessions with the team. When a family is contacted, and its socio-economic situation determined, a written report is submitted, in which are outlined the reasons for the child's escape from home. The most frequent cause is abuse, physical, sexual or mental; in some cases, it is due to a couple's breakup, with each parent forming a new family, neither of which is interested in the offspring from a previous marriage. Most victims come from very poor families. Whenever possible and safe, we try to reunite daughters with parents, and follow-up on them, to make sure no harm is done. We provide psychological support to the families, and, where appropriate, we put them in touch with an NGO that provides micro loans to help them start their own small business. In some cases, we have even succeeded in arranging basic housing.

Some may argue that the work of the Reception Center is unimportant since most children go back to the street at the end of the day. This brings up the question of defining importance and success. Should they be measured only when a girl is fully reintegrated into her family or housed in a shelter? If that were the case, worldwide statistics point to a success rate of about 30%. My argument, however, is that children who frequent a Reception Center are less likely to engage in violence or criminal activity, and more inclined to stay safe and healthy, even when they remain on the street. I strongly believe that such factors should be taken into consideration when evaluating our achievements.

An important group that we treat—approximately 60% of the children in the Haram City Shelter located near the pyramids ("Haram" is an Arabic word meaning pyramid),—consists of second-generation street children, born to girls who became pregnant on the street, resulting from rape, prostitution or sexual promiscuity. Many do not know who fathered the child, and are at great risk of death, illness, accidents and malnutrition on the street. We usually follow the girls during pregnancy, and invite them to visit the Shelter. Once they feel comfortable enough, we suggest they remain permanently in the Shelter, with an open-door policy allowing for visitors and permission to leave, as long as they notify us.

The Haram City Banati Shelter was donated by Samih Sawiris, our principal sponsor. The Sawiris Foundation covers some of the running costs for both the Reception Center and the Shelter through renewable yearly donations. At Haram City, girls live in rooms of eight, each has her own bed, and a closet for her personal effects. The rooms are arranged in pairs, with a living room and a balcony in-between, the idea being to raise the girls as a family of 16 members of varying ages who can look after each other. There is a caregiver in each room; unfortunately, some stay only for a few months or a couple of years before returning to their village. Their departure can be devastating for the children. It is the main reason for emphasizing bonding between the children, and with the more permanent staff members, such as Hind and Abdelsamie.

Activities at the Shelter are designed and aim for rehabilitation. We deal with children who suffer from various types of trauma, including bereavement, anxiety, hyperactivity, addiction, post-traumatic stress disorder, and attention deficit, among others. They have often been victim or witness to repeated physical and sexual abuse. Those who have been on the street for longer periods are impervious to discipline. It is difficult to convince them to follow a daily time routine of sleep, meals and personal hygiene, or to give up smoking, sexual habits, and glue sniffing. The rehabilitation workshops offer a variety of arts and crafts, pottery, gardening, animation, music, singing, sewing, and origami. We are particularly gratified when the girls are publicly recognized and rewarded for their achievements. For example, one of ours won First Place for Photography in *The National Geographic* Egypt Competition in 2011; our band was repeatedly invited to perform at the Cairo Opera House; and, in 2015, Banati participated in the International Tournament for Children at Risk in Amsterdam.

All rescued children receive an education appropriate for their situation. Those below school age go to one of our four nurseries, one of which is a Montessori facility. Other students go to local public or experimental schools. In-house literacy classes are offered for those without legal papers who cannot attend regular school until they receive official documents. A community school set up by a nearby sister NGO also accommodates some of our girls. Our educational system includes a creative learning program called *Sawaseya* (an Arabic word meaning "equality and sharing"), designed to teach science through experimentation. It is particularly popular among children from other schools, as we often invite students from local and international institutions to visit, in order to bridge the gap between the girls and the outside world. Throughout the year, we take them on daytrips to various sites, and during the summer they spend a week at the beach, thus providing an opportunity to strengthen the bond among them and with staff members.

At the Imbaba Center, which we managed to recover after the attempted takeover, we now have an intermediate care unit that treats girls with severe psychological disorders who need to be closely followed for six to twelve months. They receive intensive mental health therapy, rehabilitation, and medication, if necessary. There, the rules are not as strictly enforced as they are in the other two facilities, and the education program is somewhat more relaxed.

In 2007, I succeeded in convincing the Center for Social and Preventive Medicine at Cairo University to establish a clinic for CSS called *Elbasma* (an Arabic word meaning "the smile"). Its staff has been trained in the management of physical and mental ailments of CSS by *Médecins du Monde* (Doctors of the World), a well-known French medical NGO. So far, the clinic has served more than 3000 children picked up directly from the street, or through organizations that work with them. Examination, laboratory tests, radiological investigations, referrals to specialized clinics, even surgeries, all are done at the University Hospital at no charge. The staff is trained to treat the children gently and with affection, in order to counter their ingrained fear of violence and mistreatment.

Egyptian society continues to have a negative image of CSS, although that view has recently started to change, thanks in large part to effective awareness campaigns by NGOs dealing with street children. Legislation concerning the rights of these children to legal papers, a safe environment and protection from abusive caregivers still hinders our work, especially in cases where parents are the source of danger. The Egyptian Child Law passed in 2007 has yet to be implemented, because the application guidelines have not been issued. There is still profound resistance to the idea that the State should have the ultimate word in protecting children, even from their parents, if necessary.

After the 2011 Revolution, Egyptians believed they had an opportunity to effect much-needed change in their country; as evidenced by demonstrators in Tahrir Square boasting hope and optimism. As for me, I attended the first meeting of the Egyptian Social Democratic Party on March 18 of that year. A tremendous event, it formally announced the creation of this new party, in which I was named to the Executive and Political Committees. It looked as if, indeed, a better future was about to take place, and people flocked to be part of a new dawn.

In the following year, our Party participated in the debates on the Constitution proposed by the Muslim Brotherhood, but our voice was ignored. For those of us committed to children's rights, it was a catastrophic setback. The Constitution legalized child marriage and child labor, it did not set an age to define childhood, and refused to criminalize human trafficking. In early 2013, the Muslim Brothers rushed to approve it overnight, despite strong opposition from our Party, and from Banati and other NGOs. Collectively, we then started a major campaign to denounce the ill-conceived document, and to raise awareness about its adverse consequences. Fortunately, the popular uprising of June 30, 2013, followed by the ousting of President Muhammed Morsi and the Muslim Brotherhood, led to the drafting of a new and more balanced Constitution. This time intellectuals, artists, activists, and various members of civil society joined seasoned political leaders in a "Panel of Fifty," in charge of the project. Our Party contributed two members, including Professor Hoda El-Sadda, Chair of the Rights and Freedom Committee, and my father, Dr. Mohamed Aboulghar, who drew up the part on children's rights. Thanks to NGOs like Banati and others, and with support from international organizations, including UNICEF, the new Constitution guarantees full protection to minors. At this point, what is needed are the application guidelines for implementation of the law.

Witnessing Banati grow and develop is a dream come true. At this writing, 220 girls live permanently in the Shelter, all receive a decent education, all are happy and optimistic, as they look toward a better future filled with opportunities.

Hanna in the back row with a big smile, with Banati girls at a Ramadan iftar, July 2015

Furthermore, the Reception Center serves an average of 50 children per day, and 12 girls are currently treated at the Imbaba facility. The Banati Board of Trustees includes dedicated professionals from diverse backgrounds who generously donate their time and expertise. Yousriya Loza Sawiris, the former Chair of the Board, continues her fundraising efforts; Mona Fayek, an expert in social development, reviews the proposals and reports; Iman Iskander, a Professor at Cairo University, develops and oversees the educational programs; Sahar El-Sallab, a leading banker and businesswoman (featured in the present book), is the Treasurer; and Samy Yacoub, a seasoned specialist in Management and Human Resources, is in charge of policies and bylaws.

In 2014, Banati applied for the Stars Award for Child Protection in the Middle East North Africa (MENA) Region. It was the youngest of 277 applicants for the grand prize. Following an elaborate application process, a Committee visited our facilities, and met with the girls and staff members. Over a period of several months, they conducted a complete review of our services, policies, management, and financial reports. December 1, 2014, was undoubtedly one of the happiest days of my life: Banati was announced the winner of the Stars Award! A few weeks later, I accompanied Rania Fahmy, then-Executive Director of Banati, to London, where she received two checks from President Bill Clinton: one in the amount of $ 100 000 for Banati, and another for $ 20 000 for staff training. Also present on stage was Amr Al-Dabbagh, Founder of the London-based Stars Foundation, the global philanthropic arm of the Al-Dabbagh Group. The funds are expected to be released in early 2016, after a lengthy security check and approval by the Ministry of Social Solidarity. The main priority will be to expand our services, and to reach our capacity to accommodate 250 girls.

In May 2016, Banati was recognized by another institution, the Islamic Development Bank. It was awarded the IDB Prize for NGOs in the category "Women's Role in Development." I had the honor of representing Banati at the opening ceremony of the 41st IDB Annual Congress in Jakarta, Indonesia, and received the Prize form the Vice President of Indonesia and the President of IDB.

These exciting moments were the culmination of years of hard labor, though not the end of the journey. As I look back at the past 15 years, I recall both achievements and frustrations, and overall I feel privileged to have had the opportunity to collaborate with amazing people, and to have improved thousands of lives and inspired hope. Every time I visit Banati, it feels like a breath of fresh air in the turbulent life of Cairo, and each hug from a smiling girl means a world to me!

Rania Fahmy, then-Banati Executive Director, with former US President Bill Clinton (L), and Amr Al Dabbagh, London, December 2014

Cairo, May 2016

CAN A MISFIT BRING ABOUT CHANGE?

TYSEER ABOULNASR

As a recently appointed Dean of Engineering at the University of Ottawa, and a relatively young woman, I sat at a small restaurant in awe of my meeting with one of the top high-tech executives in Canada's Silicon Valley. I had sent him an impassionate invitation to speak at the students' award ceremony, but he asked to meet me first before deciding. I sat wondering how I was going to fill the conversation over lunch with a man I barely knew, let alone impress him enough so he would accept the invitation. As the waiter left with our order, the executive looked me in the eyes and calmly asked: "How did you get to be the way you are?" I will never forget him or his question. Indeed, how did I get to be the way I am?

Everyone who knows my mother and me says the apple does not fall far from the tree, or as the Arabic saying goes, a girl turns out to be just like her mother. In many ways, I am proud to be compared to my mother. In the 1930s, when upper-class Egyptian women did not work outside the home, she challenged every norm: travelling alone to study in the UK, marrying late in life, taking on three step-children to raise, in addition to three of her own, and all the while holding a 24/7 position as a powerful and engaged school principal. She was a religious woman practicing what might be called "practical religion." For her, helping those in need was more important than perfecting the rituals of prayer. She firmly believed that what one does on a daily basis and how it is done is religion in action. As an educator, she taught me that teachers have a sacred responsibility— a lesson that has stayed with me ever since. Theirs is not just about teaching a subject matter well; rather, it is about shaping the minds of students. She instilled in me the meaning of a classical Arabic verse: "Stand up and show respect for the teacher, for a teacher comes close to being a messenger of God."

This deep sense of commitment has guided me throughout my life. I believe that whatever abilities people have, they must be held accountable for the way they use them, and for the impact they leave behind. In my family, our duty as kids was to succeed in school, and all of us worked hard to fulfill that responsibility. While I loved to study, it was also an easy way for me to get out of chores I hated. Fortunately, I was blessed with an ability to understand and assimilate the material I learned, and, more importantly, I loved to explain it to others. This led to deepening my own understanding of the subject matters, and prepared me for a career as a university professor.

My early education was in a girls' school run by British nuns. They ingrained in us a strong sense of discipline, as well as the universal values of humanity. From that time on, I learned to live being "different": as an Egyptian Muslim girl in a British Catholic seminary, among mostly Coptic Christian classmates, in a majority Muslim country. In other words, I grew up in an environment where diversity was the norm. Looking back, I credit these conditions for planting the seed of my firm belief in respecting the rights of "the other." Upon graduating from high school, I made what was then an unusual decision. Against everyone's advice, I passed up the opportunity to study medicine, the most highly regarded profession, to become an engineer. My family was liberal enough to allow us free choice. A large part of my decision was based on the fact that I did not want to be responsible for someone else's life. Little did I know that, as Dean of Engineering, I would end up having the responsibilities I tried to evade.

I followed the traditional path to an academic career: a Bachelor's degree, followed by an appointment to the first step on the tenure track at Cairo University's Faculty of Engineering. My nomination was strictly based on my high grades and top ranking among my classmates; in 1976, gender was a non-issue at the Faculty of Engineering in Cairo. This was the case throughout my five years as an undergraduate, and one year as a teaching assistant in upper-division courses. Then, I was off to Canada with a scholarship from Queen's University to work on my Master's and PhD. It was then, and only then, that—to my utter surprise—being a woman in engineering became an issue, and I realized that others regarded me as "unique," or as a "pioneer." This was 1977, less than 40 years ago. I vividly recall a conversation with a nurse during my first visit to a family doctor. Preparing to take my blood pressure, she asked the young newcomer to Canada that I was what she was doing at Queen's. "I am a graduate student," I replied. "In what subject?" she inquired. Hearing "Electrical Engineering," she stepped back and said: "Why on earth would you do a thing like that?" It was then that I realized that what was ordinary for me in Egypt was odd to some in Canada. Being a graduate student in Engineering became a secret to be shared only with close friends.

Years later, pregnant with my second child, I was appointed Assistant Professor of Engineering at the University of Ottawa. While discussing the offer, the Dean of the Faculty of Engineering confided: "We hope that by learning to respect you, students will also develop higher regard for their mothers, sisters, wives, and girlfriends." What? I thought I was hired to teach Engineering, not to serve as a social psychologist, or inspire respect for women! Did he really expect me to change the students' minds? My mother was right, indeed! Whether I liked it or not, I soon became "the" female Engineering Professor, a sample of one, the only one the students encountered. Curious students would come knocking on my door for nothing else but to take a look at "the" female professor. More gutsy than most, one took a look at me and exclaimed: "Wow! Not only are you a woman, you are brown, and cover your hair!" Notwithstanding, I learned to connect with these curious and generally difficult-to-please young people, and deeply cherished them. Over time, they did not care whether I was female, brown, Arab, or Muslim, as long as they understood the material I taught them, enjoyed the courses, and were treated fairly and respectfully. It was gratifying to know that I was not the only one to be satisfied with my teaching, and with the close relationships I built with both graduates and undergraduates.

A few years later, one day the Dean asked to see me. Nervous, I went to the meeting wondering what I might have done wrong, only to hear a surprising proposal. He asked if I would accept the position of Associate Dean for Academic Affairs, in charge of all undergraduate matters. As typical of many professional women, deep inside I was not convinced that I was good enough for such a responsibility. I bluntly asked for his motives: was I being considered just because he wanted "a woman" in a leadership position? My question to this man who really supported women engineers must have taken him by surprise, and put him on the defensive. He assured me that his decision was solely based on the conviction that I was the best qualified person for the job. Today, years later, I must admit that his confidence in me was undoubtedly greater than my own. And thus, I took the first step into academic administration.

At that point, it dawned on me that as "different" as I was, I had managed reasonably well, completely oblivious to the fact that I did not fit the typical mold of an engineering professor. I probably succeeded better than I ever anticipated because I was too busy to spend time dwelling on the matter. My years as Associate Dean were fulfilling and enjoyable. I was responsible for shaping the curriculum, setting the standards, providing the students with the support they needed to meet or exceed the criteria, as well as advising them should they no longer be eligible for an

Engineering degree. Unfortunately, this satisfying mandate did not last long. The Dean moved on, and I was asked to serve as Acting Dean for six months, until the permanent position would be filled: the six months turned into six years.

Generally speaking, I was warmly welcomed as a young female dean, despite my Arab and Muslim origin. It was a novelty in Canada, a reason for the University of Ottawa to boast its progressive policies, and its promotion of women and minorities. However, past the initial excitement, faculty had to do business with a person who had a different way of getting things done. For those used to dealing with men in a certain "manly" way, it was confusing, and at times problematic. Two situations come to mind. In one case, after an especially intense executive meeting with the department heads, one of them was particularly aggressive, making preposterous comments. I was alone responding to him, although most of those in attendance agreed with my position. After the meeting, another head quietly said to me: "He would have never dared to say such things if you were a man. I am sorry that I could not speak up, we go back many, many years." This was my introduction to the reality of the "good old boys' network." On a more positive side, I recall the second incident that occurred as I addressed a Faculty Assembly of professors and staff. After discussing the usual issues of budget and enrollment, I spoke of the values and principles that should guide us, ending my remarks with comments on the importance of treating each other with dignity, courtesy, and respect. I reminded the audience that the use of simple phrases such as "please," "thank you," or "I am sorry" can contribute to a more amiable and collegial environment. The room went silent; clearly, no one expected the Dean to give a "motherly lecture." After the Assembly, the Founding Dean of the Faculty, the man who had hired me 15 years earlier, was highly supportive. He told me: "No man could have ever spoken like that. It needed to be said, and you said it. Thank you." While men were ambivalent about my administrative approach, women's rights advocates had a more determined opinion of me. Because I was not as focused on increasing the enrollment of women in engineering as I was on making the environment more hospitable and more accessible to students of all backgrounds, I was perceived as "leading like a man." It did not endear me to some in that camp.

Being the first woman Dean of Engineering at the University of Ottawa, and one of the first in Canada, opened up amazing opportunities. However, leaving that office was just as refreshing and transformative. I enjoyed the responsibilities and respected the position I held; therefore, I purposely did not engage in community or political activity, so as to avoid making remarks that could be viewed as controversial or inappropriate. After September 11, 2001, the world changed for Arabs and Muslims in North America. Traditional community associations failed to reflect effectively a true image of Arab and Muslim Canadians; many community members started to step forward and speak up. As Dean, I opted for self-restraint, in order to forgo mixing my own politics with my status at the University.

Upon returning to a regular professorial position in 2004, no longer constrained by the deanship, I felt like a genie out of the box, and threw myself wholeheartedly into community action. On the one hand, I strongly advocated for equal rights for Muslims and Arabs, and worked closely with Canadian national security officers, in order to help improve understanding of Muslim and Arab communities within the security apparatus. On the other hand, I put a mirror to the face of the Muslim community to reflect our own failures, urging them to stop acting like helpless victims, and start taking responsibility for addressing the new challenges. As a high profile professional Canadian, recognized among the 100 most influential people in Ottawa (2001) and recipient of the Order of Ontario (2004), I was able to articulate my thoughts comprehensibly and convincingly, and managed to find an appropriate space between the two cultures. For both sides, my credentials were uncontestable, and my criticism sanctioned, as it emanated from someone who cared deeply. I was amazed to be invited by a major political party to run for office. While flattered and honored, I did not take the plunge.

Joining Potlucks for Peace, a group aiming to create a "safe space" for fair-minded Jewish and Arab Canadians, was one of the most enlightening and gratifying experiences of my life. Membership required understanding of "the other side" without any preconditions, or giving up one's own principles. At first, it was very hard for me to remain silent in the meetings. It was also painful to listen to the Jewish perspective. Gradually, however, being quiet due to fear of being unable to control what I might say, turned into actual listening, which, in turn, resulted in understanding. Eventually, when I did speak, what I said was far better articulated because it was based on appreciating where "the other side" was coming from. While my fundamental convictions did not change, I most certainly understood theirs. I also learned two lessons about conflict resolution: first, I should not focus as much on the words of my opponents as much as where these words come from; second, it is my responsibility to find a solution for my opponent's problem, because failing that my problem will never be resolved. Potlucks for Peace taught me that listening did not only help me to understand the other side, it enabled me to better articulate my own side in ways the other side could understand it. To this day, I value and treasure this experience.

Alas, these exciting times abruptly ended when the University of British Columbia came knocking at my door, in their search for a Dean of Applied Science. I had comfortably resettled into my role as professor, and was thoroughly enjoying my post-deanship freedom and community engagement. However, a very talented and convincing headhunter company was determined to get me to Vancouver. To my own amazement, after a long and persuasive courtship, I packed up and crossed the country, leaving behind my rewarding life in Ottawa.

Moving from one part of Canada to another was a cultural transition of equal magnitude as that of moving from Egypt to Ontario, 30 years earlier; it was even more stressful now I was thirty years older. Vancouver and the University of British Columbia were as beautiful and as impressive as I had imagined, but the cultural contrast with Ontario and University of Ottawa was unexpected. Here, accepted principles in my previous world were regarded by some as political correctness or barriers to innovation. Ill-placed jokes about women and minorities took me back 25 years earlier. Even, the Muslim community was reminiscent of what I had experienced decades ago in Ottawa. It took me no time to learn that the perceived self is not always the real self, and the difference can be significant. While I treasured the experience in Vancouver, halfway into my mandate, it was time to part ways.

As always in my life, when one experience concludes, a better one materializes. Ending my contract as Dean earlier than planned opened up an exciting new chapter. Following British Columbia, I returned to Egypt, initially for a year but that year kept stretching. I was blessed to share some of my native country's most turbulent and most exciting times, post 2011. Now back home, I did not fit. I was perfectly Egyptian in many ways, yet very uniquely Canadian in others. I never seemed to see in myself what others found in me. Surprisingly, much of what clashed with the views of fellow Egyptians appealed to many others. I embraced my newly gained freedom in what gradually became retirement, determined to enjoy life to the fullest, while trying to contribute my best. I managed to find a place in the scientific community of Egypt, supporting initiatives by government, universities and NGOs to ensure that research and innovation address real problems, empower inventors to take their ideas to market, and improve people's lives. And on a personal basis, I traveled and visited every corner where I could go, carefully observing my surroundings, recording and sharing the small beauties that others might have missed. Now, every chance I get, I urge my fellow citizens to take responsibility and assume the charge of shaping their own future.

Back to the question of my high-tech executive years in Ottawa, how did I become who I am? I have no idea. At least now, I know who and what I am. I am too Canadian and not Canadian enough. Too Egyptian and not Egyptian enough. Too staunchly Canadian for some, too critical of Canada for others. Too much of a woman for men, and not woman enough for women. Too practicing as a Muslim for some, not practicing enough for others. Too traditional for some, not traditional enough for others. A true misfit. But somehow, I have come to terms with the fact of not fitting. Is this not what balance is supposed to be? To avoid the extreme on any side? To be able to see both the good and the bad on both sides? Could it be that, by definition, "fitting" means choosing a side, while misfits do not belong to either side, and serve to bring both sides together? Could balance be just another word for not fitting? I do not know for sure,

Tyseer reconnecting with her roots on the Nile, Cairo 2015

but I have come to believe that fitting comfortably lulls us into accepting the status quo, and disregarding change. While you may be unwilling to accommodate disgruntled people, having a few misfits may be a blessing, for they ask the difficult questions that never occur to those who fit comfortably. As such, misfits can force serious reflection, and initiate change for the better. So to answer the initial question in the title of this chapter: "Can a misfit bring about change?" I have come to believe that not only can misfits effect change, they can initiate it!

Tyseer practicing Taekwondo by the Pyramid in Giza, 2006

My mother never fit the stereotype of the women of her time. She created a new role model, and taught people to respect it, even when they disagreed with some of its aspects. She never realized how different she was, or what impact she left behind, too busy to think about these matters. Long after she passed, her influence has not been forgotten by those who crossed her path. As for me, I hope that, as the saying goes, the apple will not fall far from the tree.

Before closing this chapter, I am proud to boast two achievements that are very close to my heart: being a Black Belt in Taekwondo, and an avid motorcyclist. In case readers wonder about my personal life, I wish to assure them that it has been as fulfilling and as satisfying as my professional career, but I prefer to keep it private. I am grateful for every failure I endured and every chance I had to make a difference.

Ottawa and Cairo, November 2015

WAVES OF MY LIFE:
FROM THE SEA OF ALEXANDRIA
TO THE LAKE OF GENEVA

FAWZIA AL ASHMAWI

On a beautiful and sunny October morning, in a little house facing the Mediterranean sea in Alexandria, my mother gave birth to her third daughter: me. I always knew that she was not happy to have another girl, she would have preferred a boy. This feeling caused me tremendous hurt and was the source of profound sorrow, but my father tried his best to compensate with his affection and generosity. Although my mother clearly favored my younger brother, I loved him, and both of us always maintained a fine relationship. Throughout my life, I struggled to prove to my mother that a girl was just as good as a boy, if not better. It was quite a challenge, and I wonder if I ever succeeded.

In school, I strived to be the best, but my mother could not read my remarkable results because she was illiterate. Passing the French baccalaureate exam with the highest grades of all the French schools in Egypt was no reason to celebrate, because my younger brother who was in a different school had failed a similar exam. Then, my father had major surgery that left him unable to supervise the work in his factory of aluminum cooking utensils. Therefore, I decided to teach French in my former high school, in order to pay for my studies at Alexandria University. During four years, I was a teacher in the day, and attended evening courses in the French Department of the Faculty of Arts. Shortly before the graduation exams, my father passed away. I was deeply afflicted and could not perform at the level required to be named to a lectureship in the French Department. It was a double tragedy: not only had I lost my cherished father, but my dream to become a university professor had also crumbled.

Fawzia in the 2nd row, 2nd from the R, La Miséricorde School, 1954.

In the meantime, my mother tried to arrange a traditional marriage for me with one of her cousins—a civil servant. I refused, preferring instead a young colleague with whom I was in love during our four years at the university. My mother was furious, and could not understand that I would turn down a suitor who was well established and had a steady position, in favor of a recent graduate. She tried to prevent the marriage and threatened to stop her financial support. It did not matter, I had saved enough money for the two of us. My classmate and I decided to elope and get married.

Eventually, we moved to the small town of Damanhour near Alexandria, where my husband found a teaching job in an Islamic school, and I worked as a secretary in a new carpet factory. In view of our determination and my uncles' support, my mother finally accepted our marriage. Shortly thereafter, through influential relations, my husband was appointed to a teaching position at the Islamic University of Al Azhar in Cairo, and I had to look for employment in Egypt's capital. I applied for many jobs, responded to newspaper ads and sent my CV, but never received an answer. Finding work in Cairo at that time was almost impossible without good social connections. Finally, through my previous director who recommended me to a friend—the manager of a small textile company in southern Cairo—I was hired in the archive division.

We had limited resources, and our families refused to help since we had settled in Cairo, far away from them. My husband's brother, a distinguished diplomat living in Madrid, lent us his apartment in Cairo; but when he returned to Egypt three months later, we had to move. Like all Egyptian women, I had some jewelry, and had to sell it, in order to put a down-payment on an apartment in Nasr City—a distant and yet-uninhabited suburb on the northern periphery of Cairo. Our new living conditions were extremely hard. We were isolated, had few household goods, no friends, no TV, no car, nor could we afford to go on vacation. My husband tried his best to improve our situation, but it was almost impossible. Once again, his brother came to the rescue, and was able to assist us through his diplomatic relations. He recommended my husband as a translator for two part-time positions: one in the press office of the Egyptian Intelligence Division, the other in the Middle East News Agency. Pregnant and unable to take a second job in the afternoon, I stayed home, and tutored our next-door neighbors' children in French. For six years in Cairo, we struggled to live with our two sons on a modest budget. By working continuously from 8 am until 12 midnight, my husband wore himself out and became terribly ill. He developed rheumatoid arthritis and could not move for six months. Fortunately, the long ordeal finally ended with an unexpected heaven-sent reward.

In 1971, Al Azhar University nominated my husband for a four-year scholarship at the University of Geneva, to work on a PhD in translation. In two months, he completed the paperwork and flew alone to Switzerland, leaving our two sons and me with my mother in Alexandria. I was elated to return to my beloved city, to renew my contacts with family and friends, and to immerse myself in the cultural circles I had so missed. But it was not to last long. In order to allow me to join him, my husband enrolled me for graduate studies in French literature at the University of Geneva. He knew that I dreamed of being a university professor, and gave me the opportunity of a lifetime. I welcomed the proposal with enthusiasm, although it was sad to bid farewell to my cherished Alexandria.

In Switzerland, I immediately fell in love with the wonderful and peaceful city of Geneva. I was impressed with the famous fountain, the manicured gardens, the majestic mountains, the luxurious palaces, the neat crafts, and the quaint streets of the old city. Standing by the great lake of Geneva took me back to the Mediterranean sea in Alexandria. For a moment, the view would make me feel as if I were in my birthplace; it would bring back my dreams, my childhood memories, and my younger

Fawzia by the sea in Alexandria, 1956

years. In no time at all, I embraced my new life in this multinational and multicultural city. Unfortunately, the same attitude was not reciprocated by the Swiss authorities. As university students, my husband and I were granted annual residence permits, but not our two sons. In the 1970s, Swiss law did not allow students to be accompanied by their spouses or their children. In order to comply with the law, we would have had to send our two- and five-year old sons back to Egypt, something I absolutely refused to do. We initiated procedures against the Swiss Office of Population, but lost our case. Then, a Saudi friend lent us a helping hand. He offered me a job as an Arabic translator at the Saudi Permanent Mission to the United Nations in Geneva. As a local employee of the Saudi Embassy, I received diplomatic residence permits for my sons and myself, a miraculous solution had been found.

For seven years, I worked at the Saudi Embassy from 9 am to 5 pm, and attended evening courses at the University of Geneva. Although my husband and I had a B.A. in French literature from Alexandria University, the Swiss Universities' Academic Committee on Degree Equivalence did not recognize our degrees, and gave us partial credit only. We had to take additional courses to complete the requirements. After a year of study, we registered for the Master's degree, and after another two years we signed up for the PhD. At the University of Geneva, we discovered that our French literature program at Alexandria University was antiquated, it lacked important analytical and critical dimensions. Our Swiss professors taught us to read and interpret texts methodically, and to approach them in light of various schools of literary criticism.

It took me seven years of arduous work to complete the doctorate, not in French literature but in Arabic. This was an altogether different story. I wanted to register a dissertation topic on Swiss/French Enlightenment philosophe Jean-Jacques Rousseau. My advisor, the renowned scholar Jean Starobinski, called me in to say that there were hundreds of theses on Rousseau, and recommended instead that I study an Arabic author, because there was very little research on Arabic literature at the University of Geneva. This conversation was to change the course of my life. After considerable thought, I decided to focus on Naguib Mahfouz, whose novels portrayed realistically life in old Cairo in the early twentieth century. My dissertation would be entitled "The Evolution of Egyptian Women and Society in the Novels of Naguib Mahfouz."

In the 1970s, Mahfouz was not well-known in European literary circles, and I could not find sufficient documentation about him in the libraries and bookstores of Geneva or Paris. Therefore, I decided to meet Naguib Mahfouz in person. I sent a letter to his office at the daily Al Ahram where he had a regular column, and asked for an interview. A month later during summer vacation, I met him at Café Petrou in Alexandria. Our discussion was both fruitful and fascinating. He spoke about his childhood, his studies, and his first achievements as a young writer, then as a celebrated novelist. In the course of the conversation, he recommended important sources, including the first dissertation on his novels, which had been undertaken by a student from Israel and published by Tel Aviv University Press. I was surprised to learn that his work had been more appreciated by an Israeli student than by one from our own country. This was even more astonishing because it happened prior to the 1979 Camp David Peace Accords between Egypt and Israel. Finally, in February 1983, after many years of intensive work, I received the PhD with Honorable Mention, and was gratified with an appointment to a faculty position at the University of Geneva, in the Department of Arabic Literature & Islamic Studies. Five years after the publication of my dissertation, Mahfouz received the Nobel Prize of Literature in 1988.

During my 27-year academic career, I tried to promote the image of dignified and accomplished Muslim women. At the same time, it was rough to balance my own personal and professional responsibilities. Along the way, an unexpected surprise occurred: I became pregnant, and gave birth to a healthy and beautiful girl. It was not long before the happy waves of my life took a turn for the worse, and led to a mighty storm. While

Fawzia with Naguib Mahfouz in Cairo, August 2005, one year before his passing

I was facing innumerable hardships and attempting to complete the doctoral program, my husband gave up his academic ambitions, preferring instead to work as Press Attaché at the Embassy of Kuwait. At home, he became jealous, and resented the fact that I was now more educated and more professionally successful than him. Malevolent comments by acquaintances and colleagues did nothing but increase his anger and frustration. Gradually, our relationship deteriorated and divorce was inevitable. The impact of the break-up on me was devastating. To be separated from the only man I had loved for twenty-five years was much more difficult than I had anticipated. It was especially humiliating when he married a younger illiterate woman; it felt as if I had just been slapped on the face. Nonetheless, I pulled myself together, and devoted my total energy to the education of our three children and my academic career. Thanks to my determination and faith, I found the courage to move on and achieve my goals.

Immersing myself into various research projects, I continued to focus on improving the image of Islam and Muslim women in the European media and textbooks. In the 1980s, the Iranian Revolution and Salman Rushdie's *Satanic Verses* inspired an attitude of antipathy toward Muslims and Islam among many Europeans. In Switzerland, TV shows and newspapers started to spread offensive information about them. I could not keep silent. Reacting to a cartoon representing the Quran falling on the heads of Salman Rushdie and Bangladeshi writer Taslima Nasrin—author of *Shame,* a book blasting Islam—I published a piece titled "Hands off my Quran!" in the most reputable Swiss daily, *La Tribune de Genève.* I decried the two authors, and charged them with apostasy. My text was maligned, and I was blamed for inciting hatred. The University of Geneva President sent me a letter of reprimand for defying Swiss neutrality and disregarding the impartiality required of Swiss officials. He threatened to dismiss me if I did not apologize and retract my words. Naturally, I rejected the accusations and refused to apologize. Little did I know that the matter would take on much larger proportions. The Permanent Mission of the Arab League to the United Nations in Geneva convened the Ambassadors of the Muslim States to the UN to back me up. The controversy caused the winds to start turning in my favor, and the crisis ended with a note from the President of the University of Geneva, in which he asked me to avoid such outbursts in the future. The incident became known in the Swiss media as the "Ashmawi Affair," and raised questions about freedom of expression in Switzerland.

Once again, I raised my voice when the Danish cartoons of Prophet Muhammad were reproduced in the French magazine *Charlie Hebdo*, and the daily *La Tribune de Genève.* I published another letter inviting Muslims in Switzerland to boycott the paper. Facing financial loss, the newspaper editor asked the main Swiss television station to have an on-air discussion with me, hoping to end the campaign against his paper. During the show, I spoke of Prophet Muhammad's life and achievements, and compared them to those of non-Muslims, referencing the writings on Islam and the Prophet by European personalities and philosophers, such as Voltaire, Napoleon, and Schopenhauer. Two months later, the newspaper editor had to resign.

In 1996, I was invited to participate in a project launched by the Education Bureau of UNESCO in Geneva, entitled "The Image of the Other in Seven Mediterranean Countries." The purpose of this comparative study was to survey the portrayal of "the other" in history textbooks of 5th and 6th graders in three northern Mediterranean nations (Spain, France, and Greece), and four southern Mediterranean countries (Egypt, Jordan, Lebanon, and Tunisia). The research provided evidence that, in the north, textbooks tended to omit or conceal some historical truths related to the south; while in the south, they overstated the Muslims' past glory. The materials depicted "the other" in a distorted and biased way, creating stereotypes, and spreading misunderstanding. In the north, they misrepresented the image of Muslims in the minds of young people, while in the south, they gave hope that payback time against the West may come someday. The report was translated into more than seven languages, and widely distributed in many countries. As a specialist of Islamic Studies, I have been invited to participate in more than one hundred international conferences and workshops throughout the world. The most significant for me was the annual conference of the Supreme Council of Islamic Affairs at Al Azhar University in Cairo. To be recognized by the highest and most prestigious Islamic institution in the world was the most meaningful reward of my career. For ten years, I was invited to speak at this conference, and presented papers on major concerns for the Muslim world. It was a real honor to be the only woman sitting among these most distinguished dignitaries, the only woman to whose ideas they listened and paid attention.

Through the years, my research and publications established my reputation in academic circles in Europe and beyond. In 1997, researchers from six European Union nations conducted an important socio-economic project sponsored by the European Commission. It was entitled "Muslim Voices in the European Union: The Stranger Within. Community, Identity and Employment." This anthropological study focused on the presence, visibility and contribution of Muslims in Europe, and the difficulties they encountered as they attempted to integrate into European societies. The research was undertaken in conjunction with the UK Runnymede Project on the rise of anti-Muslim attitudes in Europe.[1] Part of the study related to Islamic voices in Switzerland was published in French, in a book titled *La condition des musulmans en Suisse*.

Ten years later, I participated with a group of five Arab and European experts in an international project supported by UNESCO, the Arab League, the Anna Lindh Foundation, and ISESCO. It consisted of preparing a guidebook designed to assist authors of history textbooks who write about encounters between Europe and the Arab world; it too was later published under the title, *Learning about the Other*. My work on the rights of Muslim women led to my selection as a contributor to the 2007 *UNESCO Encyclopedia of Islam*. A year later, during the annual conference of the High Council of Islamic Affairs, Minister of *Wakfs* Hamdy Zakzouk[2] announced that Egypt had recognized my contributions to Islamic research by bestowing upon me the Medal of Merit in Arts and Sciences—Egypt's equivalent of France's Order of Arts and Letters—one of the nation's highest honors. Receiving the award from then-President Hosni Mubarak, I burst into tears as I remembered my mother who had died ten years earlier. I was hoping that she would now be glad to have

Fawzia at the Conference of the Supreme Council of Islamic Affairs, Al Azhar University, Cairo, 1998

had a daughter instead of a son. My younger brother, who was in attendance at the ceremony, was also crying. He took me in his arms and whispered: "I am proud to have you as a sister!" I was grateful to my mother for having given me a wonderful brother, one who has always encouraged and supported me in all the circumstances. In fact, I often had the feeling that he was my father, not my younger brother.

Geneva, September 2015

Notes

[1] The Runnemede Company is the UK's leading independent think tank on race equality. It conducts a large range of projects that address key issues related to race equality and challenges for public policy.

[2] In Islamic law, *Wakfs* are a type of religious endowment donated to a trust held for religious or charitable purposes.

PLAYING AN ACTIVE POLICY ROLE WITHIN THE GOVERNMENT

RANIA A. AL-MASHAT

Given my upbringing in an academic family, with a father who is a professor of Political Science at Cairo University, and a mother involved with Ain Shams University, our house was a frequent meeting place for intellectuals, professors, journalists, and national and international leaders. The common theme of discussion during their visits was often how to improve conditions in our country through better policy formulation.

As a child, I internalized these stimulating discussions, tried to understand the arguments, and just dreamed of participating in the conversations later on. I was also inspired by watching my father expound on important national issues on radio and television shows. What had become apparent to me was that one had to build his/her credibility through higher education and the right educational credentials. Most of our visitors whether women or men were PhD holders. Among these distinguished visitors were Dr. Mohamed Saeed, an intellectual, lecturer and former Deputy Director of Al-Ahram Center for Strategic and Political Studies; Dr. Ali Eldin Helal, Professor of Political Science, Dean of Faculty of Economics and Political Science and former Minister of Youth; Dr. Wadouda Badran, Professor of Political Science and former Director of the Arab Women Organization of the League of Arab States; and Dr. Amany Kandeel, a leading figure in NGO activities, and Director of the Arab NGOs Network. These were only a few of the many outstanding guests I was privileged to encounter at home while growing up. So by the age of 7, I had decided that I would have to become Dr. Rania Al-Mashat. At that point, it was not clear to me in which discipline I would specialize, but the goal was already set at that early age. Obtaining a PhD was the first pillar of fulfilling my dream.

When I entered the American University in Cairo (AUC), it took me a while to realize that my true passion was for Economics. I started off as a Computer Science major, a fairly novel field in Egypt at that time. Despite being a top student in class, two years into the program, I did not feel passionate enough to graduate with a Computer Science degree. I did not think that I would innovate in that discipline, because I was not eager enough to program unless it was part of an assignment. That motivated me to explore Business Administration, another option that was very popular; but I still could not find my heart in it. It was one of our regular home visitors, Dr. Mohamed Saeed, who assisted me in finding the right field. He directed my attention to Economics, and convinced me to pursue it as a major.

Labeled the "dismal science," Economics is a discipline that attempts to explain the behavior of consumers, businesses, and, of course, governments. In my courses, I was inspired by Professor Galal Amin, who taught us the principles of economic development and the role of government in ensuring the interests of all stakeholders in the economy be safeguarded. I was also influenced by Professor Adel Beshai, whose lectures on international trade shaped my passion for exploring the concept of comparative advantage, the role of international institutions in influencing the economy, and the people's welfare in developing and emerging markets. During my last summer at AUC, I interned at the Economic Research Forum for Arab Countries, Iran and Turkey, which was set up and run by Professor Heba Handoussa. Through our close interactions, I developed a great deal of respect for her, and looked up to her as my role model. I also participated in a project that examined the role of the General Agreement on Tariffs and Trade (GATT) on developing economies, which exposed me to renowned economists who wrote in that field, including Nemat Shafik.[1] Combined, these experiences exposed me to the international dimension of Economics, and the reactions of governments to foster the welfare of their people. They also reinforced my decision to pursue my studies in that direction.

In addition to my academic work at AUC, participating actively in extracurricular activities was a keen interest of mine. I was involved in the Arab Cultural Club, which organized economic and political lectures for students, and I ran for the Student Union elections in 1994 to become the Representative of majors in Economics. As such, I was in charge of looking after the students' interests with the school administration. During my senior year, despite tempting job offers, the straight A student resisted, determined to follow the dream and get a PhD. My parents opposed my decision to study abroad, for they did not accept the idea that I would be living alone overseas. Instead, they asked me to spend more time in Cairo after graduation, before enrolling in a PhD program. This was a true setback for me, but fate would play an unexpected role in my favor when my father was asked to be the Egyptian Cultural and Educational

Counselor at the Egyptian Embassy in Washington, DC. In January 1995, he travelled to the US alone, and the family was to join him after my commencement. Six months later, I graduated at the age of 20, and was on a flight to DC with the whole family on July 4, 1995—US Independence Day. In the metropolitan area, the University of Maryland at College Park (UNCP) was well-known for its International Economics program. I applied, was admitted, and started the MA/PhD program in August 1995—two months exactly after graduation.

After taking a course in International Finance with two prominent professors, Guillermo Calvo, Former Deputy Governor of the Central Bank of Argentina, and Carmen Reinhart of the International Monetary Fund, I decided to specialize in International Economics with a focus on monetary policy and public debt management. In DC, I was able to secure two internships over two consecutive years: the first at the World Bank (WB) and the other at the International Monetary Fund (IMF). At the age of 23, I was the youngest summer intern at the IMF. It was the summer of 1998, the Russian crisis loomed, with disagreements between the WB and the IMF on the way to approach it. With my intern cohort, we met with Stanley Fischer, the First Deputy Managing Director of the IMF, and Joseph Stiglitz, the Chief Economist at the WB. Being exposed to two of the highest-ranking economists in the world was very special and very enlightening, indeed.

By then, it had become clear to me that if I received an offer from the IMF upon completing my degree, I would remain in the US to get first-hand experience in economic policy management within governments. This was exactly what happened. In 2001, I received my PhD at the age of 25, and was among the youngest economists to join the IMF. The door toward shaping policy making for governments had finally opened for the 7-year old planner. This was the second pillar of my dream.

During my tenure at the IMF, I worked among talented economists who believed in the institution's mission of maintaining global financial stability. I traveled extensively and worked on different country cases, interacting with the authorities in The Gambia, Vietnam, India, and Micronesia, among others. Close engagement with colleagues and country counterparts provided the appropriate training needed to convert academic experience into first-hand on-the-job practical application. Country experiences were diverse and rich in terms of both theory and practice. I had the opportunity to observe how central banks in these countries functioned, handled crises, and moved from fixed to floating exchange rate regimes. During the missions, I learned to interact with policy makers, and

Rania surrounded by her mother, Nagwa El-Attar, and her father, Dr. Abdul Monem Al-Mashat, on graduation day, University of Maryland College Park, 2001

contributed to the policy-making process. A very important lesson learned was that every policy maker claimed his/her country was different. The challenge was how to take into account each country's specific circumstances, and try to deliver advice that worked elsewhere. Moreover, it was also during the frequent country missions that I discovered the fascinating cultures of Africa and Asia.

Rania (lower row, 2nd L) at the meeting of the IMF International Monetary and Finance Committee, among global central bankers and ministers of finance, Washington, DC, 2012

My tasks in India included interacting directly with the Reserve Bank of India, monitoring development, and examining the monetary transmission channels. In Vietnam—a nation concluding an IMF program—the focus was on exploring the country's real monetary performance. In the small African nation of Gambia, my responsibility was to examine its external sector, in order to identify the sources of financing, and to link them to banking reform. The case was similar in Micronesia, an island in the Pacific that mainly depended on inflows from other countries. In all these missions, IMF professionals collaborated with each other, hence the outcome was a true team effort. This operational style was fundamental in shaping my own work ethics.

While time on the missions was always packed and hectic, interacting with the locals gave the job a pleasant dimension. There are endless anecdotes that I collected during my travel experiences. In Gambia, I visited local schools, and on following trips I contributed to secure funding to build additional classrooms, and a water pump to protect the young students from falling into a well. The humanitarian dimension of the job made it even more rewarding. While on mission to India, I visited the historic Taj Mahal, and observed how a man's love for his late wife translated into a timeless monument directly influenced by Islamic art. In

Cambodia, the visit to Angkor Wat was both enjoyable and enlightening, as it made clear to me that its architectural style was similar to that of the Baron Palace in Cairo, notwithstanding the difference in scale.

However, the most memorable incident happened in Hanoi at the end of a lunch at the famous Bobby Chinn restaurant, overlooking the Hanoi River. During the meal, owner Bobby Chinn came in person to entertain members of the mission, as he had been a stand-up comedian in New York prior to opening his restaurant in Hanoi. Before leaving the group, the Asian-looking 40-year old gentleman asked me: "Are you American?" I replied: "No, I am Egyptian." I was in for a huge surprise when he responded: "My mother is Egyptian, too!" I was stunned: one of the most famous chefs in Asia today, Bobby Chinn, has Egyptian roots. He invited the team and me to a special Chef's Dinner that evening during which not only did we savor delicious food, but also enjoyed Om Kalthoum's voice in the background. Eating Asian specialties while listening to our most famous Egyptian singer in Hanoi was an evening I will never forget. This story is one I often like to tell.

I was into my fifth year at the IMF when the reformist government of Egypt went looking for well-educated and experienced Egyptians living abroad, in order to encourage them to go home and contribute to the development of their country. The Minister of Investment at that time, Dr. Mahmoud Mohieldin, was familiar with my academic and operational work on monetary policy and public debt management, as well as my IMF policy work with various governments. He recommended me as a potential candidate to Tarek Amer, the then-Deputy Governor of the Central Bank of Egypt (CBE). I was approached by Amer at the end of 2004, to lead the effort of modernizing the monetary policy framework in Egypt, and to establish the department and build its capacity. He convinced me to return to Cairo, and participate in the CBE's reform effort, and the country's economic transition.

When I started to share this information with my colleagues at the IMF, they were very proud of me and extremely supportive. However, they were also quite concerned about possible gender bias in Egypt. I then reminded them of the historic role of Egyptian women through the ages, and spelled out my "4 Cs" of success: Competence, Connections, Confidence and Charm. I underscored that continuing to build one's competence, maintaining connections, remaining confident and delivering messages in a charming way would be the magic steps toward progress and success. Actually, in this case what might have been more of an issue than the "gender factor" was the "age factor": I was not quite 30 yet. However, I believed that with my experience and contributions, the focus on age would dissipate and competence would prevail. The years that followed proved me right. Despite enjoying tremendously my job at the IMF and being promoted rapidly, I joined the CBE on August 2, 2005, at the age of 30. Although it was difficult to leave an exciting and important position at the IMF, the offer from CBE was the third pillar on the way to achieve my dream: playing an active policy role within my own government. I was ready to embrace this challenge and serve my country.

The CBE Board had launched a reform program for the banking sector based on three pillars, namely strengthening banking supervision, addressing distortions in the foreign exchange market, and modernizing Egypt's monetary policy. I was entrusted with the task of identifying the CBE monetary policy strategy, and assisting in its endeavor to adopt an inflation targeting regime. Here was the perfect opportunity for me to implement in my own country what I had been advising policy makers to do in other nations; thus becoming a policy maker myself. Over the years, the assignments broadened to include, among other responsibilities, participating actively in the country's macroeconomic management through the design and update of the macroeconomic framework, in conjunction with other ministries and government entities. I became the CBE liaison with the IMF and Sovereign Rating Agencies, and was also in charge of representing the country's monetary authority at national and international conferences and forums, including hearings on monetary policy and IMF related issues at the Egyptian Parliament. I was then promoted to Sub Governor for Monetary Policy in June 2012, the youngest Sub Governor in CBE history.

I have witnessed Egypt's economic transition over the past 11 years. These included time prior to the 2011 Revolution, the 2011 Revolution, the short political transition that followed, the 2013 Revolution, and finally the relatively more tranquil current times. The role of CBE in smoothing the political transition was an important part of Egypt's history, and makes for a good story to tell colleagues all over the world. If it were not for the reforms that took place between 2004 and 2011 and the build-up of credibility that followed, there would have been a full collapse of the banking sector and, in turn, to the economy. The CBE performance during the reform period translated into a resilient banking sector able to weather the political shock. In the early days of the 2011 Revolution, CBE worked closely with the army: physical banknotes were carried in tanks to the airport, and delivered with helicopters to the various governorates, to feed banks nationwide. Having been part of the team that helped to reform the banking sector and prepare it for such unexpected shocks has, indeed, been a source of great pride.

Moreover, between March 2011 and November 2012, Egypt was engaged in IMF program negotiations, and we concluded two staff-level agreements. I was leading the effort from the CBE side, and was called upon to explain the details of the program and the monetary policy to the Economic Committee at the Parliament, which was dominated at that time by the Muslim Brotherhood. Skillfully, I was able to obtain a letter of endorsement from the Parliament, which was required to secure Egypt's access to the IMF Program Disbursements—a challenging task that will remain engraved in my memory.

Beyond CBE, I currently serve on several Boards, including the Egyptian Stock Exchange, the General Authority for Free Zones and Investment, the Arab International Bank, the Middle East Economic Association, and the Dean's Strategic Advisory Board of the AUC School of Business. Previously, I was also a Board Member of the Arab Investment Bank. My passion for the region has also prompted me to accept responsibilities in various regional initiatives. For example, I am a Research Fellow at the Economic Research Forum for Arab Countries, Iran and Turkey; a lecturer at the Egyptian Banking Institute; and an Adjunct Professor of Economics at AUC.

My efforts have been rewarded by several national and international organizations. In 2015, I was selected among the Top 50 Most Influential Women in the Egyptian Economy. Earlier, I was recognized by the World Economic Forum among the 2014 Young Global Leaders (YGL), by the Institut Choiseul of France in 2014 and 2015 among the Economic Leaders for Tomorrow in Africa, and was named among the 2014 Most Powerful Women in the Egyptian Banking Sector. In 2013, I was invited by the Government of France to participate in their International Visitor Leadership Program; and received the Distinguished Alumni Award of the AUC School of Business.

Recently, I have been appointed by the International Monetary Fund to a management-level position as Advisor in the Immediate Office of the Research Department, to work closely with Chief Economist, Maurice Obstfeld. My new responsibilities are designed to tap on my years of experience managing Egypt's macroeconomic transition in the most challenging periods of its recent history. I will be involved in supporting the IMF's multilateral surveillance activities across emerging countries around the globe.

Rania awarded a certificate recognizing her among the 50 Most Influential Women in the Egyptian Economy, Cairo, 2015

Beginning August 2016, exactly 11 years after joining the CBE in August 2005, I will be at my office in Washington, DC. This professional move will be an instrumental step in my life journey. The broader internatonal exposure will certainly equip me for my eventual return to Egypt to assume higher responsibilities in my country's economic policy management.

Today, I am living the dream I developed in my childhood, playing an active role within government, and fostering relationships with national and international stakeholders. Nationally, this includes close ties with the business community, political leaders, parliamentarians and the academic community. Internationally, the ties are with various global financial institutions. Serving Egypt by contributing to policies that would make the riches of the Nile flow to all its citizens is not only a mission, it is a passion. The years between the 7-year old dreamer and the CBE Sub-Governor and IMF Advisor have not always been easy, but they have been enriching personally and professionally, and brought an enormous amount of happiness and fulfillment. Achieving this dream would not have been possible without the continuous encouragement and unconditional love and nurture of my family, particularly my mother and my father, to whom I owe every bit of my success.

Cairo, June 2016

Notes

[1] Alexandria-born Dame Nemat Talaat Shafik is Deputy Governor of the Bank of England since 2014, having served at the IMF between 2011 and 2014. In 1998, she was the youngest ever Vice President at the World Bank, at the age of 36. At the end of February 2017, Shafik will leave the Bank of England to become the Director of the London School of Economics.

ME? A BANKER? YES, AND I LOVE IT!

NAYERA AMIN

Growing up in Alexandria provided me with an unforgettable childhood, as it opened my eyes, ears, brain, and all my cells to the concept of diversity. In the early 1960s, Alexandria was still "the bride of the Mediterranean." Many nationalities, cultures, religions coexisted, creating an excitingly rich intellectual and cultural life. It was a real melting pot where everybody spoke at least three or four languages, and celebrated each other's religious and social holidays. In my class at Notre Dame de Sion, we were 30 girls of 17 nationalities. Alexandria was beautiful and elegant. Its long Corniche, extending from the port harbor in the west to Montazah Palace in the east, was flanked by attractive villas and fine buildings in different architectural styles. The landscape featured Art Deco, Baroque, English, Italian and Greek, all blending without a glitch. Only one adjective comes to mind to describe it: superb.

We were a small upper-middle class family: my father was an engineer, my mother a housewife, with my paternal grandmother living with us. Ours was an Italian-style house in Rouchdy, with a beautiful garden—the pride and joy of my parents. My younger sister and I studied at the same school, and had a lovely and uneventful childhood and adolescence, surrounded by much love, yet strict rules had to be followed. Our opinions were heard, but it did not mean that real democracy prevailed; there was freedom of speech as long as we spoke politely and with decorum. My parents embraced the concept of diversity, respecting the other, understanding and accepting differences: these values became ingrained in us.

High academic performance was expected, and sports, ballet, theater, and music were part of our extra-curricular activities. We were encouraged to participate in those programs offered at the school or the club, all contributing to a well-rounded education. The extended family was very important. Summers were spent with cousins, uncles, aunts who came to Alexandria to enjoy the beaches at Montazah and Agami. In winter and for Christmas vacations, we used to spend a week in Cairo first, visiting with family, immersed in cultural activities. Mornings were devoted to visits to museums and historical monuments: pharaonic, Coptic, Islamic and Jewish. In the evening, it was entertainment: theater, opera, and special shows. My mother was keen on exposing us to Egypt's diverse heritage and culture. The next stop was the Old Cataract Hotel in Aswan, where we enjoyed the most spectacular Nile view. After lunch, we would take rides in small boats called *felouka*, before sipping tea and juice on the hotel terrace as we watched the spectacular sunset. Life was good!

On June 5, 1967, war broke out. We lived the worst days of our lives listening to big lies, followed by President Nasser's resignation, and the uprising begging him to stay. These were indeed confusing and traumatic times. Sadness fell upon the entire nation, causing anger and bitterness. Many Egyptians and foreign nationals left Egypt, starting an unprecedented brain drain that included many friends and family members. My childhood came to an end, the carefree days were gone forever, and our lives changed drastically. My dad was transferred to Cairo to head the Iron & Steel complex: bye-bye Alexandria, home, school, friends, beach; hello Cairo, new home, school, friends, no beach. I was devastated and missed my life in Alexandria, and stayed in touch with my former school friends.

Cairo was not bad, after all. It was more vibrant than Alexandria, but more restrictions were mandated by my parents, especially in the early years. The Sacré Cœur was the new school, where I passed the Franco-Egyptian baccalaureate, specializing in science. Then, I enrolled at the American University in Cairo (AUC), a great institution with an educational system quite different from the more classical approach of French schools. Choosing a major was important, but we were exposed to other disciplines through the electives and other requirements. Among others, I took courses in Science, Math, Art, History, Political Science, Anthropology, Sociology, and Psychology, which expanded my knowledge and broadened my horizons. Majoring in Economics and minoring in Management provided a solid foundation for my future career as a banker. I enjoyed the student life, made new friends, and worked part-time to earn some pocket money. It made me feel proud and mature, as this was my own initiative, not my parents'. During my European summer trips, I learned the value of work and independence. Students working to pay for school and earning a living was unheard of at that time in Egypt.

That was also the age of dating. Sooner than expected, I fell in love with my husband-to-be, Hussein El Zayat. We were at totally opposite poles, nobody believed it would work, me included. We got engaged during my junior year and married after I graduated from AUC with High Honors, but before starting my career. Hussein, too, had just graduated from medical school, and was an intern preparing to specialize in Obstetrics and Gynecology. Together, we embarked simultaneously into marital and professional life. My graduation gift was a trip to the US, where I stayed with one of my best friends, the daughter of a respected diplomat, and acquired first-hand exposure to American life. I was familiar with Europe, but not North America, and was amazed by what I discovered: everything was beautiful, clean, different, extra-large, even the sky!

Back in Cairo, my father had lined up a couple of job interviews for me, at the Ministry of Planning and Finance, and Chase National Bank—a joint venture between the National Bank of Egypt and Chase Manhattan. Arguments flew back and forth between us: he, pro-government, one of its by-products; me, a daring and unconventional young woman who totally believed in the private sector, but, more importantly, wanted to know what she was worth, based on her own merit. A compromise was reached: I accepted to show up for an interview at Chase. I did, was offered a position, but had a strange feeling that it was not what I was looking for, yet could not quite nail the exact reason. During the visit, I happened to bump into a few AUC graduates who were working there. In the course of the conversation, an Indian manager called on one of my friends, and reprimanded her: "Miss Rita, you've been away from your desk for five minutes!" I apologized, and quickly left to save the employee from further criticism. Wandering in the street maze of Garden City, I found myself facing a building with a big "Citibank" sign. To this day, I do not know what prompted me to stop and request a job application. In less than five minutes, I had completed the form, and was ready to leave, when a smiling lady asked me if I had a few minutes to meet Mr. Jack Goodridge. Sure, I accepted, having no clue who was the gentleman.   Here I was unannounced, a 22- year old AUC graduate in the office of the Head of Citibank Egypt: a 50-year old American. Chatting for God knows how long, he asked me if I had a valid visa for Greece. Curious, I replied: "No, but why?" He went on: "Get it quickly to meet with the Executive of the Middle East North Africa Division (MENA) for further interviews." Wow, I did it on my own, YESSS!!

President Sadat's open-door economic policies had just been promulgated in 1975, and Egypt was in the midst of shifting from a socialist to a capitalist system, with ensuing major changes in the social, political and economic environment. I believed in the market economy, and longed to work for the private sector, dreaming of an Egypt similar to Europe and the US, where my work would contribute to achieve that goal. I joined Citibank in February 1976—incidentally, its 40-year anniversary in Egypt was celebrated in November 2015—part of its first-generation employees. After a few months of on-the-job rotation in Cairo, I was sent to their Training Center in Athens for the super-tough credit course, which I passed with flying colors.

Back home, I started my corporate banking career, was promoted fairly quickly, moved into different departments, and received more training nationally and internationally. There was never a dull moment. The realities of work proved that I had lived in a bubble within my own society. The outside world was shocking, as I discovered there were not one but many codes of ethics. Frustration and anxiety were about to overcome, but I did not succumb, and learned to handle sensitive situations. Banking was my passion, and I was determined to pursue my career and excel in it. Citibank was a great school, and a fabulous employer. Never was I treated as an employee, rather like an entrepreneur despite my lack of experience. Mistakes were allowed, as long as we learned from them. We were always pushed beyond our limits, but I enjoyed the challenge.

Building my family and career while discovering the world through a job requiring extensive travel, much reading, new responsibilities, and adjusting to new cultures, was instrumental in shaping my character. Believing in youth has kept me young in spirit and heart. Working and living in different environments gave me a sense of perspective, and made me a pretty liberal and progressive person. I learned to adapt, but never to compromise. These values have helped me achieve a successful and gratifying career, despite conflicts between the more typical Egyptian conservative environment and my own views. In the process, I was blessed with two sons, Mohamed and Omar, while juggling wifehood, motherhood, and "bankhood"—I just made up this word, with apologies to the Webster's English Dictionary! Six months after Mohamed was born, I completed the Master's degree, working full time and very long hours, taking care of a newborn baby, and teaching part-time at AUC. My mother helped when she could, due to her precarious health. Omar was born in 1985, another joyful and blessed addition to our family. By then, Mohamed was going to the Jesuit school and the rollercoaster was going full speed. We were a happy family.

On August 1, 1991, Hussein died suddenly of a heart attack, at age 40. I thought my life would end, everything around me seemed to have crumbled. I was scared, angry, bitter. I felt robbed, and wished I were Indian to be cremated with my husband. While depressed, I did a lot of thinking and soul searching, and finally convinced myself to snap out of the dumps, as I realized that I did not have the luxury of feeling down.

Family picture. (L to R) Mohamed, Hussein, Nayera and Omar, Cairo, 1988

I decided to pursue my career, and work even harder. It was definitely not easy, but my support system helped: parents, sister, family, in-laws, friends were always there to inject the needed strength, which allowed me to face the unchosen challenge. A week after the tragedy hit, I was back at work.

In 1993, Citibank changed its status from an offshore to an onshore bank, in order to increase its role in the local market. It was a timely decision as we were marginalized and losing market share, since we were not authorized to deal in local currency. Following approval of the Central Bank of Egypt, numerous customer and staff events were organized, attended by all the bank senior executives, including Shawkat Aziz, who later became Prime Minister of Pakistan. For us, a bigger challenge was ahead, with more exposure and competition as we were latecomers to that business, but we caught the train while running, by offering new products and technological advances, competitive pricing, and high quality services. position opened as Corporate Bank /Risk Management Head at Citibank Tunisia. Being trilingual was a definite advantage and my profile fit, I was selected for the job. In Tunis, new life, friends, and challenges would lie ahead, but it was an amazing seven-year experience. My family integrated very well into Tunisian society and the expatriate community. One of the highlights of that time was meeting Nelson Mandela at a South

African Embassy reception. Meanwhile, I was promoted to CEO for Citi Tunis.

Citibank gathering, Nayera, 2nd row, 4th from R; 3rd row, 4th from R, Citibank CEO; 5th from R, Shawkat Aziz

Later, I was transferred back to Cairo as Regional Risk Manager for North Africa, a responsibility requiring more travel, often up to three weeks per month. Three years later, I took over the Corporate Citibank in Egypt for a few years. In the meantime, things were rapidly changing at the New York head office, with frequent re-organizations, new policies, and more restrictions. Our corporate culture was modified again after the merger of Citicorp with Travelers, from one focused on a customer/product/relationship, to one driven by transactions. Citi was going through tough times in the US, with repercussions on its worldwide activities.

This was happening as I was approached by Banque Audi, a Lebanese bank seeking to streamline and grow its newly acquired local business. The challenge appealed to me, and after 30+ years at Citi, I took the plunge and resigned, leaving behind my comfort zone. There was more hard work ahead, a different environment, an interesting experience for sure, but the politics were mindboggling, and counterproductive. Clearly, we were not on the same wavelength, so after 18 months we parted in good terms. Along came Piraeus Bank with an even bigger challenge: it was losing money, and needed a major clean-up and overhaul, in order to turn it into a growing and profitable business. After considerable thought, I accepted to become Piraeus Bank Chief Executive Officer and Managing Director.

Nayera with Nelson Mandella, at South African Embassy in Tunis, 1998

My responsibilities at Bank Audi and Piraeus were the ultimate tests where I had to put into action all that I had learned, though in a different work environment and culture. I must recognize, however, that Citibank, as a multinational institution operating in over 100 countries, had well-defined policies and procedures—a buffer zone in itself. Hence, the management skills, business techniques, vision, strategy, and social skills I had acquired in my many years at Citi came in handy. Building a good team of professionals, empowering them, and collaborating toward achieving our goal were the basis for our success, despite two Revolutions in 2011 and 2013, a year of Muslim Brotherhood ruling, an economic downturn, and an unprecedented Greek financial crisis. Although the double negative local and international calamities delayed our original plan, the goal was achieved in 2014, when Piraeus finally became profitable. Given the exacerbation of the Greek crisis and the EU mandate to restructure and recapitalize the Greek banking system, banks were required to sell all their international subsidiaries, which also included Egypt. The process was started in June 2011 by Standard Chartered Bank.

I do not wish to bore readers with technicalities, but from then on until November 10, 2015, notwithstanding the political and economic turmoil in Egypt and Greece, we went through five due diligence exercises. In the process, we saw it all: investors getting cold feet at the last moment and wanting to change the business model; a plan turned down by the Central Bank of Egypt; or the offering of an unacceptably-low price by a potential buyer believing it was a distressed sale. These were but a few of the problems encountered. Finally, the Ahli Bank of Kuwait came along with a reasonable offer. The acquisition represented a mutually strategic fit, and the deal was successfully concluded: a win-win situation for both parties. This is where we actually stand, undergoing the post-sale integration and alignment.

(L to R) Piraeus Bank Representative and CEO of Ahli Bank of Kuwait with Nayera, at a press conference announcing the sale, Four Seasons Hotel, Cairo, November 2015

Does this not sound like a smooth career path marked by some family tragedy? Perhaps. But I can vouch it was a tough ride. The success chart was not always moving upward, it was more like a rollercoaster, all parts contributing to an amazing experience. If one were always successful, it would not be enjoyable for failures are important to savor success. Mistakes are one's best teacher, but the trick is to learn from them, and avoid repeating them. My motto has always been: surround yourself with smart and creative people, guide and train them, invest in them, and everyone will be a winner. Remember the process: work hard, be passionate, laugh a lot, have fun, do not take life too seriously, and, more importantly, do not take yourself too seriously. No one wins alone. The

Beatles remind us that "Everybody needs somebody." Perseverance and focus on targets, together with help from a good team, can work miracles.

Along my way, there were situations and bosses that were stumbling blocks. Did I encounter failure? Sure. Discrimination? Sometimes. Here is a 20-year-old incident that I will never forget. I was recommended for an opening at Citibank Geneva, Private Banking. In a telephone interview with the executive who was to be my superior, following the technical/business conversation, we had the exchange below, starting with his comment:

— "You understand, of course, that the bank does not pay for a nanny."

Taken by surprise, I retorted:

— "Of course not, but why this question?"

— "You are a single mother, the workload is heavy, excluding the frequent travel, how will you handle it with two young boys?" I was fuming, and glad it was a phone interview, not a face-to-face encounter.

— "Sir, would you have asked this question of a single father postulating for the job?" He was embarrassed, started to mumble and added:

— "Don't get me wrong, it's out of concern for you." Too late, the damage was done. It did not take me long to respond:

— "Sir, you don't know me to show concern, but if this is your perception, then I don't think I'm interested in joining your team."

— "No, no, you're overreacting. It was a genuine remark and I'll see you next week in Geneva, right?"

— "No, I won't come, and thanks for your time."

The incident upset me tremendously, maybe because until then I had not experienced serious sexist comments, or anything even close. After a while, I brushed it away, and went on with my life. This shows that despite the institutional culture, humans have their own beliefs, fears, and idiosyncrasies that do not always match those of the corporation. It was not the only time I heard discriminatory remarks, but after this conversation, I learned to pay no attention to them, pretending the sexist person was speaking to me in a foreign language.

My professional achievements were crowned by the personal satisfaction of having led my young sons through adolescence into healthy and balanced adulthood. They adopted my ethical values to which they added their own, learned from their exposure to different cultures to be adaptable and able to cope, and succeeded in their professional careers, entirely on their own. Nothing could mean more to me.

Furthermore, throughout my life, helping has always been a mission close to my heart, especially what concerns education. My father used to tell me: "Money comes and goes. It is important, but what is more important is your ability to make money, which only comes with education. This is my legacy to you and your sister." He was true to his word. I appreciated that privilege, and his message continues to ring for me. When I was asked by one of my AUC graduate professors to offer MBA courses in Banking, Treasury and Marketing, on a voluntary basis, I beamed with joy and did so for close to five years. It was a gratifying yet time-consuming experience, but the personal satisfaction and fulfillment were immeasurable. As a senior banker, I always lobbied to ensure that education would be one of the corporate social responsibilities. Later, I felt that I needed to be more involved. The opportunity presented itself when I was invited to sit on the Advisory Board of the AUC School of Business, to help enhance the curriculum. My extensive experience was put to work, to make sure that students would have better chances in their professional careers, and the school would fare safely toward accreditation.

Women were another high priority for me. Despite being the bread winners in 60% of the households in Egypt, they continue to be discriminated against and disregarded in some areas. Yet, without them the January 2011 Revolution and the toppling of the Muslim Brotherhood would not have been possible. At every opportunity I have and in every presentation I make, I emphasize the importance of women's empowerment. After a recent lecture in which I spoke of gender equality, a group of students from the Canadian University in Dubai wanted to pursue the discussion, and told me how inspired they were by my words. It was one of the most heartening compliments, as my goal was precisely to communicate my principles to a younger generation.

At this juncture, I would like to pay tribute to some who have impacted my life, and contributed to make me who I am. First and foremost were my parents. The love, understanding, support, and values that my sister and I received were primordial in shaping our characters, personalities, and consequently our achievements. My husband always believed in me, and encouraged my professional advancement, which was instrumental in my successful career. Unlike some Middle-Eastern men, he was proud of my accomplishments, and never felt threatened by them. Two of my Economics professors, Dr. Mikhail and Dr. Galal Amin made me passionate about Economics, and prompted me to excel. My graduate professors Dr. Sabry El Shabrawi, Dr. Amr Mortagy, and Dr. Bazaraa, taught me to be resilient and daring, and to stand for my beliefs. I would also like to recognize the many Citibank colleagues and supervisors who were my sounding board and life coaches.

Nearing the conclusion of this chapter, I would like to share some thoughts about the concept of success. I believe it is holistic, as it cannot be parceled out into separate compartments, it is made up of small steps that add up to complete the larger picture. For example, being a good mother, daughter, sister, cousin, friend can impact one's environment in many positive ways, and make a difference on the human level. It is at least as fulfilling and gratifying as professional success, yet less measurable than being the best bank president, minister, actor, writer, or scientist. Evaluating success in business is fairly easy because it is measured against acceptable benchmarks. These were used in assessing my performance, and as a result, I have been recognized and honored, most recently in February 2016, when the Government included me among "The 50 Most Influential Women in the Egyptian Economy." This latest award epitomized my lifelong quest for excellence; however, my greatest sense of achievement emanates from another source. When I see young members of my team, including some who considered me their role model, climb the ladder to senior positions in banks, companies, or government, I feel proud to have contributed even a small part to their progress.

All along, I have strived to do my best on the personal and professional levels, because I believe both are complementary. Moreover, I relish continuing to learn, understand the world around me, be creative, and help those who need me. By so doing, I hope to enhance my own life, and be a catalyst for change in the greater society and country where I live. The improvement I seek to achieve will likely not show immediate results, these will happen in the long term, and will hopefully make the world a better place for my children and grandchildren.

Cairo, January 2016

A LIFE DEDICATED TO HELPING THE MARGINALIZED AND BEYOND

MARIE BASSILI ASSAAD

IN COLLABORATION WITH

CHRISTINE ASSAAD[1]

Born in 1922 into an upper-middle class family of five siblings, I was an unwanted fourth girl. I came to life at an inopportune moment when my beloved maternal grandfather has just died, and the family was grieving. My parents would have preferred a son instead of a daughter. My brother, born in 1924, was welcomed with joy. I was also darker than my sisters, which gave me a lower standing within the family. It was a blessing in disguise that developed my stronger "fighter" personality, and increased my compassion toward the oppressed and neglected.

My mother was an only child who had been quite indulged by her maternal family. Despite her lack of interest in education, she was quite intelligent and influential throughout our lives. She decreed that I would not go to kindergarten; thus, I stayed at home until I was seven, and ready to go to school. Like my sisters, I was supposed to join a French private Catholic school, the Mère de Dieu, but the school had strongly tried to convince my eldest sister to become a nun, so my mother, a Coptic Orthodox, refused to send me there, and withdrew my other sisters who were privately tutored for a few years. As for me, mother decided to send me to a public institution, the Ghamra Primary School. Extended family members looked at government schools with disdain and made me feel like a black sheep. I tried to imitate my sisters, and made an effort to learn French on my own so I could understand them when they spoke that language at home. Nevertheless, we were a close-knit family where all the siblings played well together, despite our age difference and our mother's stiff personality.

In the public school, I stood out for two reasons: I came from a more privileged socio-economic background than the rest of the students, and I was Christian. Religious discrimination was not as pronounced as it is today; it existed, nevertheless, as there were only two Christians in the class. Despite these challenges, I did very well and had many friends. My eldest sister married at age 18, and her husband who had studied in the US eventually talked my mother into putting all of us at the American College for Girls. At first she resisted, believing that American education was too liberal, but she finally gave in.

I struggled when I joined the American College because I was much better in Arabic than the other students, my French was barely adequate, and my English poor. I worked hard to reach the required level, and became the one in charge of every single extracurricular activity, and the editor of the school newsletter. This created jealousy among fellow students who complained to the headmistress; she asked me to give a chance to others. I was a sensitive 17-year old, her words put me on the defensive, and I soon realized that it was the wrong approach to life.

By the time I was ready to go to university, my sisters had paved the way for me, convincing my mother it was important, despite her objection to its being mixed-gender. She was also conservative in her notion of marriage, and wanted to arrange marriages for each of us. My eldest sister married young, my second sister married a colleague of hers in the School of Social Work against my mother's wishes, and my third sister graduated from the American University in Cairo (AUC), and worked in an American organization where she met her American husband. My mother was categorically against that marriage, but my older sisters and their husbands finally convinced her to accept him, on condition that he learn to speak Arabic and become Orthodox.

At an early age, I developed an urge to help marginalized groups, especially women and girls. I volunteered to tutor in literacy classes in poor neighborhoods, in addition to serving as a social worker at the Young Women's Christian Association (YWCA), and in an NGO that dealt with families of TB patients. My job required that I collect information about them, and I learned to handle tough situations that I would not face in my privileged circles. I remember trying to find an address in Imam Al-Fateh, before realizing that I was actually looking for a family living in a tomb in the "City of the Dead." As an upper-middle class woman, I was naive about the dangers I could encounter in unsafe areas, and learned to protect myself while doing fieldwork.

After graduating from high school, I went to AUC and earned a B.A. in Sociology, Anthropology, Psychology and Education, but did not have a clear direction in mind. In September 1945, I was invited to travel to Ramallah, in Palestine, as a junior leader at the YWCA. I was asked to give an honest assessment of the YWCA Egypt, and impressed the Board members with my critical comments. Upon returning to Cairo, I was offered a job that I declined at first, but eventually joined the organization in 1946, after successfully negotiating a salary befitting a university graduate. The position at the YWCA allowed me to gain confidence, and taught me the importance of forming alliances at work. In 1948, my colleagues and I managed to merge the British and Egyptian chapters of the YWCA in Egypt.

Four years later, I was invited to attend the World YWCA Meeting in Geneva, at a time when they were looking for a junior staff member. I was invited to take the position for sixteen months, and thus became the first Egyptian on staff at the World YWCA. As a Program Assistant, I attended a closed meeting of the Commission on the Status of Women, where the subject of female genital mutilation (FGM/female circumcision) was discussed. It was a shocking revelation for me, as I had always felt the odd one out in my family. My mother had not circumcised me, unlike my sisters, because I was born at the time of mourning my grandfather and, according to tradition, I was never going to be married. That meeting made me realize that I was actually privileged not to have been circumcised, and I began to broach the subject with friends upon returning to Cairo in 1953. The friends with whom I spoke about this brutal and primitive practice thought I was crazy because this was a well-established tradition, but then I realized that these friends had Turkish mothers and had not been circumcised, according to an Egyptian tradition. Gradually, I was able to convince a few women not to circumcise their daughters. Although at the time I did not think of myself as a feminist, these experiences sensitized me to the different treatment of men and women in a patriarchal society. Injustice has always made me angry and prompted me to defend the weak and oppressed. Studying my environment, I also noted that more women than men were oppressed and mistreated.

After my initial assignment, I was offered a permanent position with the World YWCA in Geneva, but the Cairo YWCA opposed it as they wanted me back in Cairo. I was upset because I would miss the opportunity of being the first Egyptian permanent staff member travelling around the world. However, the World YMCA Secretary General was a wise person; she told me that she regretted the Cairo decision, but could not take me away from my original post, and advised me to leave everything in the hands of God who would lay the best plans for me. These words of wisdom have stayed with me throughout my life. In an effort to encourage me, she facilitated my attendance at the National Convention of the YWCA in Canada, and arranged a UN internship for me in New York, in summer 1953. Upon returning to Cairo in 1954, I became the Secretary General of YMCA Egypt. The next year, I got married and resigned my official position, although I continued to volunteer unofficially for several years.

Initially, I had no intention of getting married, and did not take the decision to marry lightly. In fact, I thought that I belonged to a group of empowered women who worked and spoke their mind, and men would be afraid to approach me. My husband, Assaad Abdel Motagalli Assaad, was someone I had always known. He had been a widower for twenty years, with two adult children who were my personal friends. His first wife died very young, and he did not intend to woo me due to our age difference, but his children urged him to marry me. In this and in many decisions in my life, I felt guided by a power beyond me. I prayed and eventually felt that it was God's will, and the marriage would be blessed. My mother and sisters were very keen, as Assaad was a wonderful man. He was 47, I was 33. I threw myself wholeheartedly into my family life, had two sons, and stopped working for ten years to dedicate myself entirely to them. In the meantime, I also worked on my Master's degree, and volunteered with several organizations. My husband was an unusually supportive partner who always encouraged me and helped with the children. Ours was a partnership of equals.

When I began Master's studies, my second child was entering kindergarten, and I was going to quit because there was too much pressure. However, my husband categorically refused to let me drop out. He insisted that once I started something, I had to see it through. I am eternally grateful to him for his encouragement, as this was a critical juncture in my career. I earned an M.A. in Sociology from AUC in 1969, and was invited by the Director of the AUC Social Research Center (SRC) to work with them. First, it was on a part-time basis, then full-time with full pay and benefits, and a flexible schedule; she knew that family was my priority. This was crucial, as it helped me a great deal when my husband passed away in 1974, while my sons were about to graduate from high school and wanted to study abroad. Throughout my husband's illness, people told me that I would not be able to send my sons abroad. I insisted that nothing would change the plans and that I would help my sons as best as I could. One went to Toronto in 1975, the other to Stanford in 1976.

I have been blessed by many great opportunities in life. At SRC, I worked on several issues and wrote a seminal paper about FGM practices in Egypt. In 1976, my colleagues unanimously recommended me for a WHO scholarship that would allow me to earn a graduate diploma in Population Studies from the University of Exeter in the UK. Upon returning in 1977, I resumed work at the SRC for three years, before being guided into another decision to join the World Council of Churches

(WCC) in Geneva, at the time when a women's movement was budding within the organization. In the 1970s, it had organized a conference about sexism, the first event in which the issue of unfair treatment of women was addressed, and a decision was made that one of the three deputies of the WCC Secretary General would have to be a woman.[2]

At that time, I was on the WCC Christian Medical Commission, headed by a friend from Barbados, Dame Ruth Nita Barrow. She came to visit in Cairo, and broke the news to me that I had been nominated for the post of WCC Deputy Secretary General, and had to give my answer in two days. This was a very big decision to make. I reflected and prayed before acknowledging that the opportunity must have been sent my way from above, so who was I to close the door? My sons urged me to accept; I also consulted Bishop Samuel of General Services, Egypt, who beamed when I told him the news. He knew about the discussions within WCC to appoint a woman deputy, but never dreamed that an Egyptian would be selected. Aware that I had been instrumental in starting the ecumenical movement in Egypt while at the YWCA, he could not think of anyone better suited for the post. The Coptic Pope gave his blessing as well, and I went to Geneva in 1980.[3]

It was a difficult move for me. I had never studied Theology and was not interested in the bureaucracy of churches. I was a petite woman in the midst of big men in the Secretariat General, the only one from the developing world and from the Coptic Orthodox Church. My two biggest strengths were my knowledge of different cultures and my good communication skills. I held the post of Deputy Secretary General from 1980 until 1986, and became the Director of the Unit on Education, which included many programs on women and youth. I was aware of the bias against women by the heads of churches, which made me work harder to prove my gender's capabilities. I remember the many sleepless nights I spent reading documents and preparing reports. Despite the bias, church heads wanted me to be present during deliberations and meetings with dignitaries such as the Archbishop of Canterbury and Bishop Desmond Tutu. I was always asked to sit at the right of the guest: it was a clear message that women were to be included at the forefront.

I am proud of two important achievements to improve the image of women at the WCC. The first was preparing the 1983 General Assembly in Vancouver. With my unit, I made sure that women's issues were on the agenda throughout. It was said that this meeting would be remembered by "two Ws": women and worship. As a result, when I left the WCC in 1986, two women became deputies. The second achievement was a book

Marie, Deputy Secretary General of the World Council of Churches, on an official WCC visit to Lebanon with representatives of various Christian denominations, c. 1983

published by the WCC entitled *Women, Religion and Sexuality: Studies on the Impact of Religious Teachings on Women*, in preparation for the Decade for Women and the Nairobi Conference in 1985. The book brought together various women theologians, anthropologists and scholars who delved into primary religious sources, and interpreted what different religions had to say about women, their bodies and their sexuality. It was a revolutionary idea in the Secretariat, but my initiative was supported and encouraged by the Secretary General, Philip Potter. I secured funding for the study and after almost a year, managed to identify eight women scholars from different regions of the world who would contribute to the book. The main conclusion was that despite the differences in religions and cultures, the similarities in interpreting women's status were striking. In every religion, Hindu, Buddhist, Muslim, Christian and Jewish, women's bodies and their sexuality were defined by men. Furthermore, women were lifted up to spiritual heights like the Virgin Mary, while at the same time considered second-class citizens.

I returned to Egypt in 1986 intending to retire. No longer interested in a paid job, I wished to dedicate myself to volunteering. A close friend of mine, Yousria Loza Sawiris, suggested that I might consider a newly formed NGO called the Association for the Protection of the Environment

(APE) active in the garbage collectors' community, the Zabbaleen in Moqattam,. When I visited it, I was impressed and decided to join the Board as an entry point for my development work. During the first two years, I did extensive fieldwork in the community to familiarize myself with the conditions, and learned a great deal. I served two terms on the Board, then resigned but continued as an Advisor to the President of the NGO. I also chaired the Health and Development Committee, to assess the health needs in the community, always making myself available to staff and volunteers who sought advice. I also worked on a project promoting garbage separation at the source, in order to make the process of garbage sorting easier and more hygienic for the women in the Zabbaleen community, and encouraged APE to focus on income generating activities for them. This included rug weaving, patchwork, and recycling paper products. My biggest contribution to APE was the enhancement of people's skills and the development of dignified livelihoods, especially for women. Working closely with APE volunteers, we promoted a comprehensive human development model for recycling projects, including health and education components. With its heightened focus on the well-being of women and children, APE has successfully raised the status of entire families, thus positively impacting society as a whole.

Marie with Jane Fonda on a visit to the garbage collection settlement, during the 1994 UN Population Conference in Cairo

My work with the poor in Manshiet Nasser led to my appointment by ministerial decree to the Committee for the Preparation of the International Cairo Population and Development Conference (ICPD) in 1994. I was approached by a Sudanese physician, Dr. Nahid Toubia, who knew about my previous research on FGM, and wanted me to become the Coordinator of a National Taskforce to Combat FGM. During the Conference, video footage was aired by CNN of a little girl's live circumcision. It shocked everyone, but brought our cause out into the open and gave it legitimacy. The Taskforce included representatives from various NGOs and funding agencies, including CARITAS, UNICEF, the Danish Embassy, the Ford Foundation, as well as individual researchers committed to combatting FGM. The Taskforce meetings were held at my home, sometimes gathering 30 or more people. Many donor agencies were willing to fund research and advocacy projects to help promote change. The Taskforce worked with local grassroots NGOs to influence religious leaders at the local level to speak out against this practice. It also participated in advocacy efforts with the government to criminalize the procedure. As a result, the National Council for Childhood and Motherhood (NCCM) adopted the fight against FGM, and ran high profile media campaigns to change public perception of the practice.

From L to R, Viviane Fouad, Bishop Youaness, Laurence Moftah, and Marie, on a visit to BLESS that Marie was advising on development activities, Cairo, 2005

I have always had an interest in gender sensitivity and equality based on my definition of feminism, which is liberation for everybody: women and men. My hypothesis is that the key to development and poverty alleviation is the empowerment of women, and I have committed my entire life to helping them improve their lives. As part of this mission, I have chosen to dedicate most of my efforts to combating female genital mutilation (FGM). It is part of a patriarchal culture that harms not only the bodies of women, but also their human integrity, their dignity, and their right to preserve their physical well-being. From my research at AUC in the 1970s to my work on the National Anti-FGM Taskforce in the 1990s, I have always strived to eliminate a procedure that devastates the lives of young girls in the name of tradition, and strongly advocated and fought against it everywhere, in Egypt and beyond. In fact, my profound commitment has earned me the nickname "FGM Diva," and my efforts, along with those of the Taskforce, have succeeded in criminalizing the practice and maintaining the issue high on Egypt's social agenda.

I have always enjoyed advising, mentoring and encouraging people who had good ideas or socially useful projects. I would spend countless hours discussing with them what they wanted to do, and how they could strategically do it. With my close friend Dr. Magda Iskander, I supported her initiative "Care with Love," an NGO designed to provide home health care—a first venture of its kind in Egypt. My proudest achievements, however, are the loyal lifelong friendships I have developed over several generations, including women such as Aziza Hussein, Aida Guindy, Laila Doss, Leila Al-Hamamsy, and many pioneers of social development and public service in Egypt and the world. I like to break down age barriers, and cherish my relationships with those in their 20s, 30s and 40s—the age of my granddaughters—who seek my advice, and I feel gratified to see the change I can make in their lives. My relationship with my children and grandchildren is very close, as I strongly encourage intergenerational communication. In advising younger friends, I emphasize open dialogue, and careful thinking before making decisions. My role has always been to empower people; it is part of my belief in the following fundamental concepts: use your social capital, the three Cs: depend on your Community of love, make sure you are clear in all your Communication, and benefit from Collective wisdom. I strongly advocate volunteerism as a vector for social development.   Looking toward the future, I hope that younger

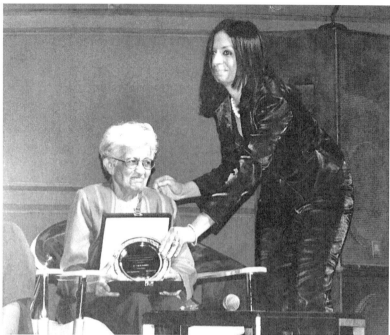

Marie receiving an award from UN Women on Women's Day, March 18, 2012, in Cairo. It is presented by Maya Morsi, in recognition of Marie's efforts to combat FGM.

volunteers will broaden the path I have established, in order to enhance the quality of life for all Egyptians, women, men and children.

Cairo, January 2016

Notes

[1] Special appreciation is hereby expressed to Viviane Fouad for providing archival documentation for this chapter.

[2] The World Council of Churches is made up of 345 member churches. In its own words it is described as "the broadest and most inclusive among the many organized expressions of modern ecumenical movement." It seeks to foster renewal in unity, worship, mission, and service.

[3] I have always been deeply rooted in my Coptic Orthodox faith, tradition, and spirituality. They have played a major role in guiding my life decisions and my commitment to help the poor and marginalized, and save Coptic heritage.

MY ROAD FROM ACADEME
TO VOLUNTARY WORK

HODA BADRAN

My childhood environment was special in many ways. My father, a professor of History, belonged to the intellectual elite of his time, and included among his friends the Chief Rabbi of Egypt and the Pope of the Coptic Church. Mastering the English and Arabic languages enabled him to translate nearly a hundred books, including *The Story of Civilization* by Will Durant. The most important place in our home was the library where my father spent the greatest part of his time. Thanks to him, I acquired a set of values based on toleration, acceptance of differences, and respect for learning and education. My mother was an upper-class beautiful woman of Turkish descent, with different interests, and an unusual personality. I was the oldest of seven children; the boys were clearly favored by my mother, but not my father. I attended both public and private schools, and was always the head of the class.

I had barely graduated from high school when I accepted to marry a man twenty years my senior, immediately got pregnant, gave birth to my daughter Fatma, lost my husband shortly thereafter, and became a widow at age 18. Back to live with my parents was not difficult for either my daughter or me, because I had not been away from home for long. As the first granddaughter, Fatma was treated like a princess. My mother took very good care of her, thus allowing me the leisure to develop a number of hobbies. I took music lessons to learn to play the *Oud*—an oriental musical instrument—started to paint, and practiced dressmaking, and embroidery, all of which contributed to my appreciation for the arts, and added a new dimension to my personality. In the evening, I often accompanied my parents to special receptions or dinners with their friends.

One day, I happened to be seated next to the Dean of the College of Social Work. During the conversation, I told her about my situation. She felt sorry for me, and expressed regret that I had not had a chance to go to university—a few words that were to change the course of my life. For the next couple of days, I could not stop thinking about our discussion and my excellent performance at school, and yearned to be a student again. Without telling anyone, I went to the School of Social Work and asked to meet the Dean. It was December, the academic year had started three months earlier, but I was sure I could make up the missed classes. The Dean was surprised that her comments had such an impact on me, and advised me to wait until the following year. Everyone was pleasantly surprised at my decision to go to university, except for my mother who had other plans for my future.

The following fall, I started university studies, as my daughter entered kindergarten. During the next four years, a special relationship developed between the Dean and me, and she was greatly satisfied with my top grades. My results encouraged me to consider graduate studies in Social Work, but that level of instruction was unavailable in Egypt at that time. The solution was to enroll at the American University in Cairo (AUC), and receive a scholarship to pursue a graduate degree in the US. Fortunately, I was able to coordinate my studies at the College of Social Work with my courses in the Sociology Department at AUC, thus graduating with two degrees: one in Social Science and another in Sociology, which enabled me to combine theoretical knowledge with practical skills. Unexpectedly, my plans took a different turn when I received a government scholarship through the College of Social Work, instead of AUC. Most Egyptian scholarship recipients favored Columbia University; however, a friend advised me to apply to the School of Social Work at the University of Louisville, in Kentucky.

I was in my twenties, and this was my first time outside Egypt. One early morning, after kissing my daughter and saying goodbye to the family, I headed to the airport, uncertain if I had made the right decision. I felt better, though, when I saw my brother, an intern in Bellevue Hospital in New York, who came to pick me up from JFK. We spent a nice week together in the city before I went to Louisville. I discovered that I was the only Egyptian not only on campus but also in the whole town. For two months, I lived in a university residence until two Egyptian women enrolled in my school, and the three of us decided to share an apartment. During my two years at Louisville, I was totally focused on my studies and did not allow myself to enjoy the American student life. I was anxious to complete my degree, and go back home. I missed my daughter although we exchanged letters twice a week, and I was worried about my father's health. I did, however, make some good friends, and had a chance to attend the famous Kentucky Derby. My grades were excellent, and thanks to the Foreign Student Advisor, I found a summer job as a medical social worker, which added some extra funds to the government stipend that paid for basic expenses, and enabled me to send a few gifts to my daughter.

Upon receiving the Master's degree, I was offered scholarships to pursue doctoral studies by both the university and the government, but I turned them down. Shortly after going home, I learned that my father had developed cancer, and I was glad for the opportunity to be with him during his final days. I did not realize how much I loved him until after his passing. Missing him during my two years in the US was different from missing him forever. In Egypt, I returned to the School of Social Work, and joined the Department of Community Organizations, headed by one of my former professors, a distinguished man with whom I was fortunate to work for three years. When I decided to go back to the US to get the PhD, he was in full support, and helped me to be admitted to Case Western Reserve (CWR) in Cleveland, Ohio. Since it was unusual to receive two government scholarships to study abroad, I thought I would have to pay for this degree with my own resources. Surprisingly, however, I received a second government scholarship for four years.

The experience in Cleveland was quite different from that in Louisville. I was enrolled in the School of Applied Social Sciences, well-known for its outstanding faculty and reputation. I worked as a graduate assistant for one of the professors, and a research assistant in a study funded by the Ford Foundation—two assignments that expanded my knowledge and experience beyond the classroom. I was in the US during the 1960s Civil Rights movement, and was privileged to participate in the demonstrations organized by the famous Dr. Benjamin Spock, a professor of Pediatrics at CWR. While I was in Cleveland, my daughter continued to live with my mother in Egypt, and came to visit me twice. The first time, she stayed only for the summer as I was busy preparing for my first qualifying exams; the second time, she spent a whole year. I managed to enroll her in a couple of courses, and the dean of my school helped her to find a job at the university library. Although I was working, studying, and helping Fatma with her own studies, I found the time to accompany her to cultural activities, and enjoyed various shows and events. We also took several trips to New York and California in my small VW, stopping for a day or two along the way to visit friends. Upon graduating, I worked for the Urban League in New York, an NGO headed at the time by Whitney Young. The Cleveland years have a special place in my memory, and I like to go back to that city whenever I have a chance.

When I returned to Egypt, I noticed a general deterioration of the environment, the shops and streets were in disrepair; even the expressions on people's faces seemed to have changed. At home, three of my brothers and a sister had married, and we would soon lose a brother in the 1967 war. My school had changed, the number of students had tripled, and a new building was standing where a beautiful park used to be. On a more positive side, my Department Head was still there, and with his encouragement, I published my first book. Every Wednesday evening, three colleagues and I would go to Alexandria to teach for two days at the Higher Institute for Social Work. These weekly trips created a special bond among us, and I never felt discriminated by them because of my gender. Eventually, one of them left Egypt for a UN post in Ethiopia, and another found a position with UNICEF in Cairo and later recruited me to carry out a study on women for the first International Conference on Women in Mexico in 1975. The report was presented at a regional conference sponsored by the Arab League and UNICEF. Among others in attendance were Helvetia Sepila, the UN Assistant Secretary General, and Jihan Sadat, the then-First Lady of Egypt who gave the keynote address. It was my first contact with her, we have remained friends ever since. My presentation was well received at both the national and international levels, and I was invited to address the international conference in Mexico, and offered a position at the UNICEF Office in Cairo, then promoted to Regional Advisor for Women at the UNICEF Regional Office in Lebanon.

Defense of a doctoral dissertation: Hoda (L) with Dr. Nazli Moawad (R), Cairo University, 2000

I never planned to leave my university position before retirement age, and managed to teach a course while working at UNICEF in Cairo; but I had to resign from the School of Social Work when I moved to Lebanon. During my six years as Regional Advisor, I had the opportunity to work on the status of women in all the Arab countries. My academic background was a definite asset, as it facilitated my contacts with universities and research institutions when I needed their cooperation. One of my most important projects was the establishment of a maternal clinic inside Al Azhar University. My non-traditional thinking and approach were appreciated not only in the Regional Office, but also at UNICEF Headquarters. My next promotion introduced me to the fascinating cultures of Asia where I was posted for four years as Resident Representative in Sri Lanka and the Maldives. This was a new professional experience where I had to learn a great deal. Now I had to administer a large staff and a budget in the millions of dollars, a responsibility for which none of my previous positions as professor, UNICEF officer or regional advisor, had prepared me. In addition to the regular daily tasks, there was a busy schedule of lunches, dinners and receptions I had to host or attend. Strictly speaking, these were not purely social events, as a sizable part of the work was concluded during those functions, in a less formal atmosphere.

Hoda with President J. R. Jayawardene of Sri Lanka (C) and Minister of Foreign Affairs A. S. Hameed

The wife of the Regional Representative generally plays an important role handling the entertainment activities. Unfortunately, I did not have the luxury of a wife and had to handle both jobs myself. I also discovered that the golf course was a favorite place to discuss business with the donor community. I did not particularly enjoy getting up early to play golf, but I was able to reach many agreements in-between shots. The Minister of Foreign Affairs and another two members of the cabinet had studied at Al Azhar University in Egypt, which helped to create a special relationship between us and facilitated my work. One of the measures of success for the UN Representative was determined by the number of high-ranking officials who attended the functions s/he hosted. In my case, the presence of at least three members of government was a good indicator. These were also instrumental in allowing me to establish direct contact with the president of the country—another positive sign of the quality of my work. When *The Wall Street Journal* mentioned that one of my conferences was attended by the president and five eminent international personalities, I received a congratulatory note from the UNICEF president, in recognition of my exceptional work.

Sri Lankans tell an interesting story about the way God created their country. It claims that a leaf fell from a tree in Heaven, swirled and dropped in the ocean, and became the island of Sri Lanka. Sri Lankans believe that their country is very special, and in many ways it is. I blended easily among the various groups. The culture was gender-blind, thus a number of embassies were headed by women. The Egyptian Ambassador at that time was a man, and I related well to him and his family. Although the country was poor, it had very good social indicators: the infant mortality rate was lower than that of Washington DC, and the literacy level very high.

Meanwhile, my daughter had married and given birth to a son. During my posting in Asia, she and her family came twice to visit. I missed being close to them, which was one of the reasons that I resigned from my job; the other was a disagreement with my boss regarding my next assignment. I was in my fifties at that time, with no job back home. The Dean of the School of Social Work had just retired, and I was asked to replace him. My preference was to go back to teaching, with no administrative duties. An agreement was reached, and I was delighted to return to academe.

One day, while teaching a graduate course, there was a knock on the door. Interrupting an ongoing class was no ordinary matter. I opened the door, and found the departmental secretary apologizing, and informing me that the Prime Minister was on the phone asking to talk with me. Without much of an introduction, he set an appointment to see him the following day. At the meeting, he offered me the position of Secretary General of the National Council for Childhood and Motherhood (NCCM), which had just been created by presidential decree, and I was expected to transform the paper decision into reality! The Prime Minister provided some information on the procedure to follow in order to get started, and the names of a few people who might be able to assist me. The offer did not come as a total surprise, as I had been consulted about the potential creation of that body by then-First Lady, Suzanne Mubarak, who was strongly behind the project. Several candidates were competing for the post, all highly qualified and recommended; later, I found out that Mrs. Mubarak was the one who suggested me, based on our previous encounters.

Hoda (L) and First Lady Suzanne Mubarak (R) leaving the National Council on Childhood and Motherhood, Cairo, 1990

To manage a government institution of that level was yet a new experience for me. Although the Prime Minister was my official boss, the real one was Mrs. Mubarak. The administrative structure of the Council made the unusual situation uneasy to handle. However, I consider my five years as Secretary General of the Council the best part of my professional life, because not only did I received the full support of my real boss, I also enjoyed her guidance and could put into action her creative ideas. While my work at UNICEF introduced me to international circles, my position at the Council placed me at the highest national decision-making level. During that period Egypt was elected on the Board of UNICEF, and I was its Representative, in my position as Secretary General of the NCCM. Moving from a UNICEF executive position to that of member of its Board provided far-reaching insight. Twice a year, I had the pleasure of going to New York to attend Board meetings, and saw my former colleagues in the familiar UN environment. My past experience in the organization gave me rare depth of perspective in the discussion of projects and programs.

During that period, exciting decisions related to children took place at the international level, including the proclamation of the International Convention on the Rights of the Child (CRC), and the convening of the World Summit for Children. Egypt, and Mrs. Mubarak in particular, were the principal instigators of these events. The Council organized an international conference to advocate for the CRC, and Egypt's First Lady was the keynote speaker at several international meetings, in support of these proposals. Egypt was one of six countries planning the Summit for Children, in which I was also deeply involved. The role played by Egypt and Mrs. Mubarak, and my experience as a UNICEF executive gave me a strong voice on the Board, allowing me to recommend our First Lady for the Morris Pate Prize, a recognition she highly deserved. My role as mediator between UNICEF and the Egyptian Ministry of Foreign Affairs was crucial in the preparations for the award ceremony.

During those years, I was also Egypt's representative on the international committee monitoring the implementation of the CRC, and was elected president of a committee of ten experts. These responsibilities took me to Geneva twice a year, to question state parties about their nations' efforts to implement the CRC. It was heartwarming to see school children, accompanied by their teachers, sitting in the UN balcony to hear about their human rights, and listen to their implementation in different parts of the world. My retirement age was reached at a time when a number of projects at the Council were about to end, and my boss wanted me to bring them to conclusion. My mandate was thus extended twice, bringing to a happy end my professional life as a government official.

In 1986, in a meeting with some Arab and Egyptian friends, we decided to establish an NGO, the Alliance for Arab Women (AAW), which would bring together various groups working on women's issues. I was elected Chair, but did not have much time to devote to it while professionally active. Upon retiring, however, I was able to give it more attention. At first, AAW had a modest budget of about $ 35 000, but as it gradually gained respect and recognition among the community of donors, its yearly budget climbed to $ 3 million. After the January 2011 Revolution, when Egyptian women felt marginalized, AAW convened a conference attended by 300 NGOs to express the need for a larger coalition to defend their rights. The conference decided to revive the Egyptian Feminist Union (EFU) that had been established by early feminist Huda Shaarawy in 1923, but was frozen after the July 1952 Revolution. The AAW became a member of EFU, and I was elected to chair it. The EFU started with 15 NGO members, and has now grown to 300. It is the only feminist entity with presence on the ground in all the governorates of Egypt, and has the power to mobilize millions of women when needed.

Through its activities, the EFU was able to bring to Cairo the Secretariat of the General Arab Women Federation (GAWF). The Federation embodies the national women's unions of all the Arab countries, including the EFU. It was my great honor to be unanimously elected President of the Federation; however, I found my responsibilities heading three organizations to be excessive, so I resigned from chairing AAW in 2015. Since its establishment in Egypt, the GAWF has become more influential, and was mandated by UNWOMEN to produce the Arab Shadow Report on Beijing+20, which was discussed at the meeting of its Commission on the Status of Women (CSW) in New York, in March 2015.

Looking back at the various chapters of my life, I feel privileged to have been involved in an unusually large variety of professional activities: academe, the UN, government, and voluntary work. Each of these took me in a different direction that I never expected, all providing a great sense of fulfillment. At this point in my life, I am particularly gratified to have had the opportunity to put my knowledge and experience at the service of my country and my fellow citizens. Moreover, I am honored to have invested my expertise in the cause of women, those of Egypt and beyond.

Cairo, January 2016

BREAKING WALLS AND BUILDING BRIDGES

MAYSAA BARAKAT

I was born and raised in the Cairo suburb of Heliopolis. As my first and foremost significant role model, my mother was but one of a series of strong women who have impacted my life. My father, a mechanical engineer and a general in the Egyptian army, together with my brother, my husband, and my two daughters are my main anchor and support group. Born in the mid-1960s, going to school in the 1970s, and attending college in the 1980s, I shared the middle-class values of my generation: education, hard work, fairness, and, most importantly, level-headedness, to which my parents added empathy. While weaving the fabric of this chapter, I will reflect on the influence that my background has had on my career choices, and led me to focus on the importance of cultural competence and its crucial impact on future generations.

In the 1960s, Heliopolis was developing into an upper-middle class neighborhood, with Indian laurel and royal poinciana trees on both sides of the streets, high-rise residential buildings, and a pleasing architectural environment. Heliopolis residents were generally well-educated professionals, whose lifestyle was a happy medium between modernity and tradition. The English school I attended for 12 years mirrored our Heliopolis culture. Secular, co-educational and private, it was unique among a myriad of public and Catholic schools, single sex, and private language institutions. My schoolmates and I had similar family backgrounds, our parents looked and dressed alike, and shared the progressive values of their era: open-mindedness, common sense, and healthy appreciation for responsible freedom, as well as respect for cultural traditions and moral standards.

Sheltered in the magnificent school campus and its majestic buildings, rumored to have been standing since the early years of British occupation, I spent my formative years engaging in classroom debates, attending gatherings in the assembly hall, singing in the choir, proudly displaying my art creations, and, most of all, playing basketball on the outdoor courts. I was among the highest achievers, and a permanent fixture of the elite "class A" group; however, I did not stand out. During those years, I blended nicely with most of my peers, and was clearly visible to a few good friends.

An incident stands out in my mind as I remember my adolescent years. On the eve of the final exam for the year, my parents were peacefully enjoying the pleasant breeze of a May evening on the balcony of our seventh-floor apartment, in a beautiful and tall building. From there, I could see my entire world: my school stood majestically two blocks away, and in the turnabout was the metro train that took me to the club where I also played basketball. Relieved that the academic year was coming to an end, I asked my parents for permission to go out with my school friends after the final. My father casually asked if we would be accompanied by a teacher. "No," I replied, we were in tenth grade and did not need a chaperone. My parents exchanged one of their familiar looks, then my dad firmly ended the conversation by saying that I could not go in the absence of an adult, adding: "What do you think? We are not in America!" Little did he or I know at that point that I would be spending more than half of my adult life striving to bridge the cultures of Heliopolis and America.

In contrast to the homogeneous nature of my school and neighborhood, my parents' family backgrounds were quite different. My maternal grandparents had settled in the prestigious suburb of Zizina, in Alexandria, after years of traveling throughout Upper Egypt where my grandfather was a judge. He held my grandmother in very high regard, only referring to her as "El Hanem," a title reserved for female members of high-ranking families. Indeed, she was a sophisticated and charismatic community leader, who contributed to multiple charities and organizations. She spoke French fluently, was very creative, and had an impeccable sense of fashion, and exquisite taste in home furnishings. She was an important member of a long line of strong women who influenced my life. Competing with her for the title of "Alpha female of the household" was "Amma" Zeinab, the housekeeper and nanny who helped to raise my mom and her two brothers, hence the qualifier "Amma," a familiar way to address an older person in Upper-Egypt. Amma Zeinab was a single illiterate woman who refused to ever get married, rejecting the authority of a husband. She was the matriarch of her extended family and the breadwinner for her many nieces and nephews. My mom and uncles loved and respected her, and, yes, also feared her. Even though Amma would never allow herself to sit down in the presence of my grandmother— implicitly acknowledging their class status—the power struggle between the two was real, and all of us learned to stay clear whenever a face off was looming on the horizon. These two distinct yet similarly strong and outspoken women were in vivid contrast to my kind, timid, and soft spoken paternal grandmother, "Teta."

On my father's side, my grandparents lived in Shamshira, a beautiful small village on the Rosetta branch of the Nile. I fondly remember our family gatherings during the "Eid" holidays, six uncles, two aunts, and many cousins. Teta would try to hide us, and instruct us not to be seen for fear of the evil-eye. As children, we had the best time fishing, riding donkeys, and getting on small row boats on the Nile. We were treated like celebrities because my grandfather was the "Omda," the most important person in the village, the equivalent of a mayor. We were also special because we were urbanites who came from the capital city of Cairo, and dressed and spoke differently. I was always fascinated to watch my dad switch to his rural dialect whenever he met with his siblings and cousins who all did likewise; it was as if they were bilingual within the same language. As I grew older, the patriarchal nature of mentalities in Shamshira became obvious to me, as well as the subtle sexist comments and gender roles. However, even in the 1950s in Shamshira, there were enlightened people, and my grandfather, the omda, was among the most progressive. He fully supported the education of women, thus his eldest daughter, my aunt, became the first woman in the family to receive a university degree.

Embraced by my family on both sides, I developed an early awareness and sharp sensitivity for cultural differences, norms, behaviors, and expectations. Proud of my heritage, I used to share my knowledge of life in Egypt's villages with my big city friends. I showed off my skills by imitating my dad's and uncles' rural dialect, and bragged about our family roots. My interest in diversity and fascination with cultures were encouraged by my mom who took after her own mother. A polished and refined graduate of the elite school Notre Dame de Sion in Alexandria, she was able to reach out and relate to people from all walks of life. It was pure pleasure to hear, quote, and comment on the innumerable Egyptian proverbs that accurately mirrored Egyptian life and mentalities.

When I received the Bachelor's degree in Architecture from the Faculty of Engineering at Ein Shams University in Cairo, my dad was boasting with pride. While considering employment opportunities, I had concerns about working in the field, and expressed definite preference for more sheltered environments. My dad was disappointed in my attitude, and encouraged me to pursue the most challenging positions, confident that I could do anything. I applied for a job at the National Authority for Tunnels (NAT), created in 1983 to carry out the construction of the first underground metro line in Cairo, in collaboration with the French government. In 1987, I was the youngest architect in the Department of Technical Studies, headed by a small-framed woman but a giant in her field, Shoushou El Bedeiwy. She was a competent and strong engineer who had broken the glass ceiling in her male-dominated profession. During my years at NAT, she was a role-model who afforded me countless learning opportunities, including collaboration with the international architects of the *Société française d'études et de réalisations de transports urbains* (SOFRETU), the French consulting firm in charge of the project's development. I also worked with iconic Egyptian artists, especially Dr. Salah Abdel Karim who coordinated the selection and acquisition of numerous art pieces to decorate the underground metro stations. In 1987, I was selected to represent my department in the ribbon-cutting ceremony celebrating the inauguration of the very first Cairo metro line, and presented the scissors to French President François Mitterrand who was present for the momentous occasion.

For three years, I enjoyed my short and exciting career as an architect, until I fell in love head over heels with a tall and handsome engineer, Essam Abou Zeida. We married in 1990 and moved to Columbus, Ohio, where he pursued doctoral studies. In our new environment, not blending with ordinary people, I stood out. Overnight, I found myself in the spotlight, out of my comfort zone. Eventually, I accepted the situation and used my status as an exotic person to advocate for my country, and promote a better understanding of its people and their culture. I felt like a living version of the proverbs that my mom loved to quote, which carry the wisdom of centuries of human experience. They reflect the inherent patience, and deeply rooted faith in God shared by Coptic and Muslim Egyptians alike.

Soon after moving to the US, we had two beautiful daughters: Farida and Aliah. Through them, I became even more sensitive to cultures, constantly reflecting about the embedded values they carry. In an effort to help my children integrate into American society and ease their transition into school, I applied for a job as a teacher in the Learning Center of Westerville (LCW), a private preschool where they were enrolled. I was hired, and, surprisingly, loved being a teacher. Actually, an architect and an educator have more in common than most people might think. Both professions require creativity, critical thinking, problem solving skills, the ability to focus on the big picture while tending to details, and taking culture and context into account.

I attended many professional development sessions to better prepare myself for my newfound passion, and started thinking about education as a second career, not just a temporary job. During my time at LCW, I was able to combine my personal and professional experiences to educate my colleagues and my daughters' classmates about Egyptian culture. The girls knew that, as a family, we were somewhat different: we spoke Arabic at home, and had no relatives in America. They were not allowed to eat the red slices of meat on pizza, and learned to say: "We are Muslims, we don't eat pork." It was also beneficial for my daughters to learn and talk about their Egyptian roots. I worked at LCW for four years, during which I became head teacher and was assigned some administrative responsibilities. By then, Essam had successfully completed his PhD and it was time to go back to our native country.

Upon returning to Egypt in 1996, I accepted to be in charge of establishing a preschool program replicating the LCW model in one of Cairo's new and fast growing private schools. The principal, a powerful woman, gave me the authority: (1) to design and supervise the preparation of the physical space of the Child Development Center; (2) to create and execute a marketing campaign for the Center; (3) to hire qualified teachers; (4) to develop the curriculum and needed technology, and order textbooks and learning materials; and (5) to interview parents and enroll their children. It was both the best and the most testing of times. I appreciated the autonomy and challenge, as well as the opportunity to sharpen my knowledge and skills, both as an architect and an educational administrator. Essam and I enjoyed the novel situation of having a village of parents, family and friends, to help care for Farida and Aliah, and I was able to commit heart, mind and soul to bring the Child Development Center to fruition. I ran the program for about three years filled with many successes, and a few frustrations; overall, however, it was a fulfilling learning experience.

Based on my work at the Child Development Center and my experience in the US, I was offered the position of Assistant Principal of the new American division at the school. In addition to the skills I applied in developing the Center, the job required effective communication, conflict resolution, and sound advocacy, since I also served as liaison between the Egyptian school administration and the American principal and teachers. The school principal, Dr. Gary Kenny and I collaborated on the launching and development of the procedures needed to obtain accreditation of the school. Navigating through many layers of cross-cultural bumps and conflicts, and administrative and educational challenges, I emerged as a more seasoned and competent school manager. For 12 years, I assumed leadership positions and served as a consultant for several prestigious international schools, spearheading improvement projects, self-study programs, and accreditation efforts. For my role as

Head of the International General Certificate of Secondary Education (IGCSE) in one of the schools, I was honored by the British Council in Cairo with the Beacon Award for Coordinators, from the Cambridge International Examination.

By 2008, I had hit the glass ceiling of school leadership in Egypt, and time had come for a new venture. We returned to the US where Essam was appointed Visiting Scholar at Auburn University in Alabama. Farida started college, Aliah entered high school, and I tagged along with no real plan, but confident that good things would happen. Shortly thereafter, I met Dr. Samia Spencer, a compatriot, an old friend and neighbor of my mom, and an accomplished and well respected member of the Auburn University faculty and the community. She became a mentor who inspired and guided me, as I embarked on a journey toward my third career as a university professor. Based on her advice and invaluable recommendation, I was admitted to the Master's program in Educational Leadership at Auburn University, and awarded a teaching assistantship. In May 2010, I completed the degree, and received the PhD four years later.

Being a graduate student was a different and invigorating experience, highlighted by the vivifying level of maturity and experience that my professors and colleagues brought to the table. We were immersed in theory, dialogue, debate and self-reflection. These stimulating exercises allowed me to acquire and assimilate the theoretical foundation that I was lacking. When I integrated this newly-gained knowledge with my extensive experience as a practitioner, my thoughts gradually started to align and make sense. Thus, I was able to excel in my studies, and earned many honors from the Department, the College, the University, and various professional organizations. I was appointed Graduate Student Ambassador, and recognized as a David L. Clark Scholar, in addition to receiving the Outstanding International Graduate Student Award, and another from the Alma Holladay Endowment for Academic Excellence. Thanks to institutional travel funds, I presented papers on cultural competence and educational leadership at State, National and International conferences. Clearly, Auburn University appreciated the unique and valuable perspective I brought to its programs as a mature and experienced international student.

I will forever be indebted to my professors and the members of my dissertation committee for their impact on my professional development, and their invaluable advice while preparing for the job market. However, I must single out Dr. Fran Kochan, professor, dean and mentor, whose influence on my life remains quintessential. An educator, scholar, and pioneer in her field, she was instrumental in breaking the glass ceiling in her profession, paving the way for other women to follow in her footsteps. Like my mother, she was strong in a gentle way, leading with competence and empathy. As a professor at Florida Atlantic University, I aspire to follow the example of Dr. Kochan, and apply the principles and values she taught me, as I mentor my own students.

Sailing between countries and careers, personal life and professional experience continued to merge, providing a deeper and broader understanding of humanity. In this present day and age, perhaps more than ever before, and in a world where conflict, violence, mistrust, and misunderstanding are widespread, there is an urgent need to reverse the trend, and reject prejudice, discrimination, and hatred. Through my teaching, research, and collaborative work, I seek to promote enlightenment, understanding, acceptance, and toleration. In short, in light of my multicultural background, my interdisciplinary education, and my vast experience crossing two centuries on two continents, I am unconditionally committed to breaking barriers, fighting ignorance, advancing dialogue, and building bridges. And even though the bridges are sometimes abused, nevertheless they are an important and much needed asset. As I view it, this process starts as an intrapersonal endeavor that engages the self in reflection, and challenges deeply rooted beliefs.

During my journey, I drew wisdom and strength from the lessons I learned from many powerful women who surrounded me as I was growing up, starting with my mother, grandmothers, and mother-like figures. I also owe much to my two daughters who have shown strength as they morphed from being culture-conflicted kids to mature and confident global citizens. My role models also include women I was fortunate to encounter along the way: acquaintances, lifelong friends, mentors, teachers, supervisors and colleagues, from all walks of life. There were homemakers, politicians, educators, engineers, ambassadors, TV directors, writers, some of whom were highly educated, others barely literate. Among those who influenced me some were Egyptians, others were not, which leads me to conclude that strong women are not necessarily from the East or the West, and do not follow principles associated with a particular culture or country. The extraordinary personalities that stand out in my mind were individuals who believed in basic human rights, and acknowledged that everyone, regardless of gender, must enjoy the freedom to make choices for themselves, for there are no books or movements that provide a mold that fits all.

In short, to my daughters, and to all the young women in Egypt and beyond, I say: be true to yourself, make decisions wisely while weighing their consequences, and surround yourself with enlightened individuals who know you, appreciate you, and are committed to help you spread your wings and reach your goals.

Boca Raton, Florida, October 2015

The Mulberry Trees on Rue Stross

Magda El-Nokaly

Wise as you will have become, so full of experience, you will have understood by then what these Ithakas mean.

Cavafy[1]

Let the title be about trees, suggested pensively my lovely young friend, because you are a tree. I was stunned at her insight! How could she have known I wrote an essay about wanting to become a tree at age 14? A tree has strong roots, stands tall and proud, aspires to the skies, dares to go out on a limb, and generously bears fruit. When chopped, it continues to give, repeating the cycle of life. In their essays, my schoolmates had dreamed of getting married, having children, and becoming rich—all mundane wishes. A grade of 2/20 was my punishment from a favorite nun for daring to be different. Back then, I desperately wanted to be accepted, not unique or different. Fifty-five years later, my friend confirmed I had unconsciously achieved my goal. I had become one of a kind, hopefully a fruitful and majestic old tree. The circle is now almost complete. My voyage, destined to be different from day one, took a lifetime to accept.

The first image that comes to mind when reflecting upon my childhood is one of a serene scene under a huge ficus tree. It is in my maternal grandparents' home in Rouchdy, Alexandria. My gifted older cousin Mona and I are having a drawing lesson. Our teacher is an old, thin, white-bearded man, always in a black suit. He speaks only Italian, and must be one of the numerous Jewish European refugees in our then-hospitable and cosmopolitan city. He focuses exclusively on Mona. I am an observer, and feeling the warmth of those sunny afternoons.

My grandparents' home was my fortress, my "Jalna," a 1930 Mediterranean-style villa decorated with red tiles, typically built for the Egyptian upper classes. [2] It sat high on Stross street, then-called rue Stross, after a British colonial official. Due to its proximity to an ancient Roman camp, the children fantasized about a treasure buried underneath it.

After the 1952 Revolution, the street name changed to Alfred Lian, a physician of Lebanese descent. Once again, it was renamed Samir Zada, to memorialize an Egyptian hero of the 1973 Israeli-Egyptian war. Four beautiful mulberry trees towered majestically over the villa's entrance.

Two of the mulberry trees on rue Stross

They were among those rare trees in Alexandria changing with the seasons, each bearing a different colored fruit. During the quaint Stross years, children would politely request leaves to feed their silk worms. As times changed, children no longer asked permission, breaking stones from the wall and targeting the berries. Two trees died and the remaining cut short, never allowed to bear fruits. Mulberry trees are dying in Egypt, mirroring the fate of old cosmopolitan Alexandria. I was born on rue Stross, and will probably die on Samir Zada street. I have witnessed the British protectorate, King Farouk's reign, Nasser's Revolution, nationalization, socialism, capitalism, four wars, and two recent revolutions.

The reason for my "difference" started before my birth, upon my parents' divorce. I was the only fatherless child in my mother's extended family. My grandfather was my father figure without fulfilling the role. A good looking, witty and renowned economist, he was appointed twice

Minister of Finance during King Farouk's reign, and was decorated by France and Great Britain for services rendered during WWII. He was multilingual, attended the League of Nations, corresponded with Bertrand Russell, met Yugoslavia's President Tito, and India's Prime Minister Nehru, among others. He is remembered in History for refusing to fund the restoration of King Farouk's yacht from an empty government treasury. This act of courage, rare in Egypt at that time, was rewarded by a position in Nasser's government after the 1952 Revolution. He was appointed Head of the Production Council, in charge of drawing economic strategies for Egypt's development. A Renaissance man, larger than life, he and Alexandria were dreams that all of us in the family tried to relive in our adult lives. However, the time of great men and Alexandria seems forever gone. Throughout my life, I searched and never found a place close to our mythical city, with its cosmopolitan communities living together peacefully and harmoniously.

Grandfather predicted that Egypt would soon be on the road to socialism and nationalization. When time came to choose between studying science or humanities, he advised me to go for a career ensuring a comfortable life anywhere in the world. His prediction proved accurate. Suddenly, we all became poor. Following his advice to the letter, I became a PhD chemical engineer, and worked for a multinational company across the globe.

I married shortly after graduating from Alexandria University. Both my husband and I enrolled at Northwestern University, in Evanston, Illinois, a suburb of Chicago. In 1968, I was the first woman in the graduate program of the Chemical Engineering Department. Years later, I was told that the women, all secretaries, had bet on my success, against the all-male professors—there were no women on the faculty then. Needless to say, who won. I also worked in a chemical company in downtown Chicago during the terrible 1968 riots, witnessing its ghettos aflame the night of Martin Luther King's assassination.

Not expecting my marriage to last, I focused on getting a Master's at the expense of starting a family. After completing our degrees, my husband and I returned to Egypt where I joined the Egyptian National Starch Company, a public sector entity. It provided great insight into the Egyptian industrial environment. Witnessing the dedication and sacrifice of Egyptian workers, I acquired a great deal of respect for them, but was disappointed with the carelessness of the supervisors for safety. Enthusiastically, I fought to apply the general scientific safety guidelines I had learned in the US. I won some of the battles and lost many.

In order to pursue doctoral studies, I joined the Colloid Chemistry division of a newly founded UNESCO Research Center in Alexandria. My husband judged me not PhD material and gave me no support. A

Magda El-Nokaly shaking hands with Egyptian Prime Minister Mamdouh Salem, Alexandria University Research Center, 1975

Swedish visiting professor at the Center came to my rescue. Bashfully, I asked him if I was capable of getting a doctorate. A spirited man, he answered: "Your husband must be very cruel. Anyone can do it, if they put their mind to it." It helped me to persevere and succeed against all odds. The inevitable divorce was the onset of my lonely voyage. Another deterrent was the attitude of my Egyptian PhD advisor. He asked me why I was in a hurry to complete the degree, I was too old anyway at age 30 to remarry or start a career. Years later, he would boast about having been my advisor. Such stance would be a pattern in my personal life and my career, with important exceptions: the great Egyptian actor Mahmoud Morsy, the French Nobel laureate Pierre-Gilles de Gennes, and two great General Managers at the Procter & Gamble Company. They were exceptional men and wise mentors, not intimidated by my talent, and having no need to prove their superiority by debasing others. I owe them my sanity and success. I am also grateful to another person who rendered me a great service. During a P&G training course, he criticized me viciously in response to what I thought to be a simple question. Later, he kindly admitted: "As a middle-aged man not going anywhere in my career, I felt threatened by a highly intelligent woman like you." His acknowledgment released me from the insecurity of not understanding why I had deserved such treatment. Until then, I always blamed myself for not being good enough.

Having missed the support and encouragement of a father, I did not developed self-confidence until much later in life. Whenever put down, I tried harder, causing more intimidation. My role models being the truly independent women of my family, I did not learn subtle feminine manipulation. Unfortunately, throughout my career, I met very few women who were supportive of their gender in the workplace. Fierce competition was the name of the game. Women and minorities hurt me the most, yet they were the ones I always protected and encouraged. A true Capricorn, I was disciplined, hard-working, and perseverant. The only unfailing support I enjoyed came from my mother, a strong woman who attributed her unhappiness to the lack of a university degree. She returned to high school at age 42 to attend classes with students my age. Then, she proceeded to fulfill her dream of acquiring a BA in English literature. She introduced me to Shakespeare and Anglo-Saxon writers whose works were not taught in my French school. Working in a man's world, she and her sisters were recognized as Egyptian pioneers of their generation.

For seven months after receiving the PhD, I searched in vain for a job in Egypt. Research was conducted only in academe, and I had not risen through its ranks. Even provincial universities would not give me a chance. Timing was bad and money tight. Nasser's socialism was waning, and Sadat's capitalism not yet fully fledged. Nationalization had left us with valuables from a bygone era that no one could afford to buy, and no cash. I needed a job to put food on the table for my mother and myself, so I accepted a post-doctoral position at the renowned School of Mines of the University of Missouri at Rolla. During three years on that campus, I received the US Green Card, published my first papers, and taught my first classes. At first, it was hard for me, a city girl, to adapt to country life. I remember exactly the moment when I converted into a country girl: it was on my first White Water canoe trip. I learned to enjoy the Ozarks, country living and music. I loved teaching, and my students reciprocated the feelings. Very little attention was needed to motivate them, and keep them focused. A student dedicated to me a poem that I still cherish.

Preparing to return to Egypt, I received an offer I could not refuse: an industrial position in San Francisco. The minute I set foot in that city, it was love at first sight. It is there that I registered my first US patent for formulating a lethal organophosphate pesticide that may be at the root cause of an autoimmune disease I contracted later. Being too young and earnest, I never worried about its effect on my health. In California, I drove for hours through Napa Valley or Carmel, never feeling homesick. In my second year in that post, I was promised a research job in Egypt where my mother and my brother needed me, and I felt compelled to return. I resigned, hating to leave San Francisco. Nevertheless, being cautious, I accepted an offer from the Procter & Gamble Company in case the promised position in Alexandria would not materialize. My precaution was well-founded.

The job in Alexandria never materialized. Like many expatriates, I faced discrimination upon returning to serve my homeland. It was very sad, indeed, that well-educated Egyptians were not able to transfer to their country the knowledge they acquired in highly industrialized nations. Each year, I would look for a job in Egypt, but would find another in the US. Finally, I realized that I needed to count my blessings, as many people yearned for my status. It was then that I stopped feeling in forced exile. Little did I know that Cincinnati, Ohio, and P&G would become my home for the next 28 years.

The tragic death of my mother soon after I joined P&G left me depressed for years. In the meantime, I dedicated my life to work and innovation, making some great discoveries related to Colloids, Nanoparticles, Polymers and Product Formulation, all registered in numerous patents I was awarded. My Master's thesis in Polymers and my doctoral dissertation in Colloids were complementary. These were still unchartered territories making me a true pioneer in industrial research. I had stumbled onto them by pure luck. This expertise gave me a unique background, and supported my entire career. Colloid chemistry, presently labeled Nanoparticles, is a combination of many disciplines. It is still more of an art than a true science, needing imagination and diverse capabilities, especially in Formulation. Most of my colleagues had been thoroughly trained in one discipline, and had trouble connecting them to each other. Being creative and having an interdisciplinary background, I first encountered strong resistance from my peers. When "innovation" became a crucial need for companies to advance in the global economy, enlightened managers realized that I possessed the perfect skills and profile.

For the first time during these difficult years, I experienced the subtle nuances of racism. I remember complaining to my African-American manager that my ideas and contributions were disregarded during our meetings. He explained it as racism. I could not understand why anyone would look down on me. I was competent in my field, multilingual and possessed many talents, and refused to believe then that it was due to the color of my skin and my accent. So I kept trying to please, to no avail. It was tough to be alone, without family or a support group. I did not fit in either the black or the white community. Having had a French education and traveled extensively in Europe, I related better to Europeans and Latin Americans. Unlike Italians or Greeks who come to America from the same villages and cultures, Egyptians carry their class issues in exile. Very few Egyptians gave me the moral support I needed during my ordeals. I was probably repaying the debt of my class back home. Today, those who stood by me are forever special friends.

I had not come all this way to fail, and had no place to go but up. Gradually, the company I had joined at age 40—an unusually advanced age for a P&G new employee—became my family. Having no children and being older than most peers, I developed an extended family of sons and daughters. At P&G, I was first to introduce the concept of "Communities of Practice," later adopted by other companies. Since I loved to teach and my expertise was valuable and scarce, I toured P&G subsidiaries overseas to train technologists all over the world. The experience gave me great insight into humanity, and made me a true citizen of the world—something for which Alexandria had initiated me well.

In Corporate Research, I was responsible for technical innovation for all P&G product categories. I created technologies to stabilize formulation and deliver active compound from products such as moisturizing lipstick, longer lash mascara, detergent, wet-wipes, food, among others. I was awarded more than 35 US technology patents, 30 published applications, in addition to contributing 22 articles to scientific journals. Formulating the cosmetics I always loved to wear was fun. After all, it is the ancient Egyptians who invented the tradition, especially enhancement of eyes with black kohl. I introduced science into the art of formulation, and was famous across the company for promoting the use of liquid crystals and gel networks as delivery and stabilizing systems. In my "Research Fellow Promotion Announcement," the Chief Technology Officer fondly called me "Magna Liquid Crystals." Many mispronounced "Magda" as "Magna"—a name I disliked; so, teasingly, it stuck as my company nickname.

Throughout my career, I organized and attended numerous national and international Symposiums in Science. I associated scientists from complementary fields and different nationalities, thus breaking the norm and usual alliance of Americans versus Europeans. This led to successful meetings and more advances in the field. I was active in the American Chemical Society, for which I edited four books. At that time, women scientists were globally a rare breed, and an outspoken Egyptian scientist was quite a curiosity. At P&G, they called me "The Legend." Everyone knew and sought after the Egyptian researcher. Even competition such as L'Oréal complained about this Magda El-Nokaly who was not leaving any space to patents in lipsticks.

Two tragic incidents marked my years in Cincinnati: my mother's sickness and subsequent death, and my brother's long stay in its hospitals. He had broken his legs in a very serious motorcycle accident in Egypt. I faced these situations alone shortly after my arrival, when I had yet to form a supportive network. I do not know how I survived—divine intervention, perhaps, especially in the case of my brother. He was meant to live. One day in the hospital, sitting in despair next to him, a nurse walked in greeting us in Arabic. She was born into a missionary family in Alexandria. I knew right then that he would be saved. Thanks to her, the racist and stereotyping mindset of some caregivers we had encountered in the ward was changed into acceptance and suitable treatment.

In Cincinnati, I loved my condominium on Bedford Avenue, which was overlooking a golf course and a beautiful mansion. It was centrally located, close to downtown, the highway, and the shopping areas. No one believed that it reminded me of Alexandria. After all, Egypt was about tents, desert, and camels. In my early years in Rouchdy, our home offered a similar view on the palace of a princess. It was turned into a hospital after the Revolution, then into an ugly concrete condo building whose occupants peeped onto our every move—one of many such destructive acts changing Alexandria. While in Cincinnati, I had no time for "work-life balance." Years passed by very quickly. Same-minded fellow employees became my friends, forming an enduring P&G bond. Conservative Cincinnati was a manageable-size city for singles. It was renowned for safety, and now boasts its diversity, thanks to numerous multinationals established in its surroundings.

The Procter and Gamble Company offered me a generous stipend and retirement benefits. More importantly, it allowed me to mature professionally through exposure to great scientists, travel to many countries, and involvement in global research. Enlightened managers, appreciating my thirst for knowledge and freedom, mentored me to develop my talents fully, while achieving company goals. The Management and Diversity training I received continues to be useful tools in my daily life. Occasionally in an Egyptian bank, I am glad to recognize the training being applied by a young employee.

It took me five years after retirement to sell my home and leave Cincinnati. Working for P&G gave me the protection I needed as a single woman in a foreign country. It was my haven. I had lived my exile dreaming about going back to the safety of the house on rue Stross. By some miracle, the family of my youth would still be there. For me, time had stopped in Egypt the day I left in 1979. Now, I was faced with the realization that, after more than 35 years, I was returning to an unknown Egypt. The older generation was gone. I am now among the "elder." The cousins who had stayed behind had become alien to me. Fortunately, almost all had regained the wealth and stature lost by nationalization during their parents' era. Professional success must be ingrained in our genes, the legacy of our grandfather. Like me, they had chosen survival, leaving little room for happiness. Though the price was high, the journey tough yet exciting, occasionally enjoyable or dreadful, I did it. Today I am retired comfortably in a Mediterranean-style home, surrounded by trees, flowers and cats, my own Cairo "Jalna."

Cairo, October 2015

Notes

[1] Constantine P. Cavafy (1863-1933), a Greek poet born in Alexandria, wrote more than 150 poems, the most popular after age 40. In *Ithaca*, inspired by Odysseus's return to his home island, Cavafy suggests that life is a journey, and the experiences we acquire along the way make us wiser. See *The Complete Poems of Cavafy* translated by Daniel Mendelsohn (NY: Harper Press, 2013).

[2] "Jalna" is the home of the Whiteoak family from 1854 to 1954, in the 16 best-seller Jalna novel series by Canadian author Mazo de la Roche (1879-1961). The 13th, *Return to Jalna*, takes place when family members reunite after many years of absence (Boston: Little, Brown, 1946).

Achieving a Lifelong Dream: Leading Egypt's Most Prestigious Academic Institution[1]

Hala Helmy El Said

The events in our lives happen in a sequence in time, but in their significance to ourselves they find their own order, a timetable not necessarily—perhaps not possibly—chronological. The time as we know it subjectively is often the chronology that stories and novels follow: it is the continuous thread of revelation.

Eudora Welty,
One Writer's Beginnings[2]

The Early Part of Life

Throughout my life, I have made it a point to recognize the people who deeply influenced me, especially my parents, Helmy El Said and Soad Farahat, who had a great impact on my career. My father was my mentor and my role model. I looked up to him, and fondly remember his kindness, fairness, and affection. He established the Central Agency for Organization and Administration, and was Minister of Electricity and the High Dam. He raised me according to his values, ethics, and conservative Egyptian traditions, but also with an appreciation for modernity. I remember him as a gentle and religious man who encouraged me to be a leader, and to take an active role in public life. Despite his busy schedule, he always found time to check on my studies and be engaged in my activities. His relationship with the family set a high standard for all of us, and neither he nor my two brothers would have ever considered discriminating against me because I was a girl. My mother treated us with affection, and always answered our questions with love and understanding. This privileged childhood determined who I am today. Being part of a caring and supportive family put me on the right track in life, and provided a perfect example how to raise my own family.

Hala with President Gamal Abdel Nasser (L) and her father (R), Cairo 1962

School played a vital part in my early years, and I managed to be at the top of my class, in order to meet my parents' expectations, and maintained a balance between working hard and having fun. In high school, I represented my class in the student union, and was selected by the school principal to be President of that organization. In that role, I had many responsibilities, the most important was to serve as a bridge between the students, the school administration, and the community. With my parents' support, I successfully accomplished that assignment, and won an award as Best Student Union President, while graduating with honors, ranking 6th best student nationwide—a record never before achieved by anyone at my school. Then, it was time to join the prestigious Faculty of Economics and Political Science at Cairo University—the first step in my academic career. Among my outstanding professors, I was fortunate to encounter two intellectual giants: Boutros Boutros Ghali who would eventually become Secretary General of the United Nations, and Amr Mohieldeen, one of Egypt's leading economists of his generation. They provided great inspiration, as I rose to lead my alma mater, champion the cause of women, and connect academe and society at large.

As a university professor, and later as dean, I instilled in my students the value of rigorous study and serious discipline, crucial for their intellectual development, and encouraged them to benefit from experiences they acquire in real life. In applying this philosophy of education, I offered them a variety of opportunities to broaden their minds. For example, I arranged for lectures that brought to campus distinguished political, economic and cultural leaders, with whom young minds could mingle in social gatherings that promote learning in a relaxed atmosphere. I felt a special responsibility toward the students in my institution, many of whom were likely to become future leaders, in our country and beyond. For their sake, I set up committees to provide them with assistance and support when they need personal attention and help, treating them, in fact, as if they were part of a large family. This profound concern for both students and my family earned me the 2015 "Mother of the Year" award of the Al Maktoum Foundation.[3]

Hala, (3rd L), recipient of the "Ideal Mother Award" from Al Maktoum Foundation, March 2015

No life is free from obstacles, and mine met its share of them along the way. However, thanks to my father's advice, I was often able to overcome the difficulties I encountered at various junctures in my life and my career.

He taught me how to reach the right decisions by evaluating my strengths and preferences, and deciding accordingly. For example, when I had to choose between two great opportunities: a position in the investment department in one of Egypt's renowned regional banks, and a university position leading to an academic career, I had to ask myself: "How could I best serve my country and improve the lives of its citizens?" After considerable thought trying to answer this question, I opted to pursue my studies and go for a career as a university professor.

An Important Milestone: The Egyptian Banking Institute

For several years, I was an educator, reaching the rank of Associate Professor of Economics and Political Science. I taught courses in my discipline, gave papers at professional conferences, initiated student activities, created simulation models, and organized employment fairs. Then, came a time when I found that rigidity and inflexible administrative bureaucracy were hampering my efforts, I made the difficult decision to shift professions, and accepted the position of Executive Director of the Egyptian Banking Institute (EBI)—the training arm and think tank of the Central Bank of Egypt. The move from academe with its flowing routine of teaching and research to the more active fast-paced life of a manager was a huge step, and an invaluable component of my career. The EBI had great potential, and my goal was to transform it into a hub of knowledge and expertise for the banking and financial sector, and a rich source of human capital.

A few months after accepting the position, the Governor of the Central Bank announced a major plan of reform, in which I would have a leading role. I was in charge of preparing members of the management team, upgrading their professional capacity, raising awareness, and establishing the needed policies. The plan was ambitious and extremely difficult to achieve, because it required changing the mentality of government employees whose bureaucratic habits were deeply rooted. However, with dedication and a strong commitment, I was able to turn things around, gradually transforming the inefficient Training Center into an internationally accredited institution, in which bankers competed to be involved. Within a short time, its yearly budget increased from 4 million Egyptian Pounds to 60 million Egyptian Pounds. From training 1000 bank employees a year, it grew to serve 50 000, including not only bank employees, but also government officials. The Center was completely remodeled and transformed into a nucleus where knowledge, creativity, and activity converged.

During that time, I had the privilege of working on many successful projects with some of the brightest minds, the boldest bankers, and the most talented financial experts. Our initiatives included, among others, creating an anti-money-laundering task force, preparing to meet international standards, educating bank employees and equipping them with the necessary tools to improve their performance, and enhancing knowledge and awareness about the market at large. After years of hard work, our team succeeded in highlighting the reputation of Egypt's banking industry: I could not be happier or more proud.

One of the most critical goals achieved during the reform period of my tenure was to revolutionize the professional culture and revamp the procedures in several banks, including the Central Bank of Egypt. Another important goal was to redesign corporate governance, standardize operations, determine roles and responsibilities within various units, and set up objectives and adhere to them. This required putting the guidelines in writing, raising awareness for these novel concepts, and preparing the banks and their employees to accept new ideas and procedures. For these monumental efforts and the remarkable transformation within the EBI, I was honored with a Certificate of Recognition from the Central Bank of Egypt.

Good governance is crucial not only for the financial sector, it also benefits society at large. It involves making and implementing appropriate decisions, and the means to reach them. It can also impact various facets of local government in positive ways, by setting up policies and practices for consultation, establishing procedures for board meetings and protocols for quality control, defining roles for council members and officers, and promoting cooperation among all parties concerned. Good governance is essential for the long term survival and success of any institution, and it greatly depends on the skill, experience, and knowledge of its leaders. Corporate governance involves the manner in which business is conducted at individual banks, the objectives set up by their senior management, the way they are ruled by their Boards of Directors, the consideration given to the interests of their stakeholders, and the protection of their depositors' assets.

Building a national strategy for microfinance was another important goal achieved during my tenure. This project established a strategic framework for increasing the efficiency and effectiveness of government, non-government, and donor efforts to develop microfinancing in Egypt. As an economist keen to involve the banks in this endeavor, I established a unit especially designed to promote entrepreneurship, work with small and medium enterprises, and facilitate their access to capital. Thus, this untapped source of growth and prosperity could be used to accelerate employment, spur economic growth, ensure stability, and combat poverty. In cooperation with various government entities, I created the first national database on small and medium enterprises, and started a program of financial education to assist individuals in accessing and using appropriate financial products. However, obtaining international accreditation for the Institute after many years of hard work was, undoubtedly, the highlight of my career at EBI. Our training center was the first in the Middle East to meet the required international standards, and remained the only one for five years. In 2011, in view of these efforts and my prominent role in public service, I was recognized among the 50 top influential women in the region, and was further acknowledged in 2015 by CBC news as the most influential figure of the year, having had the most impact on the economy.[4]

Hala recognized for achieving International Accreditation for the Egyptian Banking Institute from the Accrediting Council for Continuing Education & Training (ACCET). To her left are Roger J. Williams, Executive Director of ACCET, and Farouk Okdah, Governor of the Central Bank of Egypt, May 2009

Achieving a Lifelong Dream

Another turning point in my career occurred after the 2011 Revolution, when laws and regulations governing the appointment of deans at

Egyptian universities were changed. As of August 2011, deanships were to be filled through an election process, whereby applicants would present platforms outlining their programs, and faculty members would vote, accordingly, for their favorite candidate. By law, deans are responsible for managing the scientific, administrative and financial affairs of their institutions, according to national laws and regulations, and they report directly to the University Council. When the deanship of the Faculty of Economics and Political Science became available, my former colleagues and professors urged me to apply. It was particularly heartwarming because all the other applicants competing for the position were active faculty members, I was the only candidate who had been away from the Faculty for eight years. It took me three months to think about it and make up my mind. In the end, I decided to run for election, knowing that it was my late father's wish, and my own lifelong dream.

There were considerable issues to ponder, especially the fact that the country was governed by the Muslim Brotherhood, well-known for its discrimination against women. Once again, hard work, dedication, commitment, and determination were the keys to my success. I appointed a strong team to advise me, and together we studied the situation at the Faculty, and carefully developed a plan to remedy institutional weaknesses, and prepare it for a better future. The strategy was based on three major points: 1) to modernize the curriculum to meet international standards; 2) to engage the faculty in all administrative and institutional decisions; and 3) to extend the role of faculty into public and civic life. Evidently, my colleagues appreciated the vision and goals outlined in my platform and the means to achieve them, and decided that they needed someone like me to lead them. They voted overwhelmingly in favor of my candidacy.

My first three years as Dean were the hardest, in light of the political turmoil in the country. I was particularly concerned about the students during that troubled period of our history, and tried my best to engage them responsibly in political action. On the job, one of my first priorities was to develop an institutional framework that allows full participation of the faculty, and ensures a high level of transparency. A number of committees were named and put in charge of monitoring administrative and financial procedures. Among others, these included the following: Transparency; Disclosure and Financial Matters; Development of Organizational Structure; in addition to a Council on Lecturers and Teaching Assistants. For the first time in that institution's history, membership on these committees consisted of faculty of various ranks, disciplines, and departments. The diversity of perspectives added depth to debates, and helped to reach acceptable solutions. As a result, administrative procedures were enhanced, and junior faculty gained important insight.

Two committees had particularly significant roles. The Nominations Committee was in charge of setting up the criteria for gaining leadership positions within the institution. The Governance Committee established proper rules and regulations of governance, including: rights and duties; disclosure and transparency; accountability; and avoidance of conflict of interests. A faculty board created a code of conduct and ethics for students, staff, and faculty members.

Gradually, the Faculty of Economics and Political Science extended its services beyond teaching and research, to engage in public discussions of domestic and international policies, to study political and economic development, and environmental problems, and to heighten awareness about these issues at all levels of society. Faculty members, departments, and research centers within the institution organized conferences, workshops, and seminars to study problems plaguing the country, and recommended solutions. Faculty research was thus put to good use by addressing practical societal needs, and guiding the government and its agencies. Promoting faculty and student participation in volunteer work and public service programs strengthened the bonds between academe and society at large.

Throughout my life, one of my highest priorities as a professional woman, dean, and member of the Board of Directors of the Central Bank of Egypt has been to advocate for gender equality at all corporate levels. Such effort must start at the grass roots, and involve all facets of life, including education, training, and employment. All women and men must be treated fairly, with respect, and receive equal pay for equal work. Despite recent efforts to improve the status and condition of Egyptian women, they continue to face serious obstacles, especially in social and economic life, and are less likely than men to receive a quality education, and to benefit from important contacts and resources. There are still structural barriers that limit their access to elected office, and leadership positions. Although some individual women have succeeded in overcoming these obstacles, and have been recognized for their contribution to society, women on the whole do not compete on a level playing field. Legislative reforms are needed to ensure women's fair access to markets, services, and flexible working conditions. For my part, I collaborate with national teams on programs that aim to create a culture that values women's professional contributions, and to provide them with equal decision making power. Both women and men, young and old, need to be engaged in advocacy for gender equality, in order to make it a

Hala receiving an Award of Distinction from Gaber Nassar, President of Cairo University (L), and Gamal Esmat, Vice President for Graduate Studies and Research, Cairo University

central issue in public policymaking, as recommended by the United Nations Women and Development Program.

In Egypt, concern for women's economic empowerment has been a priority on the agenda of many national and non-government institutions, as well as international organizations. Furthermore, the recent Constitution stresses gender equality. However, despite these efforts, challenges and gaps persist and limit their full participation in the labor market and economic life. For example, unemployment rates for women is three times as high as those for men, and among the country's population made up of over 60% youth, 50% of women graduates are unemployed.

Balancing Personal and Professional Life

When my children were young, I was privileged to be a university professor with a flexible schedule; when necessary, I could leave them with my mother or my sister. I embarked on an executive position only when my youngest daughter went to school, and I do not regret turning down international assignments or after-hours consultation during their early years. I felt that it was important to be around for my children when they came back from school. When they were older, I was able to engage fully in time-consuming executive positions, with the support of my family. My husband also understood the demands and pressure of my responsibilities, and collaborated fully while the children were growing up. It was very hard to balance personal and professional life, but I was fortunate that my family was involved in my decisions and activities. A support network is crucial, for the path to success cannot be walked alone.

Today, there are plenty of role models for women, yet it is hard to pin down who is a "role model." Women with influence and power are able to transform a generation, as do their male counterparts, but they are often placed at the extreme ends of the spectrum. Successful women are either put on a pedestal as perfect paragons impossible to attain; or viewed by others as a corrupt moral force. However, role models for women all over the world are diverse and unique, many achieve that status by being courageous, equitable and upright, and do not fear fighting for what is right. My own role models are not on a pedestal; they are fellow colleagues and friends, professors and cabinet members, women I admire for their commitment and fortitude, who inspire and challenge me. Today, some of my students and my children's friends consider me a role model for a new generation, it is a compliment I humbly accept.

Cairo, December 2015

Notes

[1] Ever since its creation in 1960, the Faculty of Economics & Political Science at Cairo University has been considered a preeminent source of learning and training in economics, political science, and management. Its graduates hold some of the highest positions in business and government, nationally and internationally. More information is available at www.feps.edu.eg

[2] Eudora Welty, *One Writer's Beginnings* (Cambridge, MA: Harvard University Press, 1983)

[3] The Al Maktoum Foundation was launched by Sheikh Mohammed Bin Rashid Al Maktoum, Vice President and Ruler of Dubai. It seeks to establish Dubai and the United Arab Emirates as a center for knowledge and research.

[4] More information on the criteria that led to my selection is available on http://m.youtube.com/watch?/feature=youtu.be&v=XIv8GnEJSSQ

CHALLENGES ON THE WAY TO SUCCESS

SAHAR MOHAMED EL SALLAB

As I reflect on my life and my career, I realize that I can attribute much of who I am today to the special atmosphere of my childhood home, and to my father who was a strong supporter of women's education. Along with academic success, freedom was an important value in our family. All of us were free to think for ourselves, enjoy life, and socialize with whomever we liked. In the progressive multicultural society of Lebanon where I grew up, I was never subjected to discrimination, and was able to develop great ambitions that I eventually achieved. One of these was having the opportunity to complete a management course at the Kennedy School of Harvard University, which I did later in life. Determination, hope, and faith were instilled in me from a young age, and I am forever grateful to my parents for that upbringing. Their values helped to shape my positive outlook, and established the solid foundation that allowed me to handle difficult situations, and overcome obstacles I would face. My years at university also played a major role in the development of my personality. I enjoyed participating in student activities, and fondly remember those years as a catalyst for my future success.

I was inspired to get into banking because it was my father's profession. I was glad to have opted for business school, and was convinced from the start that I would excel in my chosen field. I took my education seriously, studying theory while gaining practical experience. I always tried to acquire as much knowledge as possible, and challenged myself in order to grow. The educational process I experienced in Lebanon was extraordinary. My professors encouraged me to question everything until I reached the next level of understanding. Education at the American University in Beirut (AUB) was and continues to be the source of success for many women leaders in the Arab world. During my years at AUB, not only did I dedicate myself to my studies, I also took part-time jobs that enabled me to enjoy life while gaining valuable hands-on experience. At that time, women from various parts of the Middle East flocked to Beirut where they challenged themselves and excelled in many fields. Personally,

I felt empowered by the financial security my part-time jobs provided, and the quality of education I was receiving.

My father introduced me to the bankers with whom he was associated, so I could learn from them and be exposed to leaders in the industry; in fact, some of them have remained friends to this day. At the same time, I was elected Treasurer of the Business School Council, a responsibility that strengthened my contacts with students, professors, and the school administration. Being involved in a wide range of activities, I encountered valuable opportunities, and gained priceless insight. I was learning immensely from people with different perspectives, which allowed me to acquire a better understanding not only of business practices, but also to realize the importance of working well with people. Life was moving along very nicely until the spring of 1975, when the civil war broke out in Lebanon, and our world fell apart. It shattered lives, separated people, forced numerous families to flee the country and settle elsewhere, spreading their energy and talents all over the globe. Many dreams were disrupted, mine included.

I had to return to Egypt, a homeland largely unfamiliar to me. As a fresh business school graduate, I saw great economic potential. With its recent open-door policy, Egypt seemed ready to welcome and embrace new business. On the personal level, however, settling in the new country was difficult. In Beirut, I was used to living freely, dressing and going out as I pleased. In Cairo, I was a bit surprised and unprepared for the conservative and traditional society I found at that time. My colleagues did not look kindly at my clothes or my leisure-time activities; I realized that I would have to make adjustments in order to fit into that environment. I was not particularly happy about it, but I thought it would be easier to change my outlook than to attempt to change the society.

I accepted my first job at CitiBank believing it would be a short-term assignment to hone my technical skills and gain experience in the banking industry. Although I was doing chores such as filing and photocopying, I was grateful for the opportunity. Others with my background and education might have scoffed at the seemingly menial tasks, but I came to welcome every opportunity as a chance to grow, believing in the importance of developing a good foundation. Learning to master a job requires starting from the bottom up, while being always ready to benefit from new experiences. Looking back, I must give much of the credit for my success to those who were there for me in the beginning, who believed in me and gave me a chance. I had a wonderful boss, May Sadaka, a Lebanese lady with whom I had much in common. Not only did we connect well personally, but she also made me love my profession even more.

As a credit analyst, I decided to plant the seed for my future success: to think, listen, speak, and act assuredly and with determination. My first major initiative was to create a first-of-its-kind credit policy. It revealed my potential to others in the bank, and I was selected for a five-month credit training program in Greece. Before traveling, I got engaged to Mohamed Nofal, the man who would continue to support and inspire me to this day. The course was beneficial and reinforced my belief in the importance of training to build a solid foundation. Back from Greece, my career continued to advance, and I became even closer to May who introduced me to Roger Crevier, the Managing Director of Chase Manhattan Egypt—later to become Commercial International Bank (CIB). He offered me a higher position with much responsibility, as head of an important credit department with about 25 people reporting to me, most of whom were older than me. I owe my boss there, Salman Abassi, much of what I learned during that period: he taught me, trained me, and trusted me. It is crucial to recognize the colleagues who had a positive impact on me, because it is thanks to them that I was able to handle many challenges in the workplace.

For me, the actual work was never a problem. I loved planning, policymaking, and numbers, and was good at them. The obstacles I had to overcome were related to colleagues who wanted to interfere in my work. It was not easy to manage people who were older, especially those who questioned or criticized my performance for seemingly no reason. It was difficult to work in an environment where some were putting me down, in order to get ahead. While these actions and the general atmosphere bothered me, they did not deter me. I was motivated to succeed, quickly moving to achieve my goal. In Lebanon, we spoke a mix of Arabic, French and English, and most of my education was in English. For this reason, my Arabic was not as free-flowing as that of my Egyptian colleagues, I had to make progress quickly to avoid letting this gap disrupt my career. Traveling to New York, London and various countries in Europe for additional training, I was meeting senior bank officers, and making a name and a future for myself; thus, in less than two years I became a senior manager.

Just before joining Chase Manhattan, I had a son, Karim, and found myself having to juggle a rising career, a home, and a family. In addition to recognizing the influential bosses I had, I must give even more credit for my success to my husband, Mohamed, a strong proponent of women in the professions. He was unequivocally supportive, and as determined as I was that I must succeed in my career. I am forever grateful for his cooperation, which means a lot to me. This leads me to emphasize another firm belief in the importance of teamwork. I never doubted the value of the input of others; it is the reason I put together high-minded teams with amazing colleagues, and in so doing I created a congenial atmosphere in which all could thrive. I am of the opinion that one should listen twice as much as one speaks: this is why we are created with two ears and only one mouth!

In 1984, having climbed the corporate ladder, I was selected by Chase Manhattan to go to London for a six-months training for a senior position. I accepted the challenge, hoping the difficult period away from home would ultimately benefit my career. I took my baby son Karim with me, and spent most of my salary on childcare. The training was rigorous, I was exhausted, but the knowledge I gained was priceless. Fortunately, my sister Samar was living in London at that time, and through her I met interesting and inspiring people from all over the world. My classmates and my colleagues became my friends, that experience reinforced my belief in the importance of building a rich network.

After completing the training in London, I returned to Cairo where I was elected to a senior position. However, in 1986 Chase Manhattan decided to pull out of several countries, Egypt included. This move prompted many young men who worked for the bank to seek employment in other Arab countries, and left the women to become the leaders of the banking industry in Egypt. I headed the Risk Management Department— the core of any bank—at CIB, a job to which I became almost addicted! From there, I was promoted to Managing Director, then to Vice Chair and Managing Director. Now I was visible not only in the business community, but also throughout Egypt and the Middle East. Besides being a successful businesswoman, the birth of my second son, Hatem, made me a happy mother of two. Juggling motherhood and a career was definitely not easy but I was determined to keep on. In a short period of time, my bank went from being nationally ranked 3rd to 1st. I became a strategist, and the reports I wrote were syndicated for the entire industry. Government projects and privatization contracts were concluded in my office; I was named among the top executives and most powerful women in the region, profiled in many magazines, including *Forbes*. Not a day would go by without an interview with me in the media, or an appearance on the news. I held meetings with government ministers, headed tables at high-powered luncheons, and graciously accepted the honors and awards that came my way.

Number 5 was dedicated to Sahar Sallab, an Egyptian woman who has served on the boards of the National Council for Women and the American Chamber of Commerce in Egypt. Yet, these are only her so-called "extra-curricular" activities. For 25 years, Sallab worked for the Commercial International Bank (CIB), becoming the bank's Vice Chairman and Managing Director. For a while, Sallab served in the government as a Deputy Minister for trade until March 2010. She was also chairman of CI Capital, one of the biggest investment banks in Egypt. Having gained experience in both London and New York, she has later moved on to become the chairperson of HitekNOFAL, a family-owned business that works in high technology solutions and networking engineering. Sallab has a degree from the American University in Beirut.

Sahar recognized in *Forbes* Magazine as one of the five most influential women in the Arab region, May 2008

I am positive that my achievements would not have been possible had it not been for the team I put together, to which I delegated much work, and which provided me with valuable feedback. I believe this attitude distinguished me from many in the industry. Egypt in general, especially in the banking profession, is not team-oriented. People tend not to be inclusive or willing to listen to others, they believe it may distract them from their own goals. Unlike them, I am proud of my collaborations with others, helping them instead of crushing them on my way up. I continued to use my teamwork model when the chair of the bank asked me to head a small brokerage firm within the CIB. I recruited good people, and together we were able to turn this modest division into asset management, which eventually became the second largest investment bank in the country. Again, this could not have happened had it not been for my passion for the work, the staff I assembled, trusted and trained, and my ability to delegate tasks.

Sahar receiving the prize of "Best Banker in Egypt," by Maged Shawky, Chair of the Cairo and Alexandria Stock Exchange (R). Also shown are the President of UBS, Union Bank of Switzerland (L), next to Ashraf Naguib, Managing Director of Global Trade, Cairo, 2008

2008 was a year of major change in my personal and professional life. I made the decision to leave the private sector and move to public service, in order to put my experience toward serving the greater good of Egypt. I accepted the position of Deputy Minister of Industry and Trade, responsible for Internal Trade and Investment. On the home front, I was devastated by the loss of my older son, Karim. The pain of losing a child seemed insurmountable, but I wanted to honor the commitment to work for the government for at least two years. The transition was onerous, to say the least. I had gone from being a leader in banking, able to make decisions and see them promptly implemented, to being an official in a most painstakingly bureaucratic government. Despite the challenges, I looked ahead, remained optimistic, and stuck with the principles that had always worked for me. I recruited young people to assist me in developing a new strategy of internal trade to combat poverty. I traveled nationwide to see the obstacles for myself, and journeyed to Malaysia, Turkey, France, and Italy to see what had helped reduce poverty in those countries. I also negotiated to bring Inframed Investment Funds to Egypt. These were aimed at developing North Africa and the Middle East while being beneficial to Southern European countries. Suggested projects included, but were not limited to, solar energy, recycling, and water irrigation systems in agricultural deserts. I focused on implementing such projects because I really wanted to improve the quality of life in my country.

Sahar accepting the prize for "Best Egyptian Woman in Finance," awarded by the Egyptian Businesswomen's Association. Also shown to Sahar's left are Yumma Sheridy and Mona Zulficar, Cairo, 2014

Unfortunately, not everyone in the government shared my vision or determination. I was constantly frustrated and disappointed because of prevailing corruption, bribery, and greed. People would oppose my ideas or undermine my initiatives simply because they thought that to get ahead they needed to pull someone else down. It seemed that no matter how hard I tried or how steadfast I remained in my beliefs, I just could not get much accomplished. I contemplated whether I could even last two years, and got through that time by praying, and reminding myself to breathe, and go with the flow. It was clear that I could not singlehandedly overhaul a system that was causing me tremendous hardship, but I could adjust my attitude within it. I resisted the pressure to conform and stayed true to myself, smiling my way through the overwhelming personal and professional pain.

Working in the government is often a thankless job, and during that time, I often reminisced about my life in the private sector. More than the fame and recognition, I missed my staff, and the people I had recruited and trained. I missed the work that impassioned me. I remembered my accomplishments, especially my promotion of the economic welfare of women, approving their request for funding, creating a credit card for them, and becoming a board member of the Council of Egyptian Women headed by Egypt's First Lady. I thought about the challenges I had overcome to reach the high level of respect and visibility I had achieved in a society that is not particularly known to enable women. I tried to understand what it was about me that made me succeed. Indeed, I had help and support, but perhaps more importantly, I believed in myself and followed my passion, two factors that should not be discounted. Instead of getting down about what I missed, I became even more determined to finalize my strategy in the government and move on. I remained enthusiastic about effecting change in Egypt, and presented my proposals to various ministers, including the Prime Minister. Again, unsurprisingly, not one of them welcomed my ideas, as they were self-seeking individuals for the most part, uninterested in looking out for the greater good, more easily swayed by politics and appearances. Most of the ministers were old, with no clear vision for the future, except for my brilliant colleague, the First Deputy Minister. As a go-getter and achiever, I just could not see myself remaining in this toxic environment, a cog in a rusty machine. Even my resignation from the government took six months to be approved!

As with other challenges I had faced in my life, this one taught me an important lesson about forgiveness. I could not hold on to grudges or feelings of bitterness, contempt and disappointment, I had to let them go before they consumed me. I needed to grieve and mourn my losses: my position in the banking industry, my staff, my friends, and most importantly, my son Karim. To be able to forgive and move on felt like a rebirth, it reenergized me. In early January 2011, I started a new job as consultant and financial advisor, and by the end of that month, the Egyptian Revolution had begun. In a way, the upheaval of the system that I had experienced earlier in Lebanon and now in Egypt was symbolic of the changes that I was personally undergoing. I was experiencing my own revolution in the middle of a political revolution, and was struck by the determination of the people demanding change. They were no longer satisfied with the status quo and the ineffectiveness of the system—and neither was I. Their call to do something to better themselves and improve our country inspired me.

Shortly thereafter, I met the head of Google Egypt, at a meeting of the American Chamber of Commerce. He asked me to be a judge and mentor for 75 projects started by young Egyptians nationwide. I accepted, not knowing how different it would be from my previous professional experiences. I was a banker who determined the approval of funding for projects in the millions and billions; now I found myself deciding on grants in the tens of thousands. However, despite the difference, and much to my surprise, I loved it. Working with young people eager to make their dreams come true became my new passion. I was inspired by their commitment to be their own bosses, and impressed by their entrepreneurship; I was particularly proud that many of these enterprises employed women. After all my trials and tribulations, I was hopeful as there were some signs of positive change. I mentored several young entrepreneurs, many of whom were friends of my late son Karim. It was heartwarming to do something that honored his memory. This work was important because there were great initiatives out there that just lacked funding. By investing in our youth and their creativity, we were making progress happen.

Then, I took on other roles, as a board member in various companies, including a marine services company and a food company, where my experience and input were valued, and I was heartened to see that my passion and knowledge were benefitting others. Today, I am enjoying my new role as a non-executive chair at HitekNofal, a family enterprise, and an investor in new ideas to improve the quality of life in Egypt. I am delighted to lend a helping hand to my husband and friend, Mohamed, in his own company; grateful for our mutually supportive relationship with our son Hatem; and especially proud that he has chosen to remain in Egypt despite many offers to work abroad. It is a blessing that my personal and professional experiences combined to make the best possible life for our family.

Sahar at an Entrepreneurship Fund banquet sponsored by the European Investment Fund, with Heinz Olfers, EIB Diretor of Lending Operations (L) and Dario Scannpieco, EIB President (R), Cairo, 2015

Looking back on my life and my career, there are several things I know to be true, and would like to share with readers of this book. First, there will always be challenges, it is important to expect them, face them, overcome them, over and over again, and never be deterred by the difficulties along the way. Second, it is possible to have both a career and a family. I never regretted being focused on my career at the expense of being the best cook or the best housekeeper. I may not have spent as much time as I would have liked with my children, but we made the best use of those times we were together: quality over quantity. Third, learn to adapt without compromising your beliefs. For example, I could not completely overhaul the patriarchal environment in which I worked, but I was able to make a difference by making men think that my ideas were theirs; then, they rallied and got behind me. I did not make any concessions, I just made it look as if I did. Last but not least, it is crucial to be surrounded by a good team, to listen to wise and experienced people, and never stop learning.

Cairo, December 2015

A PASSION TO ACHIEVE AND MAKE A DIFFERENCE

NEVEEN HAMDI EL TAHRI

I must admit that I am a workaholic. I love what I do and have a relentless passion to achieve and make a difference. It has taken a bit of reflecting on the many memories, challenges and milestones I have encountered over the years, on both the personal and professional paths, to pin down the specific moments and situations that have taught me the most, made me grow, and left the biggest impact on my life. As a youngster, here is the first significant milestone I can recall while growing up. My father, a diplomat, insisted my sisters and I work every summer, regardless of the country in which we were posted. At that time, it made us angry, but as we grew older, we realized he had instilled in us a work ethic and a pride in perfecting whatever job we were assigned. Unwittingly, he bestowed upon us a gift that I later realized allowed me to take on any kind of work. This was also at the root of my passion to achieve. The string of summer jobs included being a librarian and a summer school teaching assistant, as well as delivering newspapers.

I grew up in different countries: Panama, Lebanon, Finland, England and Egypt. Coping with displacement was only part of the chore, then came the adjustment from one language to another, from a school system to another, and sometimes from one level to the next within the same country. I ended up going to eight different schools before finishing high school. It was not always easy, but I quickly learned to adapt and feel part of the community in which I found myself—an asset throughout my life. The real challenge happened when I started university. Having grown up abroad, my Arabic at the time was very weak, yet my dad insisted I go to Cairo University where the entire curriculum was in Arabic. I studied Economics and Political Science, which was a difficult experience. The first year, I barely managed to pass, it was almost a miracle. I continued my studies in Arabic and, against all odds, graduated with highest honors, and was offered an academic position at the university that I chose to decline. Being offered that post, as one of the highest-ranking graduates, was a statement that one can achieve whatever one sets his or her mind to do. I learned Arabic in the process; today, naturally, it is an asset working within Egypt's business world.

My career began in 1980 at Chase National Bank of Egypt (CNBE), the first Egyptian American joint venture bank. It was a time of rapid change in Egypt with the economy opening up to the capitalist system after decades of a state planned economy. There was much to learn, and in many ways my experience at the bank shaped my future endeavors. CNBE invested in our learning, focused on highlighting our potential, and made sure we developed our best skills. Although it was not my objective, I started as a teller, with a promise to join CNBE's renowned credit course the following year, it seemed worth it to accept. In that job, I learned about the details and inner workings of the banking process, but to my shock, when time came for the credit course, I was not included. Instead of complying with the decision, I took a bold step and demanded to meet the Managing Director to sound my fury. As a 22-year old, I had to gather the courage to voice my anger. Looking back, I realize it was kind of this man to hear me. I ended up talking with him about my background, and the condition for accepting to be a teller. The following day, I was assigned to the credit department as an administrative assistant to more than 15 officers who later became Egypt's most renowned bank leaders; finally I took the credit course in 1983. This encounter with the Managing Director taught me that "if you do not ask, you will never get"—one of my mottos ever since.

When I started the 6-month credit course, my daughter was only three-months old. I needed to work double—if not triple—the load of my colleagues. My pride was immense to be among the 17 out of 30 entrants to pass the credit course successfully. Upon graduating and after a three-month training, I realized that I was paid much less than my new colleagues because I had started in the Operations Department, unlike those who were appointed directly in the Credit Department. As a result, I made the tough decision to resign from Chase, and joined the local affiliate of Bank of America for double my salary. A year into the new position where I was promoted twice and given an even higher salary than upon entering, I realized that the job came with minimal learning. Hence, when offered to return to Chase Bank—by then it had been renamed Commercial International Bank (CIB)—with equal salary and rank as my colleagues, I jumped back in. That experience taught me two good lessons: 1) salary should never be the main reason to assess a job, and 2) working in a learning environment is of crucial importance.

I remained with CIB for the following seven years, advancing my career and becoming part of the senior management team. By 1992, 12 years after graduation, I hit a glass ceiling and was no longer enjoying the work. I decided to resign and became a housewife doing the things I never had a chance to do: learning German to be in tune with my children, doing pottery, making dried flower arrangements that I sold to a boutique next door, and going daily to the gym; but that was not to last long. I wanted to work, and my family urged me to get busy again, as they did not like my intervening in the nitty-gritty of household details. For the following year, I did consulting work for multinationals, and taught Banking & Credit courses at the American University in Cairo, on a part-time basis. Suddenly, my career path took a major turn when one of my former clients offered me the opportunity to manage a new tourism company he had just established; he needed an experienced and creative manager to run it. It was an interesting challenge, besides I was only required to commit for one year.

I had no idea how this decision would affect both my life and my career. The tourism company taught me how to run a business from A to Z, and allowed me to see Egypt through the eyes of a tourist. I was able to be innovative, and made our products distinct from those of other providers on the market. During that year, Egypt was the target of several terrorist attacks, leading to the first real crash in the tourism sector. I had to forgo my salary during the crisis, and diverted the company focus to other venues. I will always appreciate this unique opportunity to manage the company, and learn entrepreneurship on the job. The experience taught me a very important lesson: flexibility. One has to rethink strategies when the unexpected occurs, while continuing to run the day-to-day business.

In 1994, the government revived the previously renowned Egyptian stock market—one of the five largest in the world in the early twentieth century—which had been dormant for almost 60 years. The authorities finally issued the executive regulations of the capital market law with the first permissible permit license being Securities Brokerage. I was eligible to apply, leveraging the experience and confidence gained from running the tourism company. My first endeavor as an entrepreneur was to establish "Delta Securities Egypt," in partnership with a close family member—an experience I would not recommend, to ensure keeping problems away from home. After four months, the partnership ended and I found myself managing the company on my own, as the license provided by the capital market authority was in my name. Because the industry was new, everyone was learning on the job.

As a professional credit officer, I quickly realized that the capital requirement set out by the authorities to start the brokerage business was low for the risks involved. Thus, I decided that I would take a precaution by partnering with a financial institution, to give me strong financial and personal backing. I was the only woman in the field and, somehow, for the first time in my life, felt the gender difference. The market was led by men, and I thought that if I institutionalized the company it would grow faster. Looking back, that was undoubtedly one of the most important decisions I made, and the reason for much of the success I achieved thereafter.

Over the following years, I sought quite a few partnerships, always chosen with the aim of adding value to the business. My first two were with the American Express Bank of New York (AMEX) and its local affiliate Egyptian American Bank (EAB). Negotiating and dealing with lawyers was just the start of what became the norm in the many partnerships that followed. I retained a 60% majority, and after two very successful years, the banks wanted to materialize their profit, and decided to exit. Once more, I found myself in search of a partner, but this time I wanted to find one who would bring new market know-how. I approached the Dutch ABN AMRO Bank NV, well-known for its asset and fund management, in addition to having strong brokerage and investment banking presence worldwide. When the agreement was finalized, I was overjoyed: this was a bank five times the size of Egypt's GDP partnering with me. Albeit, I had to relinquish control, becoming a minority with a proviso that would further decrease my share in two years. In return, they would train all the staff abroad, as well as fulfill numerous requests stipulated as a result of lessons learned from my first two bank partnerships.

ABN AMRO established ABN AMRO Delta Asset Management, with training, manuals, and infrastructure derived from more than one hundred years of banking experience. The brokerage firm also tapped into the resources of our new partners, and its research department immediately became involved with one of Egypt's landmark public offerings, the fixed line telephone operator. Not only were we involved in the due diligence and restructuring—in collaboration with Rothschild Bank, an affiliate of ABN AMRO—to prepare it for the IPO, but also in the bridge loan provided by the bank to the first local mobile operator to purchase the mobile telecom infrastructure.

Neveen (2nd row, 7th from L) announcing the entry of ABN AMRO Bank in Egypt via majority acquisition of Delta, 1999

The ABN AMRO partnership was established in June 1999 and by 2001, ABN AMRO decided to exit internationally from many countries. Hence, unexpectedly, they requested to exit from the brokerage firm when they were supposed to become the majority owners of the business. I ended up buying back my brokerage company, yet continued to be their partner in the asset management company until 2007, when I bought them out as they were selling the bank to Royal Bank of Scotland (RBS). The ABN AMRO partnership was one of the best learning experiences for me, as not only was I their partner in the various companies, but I also became their country representative from 2001 until 2007, and followed in the same role with RBS until 2014. In 2007, I found myself fully owning the businesses, and as always thinking ahead of the next partnership that would assist me in taking the company to the next level. This time with all the international markets in distress, I sought my first Arab partnership.

In 2008, I partnered with a Gulf-based company run by many foreign-educated Arab men to whom I willingly sold 51% ownership of my three companies: brokerage, asset management and investment. Very soon, I realized there were many insurmountable cultural differences. Well-educated as they were, these men found it impossible for them culturally to allow me, a woman, to be in charge of management. I had to take one of the most difficult decisions of my career: I resigned from my own companies less than a year into the partnership. In hindsight, the best thing about that difficult move was that my departure in late 2008 was timely, as it came right before the financial crisis. Many lessons were learned from this partnership; yet, the most important was not to give away majority early on. My exit gave me the opportunity to start a new endeavor I had been contemplating for some time: working with small and medium enterprises (SME). I must admit that it was never my intention to sell my businesses, but looking back, I am surprised at the number of exits I have done: a total 17 of the 10 companies I had established, sold, and bought back at various times. In each case, the business was purchased by others who sought to take it to next level, thus being of mutual benefit to both parties.

I went on to establish the first SME-focused investment firm in the country: Delta Holding for Financial Investments. It would include one of only a handful of securities custodian licenses, a fund service company, a financial leasing company, and an incubator-accelerator for SMEs. All were founded with promising partners. With the eruption of the 2011 Revolution and the difficulties that followed, most of the initial capital was depleted, and the company had to merge with one of the larger private equity funds in Egypt. Post-merger, Delta Holding shifted its focus from SMEs to medium and large size companies, which led me to leave and start what I believed to be my final professional endeavor. I went on to establish three companies devoted to the passion and outstanding talent of young Egyptians. Having started to work with them since 2008, I sought to develop a framework to channel that inspiration into action. The Revolution left the country's economy in a state of continuous decline, massive layoffs and no job-creation. Within that context, my companies were an attempt to give back to Egypt and assist its younger generation where my experience could be of help. My aim was to empower budding entrepreneurs and guide them to succeed during the formative periods of their enterprises, and to encourage them to lead their family business where relevant.

Hence, came Delta Inspire a management company established with an excellent team possessing expertise in different business management aspects, to help entrepreneurs at all the stages to find all needed services in one place: audit, legal, financial, strategy, advisory, consulting, mentoring, raising debt or capital, etc. The model was built to select start-ups and early-phase growth companies with scalable concepts that have direct or indirect employment potential. To show our long-term commitment to that vision, we sought high profile partners that share the same passion to give back and build on our concept. Together we created one of the first venture capital/private equity hybrid fund, 138 Pyramids, harping on our traditional Egyptian heritage, which has 138 existing pyramids, our aim being to build structures that have an economic life, and become our future pyramids.

Meanwhile, one of my early establishments upon exiting from my capital market companies in 2008, Delta Shield served as the foundation for the two companies mentioned above: Delta Inspire and 138 Pyramids. Delta Shield focuses on advising family businesses, as it became evident that the millennium generation (2nd or 3rd) was shying away from working with their own families. Therefore, clear corporate governance and understanding of the educated youth had to be fostered, to create an attractive environment that would interest them in working comfortably with their parents, based on their own knowhow and applying their education, which would evidently be a step-up from the previous generation.

One of my greatest rewards was to witness the growth of companies with which I partnered, and management that went on to succeed on its own. There was always more to learn and more to perfect along the way, but one had to let go, move fast, and implement clear strategies efficiently and effectively. Creating jobs and avoiding layoffs has been my drive to success. Some of the most difficult decisions were layoffs post financial meltdowns, and the greatest joy was being able to hire back some of the former employees when the economy improved. Challenges will appear on the way to growth—which is normal and to be expected—yet one needs to know how to maneuver quickly, delegate, and depend on a good team.

This 35-year journey in business and finance offered me the privilege of sitting on many public- and private-sector boards, especially at the stages of their restructuring or infrastructure build up. I would like to highlight the ones where I felt I made a difference and widened my knowledge. In 1997, I was the first woman ever elected to the Board of the Cairo & Alexandria Stock Exchange for two consecutive terms of six years. Being selected by my male colleagues to represent them was a great honor, and validation that even in that male dominated industry it is work not gender that counts. Later, I was appointed to Egypt's Investment Authority (GAFI), and Banque Misr, the country's 2nd largest public-sector bank, both allowing me to pursue my banking passion, and the investment knowledge acquired over the years.

One of the most important experiences that kept me updated with the technological revolution the world is witnessing, was sitting on the board of the fixed line telecom operator Telecom Egypt, and heading their investment committee. Today, in 2015, I sit on the board of the Egyptian Financial Supervisory Authority (EFSA), which regulates the capital markets, insurance, mortgage, leasing industry and the micro-finance sector. This role makes me feel that I can be part of the positive changes in these vital industries, and hence of Egypt's economic growth. Continuing to keep my finger on the pulse of the on-going technological revolution and the rise of entrepreneurship, I sit on the boards of Mobinil—the local mobile operator of the French Orange—and the Suez Canal Economic Zone Authority, one the government's new build-up projects for its goals for 2030.

Growing up in an Egyptian family with two sisters and no brothers, my parents never made us feel that there was a gender difference. Working up the ladder in my banking career was never an issue, it was only upon entering as a business owner in a man's world that I may have partially felt it. I have frequently been asked by international organizations, such as the World Bank, the United Nations Women's Forum, the OECD, or the Cartier Foundation, to speak at events discussing gender issues. This is when I definitely became more aware how important it is to address these issues. I now consider my gender ignorance as one of the strengths that allowed me to grow my career without putting breaks on my potential. I believe that merit and the quality of work would always be the ultimate judge, hence my motto: "Work hard with a clear eye on the targets and you cannot go wrong, be it man or woman."

Finally, I turn to my proudest achievement: my family. Early in life, the focus is often on the dreams of a bright career, but reaching them requires clarity in one's personal priorities. It was always crystal-clear to me that family comes first. I married my teenage sweetheart and from him and my children I got unwavering support. I would have never achieved what I did had it not been for their unfailing support. I have never missed a school play, a parents' meeting, a football game, or throwing a big birthday party. Furthermore, they had to listen to my business stories every day I came home, as attentively as I had to listen to their day at school.

Neveen at the opening ceremony of the Arab World Renewal Conference at the Institut du Monde Arabe in Paris, where she spoke on "How to Foster Entrepreneurship." Here she is greeted by French President François Hollande, Paris, January 2015

Learning and education are a basis for limitless boundaries. As such, I never stopped self-development on the job, and also at the most prestigious schools. Today, I am an alumna of both Harvard Business School (HBS) and London Business School (LBS), as well as part of an executive learning organization, Young/World President Organization (YPO-WPO). Because of my passion and belief in the merits of quality education, I sought to provide my children with the best. My daughter has a PhD from Harvard Law School and is a professor at Sciences Po, one of France's most prestigious institutions of higher learning. My son holds a Master's from University College London and an MBA from INSEAD. He worked for Mckinsey Consultants, and returned to launch UBER in Egypt.

Neveen receiving the 2013 Best Corporate Woman Award from the Regional American Chambers (9 countries). She is surrounded by son Tino Waked, and daughter Dina Waked carrying grandson Moïn Khouri, Cairo

At one of my yearly HBS courses, I heard a lecture by Professor Clayton Christensen based on his book *How Will you Measure Your Life?* It made me think how to measure mine; I concluded the following: 1) in business: one has to move fast in a continuously evolving globalized world. Timing is everything. Be courageous at taking difficult decisions. First mover advantage is of great value; 2) in life: be the entrepreneur at whatever you do and follow your dream, which may not come to you on day one. On the personal front: know your priorities early on, as they shall make the difference in your overall happiness.

Cairo, December 2015

BECOMING A JEWELRY DESIGNER, RESEARCHER AND AGENT OF CHANGE

AZZA FAHMY

Beginnings

Jewelry is my karma and my dharma. It is my calling in life, which I discovered when I was 23-years old. Sometimes I wonder how far I have come, and tell myself that I have been fortunate, indeed, to have discovered what I love, because passion has been at the heart of everything I do. At an early age, I was eager to study and excel, and have never stopped learning for the following 45 years. In fact, it is one of the two secret ingredients—hard work is the other—behind the international recognition I enjoy today, and will remain at the heart of my continued success. Actually, I never doubted that I would reach the top of my profession, and still remember telling my aunt Safeya: "One day, you will see my name in the headlines."

I was born and raised into an upper-middle class family of four siblings in Suhag, a mid-size town in Upper Egypt. This is the land I cherish as the real home where I belong; it also happens to be the main source of my inspiration. My story begins in 1969, when I embarked on a journey that would lead me to become one of the most celebrated jewelry designers in the region. Surprisingly, it all started with a book that I could not read, but one that changed my life. When I graduated from the Faculty of Fine Arts at Cairo University with a B.A. in Interior Design, I was not sure which direction my life would take. I worked in a government position for eight years, while constantly searching for something that I could arouse my passion. I experimented with different projects, from ceramics to children's books, but none clicked. One day, I attended an international book fair, my very first one, and stumbled upon a book about medieval jewelry. Although it was written in German and I could not read it, the pictures came alive because of the unusual shapes of the jewelry. Those images hit me like a flash, igniting a flame and stirring an uncontrollable sense of creativity. I felt that I had finally met my destiny. Without hesitation, I spent my entire salary to purchase the book—it must have been around 18 Egyptian Pounds—because something made me realize that at this moment, I was crossing a turning point in my life.

Prior to that day, jewelry design had never occurred to me, perhaps because it was a male-dominated field, but now that I had discovered it, nothing was going to hold me back. Although I was interested in sketching and designing, I believed that the best thing to do was to start by learning the craft of jewelry-making. In the absence of a specialized school, the best place to learn was "Khan El Khalili," Egypt's most famous jewelry district. I visited some of the workshops, introduced myself, and was accepted as an apprentice in one. The next day, I put on my overalls, tied back my hair, and was ready to start acquiring the basic techniques at the hand of one of the masters, Hag Sayed. A diminutive and pious man, he was also open-minded, having accepted to take a university graduate, especially a woman, as an apprentice. Such an arrangement was unheard of at that time, and it took my family some time to understand and support my initiative. Today, Hag Sayed proudly hangs the pictures of his renowned student on the walls of his shop.

My project started with a capital of 3 Egyptian pounds, the amount I spent to buy some basic materials, since my limited resources determined the components I could afford. The first pieces I made sold for fifteen Egyptian Pounds—a considerable sum for an unknown young artist like me, in the late 1960s. With this income, I bought silver and created a few more pieces that brought in additional revenue. I crafted unusual and unconventional items that were untested in the market, but they sold well. Furthermore, over time, I befriended writers, poets, and journalists, and built a good name for myself within that intellectual community. They started to speak and write about a young innovative artist they had met. Meanwhile, I was also a frequent visitor to museums, continued to do research, and looked for inspiration in many old and modern books that filled my imagination with ideas. This intense activity caused my mind to move faster than my technique. Facing technical difficulties was one of my early challenges. I consulted my mentor in Khan El Khalili, but even Hag Sayed was overwhelmed, as my designs were much more complicated than what he used to make in his shop.

Among my friends at that time were Dr. Norman Daniel, Director of the British Council, and his wife. They were great admirers of my creations, and often included me among their guests at events and dinners hosted by the British Council. One day, in a casual conversation, Dr. Daniel asked me how things were going. I answered him frankly, shared the difficulties I had encountered, expressed my need to continue to learn and improve my technical knowledge, and deplored the absence of a school in Cairo where I could further develop my skills. Three months later, Dr. Daniel called me one day, and invited me to meet him at his office. He offered me a six- month grant to study at the City of London Polytechnic Institute—now known as the Cass London Metropolitan University. By then, I had resigned my government job, and was a full-time freelance jewelry designer. Even today, many years later, tears come to my eyes when I remember that moment. Dr. Daniel was one of the first people to believe in me and see my potential, and he made every effort to get me a scholarship that enabled me to pursue my dream. I suspect that my keen and powerful desire to achieve must have been communicable, generating cosmic support in my favor, as many people went out of their way to help me. Rarely does an ordinary woman receive as much support and as many opportunities as I did.

I packed, headed for London, and achieved in six months what most students complete in two years. I was like a sponge, learning as much as I could, because I knew that my time was limited. I was looking for information and discovered more than what I had ever hoped to find out: many new techniques for engraving, casting, grooving, and enchasing. In half a year, I took seven courses, studying continuously from 9 am to 9 pm, to the amazement of my professors. Even the Dean declared that there had never been a student as motivated and as eager to learn as I was. That experience made me realize that studying with a teacher was quite different from training with a craftsman. My instructors in London taught me how to approach scientifically any design that comes to mind, enabling me to put together multiple structures and three-dimensional forms in a single item. They taught me that the sky was not the limit, kick-starting my creativity. Immersion in an artistic and stimulating environment generated transfer of knowledge, as students learned from each other's ideas, experiments and projects. Moreover, beside my work at the college, I visited contemporary jewelry exhibitions in the City whenever time permitted. The cosmopolitan society in which I lived and breathed, and the rich history of the City added a broader cultural dimension to my experience. This trip opened my mind and expanded my horizons; I returned to Cairo with bigger dreams and greater ambitions. In the early 1970s, I opened the first of my three workshops, followed by my first boutique in 1981.

Azza, Chair and Creative Director of Azza Fahmy Jewelry, in her design room, Cairo, 2015

The Journey

Equipped with my newly acquired skilled, and armed with knowledge and determination, I sought to mirror in my creations the world's cultural heritage, especially that of my native country, and wanted to make sure that my work would properly reflect the time-honored craftsmanship of my fellow citizens. As I set out, I was faced with another challenge that turned out to be a blessing in disguise. At that time, women in the Middle East favored Western-style jewelry, and here I came as a pioneer suggesting they wear pieces inspired from their own heritage. However, I combined jewelry design with what I had learned about color, harmony, and art history, and the novelty touched the right spots.

My objectives became clearer following my early pieces inspired by the Fatimid goblets in the Islamic Museum in Cairo. The palm tree as a symbol of Egypt resonated well, as featured in another early collection titled "Houses of the Nile," next to Nubian architecture and mud houses. As an intellectual artist and designer, I started to develop collections based on particular concepts and themes that I describe as "intellectual jewelry." These pieces were inspired by particular verse or poems that I had come across, for example, some by Salah Jaheen, or by Arabic proverbs, or anything else in the environment that fancied my imagination. By the mid-1980s, my concepts had broadened, and I sought to interpret global cultures in my own special way. I started with Indian, Mogul and Victorian, sometimes merging all three in a single design. Such innovations made my creations more unusual, more intriguing, and more attractive. The Azza Fahmy brand developed along with me. In the early days, I used brass; then, I moved to silver, and eventually mixed gold with silver—my signature combination today. Throughout my career, one thing never changed since 1969: staying true and committed to the artist and intellectual within me.

As the business grew, so did the pressure on my time with increasing demands from an expanding business and duties as a single mother. Another challenge occurred when I had to move my small scale operation—a one-woman show, so to speak—to a more structured enterprise. The time had come to transition from a modest workshop to an institution, shifting from a craft to an industry and a full-scale business. I knew that I needed to expand and recruit widely, and was able to build a strong team of skilled professionals and craftsmen—people I could trust on the way to achieving the dream. Expansion continued, and by 2002, I opened a larger and more sophisticated workshop, complete with a design studio housing more than 200 artisans, still used to this day.

Throughout the growing process, I wished to remain focused on my goal of celebrating the world's heritage, while preserving time-honored craftsmanship and techniques for generations to come. The three-tier "Ottoman System" of "Master," "Worker," and "Apprentice" seemed appropriate and effective for the transfer of skills, knowledge and expertise. I decided to apply it, and it has continued to serve us well in transferring know-how from generation to generation. Basically, it has allowed me to build an educational system within my workshop, while

Craftsmen at Azza Fahmy's workshop using handpiercing technique, Cairo, 2010

introducing improved craftsmanship; these were essential elements in my effort to wed tradition with technology, in order to stay ahead of the curve and meet worldwide market demands. I started with filigree, investigating its practice in several countries, and explored executing certain motifs with techniques that allowed mobility, which had been developed in our own workshops. Jewelry from the Ottoman Empire was a major source of inspiration, and led me to travel to Turkey and Aleppo in Syria to learn the ancient techniques applied by craftsmen there. These trips further expanded my vision, exposing to my imagination the different facets and rich layers of the cultures I admired, and made me dig beyond visual aesthetics.

As the years went by, research became an essential and critical part of my work. Born and raised in Egypt, I realized that its rich multilayered heritage—from Pharaonic to Coptic, and from Islamic to Ottoman—had not yet been fully explored in contemporary art and design. I wanted to work on Egyptian and Middle-Eastern jewelry, but there were no books, no references to consult. In the absence of sources, I started to collect vintage pieces of jewelry, and searched the market to find them before they were melted and recycled; thus saving from a dreadful fate the glorious relics of a bygone era. For hours, I would sit with "sheikhs," the lords of the silver market in Cairo to learn about the historic significance of each piece, and carefully recorded the information in detailed notes. As an intellectual and an academic, I enjoyed tremendously the educational part of my work and, before I knew it, I had gathered invaluable and vast archives that became my personal library. This newly-acquired knowledge sparked my interest in discovering where these treasures had come from, and I set out on a journey of research and exploration across Egypt. It was the source of my first book, *Enchanted Jewelry of Egypt. The Traditional Art and Craft* (Cairo & New York: AUC Press, 2007), and was followed by *The Traditional Jewelry of Egypt* (Cairo & New York: AUC Press, 2015) that some have described as "an Aladin's cave of jewelry."

Over the years, cultures have remained at the heart and soul of my inspiration, and I have spent endless hours studying them to hone my artistic skills, and transfer my experience into my creations. The journey of exploration did not end with my beloved Egypt, it was actually the first of many that were carried out across the world. The dream took me to Katmandu in Nepal, and to the Himalayas where I was fascinated to see that modest Tibetans adorned themselves with fabulous jewelry of corals and turquoise, driven by their talismanic beliefs. This observation made me ponder further the significance of jewelry in India—another love of mine. I also traveled to Morocco, home of some of the most beautiful ornaments in the world. Continuing my travels to Addis Ababa in Ethiopia, I was struck by the richness of their primitive motifs. The assortment of body ornaments in Africa, using painting, textiles and traditional bridal jewelry, offered a gorgeous contrast with the people's dark complexion. Moving on to Iran, a country of unending discovery and innumerable motifs inspired by gardens, architecture, sculpture, pottery, ceramics, even rugs and carpets—my personal favorites—I was moved by their magnificence, which sparked hundreds of ideas. Traveling remains a passion, as well as a source of inspiration that allows me to experiment and innovate by blending the different cultures I discover.

As time went by, my two daughters were growing. At an early age, they were immersed in the business since, as a single mother, I had to multitask at work and home, and they were often involved in both. As a result, they became fully engrossed in the business, and decided to be a part of it. Today, I am fortunate to see them at the helm of the family enterprise, and proud to watch them as they carry on the legacy. Having closely mentored them, I made sure they worked their way up the ladder, just like I did. This training helped them to develop an appreciation for their colleagues' input, and most importantly it set an example that all employees in the company are treated equally. My eldest daughter Fatma is the Managing Director of the company, and her sister Amina is my partner in design, preparing to become the next Chief Designer.

Azza with her two daughters in her design room (L to R) Amina Ghali, Head Designer; and Fatma Ghali, Managing Director, Cairo 2010

Around 2005, global recognition of my brand was growing, and so did the demand from jewelry connoisseurs around the world. It was only natural then to set our sight on Europe. We ventured in a series of fashion, cultural and educational partnerships and collaborations, kick-starting our regional and global expansion plans. We joined forces with Julien Macdonald for *London Fashion Week* in 2006; with the British duo Preen for *New York Fashion Week* in 2010; and with Matthew Williamson in 2013 and 2014 for *London Fashion Week.* In early 2012 and 2015, we embarked on two cultural collaborations, presenting bespoke creations for British Museum exhibitions.

A Look at the Future

In addition to designing, giving back is another passion of mine. When I was starting my career a few decades ago, I had no opportunity to learn and develop my creativity in Cairo; however, I was very fortunate to be offered the possibility to sharpen my skills in London. When I came back,

I realized that we were sorely lacking jewelry education, and was determined that, some day, I would remedy this gap and give back to my community. Today, there are many young people—just like the woman I was 45 years ago—eager to grow and develop their talents. With that objective in mind, and in collaboration with the European Union, I created a series of courses, which eventually led to the launching of my design school in 2013. That was my way to contribute to the development of the jewelry industry in the region, and fulfill my role not only as a designer and historian, but also as a change-maker. I partnered with Alchimia Contemporary Design School in Florence, to establish the Design Studio by Azza Fahmy that provides the needed education for aspiring designers, prepares them to compete internationally, eventually positioning the Middle East as a hub for jewelry design.

Besides developing jewelry design as an academic discipline, one of my goals is to promote the craft sector in Egypt, and teach skilled craftsmen to use technology properly, in order to export their finely-made creations all over the world. I would also like to publish as many jewelry references as possible; in fact, I am currently researching the influence of the Ottoman Empire on the Middle-Eastern jewelry for a forthcoming book. To benefit future generations of designers, I also accepted to serve on the Board of the Dubai Design and Fashion Council.

Despite the many obstacles and challenges I faced on the way to success, if I had to start all over again, I would not change a thing. I believe there are no coincidences, everything happens for a reason.

Cairo, February 2016

COMING TO TERMS
WITH MY MULTIFACETED IDENTITY

SAFAA ABDEL SAMIE FOUDA

Beginnings

I grew up on the island of Rodah, in Cairo, in a typical middle-class family: a working father, an educated, stay-at-home mother, and six siblings. The foremost priority for the children was education where failure was not an option. While I was given complete freedom to choose my own field of education, I was not allowed to wear high heels until my sophomore year in college, or to go to movies without an older brother. Fortunately, my brothers loved movies, concerts, plays, and all forms of entertainment. Marriage was not to be considered before graduation from university. Interestingly enough, I never felt that these were restrictions or limitation of freedom, as all my friends lived with the same rules, no questions were asked. The 1952 Revolution occurred when I was still in grade school; I remember feeling proud without knowing why. After the nationalization of the Suez Canal, I wrote a composition for the Arabic language class recalling that ancient Egypt was a superpower 5000 years ago, and now after the Revolution, it had a chance to regain its standing. The teacher thought it was inspiring, and made me read it aloud before the class. A month later, the 1956 war broke out, and it was decreed that high-school girls and boys would receive military training. That class was a nightmare: I thought there were many ways to demonstrate patriotism other than holding a gun and shooting at targets pretending they were enemies. Something precipitated in me since then that I was a creature of peace.

In the second year of high school, we had to choose between a track of arts or sciences, a decision that would determine our future. The history teacher urged me to opt for the arts, as she thought I had a gift for analyzing history. I obliged, but quickly realized that it was not for me. One week later, I was in the science track specializing in physics—a defining moment in my life. My maternal uncle, a renowned orthopedist, author and philosopher, was thrilled with my decision. He encouraged me to focus on science, and pursue my love for the humanities as a personal interest, just like he did. By giving me books, he got me hooked on reading at a young age. Because I so admired my uncle, I followed his advice and aimed for a scientific career. Graduating from high school, my dilemma was whether to opt for engineering or medicine. Having two older brothers in medical school, I was terrified at the skulls and bones they brought home for their studies, this pretty much settled the issue. My grandmother, who thought that engineers only worked in construction, was bewildered by my decision to go for a profession unfit for a girl.

In the third year of college, a group of 25 chemical engineering students, 20 boys and 5 girls accompanied by a professor, had the opportunity to visit oil companies in Europe for a month—my first trip outside Egypt. Once again, my uncle played a key role, and I was allowed to go without my own chaperon. That trip was an enlightening personal experience: for the first time, I had a taste of independence, acquired practical education, dealt with boys outside the classroom, bonded with my classmates, handled cultural differences, and built meaningful friendships. Now I was a young woman, not just a diligent and keen student.

First Years in Canada

The class of 1966 Chemical Engineering graduates at Cairo University included 83 men and 17 women, five of whom myself included, married from within the class. This was only natural, as there was virtually no other opportunity to mingle with men outside the university environment. Dating or meeting in mixed-gender groups at coffee shops or theaters was unacceptable in our social circle. The other option for marriage was the arranged route, known in Cairo as "salon marriage." Like some of my classmates, I settled for the former approach. The overwhelming defeat and the subsequent political events of the six-day war of June 1967 left my colleagues and me in a state of confusion. As young graduates, many of us engaged in intense correspondence with international institutions, seeking opportunities to study abroad. Since I anticipated a career in research and development, graduate studies were the means to achieve my goal. My husband received a scholarship at the University of Waterloo in Ontario and left for Canada; I joined him ten months later as I was expecting my daughter. Not knowing what awaited us in Canada, I left my five-month old baby with my mother—a decision I came to regret to this day.

Waterloo was a quiet campus town. Many graduate engineering students were Egyptians. The reputation of their academic achievements, and excellent performance made them easily admitted. We had to get used not only to the harsh winter weather, but also to a novel lifestyle. In 1969, the world was not as globalized as it is today. The standard question I was asked was: "Do you have camels and crocodiles in Egypt?" At first, it used to bother me; then, I made a habit of showing pictures of beautiful Cairo, Luxor, and Aswan, as well as handmade crafts, to respond in a more positive manner.

One day, about a year after our arrival in Waterloo, my husband and I were at the library, and were approached by a gentleman who worked for Citizenship and Immigration Canada. He asked us if we wanted to change our visas from student status to permanent residents. At that time, immigration was not on our minds, but we saw the offer as a way to avoid the paperwork involved in the renewal of our visas. We agreed and, as the saying goes, the rest is history. It was strange to be called immigrants as we did not feel any different: we still liked the same food, read the same books—Naguib Mahfouz and Mostafa Mahmoud, among others—and were tickled by jokes, as Egyptians do. Another year went by before we arranged for my daughter to join us. With a 3-year old child, we integrated even more fully into Canadian society. I found myself helping my daughter to make Valentine cards for her classmates, dress up for Halloween, and exchange gifts at Christmas; always holding to the values I brought with me from Cairo.

The prime focus during the graduate school years was to complete my studies and look after my daughter. I was the second woman to receive a PhD in Engineering from the University of Waterloo, perhaps even in all Canada; the first obtained hers in Electrical Engineering a year earlier. She, too, was Egyptian.

Energy Research by a Woman Scientist

Toward the end of my graduate studies, I was offered a scholarship from the National Research Council of Canada, to conduct postdoctoral research at a university of my choice, which brought me to Ottawa. By then, I was a full-fledged Canadian citizen. During the two years of postdoctoral fellowship, I was blessed with a second daughter, and took care of both children while keeping an eye on the job market. As time went by, we grew to like life in Canada, and I was offered my dream job as a research scientist at Natural Resources Canada. At that point, I needed to answer two questions once and for all: shall we make Canada our home? If so, what will be my identity? The first question was immediately answered in the affirmation, with no hesitation. The second was more complicated; in fact, it is still searching for an answer.

My first day at the pilot plant building of Canada Centre for Mineral and Energy Technology (CANMET) was one of the most exciting in my life. My boss introduced me to many people, almost all men, especially the scientists and technologists. This was fine and well, until I needed to do what comes naturally when I discovered there was no ladies' room in the building. The architects who designed it in the late 1950s never expected there would be a woman scientist. I had to go to the next building when the need arose. This went on for years as I was too shy to bring up the matter; after a while I was promoted and moved to another building. Eight years later, another woman scientist was appointed, she was not as bashful as I was, and requested proper facilities for the ladies be installed in the pilot plant building. It was done, but I never used them.

The scientific research and opportunities were fabulous. In the early 1980s, energy security became a top national priority following the 1973 war and ensuing oil embargo. With Canada enjoying an abundance of coal and oil sands, I worked on optimizing technologies to derive fuels from coal, or bitumen, or a blend of coal and bitumen. I enjoyed doing research both in-house in the pilot plant building, and through contracts with universities and other research institutions. For several years, in these different settings, I was the only woman. Six months after I started, I gave my first paper on a technology called coal pyrolysis in Fredericton, New Brunswick. The conference hall was full of experts, all men except for a couple of women students. It was quite intimidating, but I gave it my best. According to my boss, the feedback came that the "woman scientist" was "impressive," he had been told by his counterparts; they did not need to name names, there was only one.

Gradually, I got used to being the sole woman. On top of that, I was the woman who did not drink alcohol or eat pork. This would come up at working lunches, or Christmas parties when the secretaries would wink at me, and point to which punch was with and which one was without. I was who I was, never imposed my ways on anyone, nor did I change this side of me to please anyone. The identity issue would surface in my mind occasionally, as I felt that I owed it to Canada to be a good citizen, owed it to Egypt to preserve its beautiful culture, and owed it to my Creator to keep my covenant. Moreover, I owed it to my gender to demonstrate that women can aspire to any profession, and perform it eminently. I owned up to these issues, and no one other than me had to be concerned about them. At times, the juggling felt like a circus act, but it was feasible.

In the late 1980s, science and technology work took on a new direction. The federal government of Canada required that research and development be relevant to industry, which meant that it would have to be funded or co-funded by industrial corporations. Performance of research teams was then gauged by the amount of cost recovery brought in from industry. My role as a scientist took a new turn. On the one hand, areas of research were selected with commercial impact in mind; generating knowledge was necessary, but insufficient evidence of success in the science portfolio. On the other hand, the stronger interaction with seasoned industrial experts opened up my horizon for more ideas and innovations. I was ready to acquire new skills, and learn how to listen carefully to partners' needs, and market my ideas to them so as to fund my work. My first involvement in cost recovery projects was a program funded by three industrial corporations—a most enriching experience, indeed.

In the early 1990s, I had to make two changes in my career. I was asked to lead a technology group that worked on natural gas conversion into liquid fuels. When my senior manager brought up this issue, my initial response was that it would be a new area for me. He quickly replied that I could "walk on water," as he was confident that I would manage well. Every member of this group was a man. The other request was to be trained as a facilitator for a corporate team building exercise that involved multiple groups. I would be one of ten facilitators to implement team building in the organization, I was not the only woman but the only ethnic Canadian among the ten facilitators. This growth opportunity allowed me to polish my soft skills which were as much needed as my technical scientific knowledge, as it required integration at a different level. Active listening, compassion, respect, openness, transparency, motivation, and change of paradigm were all part of this program. While such traits may be considered common sense, I learned that only a small part of them is really intrinsic, the rest had to be acquired in the process of honing management skills.

Gradually and with time, more women scientists were added, the drive for political correctness requiring more women in management. I was never into the affirmative action games; for me, it was important that the substance of what I undertook be congruent with my experience and my values, rather than to serve a political agenda. My role in the branch evolved to become a program advisor, a science and technology director, and a deputy director general. Somehow I managed to keep one foot in science where my passion has always been. I was able to form and lead partnerships to study natural gas conversion with multinationals from

Canada, US, France, Venezuela, UK, South Africa, and Italy. The corporations in this consortium were interested in long-term research that had the potential for breakthrough technologies, so called high-risk high-gain R&D; by co-funding they shared the risk component. Writing an agreement that addressed intellectual property issues among all these competing corporations was tricky.

I led this international program for six years. Except for a brief period when the Venezuelan representative was a woman, I continued to be the only one in this amazing community. It was important for Canada to be visible on the international scene; thus, I was invited to join an association of like-minded CEOs called Energy Frontiers International. I also went to Nigeria to speak about economic options for marketing natural gas, to avoid flaring it into green house gas emissions. When I would introduce myself at that event, I would be asked: "Are you the lady from CANMET Canada?" I was also invited along with three other authors to write an article in a special edition of *Scientific American*, addressing the end of cheap oil and the options for alternative energies. A major oil company in Milan, Italy, held a special symposium on gas to market technologies, and invited me to speak and present the wrap-up conclusions of the event. Another memorable event in which I was involved was the organization of an international conference in Alaska. The picture shows 21 members in the group of Energy Frontiers International, next to the first oil well discovered in Alaska, nicknamed the Christmas tree. I am the shortest and the only woman.

It was never clear to me whether the reputation I gained was due to the fact that I was a woman in a man's world, or an ethnic person in a western country, or simply because I was a scientist who liked her work. Something I never experienced throughout my working life, not even once, was discrimination. I have always lived with the motto that life is a boomerang: you get back what you send away. Positive breeds positive and I chose to be positive throughout. A colleague once told me: "I know why you don't have problems with other people, because you are not threatening." Whatever that was, I took it to mean that if you look for peace, you are bound to find it; and if you look for trouble, you will also surely find it. This does not mean that I never fought for my beliefs, I certainly did, but I chose my battles. I fought for employees when they deserved promotions, I fought for employment equity, I fought about budget allocations, but I have never fought for personal gain or self-serving matters. A TV producer once asked me to participate in a panel of ethnic women who encountered discrimination; I explained to him that my experience did not fit that theme. Perhaps, mine was the exception that

Safaa with members of Energy Frontiers International by the first oil well discovered in Prudhoe Bay, Alaska, June 1998

proved the rule, or perhaps discrimination was there and I was too busy to notice it. Nonetheless, I consider myself very fortunate.

Giving Back to the Community

Shortly after 9/11, a memorial service was broadcast live in the conference room at work. I still remember the looks on many of my colleagues' faces, they seemed confused knowing what I stood for. I insisted that I was not going to apologize for things I did not do, and decided to work on reaching out to the community without being on the defensive. As a member of a Muslim-Christian dialogue group established in the early 1990s, I wanted to alleviate misconceptions through knowledge sharing, and by example. A number of us went to City Hall to offer a multi-faith prayer for those who lost their lives in New York. I had a dire need to understand and be understood; clearly, no one was qualified to speak on my behalf except my own self. I wanted the world to know that my values are about peace, compassion, equality, charity, love, and justice; and the onus was on me to make it happen. I ended up going to churches, synagogues, government offices, schools, boards of education, and various societies and charitable organizations. The outreach was either through speaking, or participating in projects aimed at benefitting humanity at large. In 2005, I retired from my professional career, and became busier than ever in cultural awareness and charity work. People assumed that I had plenty of time on my hands, and within a few months I was on the advisory boards of the Ottawa Police Services, and the Royal Canadian Mounted Police. Both were looking to improve their cultural awareness, in order to ensure bias-free investigations. Moreover, I was asked to organize two courses of ten sessions each at an adult education body, the Ottawa School of Theology and Spirituality. It was an enriching experience, as the interaction with the audience sharpened my knowledge of my own culture, and my sense of identity. By the end of the second course, we formed a cross-cultural book club, which is still alive and well.

One of the most enlightening activities in which I was involved is the Multifaith Housing Initiative, a charitable organization offering affordable housing to those with limited income. Both service providers and beneficiaries come from diverse backgrounds, humans serving humans. The concept I gained and will stay with me forever is that charity, real charity, is not just about donating from surplus resources, it is about sacrifice, giving up things to help others. Being involved with my Christian and Jewish friends has enriched my value system in that way.

For the past 14 years, the Ottawa Muslim Women's Organization, of which I am a member, has held an annual fundraising dinner, and donated the proceeds to mainstream organizations such as hospitals, food banks, and university programs. The Festival of Friendship dinner is now an iconic event in the City, which brings together in one hall its diverse communities, from grass root citizens to police officers, members of parliament and city officials, with a message that unity is in diversity.

Some of my community work has been recognized. However, deep down I am convinced that helping one's community can only be accomplished through team work, by people who want to give and be rewarded by seeing the impact of their efforts on human lives. Individuals may catalyze and inspire, but recognition should be bestowed upon teams of determined and passionate people eager to serve and bring about change.

Reflections

As we get older we tend to reflect on who we are, and whether we led a meaningful life. These questions are not likely ever to be fully answered, yet we can always try. One of my friends from the interfaith dialogue group told me that she found me comfortable, and content with who I was.

Safaa receiving the Mayor's City Builders Award from Mayor Jim Watson (L) and Beacon Hill-Cyrville Councillor Jim Tierney (R), April 2015

She actually helped me to sum it all up in these few words. Living as an ethnic minority in Canada could have been difficult, but it has actually been a most enjoyable journey. One of the reasons is acknowledging the hospitable nature of this country; another is seeing no conflict between the different facets of my identity. Can the same person be a woman with Egyptian values, who adores Arabic literature and sometimes writes Arabic prose, make a career in engineering, and work closely with the mainstream community to benefit humanity? My answer is a resounding yes, as long as her values are kept intact. There is nothing at odds between Canadian values and my own. Mainstream Canadian women of my generation had three career options: be a teacher, a secretary, or a nurse. Yet, growing up in Egypt, I was given the opportunity to practice engineering, serve my community, and live my values peacefully in Canada.

Reflecting on my journey, I think that a key lesson is the importance of dialogue, this holds true on both the social and professional fronts. Learning about one another alleviates fear, removes boundaries, and builds friendships. Dialogue is more about listening than about speaking; it means hearing others with interest and compassion, assuming they may be right, and expecting to learn and be affected by them. Working together for the greater good is the most effective way to get to know one another, appreciate the kindness in each other, and alleviate misconceptions. In the process of trying to understand or making people understand, one gains better insight into oneself. Canada's newly elected Prime Minister, Justin Trudeau, recently said that Canada is a strong country, not in spite of its differences, but because of them. I could not agree more. In short, if I had to do it over again, I would not want to change a thing. My experiences made me who I am, and I am blessed to feel comfortable with that.

Ottawa, December 2015

A MASTER PLAN FROM ABOVE

MAHASSEN MALAK GHOBRIAL

Born in Assiut, Egypt, in the late 1930s, I was the eldest of nine children. My father was an engineer who worked for the government, while my mother stayed home to care for the family with the usual array of nannies and servants. I went to a private American mission school for girls, Presley Memorial Institute (PMI), which also happened to be the one from which my mother had graduated several years earlier.

At a young age, I knew that I wanted to do something meaningful with my life to help others. My goal was to go to medical school, and I tried my best to reach it. Beside getting good grades, there were a number of obstacles along the way, mainly limited school options, and strong opposition from some of my uncles. I knew that becoming a doctor would be challenging, but it was my purpose and a dream that I would never give up. Encouraged by my family, especially my father, I set out to achieve my goal. Eventually, hard work and dedication paid off, and I was accepted in the medical school of Cairo University, *Kasr El Ainy*. This came as exciting and gratifying news for the 16-year old that I was who could hardly believe it. Our family moved to Cairo that same year due to a change in my father's position, making it possible for me to attend pre-med and medical school. I wondered if God had a plan for me.

We lived in a modest apartment in Garden City within walking distance from university. To this day, it remains a family home where one of my youngest brothers and his wife continue to live. It is amazing that our entire family of eleven lived in such small space, along with a domestic staff that slept on the kitchen floor. A year after moving to Cairo, my father had a stroke at age 45. I vividly remember the moment when it occurred. One evening, he was on the phone on a business call, speaking loudly and fully engaged in a discussion when, all of a sudden, I noticed that his speech slurred and he fell down. Although he survived the stroke and slowly began to recover, he soon suffered a second one and died that same year, leaving my mother with nine children to raise, the youngest of whom were 4-year old twins.

Being the eldest meant that I would have to assume the role and responsibilities of the second parent. My father was the main bread winner and without him, we started to suffer in many ways, in addition to missing his presence and mourning his loss. All my siblings were still in school, and my three sisters were enrolled in costly private schools—a choice my parents had made to provide them with better opportunities for the future. At that time in Egypt, there were no social support programs, pension plans, or medical insurance; thus, few options were available to us. I tried my best to help the family by excelling in school, as the government rewarded high performing students with a stipend higher than a doctor's salary. It is hard to believe that as a university student I received 11 Egyptian Pounds per month, while a newly graduated doctor would receive 10 Egyptian Pounds. I worked hard, splitting my time between studies and supporting the family.

During my second year at medical school, I received a marriage proposal from a kind and gracious gentleman from a prominent family we knew since our days in Assiut. I was not sure how to handle the offer, in light of my goals and my academic pursuits. My heart and my mind were torn, but after considerable thought, I decided to leave my family and medical studies, and went to Assiut to be married. It was an extremely difficult decision to make and I had no idea what was to follow. The marriage was happy, and I enjoyed a simple life in Assiut. However, less than two years later, tragedy struck and my husband died suddenly from a brain aneurysm.

Heartbroken, I returned to Cairo to be close to my family and friends. Gradually, I regained the vigor and drive that had brought me success in the past, and the determination to resume my medical studies. Being readmitted to the university would have been impossible had it not been for my former classmates who lobbied and fought the administration on my behalf. It was almost a miracle when I received word that I could return to finish my second year. Once again, it seemed that the Master Plan laid out for me was back on track. With renewed dedication to my studies, I also enjoyed sports, and became the captain of the university teams of volleyball and ping pong. I do not know where or how my classmates and I found the time to practice, but we excelled and won numerous tournaments against the other medical school teams. We travelled to Syria to participate in international competitions—an extraordinarily satisfying experience for me. During those unforgettable years, I made lifelong friendships. Our core group of friends remained very close, and called itself "the Lotus Family." These bonds that were formed in the mid-1950s are still as tight today as they were back then. Although dispersed across the globe, we continue to stay in touch and rarely let five years go by without reuniting somewhere in the world.

In 1959, I had another marriage proposal from a medical school graduate who had moved to the US, Wasfy Seleman Saleh. Initially, we communicated through a mutual friend, and eventually we started to write each other across the ocean to get to know each other better. The story goes that he had seen me once outside my church and immediately fell in love with me, though he never had a chance to approach me. While I was flattered to have a second chance at marriage, this time I knew that I would not consider giving up my goal to complete medical studies. Wasfy understood and agreed to wait five years until I finished my program. From these early days, his support for me and my career was evident, and his encouragement would only grow over the years, even during the most challenging of times.

Graduation from medical school was a gratifying moment, but another obstacle loomed on the horizon. At that time, all medical graduates in Egypt were required to work two years in a public medical facility. Waiting another two years to marry my fiancé did not seem fair, and by then I was anxious to be with him. We decided that it would be best to marry by proxy, so I could apply for a visa and join him abroad—an arrangement, we thought, would exempt me from the required government service. A small wedding ceremony took place in my fiancé's family home in Heliopolis, it was attended by close relatives and friends. Our priest officiated, and my father-in-law signed on behalf of his son who participated only by phone. That is how we became husband and wife.

The marriage certificate was all I needed to apply for a travel visa, and my application was forwarded to the minister of health for his approval. Coincidentally, being a friend of my father, this man had been a surgeon in my hometown and recognized my name. Knowing me and aware that I was a recent medical graduate, he refused to sign the visa application, insisting that I would have to complete the required two-year service. However, I was adamant not to wait and made several trips to meet him at the ministry to plea for my case. After countless visits, he finally signed the papers and I was on my way to a new life. Despite all of the challenges that I had faced trying

Mahassen in Cleveland, October 1964

to get the visa, the most difficult part was leaving my mother behind, knowing that she had to carry alone the burden of caring for my younger siblings. My plan, I assured her, was to be gone for only four years of training, and then return to be with her.

In September 1964, I finally joined my husband Wasfy, after five years of knowing each other only through letters. It was my first time out of Egypt on my own. I arrived at Kennedy airport in NY after a long TWA flight; walking off the plane felt as though I was floating toward a new chapter of my life. Wasfy was waiting for me with his camera, taking photos of me as I was approaching, even before I noticed him. It turned out that photography was one of his hobbies, and I was thrilled to be one of his subjects. We spent the first week of our honeymoon in NYC, and what an experience it was to be just walking the streets of Manhattan and taking it all in! We saw the Statue of Liberty, and spent several days at the World Fair visiting an array of pavilions. The most memorable were General Motors, and the World of Tomorrow which was filled with appliances of the future that blew the mind of the very recent Egyptian newcomer I was.

After that exciting week we returned to Cleveland, Ohio, where we would settle. Wasfy had been doing general surgery training at the excellent Cleveland Metropolitan General Hospital, affiliated with Cleveland State University. As a resident, he had many opportunities to perform many surgeries under amazing staff, an experience that substantially developed his career as a surgeon. He arranged for me to work in the lab of the Surgical Department until I passed the exam for foreign medical graduates, and became a resident in Pathology. Then, Wasfy decided to seek another specialization in Urology, and I opted for children's health, another turning point in my life. Both areas seemed appropriate to the needs of Egypt where we planned to return to pursue our careers. We applied to a good university hospital in Ottawa and were accepted. In July 1965, we packed everything we owned in our small VW, and drove from Ohio to Canada's capital, where only 3 Egyptian families lived—today there are hundreds. It soon became evident that training in Pediatrics would not be optimal for me in Ottawa where there was no children's hospital. I had to transfer to Montreal Children's Hospital where I was fortunate to be admitted in a four-year residency program.

As great an opportunity as this was, it also meant another separation from my husband. The challenge was compounded by the fact that we had just had our first child, Maher. In those days, medical residents were on call every other night and every other weekend—a grueling schedule unacceptable by today's standards. Wasfy encouraged me to go to Montreal while he would care for our six-month old baby with the help of a nanny. During the first year, I would travel every week back and forth between Montreal and

Ottawa, according to what my schedule allowed. Mildly put, it was an extremely difficult time but, I believe, it was also part of the Master Plan. The next year, my husband and my son joined me in Montreal where Wasfy worked on his PhD at McGill University, while I completed the remaining three years of my training. Had it not been for his willingness, support, and encouragement, I think I could not have survived that trying experience.

We had been living in Canada on student visas, with every intention to return to our native county. However, in spring 1967, war broke out in Egypt, and we realized that finding work would be difficult under the circumstances. We applied for landed immigrant visas for Canada, and remained a few more years in Montreal where our second son, David, was born. When the visas were granted, we sponsored two of my brothers to join us in Canada. In December 1968, they arrived on a blustery cold and snowy night, totally unprepared for their new surroundings, unsure what would follow. Over the years, they established solid roots in their new country, built successful careers, and founded happy families. Eventually, all my siblings came to Canada, except for a sister who married and moved to Kuwait, and a brother who still lives with his wife in the Garden City family apartment in Cairo. My mother also joined us and saw her family grow and develop a fresh Canadian identity. She was *teta* (grandma in Arabic) to 19 grandchildren, most of whom lived close to her in Toronto. She was a strong and devoted matriarch who always maintained a calm demeanor. When she passed away in 2005 at 92, I had to take over the role of surrogate parent and teta in the close-knit family. This is a role I enjoy tremendously as it gives full meaning to my life, especially when all the cherished ones come to me for advice and guidance.

In July 1970, we moved to Ottawa to be on staff at the University of Ottawa. That year I successfully passed all the specialty exams for the Royal College of Physicians of Canada, and the American Board for Pediatrics, as well as other licensing requirements. Finally, after years of hard and intensive labor, I was officially a doctor and it was time to start my career. At first, I set up my practice in our modest home, but it was soon evident that it would not work. Eventually, I had the opportunity to share an office with another pediatrician. It was a perfect arrangement that allowed me to take on weekly clinics at the newly opened Children's Hospital of Eastern Ontario. My life and career were gradually taking shape and progressing.

Mahassen and her mother, Daisy Ghobrial Galdas at age 83, in front of their church in Ottawa, 1996

Initially, it was a struggle to build up my practice as I was unknown in the medical community. Furthermore, I had the double disadvantages of being a woman and a newcomer to Canada. Speaking with an obstetrician one day, and asking him for referrals, he replied: "Why do you want to work so hard? Doesn't your husband work?" Once again, my determination prevailed. Although it took longer for my practice to grow, compared to that of a Canadian-born pediatrician, eventually through word of mouth, patients started to arrive at my door. Today, my practice is recognized nationally as a community teaching center for students and residents across Canada. I still care for children and their families through multiple generations, in the same location. They consider me one of their own, share with me their struggles and successes, and trust me with their most personal matters. Actually, a few days ago, I went to the hospital nursery to examine a newborn baby. The mother was holding her little one, and the grandmother was standing by her. I immediately remembered the older lady and her siblings who were my patients in the 1970s.

One of the most important memories of my early years in Ottawa occurred one evening when I went home earlier than usual to make a few phone calls and take care of some paperwork. A woman came knocking at the door, she explained that her 5-year old son was unwell and she needed my help. Since she could not reach me by phone, she came right to the house, having heard from a friend about an "Egyptian woman pediatrician" who lives in the neighborhood. I obliged her, and went to see her son—this was back in the days when house calls still existed. She introduced me to her parents who were visiting from Egypt. Recognizing my name, her father told me that he had worked with my own father, and that, in fact, he had accompanied him when the two of them went together to my mother's family to ask for her hand. It is in times like these that we realize that the world is indeed very small! Young Tamer had a throat infection for which I gave him a prescription. That day, a lifelong friendship started with Abla Sherif, who is also featured in this book.

Being trilingual, I had the opportunity to see many newcomers who had escaped their homelands under chilling circumstances, arriving in Canada as refugees. The nationalities differed over the years, according to world events. For example, in the 1970s, during the war in Lebanon, there was an influx of Lebanese families. Shortly thereafter, there were many Vietnamese, also known as "boat people," whom I had to treat through translators. A couple of decades later, in the 1990s, I had to communicate through translators with escapees from Kosovo. The amount of atrocities that these children had experienced in their short lives was heartbreaking. I still see many of them, and am always glad to learn of their progress and success in life despite the turmoil they had been through.

Two years after I started my practice, Wasfy received a great offer from the Sherbrooke University Hospital, in Quebec. It was a wonderful opportunity while I was still building up my practice, and finally making some progress. We agreed that he would go on his own and give it a try before the whole family would move to Sherbrooke. This meant that we would be apart again, and this time I had two young boys and another "baby"—my private practice. Furthermore, while Wasfy was hundreds of miles away, our daughter, Titi, was born two months prematurely. Fortunately, it happened on Canadian Thanksgiving day, a national holiday, while Wasfy was home in Ottawa. In the early 1970s, there was no maternity leave, so I had to be back at work a few days after I gave birth. Titi remained in the hospital for a number of weeks to grow and build strength, and I visited her every day. These were difficult times, but I held on to my faith, confident that it was part of the Master Plan.

Finally, three years later, we decided it was time for Wasfy to return to Ottawa where the family would settle for good. He started his own private practice in Urology, while mine was growing and thriving, as I continued to hold positions at various hospitals in Ottawa. It is in that city that our children ultimately grew up and established their own roots. Some of them travelled across the country or beyond for school and life lessons, but for them Ottawa will always be home. I am blessed with six lovely grandchildren who call me *teta*. In 2015, the Ottawa Hospital bestowed upon me an award in recognition of my 40 years of service. I am especially proud of that honor because it comes from a city and a community with which I feel profoundly attached. I am one of very few physicians to have remained in practice, whereas most of my peers no longer serve. The Children's Hospital of Eastern Ontario opened in 1974, and I was a member of the staff from the onset. My work was also recognized there with another award on the occasion of my 40 years of service, and I still have the privilege of being part of the institution. In 2011, Wasfy was struck by a stroke from which he recovered, but he did not survive a second one that took his life away in August 2014, a few weeks before our 50th wedding anniversary.

My story would not be complete if I did not mention some of the most personally rewarding experiences of my life, as a volunteer with a Christian Medical group, Health Team International (HTI). It all started in 2006, when my daughter reminded me that I had been talking about going overseas on medical missions after I retired; she wisely recommended that I should go now, before being too old to enjoy it. About the same time, during a visit to my orthodontist, he happened to mention that he had recently been to India doing humanitarian work with a group of professionals, and was planning to accompany them on another trip to China and North Korea. I was intrigued, asked many questions, and casually told him to let me know if they needed a pediatrician. It took no time before I received an invitation to join the upcoming mission.

Mahassen and Wasfy, a few weeks before his second stroke, October 2013

The trips are planned months in advance, in collaboration with local organizations that handle the arrangements of all aspects of our stay. The groups generally comprise physicians, dentists and dental assistants, optometrists, audiologists, nurses and other volunteers who help in any needed capacity. We bring as much of our own supplies as possible, including dental chairs and instruments, examination tables, electrical generators, and medication. Usually, we are able to source the medicine from drug companies, after going through a rigorous process of gathering relevant details about the locations where we would be treating patients, and which health officials would be involved. After the thorough evaluation, thousands of dollars' worth of supplies are donated to support our humanitarian missions.

These trips have been fascinating, and a source of great learning experiences. For example, in North Korea, officials did everything they could to isolate the people from us foreigners. They determined who we could treat, and even once prohibited a member of our group from entering the country. During a lunch break, we were not allowed to walk down the street to visit a fishing village. Our every step was monitored, making it difficult to offer the level of support we had hoped to provide to the local population. In India, my own personal and professional experience was like no other. I saw cases I had never seen before, including patients missing limbs due to leprosy, and poor and malnourished children in orphanages suffering from illnesses that I did not know existed. The nuns in Mother Theresa's famous leprosy compound were especially appreciative and helpful, and despite the extreme poverty and hardships that people endured, they were extremely kind and welcoming. Upon a midnight arrival at one of our destinations, the local women surprised us by offering to wash our feet and dry them with towels, before cooking the most amazing meal by candle light using a coal fire. In Cambodia, another fascinating country and wonderful people, we had different experiences each time we visited. The recent history of the genocide is still vivid in their memories, and affects all aspects of daily life. During some of our time off, we visited the killing fields of Phnom Penh. Our tour guide was a survivor of the Khmer Rouge massacre who shared his horrific stories while witnessing the assassination of each member of his family. He was left for dead at age six, and lives to this day to narrate the events, fully committed to doing so every day of his life. His anger and resentment were still powerful, forty years later. This was not uncommon.

These remarkable ventures inspired me to join yet another group, Coptic Medical Association of North America (CMANA), in order to give back to my birth country of Egypt. In November 2015, I had the opportunity to return to the small town of Akhmim, not far from where I was born, to assist some of my own people, coming full circle. As I think about it, I realize that I could have never planned such a life for myself, nor could I have imagined how it would turn out. I am convinced that, every step of the way, there was a Master Plan from above, one that I could not have achieved all by myself.

Ottawa, November 2015

COMING FULL CIRCLE

NIMET SABA HABACHY

Growing up in Cairo prior to the 1952 Revolution meant that I negotiated for the club's playground swings in English, got refused in French, and ran crying to my nanny in Arabic. Or I might debate the issue in French, get yelled at in Arabic, and allow the matter to be settled by a pink-faced English nanny. When not on the playground, I lived in an Italianate villa where my father listened to Om Kalthoum, the Maria Callas of the Middle East, and my mother practiced Schubert. Occasionally, my mother played for me while I sang about coming from somewhere called "Alabama with a banjo on my knee," not having any idea what Stephen Foster's song was about. On several occasions, my parents came back from New York with a recording of the latest American musical hit which I would learn by rote and parrot endlessly.

Our home was situated on what was then Sharia El Malek (King Street). My father and I took walks in the neighborhood and if we walked along the tree-lined boulevard to the right, we passed beautiful homes and gardens, a few shops and a synagogue. If there was a wedding at the synagogue, I might get lucky and be offered "*milabbis*"—I was devoted to sugared almonds. If, on the other hand, my father and I walked behind our home, it would be on a dirt road with no pavement, a "*hara*." We dodged barefoot children clothed in *galabiyas* expertly steering hubcaps with their sticks. The local baker would present us with a loaf of bread, hot from the oven—welcome on a cold winter morning—and would not accept payment, it was a gift for the Pasha, and his daughter who accepted gladly. I listened as people came up to my father and asked his advice about this or that legal matter.

In the morning, I had the run of our home. I would greet the milkman and chat up his donkey. I enjoyed watching him fill the shallow pan left on the stoop with milk that soon created a layer of *ishta* on the top, a lethal, delicious layer of pure cream—ambrosia itself—with a dollop of honey, and worth about a million calories. Next on my household rounds was Tudri who presided over the kitchen unless he shooed me away because he was about to guillotine a chicken.

One day, my mother and I drove to a big gray building far away from home, and I was presented to a formidable, tall lady, named Doctor Martin, the head mistress of the American College for Girls (now Ramses College), my mother's Alma Mater. I thought even my mother seemed a little abashed by this important American educator who was part of the PMI— the Protestant Missionary Institute. For the last one hundred and fifty years, this organization provided Egypt and other countries with ladies who taught children like me about Jane and her dog Spot who lived in a red brick house with a white picket fence, in a town that looked nothing like Cairo. I aced Kindergarten, and was able to count to 10 in Arabic and English. I thrived on fairy tales about the *Djinn* in Arabic, and Bible stories in English. At Christmas, I was to sing a solo of *Joy to the World.* I took one look at the mass of people in front of me and froze—my debut as a performer was a memorable failure.

I spent halcyon summers in Alexandria with my Granny, condemned to go about in a floppy white cotton hat to keep me from becoming too brown. The day started with a check of what color flag was flying over the beach which dictated whether or not I would be allowed into the water. A red flag meant I had to be cautious swimming, a black one signaled that armed with bucket and spade, I would venture forth to do battle with the Mediterranean, constructing castles with elaborate canal systems to stave off the encroaching waters. No matter how deep my friends and I dug or how cleverly we designed dams and dykes, our handy work was reduced to a soft, gray puddle as we were dragged off for lunch and a nap. Older Alexandrian cousins sometimes swam us out to a golden rock that glistened in the sea, and was reputed to be Cleopatra's bathtub. They would leave us there while they showed off their swimming prowess to each other for what seemed like hours, until they deigned to swim us back. By then we were frightened and could have cared less about Cleopatra or her tub.

Cousins also featured because they had great birthday parties where, in addition to lovely goodies from Groppi, the Swiss *pâtisserie,* there would be a show. Sometimes, there was a scary man who produced a doll that lived in a box, sometimes there was a "gala-gala man," a magician who made things appear and disappear. But best of all, was the occasional American musical we would be shown. There was one about a *Show Boat* that went up and down a huge river that wasn't the Nile. There was a beautiful lady (Ava Gardner) on board who, for reasons I could not fathom, got thrown off the boat.

My father made it his business to take me to important Cairo sites. The trips to the glorious Sultan Hassan Mosque had the novelty of having to put on outer slippers over my shoes which allowed me to glide happily over the smooth flooring. The Egyptian Museum boasted *Sheikh el Balad,* the leader of the community, my father's favorite statue, whom I thought of as my father's portly friend with the shiny eyes. The visit would invariably end with my requesting that my father buy me the smallest of King Tut Ankh Amun's chariots. I enjoyed those excursions almost as much as I enjoyed going out to the Giza plateau and riding a donkey around the Sphinx, whose paws had as yet to be dug up.

On 26 January 1952, I was taken up on the roof of our home to watch the grander symbols of Cairo's foreign occupation, like the Turf Club, the department store Cicurel, and the Shepheard's Hotel go up in flames. I had frequently stood on the Shepheard's Hotel veranda among the potted palms watching parades led by King Farouk in a white military uniform and a red fez standing in a red Rolls Royce convertible. On a drive through Cairo a few days after the fire, I saw the same veranda, now broken and pitted with an upturned toilet in the middle of a pile of debris.

Sometime thereafter, my father accepted a position as legal counsel to the Arabian American Oil Company and we set out to make new lives in the US. I entered the Spence School with better Arabic than English, and tried to understand about Native Americans and Henry Hudson and Dollars and Cents. Howdy Doody to the rescue! Howdy Doody was a puppet who was running for election as mayor of his TV fiefdom at the same time Dwight D. Eisenhower and Adlai Stevenson were running for the presidency of the United States. My father and I fought for television rights to watch our respective candidates.

My English improved and I gained in confidence when I realized that I thoroughly enjoyed being on a stage—any stage. I starred as Benjamin Franklin in a jingoistic piece designed to teach us American History. I went on to play a brilliant Mad Hatter in a performance of *Alice in Wonderland.* At Bryn Mawr College, I took part in more sophisticated plays and discovered that I liked character roles best because they had the better lines. The feisty Paulina, in Shakespeare's *A Winter's Tale*, is much more fun than the insipid Hermione, and Charlotta Ivanovna, the governess in Chekhov's *The Cherry Orchard*, is an exquisite eccentric. By the time I got my BA, I knew I wanted to go to graduate school in Theater. My mother, always an ally in the past, made it clear that I was on my own in breaking this disquieting piece of news to my father.

I thought about the matter from my father's point of view: here we were, immigrants in America, and instead of pursuing a useful and remunerative line of work, I was suggesting going into the most fickle and capricious profession of them all. It was all very well that my father enjoyed my spouting lines about the house, that he actually memorized some of them himself, and that he came and enjoyed my theatrical efforts, but even so I did not see him condoning my choice. At breakfast, over a soft boiled egg, I approached him with the idea of getting a Master's of Fine Arts in Theater. My father said nothing and cracked his egg. He peeled it carefully, removing miniscule slivers of shell at a time. When

Nimet in costume as Regina in Lillian Hellman's *Another Part in the Forest*, 1971

the egg was at last denuded of its shell, and my nerves quite shot, he said slowly and deliberately: "Molière was an actor." Hallelujah! Molière, whom my father enormously admired for his ability to skewer society's foibles and hypocrisies, especially in matters pertaining to the law, was making it possible for me to go to theater school.

I received my Master's of Fine Arts from Columbia University where, for three years, I was in shows and classes dealing with a cross section of western theater. The Department required that we get some practical experience during the summer. So I gamely went out and auditioned for the Straw Hat Trail—a summer theater that was unpaid and usually performed in the outdoors in a venue infested with mosquitoes. I wound up in the middle of Blue Grass Country in Kentucky with a very young John Travolta. It was a grand summer of doing plays ostensibly destined for Broadway—none of which ever made it anywhere near Broadway. But, in one summer, I played an old crone in a political drama and Lady Windermere, in an extrapolation of Oscar Wilde's *Lady Windermere's Fan.*

But now, it was time to earn a living. I landed a job as Assistant to the Company Manager at the New York City Opera, the lesser of the two New York City Opera Houses, and became the language coach for French and Italian. I took voice lessons and sang in the chorus of amateur opera companies in New York. While performing in Bizet's *Carmen,* on a postage stamp of a stage in a geriatric center, I learned from colleagues that WQXR, the classical radio station of *The New York Times*, was looking for women, languages and minorities. The newspaper had been hit with a lawsuit because it did not have more women on its roster. I fit the bill almost perfectly: I was female; I could pronounce French, German and Italian, take a good stab at Czech and Hungarian; and though I was not quite dark enough, I could pass for a minority. In later years, a senior member of the WQXR staff commented: "I knew they were looking for a minority but I didn't think they would settle for an Egyptian Copt."

For the next 27 years, I had the privilege of being host and producer of WQXR's all night program. It was my prerogative to soothe people with Debussy's ethereal, dreamlike music, or shoot them out of bed with Wagner's *Ride of the Valkyries.* I acquired a certain notoriety which I relished while leading a singular lifestyle. I would often bike down to the WQXR studios in time for a midnight rendez-vous with 750,000 listeners who were about to share with me the glorious music of Mozart, Beethoven, and Bach, among others. I would talk about some New York event and then launch into something appropriate to the moment. A rainy day inspired a hearing of Chopin's *Raindrop Prelude*, snow meant Debussy's

Des pas sur la neige. There were theme nights: a romp through the Trojan war inspired by *The Illiad* and *The Odyssey* of Homer, suggested portions of Offenbach's *La Belle Hélène*, Berlioz's *Les Troyens*, Purcell's *Dido and Aeneas*, Monteverdi's *Il Ritorno d'Ulisse in Patria,* Strauss's *Elektra*, and Barber's *Andromache's Farewell.* Not one of your lighter evenings!

I took enormous delight in programming unexpected music. On a beautiful morning, I juxtaposed the *A'dan,* the Muslim call to prayer, and a Bach Toccata to the delight of many listeners. I played the whole 20 hours of Richard Wagner's *Ring of the Niebelungen* over several nights. And there were marathons, one of Beethoven's 32 sonatas every night; excellent for tracing the evolution of a composer's genius.

A woman—even a 10-headed hydra speaking on the radio in the middle of the night in New York City—would inevitably acquire fans. I received wonderful letters over the years. There was the gynecologist who told me his life was perfect, filled as it was with Brahms and babies. One judge issued me with a summons to appear and have a cup of coffee with him. Then there was the embezzler who wrote that he was no longer juggling the books, but rather the pots and pans in the prison kitchen. I have seen Mrs. Brown's little boy through colic—Bach partitas were soothing, I gather—and several books got written accompanied by Bach and Mozart *et al* on my watch.

Sometimes, I had to interrupt the night's music to report on world events. It fell to me to tell New Yorkers that Indira Ghandi had been assassinated. And I led one program with the announcement of the death of Diana, Princess of Wales. That night, I quickly changed the entire six hours of music to requiems and other austere works. During my WQXR career, I also gave lectures on opera at the Metropolitan Opera and the Metropolitan Museum, among other venues. The lengthy symphonies of Gustav Mahler and Anton Bruckner allowed for my doing research. Scheherazade told her tales to a grateful Sultan for a mere 1001 nights, I spun records, tapes and CDs for insomniac New Yorkers for at least 7001 nights, and am still counting. At this writing, I am still on WQXR three nights a week, but pre-recorded. I managed to garner a few awards along the way, variously from the Council of Churches of New York, the Martina Arroyo Foundation and Glimmerglass Opera. But the real reward has been the kindness of listeners over the years and my involvement in their lives. I gather a generation has grown up in WQXR's company. I continue to get holiday greeting cards as though I were a member of an extended family. Who says New York is not a community?

But, in looking back, I have to say the most fulfilling coming together of my several worlds was when I, along with my sister Sue Habachy, began to sell in New York City the cottage industry products of the *zabbaleen*, the garbage collecting community in Cairo's Moquattam hills. It was the wonderful Marie Assaad, whose profile is also in this book, who introduced me to the work of the Association for the Protection of the Environment (APE). On a beautiful March day in Cairo, Marie picked me up and we drove in the direction of the Citadel. I don't think I was quite prepared for what I experienced. We descended into a ravine and then started to climb out on a narrow garbage strewn dirt road with sheep, goats, dogs, cats and pigs scampering in all directions. It was the pigs who were responsible for the creation of the squatter community that settled in the shadow of the Moquattam hills. Egyptian laborers or *fellahin,* most of them Christian, had come north looking for work. Finding none, they returned to their agrarian roots and began to breed pigs. The pigs could sustain them, and there was a market for pork. The people of the Moquattam began collecting Cairo's garbage to feed the pigs and they gradually evolved into the garbage collectors of the city.

By the time I first saw the squatter area of Manshiyit Nasr in the Moquattam, it had already been in existence for 20 years or so. The alleys were well established, here was the butcher with a hock hanging ready to be sliced up for a customer; there was the *"kochari"* man preparing his delicious dish of rice and lentils doing a brisk business over lunch time. The car kept going up and up the hill revealing hints of lives that were almost unimaginable. Dark narrow alleys went off to left and right leading to dwellings that had been built higgledy piggledy despite the choking closeness of other buildings. We were enveloped in the smell of organic matter decaying in the sun.

Finally we came to a clearing, and I saw an attractive grey stucco building with balconies. This was the Sawiris built school that houses the Association for the Protection of the Environment, established for the teaching of weaving and patchwork and other skills to the women in the community. When we first arrived, paper recycling had not yet been introduced; it would arrive a year later. There were classrooms and storerooms that led out onto airy balconies. The atmosphere was lively with young women darting in and out of sun drenched rooms. The work was beautiful and original, and often showed much imagination. It was immediately clear that there was a great deal of camaraderie and encouragement at every turn. Volunteers, mostly fellow Egyptian women, would bring up a topic and everyone would chime in. Clearly, a great deal of general information was being propounded and exchanged. Without fanfare, the volunteers were offering lessons in hygiene and literacy and mathematics and commerce, giving the girls tools that instilled confidence in a male dominated society.

Laila Iskander, former Minister of State for Environmental Affairs in the Egyptian Government, was assigned to be my guide, and we would become friends from that day on. Leila took me to all the rooms chatting up the girls along the way. They clearly adored her, and wanted to show off their latest achievements to her and to her guest. I listened, and with each moment felt keenly that I wanted to be involved in this miracle. I bought a few things and then two *zabbaleen*—one literate and one not— painstakingly made out my sales slip. I have that slip to this day, it represents so much hope and pride. At the end of my visit, I asked Leila what besides money was needed. She replied simply: "A market."

Upon returning to New York, Sue and I wondered if we dared import products from Cairo's garbage community, and sell them to our New York friends. Of course we could! But how could we deal with the paperwork for a shipment at JFK? Enter, Freddy and his employer, Eagle Transport, ably led by our ally and friend, Jerry Donnelly. Sometimes, when a project is blessed by good intentions, it flies and this one did. Of course, there was the year JFK airport would not release the goods because APE sent us aprons which did not fit the category of "local handicrafts." As far as the US Customs agent was concerned, an apron qualified as "apparel," and many phone calls and emails later, Cairo sent the required papers by DHL, then Sue and I went to the airport and collected them at 5 AM.

The first sales took place in my apartment. They soon became something of a social event, especially as we scheduled them around the Holidays. Over the years, people brought their friends. At this writing, we have a list of about 1500 people who receive our invitations to two New York sales a year. Now that we have grown, we have found larger spaces, and word of our efforts produced an article in *The New York Times*. We have also sold Moquattam goods in several cities along the East Coast. We have become good saleswomen, as have our friends who volunteer their time and effort. They can convince any New Yorker that what he or she needs desperately is a rag rug, or a quilt, or a bag made by a woman from the garbage collecting community in Cairo, Egypt.

In all this, one of the joys has been the relationships we have formed with the women and the volunteers of the Moquattam. We have become friends as we have worked together, choosing inventory, watching the girls work, hearing about their lives. We have gone together on excursions to Fayed and Alexandria. And we have kept tabs on growing children. Nineteen years ago, my friend Samia, pregnant at 13 with her first child, was climbing up and down the ladder in the store room choosing our next sales' inventory, with me begging her to stop and not endanger her unborn child. On my most recent visit to the Moquattam, Samia, now a major player in the work of the Moquattam, informed me that she had just married off her 19-year old daughter. No early marriage and pregnancy for her child. I was thrilled for them both. I am humbled by women like Samia, they have been given so little and have achieved so much. I am privileged to count them as my friends.

Sue (L) and Nimet Habachy (R) selling products of the Association for the Protection of the Environment in Columbus, Ohio, c. 2000.

I have enjoyed the unlikely juxtaposition of a career at the forefront of New York's cultural life, and my chosen sideline as a saleswoman for goods produced by the APE. I derive great joy and pride knowing I am a part of Egypt's future. I have come full circle.

New York, November 2015

A WITNESS TO CHANGE: FROM THE PRE-DIGITAL AGE TO CURRENT TIMES

FAYZA MOHAMED HUSSEIN HAIKAL

I was born on April 11, 1938. My father, then almost 50, had achieved literary celebrity throughout the Arab and Islamic world for his groundbreaking research and publications on Arabic and Islamic literatures. For his pioneering books, he was honored with the title of *Pasha* two months before my birth, and held an important position in society due to his prominent political standing. A leading member of the opposition party, *Al Ahrar al Doustoureyeen* (the Liberal Constitutionalists), he eventually became its president (1943-1952), following his first cabinet appointment as Minister of Education (1937), and ultimately serving as President of the Senate (1945-1952).

Egyptian society has traditionally preferred having boys than girls. However, although I was the fifth daughter, I was well received because of the recently awarded title of *Pasha* that had spread euphoria throughout the family. Thus I was called Fayza, the Arabic equivalent of Victoria, or more precisely, the winner. Moreover, for my father, an avant-garde intellectual and the first Egyptian to receive a doctorate in Law from the Sorbonne in Paris, having a daughter was not necessarily a calamity. I had only one brother then, but was blessed with a second soon after my first birthday.

My mother, a beautiful, very kind and intelligent woman, married very young. As was the custom for girls of her class, she went to a French Catholic school, where nuns taught good manners beside the all-French curriculum. She was happy that her husband had a French culture, and loved and admired him no end. She conveyed those feelings to us as children, in addition to the pride of belonging to an eminent family and the responsibility of living to its standards.

Despite their very busy lives, my parents always found time to be close to their seven children, especially during school holidays. Often, we spent our vacations in Port Fouad, not in Alexandria because my father wanted to avoid the political circles with which he interacted throughout the year, preferring instead to devote his attention to his family and his writing. The precious warm evenings at home, when we would play a game of dominos with our father to help him relax, or have passionate discussions with him, deeply marked our personalities.

Too many events in my later life came to overshadow my early childhood. However, every now and then, I have some flashbacks of my family's morning routine: siblings breakfasting together before going to school, under the watchful eye of my eldest sister, attentive to a large radio broadcasting the morning half-hour of Quran chanting. As soon as it was over at precisely 7:30 am, she would rush us all into the car in order to reach school on time. We all went to the Lycée Français in Cairo, because my father wanted us to have an international secular education, thoroughly believing that religion was a family matter to be learned at home. However, despite our French education and intellectual avant-garde attitude, we were, in fact, a conservative family where religion and traditions were highly respected. Another flashback from my early childhood shows me tiptoeing when passing before my father's study, not to make any noise that might disturb him; or lining up with my siblings in his study waiting with awe and emotion to receive a copy of his latest book, with a personal dedication. I also remember the weekly visits of a sheikh who used to recite verses of the Quran for a couple of hours, to bless the house and its inhabitants. Another flashback shows me at the club, swimming in the pool or playing and climbing trees with friends at the girls' club house—mostly foreigners in those days. There are also bits and pieces of memories that resulted in my growing up bilingual and bicultural.

I did very well in school not only because I loved reading, but also because my elder sister, an excellent student herself, made sure that I did my summer vacation homework in preparation for the next academic year. In my final year at elementary school, I ranked first in Egypt at the French *certificat d'études primaires*. My parents were very proud of me, and since my father was Minister of Education, I accompanied him on his school visits because he wanted to make me feel the pride and joy derived from doing well, and to set a "good example" for the children. In middle- and high-school, I became more independent, by then the roots had been solidly grounded, and I continued to do well. My second eldest sister was studying sculpture at the Faculty of Fine Arts, and I often accompanied her to the Egyptian Museum, where my early interest in Egyptology probably started. She and my parents were also responsible for my love of classical music and visual arts, which engendered my inexhaustible fascination with beauty.

When I neared high-school graduation, I told my father that I wanted to study Egyptology. Supportive as always, he suggested I travel to Upper Egypt on an organized tour with my school friends, in order to visit the great sites of ancient Egypt. He meant for me to be sure that I really wanted to embark on such a difficult career. The trip was an eye opener and I never regretted my career choice. I entered university in 1956—the same year Egypt fought a triple aggression (British, French and Israeli), after the nationalization of the Suez Canal. But, for me, 1956 was much more: it was the year I lost my father, an earth shattering event that completely changed my life. As a Middle-Easterner, I strongly believe in destiny, which may be determined by what is "written in the sky," or by genetics. Although we do not choose them, genes determine our health and character and, in turn, affect our most important decisions.

My siblings and I loved each other, and were educated in more or less the same fashion, raised as a group rather than separate individuals, so people often spoke about us as the Haikals, a clan of sorts. But, in fact, we had very different characters and later led very different lives. Going to university began to physically break this family block, as we studied different subjects and mixed with different groups of people. Unlike in school where teachers knew all the siblings, my professors knew only me, and none of my brothers and sisters. This is when I really started to develop individually, and was eager to learn and understand, not only Egyptology, but also the changed social system that had taken place, and in which we were now living. Young men and women from all social classes and from other Arab countries were studying with me at Cairo University. My courses were taught in Arabic, not in French, and living in the heart of Egyptian culture and politics, I began to develop my own identity. In fact, it is through Egyptology that I discovered my real Egyptian roots.

In the late 1950s, Egypt had a little over 20 million inhabitants, about three of whom lived in Cairo—today the population is nearly five times greater, with about 20 million living in the greater Cairo. With a relatively reasonable demography, universities could then afford to have a limited number of students. In my class at the Faculty of Arts, there were fewer than 10 students in Egyptology. Thus, our professors knew us personally, and there was considerable interaction among us. Because of my academic background and ability in foreign languages, I was ahead of my classmates throughout the undergraduate years. When I graduated in 1960—the year television was introduced in Egypt—I was recognized by President Gamal

Abdel Nasser at the "Festival of Science," an annual event honoring top graduates in all disciplines. A few months later, a scholarship for graduate studies abroad in Egyptology became available; the recipient was expected to complete the PhD and return to teach at Cairo University. I applied for the scholarship and received it, and was due to leave a year later.

In the meantime I had to find a job. The Center of Documentation on Ancient Egypt had recently been established thanks to UNESCO, with the purpose of surveying and fully documenting the monuments and archeological sites of Nubia, which were going to be flooded by the construction of the Aswan High Dam. It was the most likely place for an Egyptologist to find a job. The person in charge of the publications at the Center was Monsieur Christophe, a Frenchman who happened to be my history teacher at the Lycée Français. I went to see him and asked for advice. When he learned that I had studied Egyptology and was looking for a job, he told me that he had to return to his UNESCO position in Paris, and needed someone with my precise qualifications to replace him: knowledge of hieroglyphics and foreign languages, to collate the epigraphic work before publication, and the notes of scholars who wrote their comments in English or French. In those days digital photography and scanning did not exist, the hieroglyphic inscriptions on monuments and the scenes accompanying them were hand copied and annotated. Before publication, they had to be collated with excellent photographs to make sure there were no errors or omissions. To my surprise, I was offered a job, although I had absolutely no experience and feared failure. Fortunately, M. Christophe told me he would train me before leaving, and I immediately started to work with him before the required paperwork had been completed. Three months later, I was officially responsible for revising the scientific material prior to its publication, and the subsequent press coverage.

I loved my job and did it well, but that was not the biggest challenge I faced. I wanted to go to Nubia to visit the monuments with which I was dealing, and contribute to their documentation. That proved to be the real challenge. In those days, Egyptian women were not allowed to do fieldwork, live away from their families and mingle with male colleagues; thus, the work itself was an issue. First, I had to prove that I was a competent and reliable person, before daring to ask for permission to go. Then, I had to deploy my best arguments to convince my directors that times had changed, and that my family had no objection to my travelling and working side-by-side with men. At last, I succeeded, and can proudly say that I paved the way for women Egyptologists to work in Nubia. When I went to England, my successor was a female friend of mine, and it became normal for young Egyptian women to pursue fieldwork far away from home. I left Egypt with just 5 Egyptian Pounds in my pocket, the maximum amount of currency allowed at that time, when credit cards were not available.

My years in England (1961-1965), particularly those in Oxford, were fundamental in consolidating my personality. It was the first time I lived on my own, at a relatively young age, in a foreign environment based on total freedom, and demanding a high level of academic achievement. It was difficult to be alone, navigate and be accepted, and not fall into depression. The scholarship I received took me to University College in London, a chief center of Egyptology. Soon after I arrived, I met the Department Head, Professor W. B. Emery, my mentor and supervisor. He received me very kindly, and told me that he was leaving for Nubia in a couple of days, and I was to spend the year taking courses to improve my Egyptological background. When I asked him to include me in his team for Nubia, he spontaneously answered: "I don't take girls in my team." I explained that I had already worked there, but he replied that it was too late anyway

I spent an extremely interesting year in London, improving my knowledge of the ancient Egyptian language, studying hieroglyphics with Dr. Raymond O. Faulkner, one of the most eminent British scholars of his generation. I was also introduced to the history of the ancient Middle East, which was much more complicated than that of Egypt, because of the many city-states that rose and were destroyed, and the difficult names of their rulers. Miss Peggy Drawer, the History professor, was a lovely lady, and the first person to acquaint me with the intricacies of contemporary British culture. I had the opportunity to visit a huge number of museums and was amazed at the wealth and diversity of their art. I also enjoyed concerts, plays and films, and probably learned more in a year than I had in my entire life up until then. However, contact with my family was complicated prior to the internet-age, as letters took a long time to reach their destinations, and I did not want my mother to worry about me. Fortunately, the BBC Arabic program invited me several times to present talks on ancient Egypt and its impact on its Middle-Eastern neighbors. I used these opportunities to ask my family to listen to me on the radio and know that I was doing well.

As I realized that Professor Emery would be in Egypt during most of my stay, I decided to visit the other British universities that taught Egyptology, in order to transfer to one that might be more appropriate for my purpose. I immediately fell in love with Oxford, and decided to move there. But it was not easy, because I had to be accepted first at an Oxford

College. I wrote Dr. Jaroslav Černy, the Egyptology professor, to introduce myself and ask for an appointment. His reply started with "Dear Sir," so he was rather surprised when he saw a young woman at his door. He was willing to accept me as a student if Professor Emery would allow the transfer, and if an Oxford College would accept my application at this late date. I was lucky or perhaps destined to graduate from Oxford, as the Egyptian authorities also accepted my petition to transfer, and everything went smoothly in a timely fashion. I matriculated at St. Anne's College in 1962, and soon became President of the Middle Common Room. That position required me to escort many important visitors at St. Anne, the most prestigious was Prince Phillip, the Prince Consort.

Oxford was a fascinating experience. As I looked desperately for housing, the Vice Principal of my College offered me a room in her apartment. A very kind English literature don, she spent most of her time in the College, and I did not see very much of her. While working on my doctorate, we became friends and stayed in touch; she too introduced me to many aspects of British life. My thesis focused on publishing some of the Egyptian papyri at the British Museum, one of which had a parallel at the Louvre. Since digitized databases of museum collections did not exist at that time, the need to compare the two documents gave me a good excuse to ask for permission from the Egyptian government to obtain a French visa. Considering my background and early French education, it had always been my dream to visit France, and meet some of my former schoolmates. Thus, as soon as permission was granted, I went to Paris whenever I could. It was on one of these trips that I met my future husband, another doctoral student, during the defense of his thesis. Mohamed Abdel Halim Mahmoud, a diplomat on leave to finish his doctorate, was the son of an eminent professor at Al Azhar University, a great Sufi who later became the rector of that very old and venerable Islamic institution. Both impacted my life profoundly, as they showed me different aspects of Egyptian society, which were later reflected in my research. We married in April 1965, shortly before completing my degree. After the successful defense of my thesis, I wanted to phone my family to tell them I was now officially Dr. Fayza Haikal, and would soon return home. I had to ask a telephone operator at the post office for an appointment to make the call to Cairo, it was set for a few hours later, this piece of news was well worth the wait.

In Cairo, I lived the active life of a married woman who was also engaged in teaching and research. Whenever my diplomat husband was transferred to a different country, the family accompanied him. These new experiences taught me about life in difficult places such as sub-Saharan Africa, or in easier ones, in Europe, for example. For two years in Italy, I

Fayza at graduation in Oxford, 1965

taught at La Sapienza University of Rome because I wanted to keep in touch with academic life. There were wonderful years, with moments of great joy while others brought deep pain, when we lost cherished members of our family. First to go was my sister, then my mother, followed by my parents-in-law; there were also the sad years when Egypt was at war in 1967 and 1973. The diplomatic life came to an abrupt halt in summer 1979, when my husband passed away suddenly, a few months after his father.

Within minutes, I realized that I had become a widow with two young children just starting middle school. I had to be strong for them, and that was what saved me. My life took a sharp turn. We had to move to another house to be close to my siblings, and the children changed schools. My career became more important to compensate for that of their father. I worked hard, and destiny also helped. A few years after losing my husband, the American University in Cairo (AUC) needed a professor of Egyptology in order to establish a full major in that discipline; I applied and was appointed. Due to my growing academic reputation, I was invited to lecture in different countries, and the Ministry of Culture asked me to be president of the Fifth International Conference of Egyptology in Cairo in 1988. I accepted the honor and became more internationally known, particularly because I gave my first paper on cultural continuity in Egypt, focusing on the analogies between the ancient Egyptian language and the Egyptian Arabic dialect. Soon thereafter, I became an honorary member of the German Archeological Institute, the first of a series of such memberships in scientific organizations. In 1991, at the next International Conference of Egyptology in Turin, I was elected Vice President of the Association of Egyptologists.

Fayza at the International Congress of Egyptology in Cairo, 1988. Also shown (L to R) are Kelly Simpson, President of the International Association of Egyptologists; Farouk Hosni, Minister of Culture; and Abdel Halim Nur-Eddin, Secretary General of Egyptian Antiquities.

This new position occurred at the same time as the digging of the Peace Canal in the North Sinai, which was designed to send fresh water to this area, and make better use of the land for agriculture and settlement. The Canal was threatening to damage archeological sites that had not yet been fully excavated and had to be saved. I asked the President of the Antiquities Organization to send an international appeal to salvage these sites, and became the director of this newly created North Sinai Archeological Salvage Project; North Sinai being previously known among archeologists as the Eastern Gate of Egypt. My responsibilities included monitoring the progress of the digging, and diverting the course of the Canal when it was threatening an important site. I directed the project for many years, invited international teams to collaborate with their Egyptian counterparts, followed and encouraged their work, and solved problems they encountered until most of the sites were excavated and documented. I was accompanied by an excellent field director, Dr. Mohamed Abdel Maksoud, who had then just completed his doctorate on his excavations in the Sinai, in France. To support this intensive work and the new discoveries, and to promote international assistance, I gave lectures around the world, from South America to Japan.

Fayza presenting results of Sinai excavations, early 1990s

My friend Dominique Valbelle, Egyptology professor at the Sorbonne, had started her work in the Sinai prior to the formation of the Archeological Salvage Project, and generously offered to help newcomers to the region. She also organized a number of workshops on the Sinai in Paris, which I attended regularly, with one of the ensuing publications kindly dedicated to me. Meanwhile, I continued to work on my research on the roots of modern Egypt and the phenomenon of Egyptomania. During my visit to Paris in 1997, I lectured at the Collège de France, and was awarded the medal of the Collège and the status of Visiting Professor at this august institution.

Many additional honors followed, and I was frequently invited to international Egyptological congresses, as speaker, program chair, or honorary president. In 1998, I was elected President of the International Association of Egyptologists, the first woman to hold that prestigious post. Two years later, I welcomed to Cairo the Eighth International Congress of Egyptologists, which I also presided. In 2004, I was presented with a beautiful book entitled *Hommages à Fayza Haikal*, published by the French Institute of Oriental Archeology in Cairo. It consisted of a collection of scientific articles written by international scholars to mark their friendship and respect for me. I greatly value its significance, and consider it one of the most important recognitions I have ever received. In 2006, the École Normale Supérieure in Paris granted me a research chair for a full academic year, to promote my research on the roots of modern Egypt and the cultural transmissions from the past. During that time, I also directed a number of seminars at the Sorbonne, to present the Egyptian approach to Egyptology as part of the nation's heritage and the identity of its people, and served on the juries of several theses at this and other universities in France.

Fayza presented with a book of homage at the French Institute of Oriental Studies in Cairo, 2004. Also shown are Bernard Mathieu, Director of the French Institute of Oriental Studies (L); Nicolas Grimal (R), Professor at the Collège de France; and Cynthia Sheikhulislami, Co-Editor of the homage volume

A few years later, in 2012, I was honored when the Berlin Museum and the Frei Universität of Berlin published my lecture "Turning Points in Egypt." A few months ago, I was selected Woman of the Year by the British Council in Cairo, and recognized by the Ministry of Antiquities for my lifelong contributions to Egyptology, receiving homages of love and gratitude from a large number of former students who are now top national and international leaders in our discipline. This was a heartwarming reward for many years of teaching and educating young people not only at Cairo University, but also at other universities in Egypt and beyond.

While being recognized is definitely uplifting, it also generates many media requests, requiring constant effort to keep up my reputation and meet expectations. The future remains a challenge, but I continue to be fully engaged in my discipline, with the students who will carry on my work.

                                                              Cairo, January 2016

AN EGYPTIAN PIONEER
IN AEROSPACE ENGINEERING

AWATEF HAMED

Scientists discover the world that exists; engineers create the world that never was.

Theodor Von Karman, engineer and innovator

Born in Mansourah, a mid-size town in the Nile Delta, I was the youngest of three daughters. My father was an engineer in his early career who worked on construction projects; later, he became a teacher, then an inspector in the public education system. Every time he accepted a promotion, the family had to move. When I started first grade at the age of five, I already knew how to add, subtract, read and write, and loved school. Eventually, my parents became concerned about insufficient classroom stimulus; I was allowed to take the test for admission to middle school, successfully completed it, and skipped sixth grade. Moving on, my interest in dancing, acting and singing blossomed, while I continued to excel in math, trigonometry, and physics. In fact, I even received a Certificate of Excellence from the greater Alexandria District of Education for achieving a perfect math score in the comprehensive exam for admission to high school.

My father researched various high schools, and learned that the Secondary School for Girls had the highest rate of acceptance to top-rated faculties. At age 13—two years younger than my peers—I enrolled in that school where I knew none of my classmates. Three years later, taking the nationwide final high-school exam was a memorable and unusual experience. The test was and still is a most important milestone for college-bound students, it is the only criteria to determine college options. That year, the students had to take the exam a second time, after it was revealed that Israel had broadcasted the questions as an act of sabotage. Actually, the information my father had received about the school was accurate: I graduated and was admitted to the Faculty of Engineering at Alexandria University, in addition to seven classmates who were also accepted in Medicine, Pharmacy, and Engineering—an exceptionally high number for a girls' school at that time.

After completing the first year at Alexandria University with a rating of "excellent," I transferred to Cairo University when my family moved to the capital. Our joy at finally living closer to aunts, uncles and the extended family, however, did not last long, as my mother was soon diagnosed with breast cancer. The year of my eighteenth birthday was one of the saddest in my life, having lost my mother before I ever had a chance to know her better as an adult.

The College of Engineering at Cairo University had an Aeronautical Engineering program starting in the pre-junior year of the five-year major. I joined that Department, and graduated three years later in a class of 35 students who had survived the rigorous course of study, out of 133 who had initially started in that discipline. Degree in hand, I was immediately appointed to a position at the aircraft complex of the Egyptian General Aeronautical Organization, in the Cairo suburb of Helwan. When I started to consider graduate studies in the US, the challenges I faced to obtain the required government approvals made it a nearly impossible endeavor. Soon after the 1967 war, Egyptian authorities stopped issuing exit visas to students who had been awarded personal scholarships based on their transcripts and qualifications. Nevertheless, I was able to overcome the difficulties thanks to the advice and support of Dr. Ibrahim El Demerdash, Head of the Aeronautical Engineering Department, and Dean of the Faculty of Engineering.

Searching through layers of correspondence at his home, Dr. El Demerdash found an announcement of the Amelia Earhart Scholarship for women pursuing graduate studies in Aerospace Engineering. He provided a letter stating that, as the first woman to graduate from the Department of Aeronautical Engineering, I was the only one in Egypt who qualified for the scholarship. I applied for unpaid leave of absence, and launched the process of getting the required approvals. It lasted more than nine months, with each official in a government office demanding approval of all the others before giving his own. In short, all were reluctant to take the responsibility of granting my request. The most critical piece of advice came from Dr. Osama El Kholy, whom I encountered while waiting for final approval of the exit visa at the Educational Mission Office. He advised me to go directly to the Assistant Director of that Office and secure his signature before he left the country. With all approved documents in hand, including one signed by President Nasser himself, I was off to start graduate studies at the University of Cincinnati (UC), in Ohio. My goal was to specialize in Aero Propulsion, a field in which I had become interested following one of my assignments dealing with performance of aircraft engines.

Due to the lengthy delays in Cairo, I arrived in Ohio in late December1967, at the end of fall quarter. It was a challenge to start in the middle of the academic year and catch up on course material that had been covered during the preceding quarter. This intense situation made me appreciate the very demanding nature of the Aeronautical Engineering program at Cairo University, where students had to enroll in up to 13 courses each semester during their last three years. In Cincinnati, I was passionate about my research, and was encouraged by my advisor, Dr. Widen Tabakoff, to present my findings at professional conferences, and have them published in specialized journals.

PhD Candidate Awatef making a presentation at the ASME Gas Turbine Conference, California, 1972

Dr. Tabakoff (1919-2015) was born in Bulgaria, and received his PhD from the University of Berlin. He had been working for the Hoechst chemicals company when he was approached by the US Army after WW II to join the team of Dr. Wernher Von Braun at the US Space Program, in Huntsville, Alabama. He arrived in the US and received security clearance, but his wife was unhappy in that rural and provincial environment. While working on a project with the Army Research Lab in Cincinnati, Dr. Tabakoff visited the University of Cincinnati where he was offered a professorship in the Aerospace Engineering Department—the second oldest one in the US. Established in 1929, it was headed by a navigation expert who was recruited from McCook Field in Dayton—currently Wright Patterson Air Force Base. From the start, the Wright brothers were involved in the development of the first Cooperative Engineering Education Program in the Nation.

Upon joining the Department, Dr. Tabakoff proceeded to modernize the program, introduced classes on space topics, initiated graduate studies, and established an advanced engineering program with General Electric (GE), through which more than 1000 GE engineers completed their graduate degrees while employed by one of the world's leading aircraft engine companies. In my course of studies, I had the opportunity to know many of these engineers as classmates. I also observed hundreds of students being guided, cared for, financially supported, and their lives positively impacted by Dr. Tabakoff. His legacy has been honored by naming the University of Cincinnati Propulsion Lab after him. It was only fair, since that Lab was established with the extensive research funds Dr. Tabakoff brought to UC, and the air tanks gifted by the Federal Government to support his research on wind tunnels. As my mentor, Dr. Tabakoff urged me to apply for a Green Card, and was the reference in my application for US citizenship.

After completing the PhD, I was still very much interested in pursuing my research. Thus, when UC offered me an instructorship for one year, to be upped to Assistant Professor the following year, I did not hesitate to accept. While I did not look for other positions, I received several invitations to interview for research positions at a government research labs and Ivy League schools, including Arnold Research Laboratory and MIT. My name was most likely suggested by scientists who had attended my research presentations. At that point in my career, I became fully aware of the importance of having a mentor. Dr. Tabakoff was instrumental in my appointment to a tenure-track position; I was the first woman to achieve tenure in the College of Engineering, and the only one for twenty years. As my mentor, Dr. Tabakoff introduced me to the best scientists in the field, and supported me as I conducted exciting leading-edge research, and compiled an extensive record of publications. These, in addition to my excellent teaching evaluations, resulted in my promotion to the rank of Associate Professor in three years, and to Full Professor four years later.

Throughout my career, I had the opportunity to meet many outstanding engineers. Among others, they included Brian Rowe, the CEO of GE Aircraft Engines, and Hans von Ohain, the chief scientist at the Air Force Research Lab and inventor of the gas turbine. Astronaut Neil Armstrong, the first man to walk on the moon, was my colleague when he joined the faculty of the Aerospace Engineering Department. Not only were they extremely competent engineers, but also outstanding leaders whose remarkable visions continue to impact our lives to this day.

For many years, I focused my research on the propulsion field with the goal of contributing to faster, safer, and environmentally friendly aviation. My findings in this and other technical areas were rewarded by NASA, the Penn State University Advanced Propulsion Lab, and the Aircraft Engine Committee of the American Society of Mechanical Engineers (ASME). They also brought invitations to teach short professional courses in the US and Europe, at Cranfield University in UK and the Von Karman Institute in Belgium, which were attended by engineers from leading gas turbine engine manufacturers, and government and university research labs. In addition to these, I was also asked to lead seminars at academic and research institutions across the US, Europe, and Asia.

Commitment to research resulted in teaching innovations. For example, I initiated and taught a senior capstone engine design class with ten UC teams that won the national competitions of the Airbreathing Propulsion Committee of the American Institute of Aeronautics and Astronautics (AIAA). Research also allowed me to enrich the quality of service I render to UC, to technical and professional organizations, and to government agencies. When I was invited to join the NASA Propulsion Technical Advisory Committee, I was surprised to be the only academic person, the remaining members of the Committee represented industry and federal government labs. I served in that capacity for over ten years—the lifespan of the Committee. It is a great satisfaction to have advocated for continuing the support and funding of the Numerical Propulsion System Simulation (NPSS) software. Today, this is a powerful tool used across the aerospace industry and federal government labs, to simulate complex propulsion systems and air cycles. My graduate students and I have been using NPSS in leading-edge research dealing with finding solutions to the challenging thermal management problems in future advance systems.

My voluntary service to my discipline extends well beyond UC and NASA. It includes organizing international conferences, chairing and serving on several technical committees of the two leading professional societies in my field: AIAA, where I chair the Airbreathing Propulsion Committee; and ASME, where I chair the Fluid Machinery Committee, and the Gas Turbine Educational Committee. In addition to evaluating articles submitted for publication in leading technical journals, and reviewing proposals for the National Science Foundation (NSF), the Army Research Office, and the Airforce Office of Scientific Research (AFOSR), I serve as Editor of *the International Journal of Computational Fluid Dynamics*, and the *International Journal of Rotating Machinery*, and as Administrative Secretary of the International Society of Airbreathing Engineers (ISABE). These opportunities allow me to work with leading researchers from academic institutions, as well as managers of industrial establishments and government labs.

In addition to my research, teaching, and service responsibilities, I have collaborated with students to create a student chapter of the Society of Women Engineers (SWE), and became its faculty advisor. This chapter is a focal point for the few female students in engineering to get together for friendly support, and become involved in recruiting more women students for the College of Engineering. Upon joining Zonta International—a service society for professional women—I was invited to serve on the Selection Committee of the Amelia Earhart Fellows. In that capacity, it was a real pleasure to meet and collaborate with fellow professors and women engineers from Germany, Australia, Canada, and NASA. More importantly, I was impressed with the caliber and drive of the applicants and their achievements, early on in their careers.

Awatef with faculty and Advisory Board of the Center for Intelligent Propulsion, Cincinnati, 2012

In 2001, when my colleagues selected me to chair the Department—the first woman ever to chair an Aerospace Engineering Department—I accepted the challenge at a time of budget cuts and hiring freeze. In addition to securing external funds to support my own research, I wrote competitive grant proposals that won over $32.5 million from the State of Ohio—$19 million for research infrastructure, and over $13 million in endowment. With these resources, I was able to recruit outstanding faculty, build new research labs, upgrade existing ones, and support the establishment of the Center for Intelligent Propulsion. Its excellent facilities are accessible not only to students and faculty at UC, but also to those at the University of Dayton and Ohio State University.

Awatef receiving University of Cincinnati Faculty Career Award, surrounded by Provost Beverly Davenport (L), and President Santa Ono (R), Cincinnati, 2015

Being recognized by peers and colleagues as often as I have is a humbling experience. Among others, I was bestowed the following: in 2004, the YMCA Career Woman of Achievement Award, received at the Convention Center in the presence of local leaders and TV personalities; in 2008, the Aerospace Educator Leeland Atwood Award, sponsored by the American Society of Engineering Education (ASEE), the AIAA, and the Lockheed Martin Company; and in 2015, the University of Cincinnati Faculty Career Award, in recognition of my contributions to the three institutional missions of education, research, and service. Being elected fellow of both the AIAA and ASME is an honor reserved to very few. My AIAA Fellow Initiation Ceremony in Washington DC, was memorable. As keynote speaker, Pat Buchanan was very witty. Then, each of the seven fellows—every year one fellow is elected for each 1000 members—was introduced and walked separately on the stage. Applause intensified and was definitely much louder when I arrived. Although I did not notice it at first, I was the only woman among the honorees. Later, the women in the audience told me how very excited they were to see one of their own among the fellows. After stepping down from the stage, I was approached by an embarassed AIAA official who asked me to give him my award certificate, in order to correct the beautifully penned statement "for **his** contribution." It was later redone and sent to me by mail. When the incident was publicized on the UC campus, a female engineering student humorously wrote me: "Congratulations on becoming a fellow! I always thought you were a gal!"

Looking back, I realize that education and research have not only enhanced my career, more importantly they have enriched my personal life. In the process of organizing many seminars, presenting innumerable papers, and producing more than 300 publications, I had the opportunity to meet amazing individuals and discover fascinating parts of the world. However, my greatest sense of accomplishment derives from having had the opportunity to lend a helping hand to many in my profession and my community when they needed me, and to assist others to reach their goals.

A lifetime of hard work has taught me two important lessons: the first is the grievous reality when talent or potential for success is wasted for lack of means; the second is that the hand that enables or comforts is a source of boundless rewards. I have been most fortunate to achieve my goals and reach for the stars thanks to the unconditional support of family, friends, and mentors who believed in me. Throughout my life and my career, I have made every effort to follow in their footsteps, and to give to others what was in my power to give. as much as I could. Although an intellectually challenging discipline, aerospace engineering is an important science that greatly impacts human connectivity. Lest we forget, it contributes to ensure travel safely, and facilitates human communication through satellites. Looking at the future, it is my sincere hope that more women will be involved in this fascinating field.

Cincinnati, Ohio, February 2016

EGYPT ON THE BANKS OF THE RIVER SEINE[1]

AZZA HEIKAL

Throughout history, many influential Egyptian women have distinguished themselves and made tremendous achievements on various fronts. In recent times, many more have led brilliant national and international careers, in their own country and abroad. I am but a link in a chain of a multitude of Egyptian women of good will who are seeking to contribute to the development of their Nation while promoting peace and understanding around the world. I consider myself fortunate to belong to a generation born and raised in cosmopolitan Alexandria, when the three monotheistic religions coexisted harmoniously. Growing up, the first rule we were taught as children was never to discuss religion in public: "We don't talk about God, we think of Him." In the early twentieth century, renowned Alexandrian poet and song writer Sayed Darwish composed a popular verse that survived the test of time, and continues to inspire many Egyptians:

Don't say Christian, Muslim or Jew
Those whose homeland unites
Never will their religion separate.

In the 1930s, Egyptian theater started with translations of English and French plays adapted to an Egyptian audience, and given a local flavor. Then, famous actor and author Naguib Al-Rihani staged more typical national shows, among which one of the most successful and encuring comedies was *Hassan, Morcos and Cohen*, a perfect illustration of the gentle spirit of brotherhood among Egyptians of different religious and national backgrounds. Respect and acceptance were essential elements in the harmony among the various groups that made up the social fabric of the city. Each had its own schools, hospitals, cemeteries, and places of worship. Thus, from birth to death Alexandrians could live according to their preference and practice the rites of their own beliefs, while integrating in a community of the whole. I must have been predestined to serve as a bridge between these groups with a name that unites three languages and three religions. Haykal—the formal word from which my family derives its name—designates a temple in Hebrew; a sanctuary in Coptic; and a structure, a frame, as well as a sanctuary and a temple in Arabic.

Suddenly in 1956, the Suez crisis deeply perturbed our lives. Until then, Egypt had a good relationship with France, and the turmoil that occurred that year was totally unexpected. Our French, British, and Jewish friends had to leave the country hurriedly when, unjustly, France, England and Israel declared war on Egypt and sent their troops to invade our land. It took years for the relationship to be restored, and gradually several scholars contributed to establish the historical truth of that brief war, French historia Alain Decaux was the first among them. then other documents revealed and denounced the "Protocol of Sèvres," the secret agreement signed in that city by the three war partners, which laid out in detail the elaborate plan of the aggression. The studies clearly attributed the failed campaign to the connivance between British Prime Minister Anthony Eden and his French counterpart Guy Mollet.

After graduating from Notre Dame de Sion, a French private school in Alexandria, I was fascinated by my city and wished to focus on urban studies—a field pioneered by Hassan Fathy, an architect I greatly admired. The northern coast of Alexandria was practically unexplored and the city could have easily grown on both its eastern and western sides. At that time, its population was less than 900,000. Today, fifty years later, nearly 7 million inhabitants, mostly youth under age 20, are confined in a space that has not expanded much since. Most of the exquisite villas that gave Alexandria its elegant character have now been leveled, each replaced by several unattractive apartment buildings, with no consideration for the infrastructure or the street size, and no parks or space for recreation. For over forty years, I have been writing to deplore these serious violations and the destruction of many important remains of the Greco-Roman era, and to advocate the creation of carefully planned suburbs.

In the 1960s, the political and social climate was not conducive to the urban studies I wished to pursue, therefore I opted for French literature. At Alexandria University, the professors were French, and the students enjoyed total immersion in the French language and culture. Then in 1961, another scandal erupted. André Miquel, the Cultural Attaché at the French Embassy in Cairo, was wrongly accused of spying. Barely restored after the Suez Canal crisis, the relationship between France and Egypt now reached a new low. Instruction was interrupted as the French professors protested the false accusation against their fellow citizen, and their students supported them wholeheartedly. This was a total reversal of the situation in 1956, when the students fully backed their country which had been unwarrantedly attacked. As time went by, the Nasser regime became more repressive, socially, politically, and intellectually. It took years before President Anwar Sadat cleared Miquel's name, and invited him to Egypt as a welcomed guest. This unfortunate experience, however, did not prevent the distinguished scholar from pursuing his research and publications on Arab civilization and Islam. With his typical humor, Miquel used to say, jokingly, that he lived "for" the Arab world but, luckily, not "from" it.

On the first visit to France to work on my PhD dissertation, I met an outstanding lady with a big heart, Geneviève Morel, who had created an association to welcome international scholarship recipients to Paris. The students were invited to French homes where they met and befriended Parisian families. Her initiative, the first of its kind in the world, soon spread around the globe. To this day, I treasure the warmth and hospitality of the friends I made during those early years.

When I resumed teaching French at Alexandria University as an Assistant Professor, I created a new course entitled "International Literature," designed to reinforce the cultural diversity of the city. I wanted to expand my students' knowledge by initiating them to works of major European authors, such as Shakespeare, Goethe, Pirandello, and Stephan Zweig, as well as masterpieces of Arabic literature and philosophy. This approach enabled them to correlate the experience of humanity throughout the ages, and to dismiss the notion of "clash of civilizations."

A few years later, I returned to France where my husband had been appointed to a permanent position at the Egyptian Embassy in Paris. Shortly thereafter, I learned that Marie-Thérèse François-Poncet, wife of External Affairs Minister Jean François-Poncet, had just founded an association named "Welcome to France." Its goal was to offer a wide range of activities to the wives of diplomats posted in Paris. I was privileged to join that distinguished group from the start, and have since been invited frequently to speak before them about my country and my books. A golden rule of the association was to avoid two topics of discussions: politics and religion. The requirement aimed at avoiding unnecessary conflicts between members whose nations had divergent politics, and to focus instead on areas of common interests. I treasured my bond to this international microcosm, for it reminded me of my cosmopolitan Alexandria.

The statement by author André Malraux that a work of art belongs to the onlooker took on a new meaning for me when I became a resident of France. Because I learned to love France at an early age, I felt that the beauty of Paris belonged to me. I also became aware that in France, Egypt belongs to the millions who have the opportunity to admire its rich heritage throughout the City of Light. For example, journalist Sylvaine Pasquier established an inventory of holdings pertaining to Egypt at the Bibliothèque Nationale. It included 85 000 coins and medals, 1 500 000 engravings, 300 printed books, and 83 000 manuscripts (L'Express, 26 February 1988: 77-78). In the Louvre Museum, an entire section houses a large collection of ancient Egyptian treasures, superbly displayed so as to highlight their exceptional beauty. Moreover, in addition to the millions of visitors who view them, the precious artifacts are studied and cared for by an impressive number of researchers and Egyptologists. Among the many Egyptian monuments in Paris, the most outstanding is undoubtedly the graceful Luxor obelisk that stands majestically in the center of Place de la Concorde.

I felt the passion of the French people for Egypt even more profoundly when I was asked to teach Egyptian Arabic and culture at the Sorbonne and the Institut des Langues et Civilisations Orientales. Most of my students were majors in history, sociology, archeology, or political science, some of whom were preparing for careers as diplomats. They were fascinated by both Egypt's glorious past as well as its present pivotal role in Africa and the Middle East. Switching from teaching French in Egypt to becoming an instructor of Egyptian Arabic and culture in France seemed poetic justice. Teaching implies an exchange that always enriches both the student and the teacher. Not only did I have to inspire appreciation for my country, I had to apply myself to master a subject matter that I had never studied, my schooling having been entirely focused on the French language and culture. It was a difficult yet stimulating venture that led me on an unexpected but rewarding path. In the process, and through my students' questions and comments, I discovered the richness of the Arabic language and the greatness of its heritage. My students also remarked that in a country that owes much of its reputation to the pharaohs, the word "pharaoh" itself had gradually acquired a derogatory meaning, as it tends to be applied to autocrats and despots.

The new voyage of discovery led to my involvement in several organizations devoted to strengthening the bonds between the two countries, especially one aptly named "France-Egypte." My application for membership in that august assembly was sponsored by two eminent Egyptophiles. One was Jean Kerisel, the Secretary General of the organization, a renowned mechanical engineer who had contributed to the reconstruction of France after WWII, served as a major consultant for the creation of the Cairo metro system, and was instrumental in the project to save the temple of Abu Simbel in Upper Egypt. The second person to support my application was the famed scholar and prolific author Christiane Desroches Noblecourt, also known as "la grande dame du Nil." Egyptians will always be grateful for her strong determination and untiring efforts for the preservation of the Nubian temples—especially Abu Simbel—from flooding caused by the Aswan Dam. Endowed with a phenomenal memory, even at a most advanced age, she could cite off the top of her head the complicated names of kings, queens and dynasties of pharaohs; yet, she managed to forget my name. To remedy the predicament, she affectionately called me "Tanagra," after the elegant figurines in the Alexandria Greco-Roman museum.

Azza next to Jean Kerisel. To her left are Geneviève Morel and Isabelle Béret, Paris, c. 2000

Over the years, the expertise I acquired in Egyptian history and cultural heritage was rooted in my personal study and research, and enhanced by informal associations. Many elders and scholars took me under their wing, served as generous mentors, and shared with me their passion and erudition. My good friend Max Karkegi (1930-2011), particularly known for creating the Arabic, English and French website "Egypt in Bygone Days" had revived the history of Egypt in the early/mid part of the twentieth century. In our conversations, he would infuse interesting facts and details about the history and geography of Alexandria, Cairo, and the Suez Canal region, even their buildings and street names. Upon his death in 2012, his wife Magdeleine donated his rich collection of precious Egyptian documents, art work, postcards, newspapers and magazines to the Bibliothèque Nationale in Paris.

Ibrahim "Berto" Farhi (1917-2012) was another close friend whom I had the pleasure to meet once a month. He was an erudite on pre-revolutionary Egypt, a respected journalist, and the author of critical works on early twentieth-century Egyptian literature, in both Arabic and French. Farhi would recall details of his encounters with such writers as Ahmed Rassim or Georges Henein, and reminisce about his travels in Europe with Minister of Education Mohamed Hussein Haikal. I was proud to have introduced to Farhi Egyptologist Fayza Haikal, the minister's daughter, also featured in this book. He told her about his high regard for her father. At the time of his death, notwithstanding his age, Farhi was in the process of writing the biography of Mostafa Abdel Razek, the brilliant intellectual and enlightened Grand Sheikh of Al Azhar.

Ibrahim "Berto" Farhi with Moutapha Abdel Razek, Grand Sheikh of Al Azhar. In the background is the eminent intellectual Ahmed Lotfi El Sayed (Pasha), carrying a cane, Cairo, 1947

Last but not least, I attribute part of my academic growth and development to the lectures and cultural activities I attended at the Egyptian Cultural Center and the Embassy of Egypt, and to my meetings with renowned scholars. While it is not possible to mention all of them, their publications, or the subjects they discussed, suffice to mention a few.

A special issue of *L'Express* titled "L'Egypte passion française," prepared by journalists Yves and Loïc Stavridès, detailed the recent work of noted Egyptologists (18 December 1996). Jean-Philippe Lauer directed excavations at Saqqarah and devoted seventy years of his life to the King Djoser pyramid. Jean Yoyotte, who occupied the Chair of Egyptology at the prestigious Collège de France, spoke of his Tanis discoveries. Christiane Ziegler, Director of Egyptian Antiquities at the Louvre Museum, discussed her archeological missions in Saqqarah. Underwater archeologist Franck Goddio drew the plans of Cleopatra's royal city and discovered the underwater city of Herakleion-Thonis in the Bay of Abukir, while Jean-Yves Empereur supervised excavations and underwater missions in Alexandria. Two young architects, Milena Annaloro (Italian) and Guirémi Lange (French), devoted three years to the reconstruction of sixteen-century Ottoman buildings in Alexandria. Their work on the "Heikal Okell" is particularly significant for me, as this area has been in my family for generations. It is located near an ancient shopping area, very popular among the women of Alexandria.

Okell Heikal (Souk El Kheit), as shown in Annaloro & Guirémi, *Une architecture ottomane* (Paris: Éditions Parenthèses, 2011)

The skills that I developed through my formal and informal education, and my experience in France and Egypt, have allowed me to write on behalf of many of my fellow citizens, somehow making me their "scribe." In our animated discussions, they would urge me to send letters to the editors, at a time predating the internet, when print journalism was the main source of information and public opinion. When reporting on Egypt was unfair or partial, we felt an obligation to rectify the inaccurate comments, and respond to biased articles. I was put in charge of the task, and wrote dozens such letters. Among the many media battles I fought, one was especially important as it concerned the reconstruction of the ancient Alexandria Library. For the most part, the French media discredited the project and opposed it. Like many Egyptians, especially Alexandrians, I recognized the value and necessity of the enterprise, and wrote much and often to support it. The successful completion of the Bibliotheca Alexandrina, and its inauguration in 2002 in the presence of numerous dignitaries and heads of states was a vindication for the Egyptians who backed the project, myself included.

Humorously, French political leader Georges Clémenceau (1841-1929) fancied in remarking that the French claim to have mighty interests in Egypt, so do the British, the Italians and many other nationals. Facetiously, he would add that the Egyptians themselves may also have a say in the matter. By the mid-1990s, thinking about these wise words, I felt compelled to become an author myself, in order to express the viewpoint of Egyptians. Following the popular and critical acclaim of Lawrence Durrell's *Alexandria Quartet*, with its deceitful representation of Egyptian society, where different communities appear to be competing for visibility and influence, and native Egyptians relegated to insignificant roles, it was time for a more accurate view of my hometown, reflecting the synergy among its diverse constituencies. Encouraged by many, I published *L'Éducation alexandrine* in 1996. It was considered the first memoirs of a native Egyptian growing up in Alexandria, whose ancestry is rooted in Egypt's soil. It focused on the real involvement of Egyptians in the progress and development of their city, and the fraternity among its residents.

In my second book, *L'Égypte illustrée par les peintres du XIXe siècle* (2000), I sought to unveil a period of our heritage that had not been uncovered. For seven millenniums, Egyptians documented their history and daily life through various artistic mediums: frescoes on temple walls, pharaonic papyruses, human portraits, religious icons, wood engravings, as well as copper and porcelain utensils. However, it was thanks to Western artists that the lifestyle of nineteenth-century Egyptians was recorded. I collected hundreds of photos of paintings scattered in international museums and private collections, to recreate as closely as possible the daily life of Egyptians of all social classes during that era. In these artistic productions, there were scenes of public and private life in rural and urban settings, representing homes, dress, and traditional trades.

Each photo was accompanied by appropriate excerpts from masterpieces of nineteenth-century French and Western authors, demonstrating the major place that Egypt occupied in the literary and visual arts of that era.

In my third book, *Il était une fois une sultane* (2004), I attempted to reconstruct the life of Shagarat al-Durr (? - 1257), whose life was the stuff of fairy tales. Starting as a slave, she rose to become a sultan, the only woman ever to rule the Arab world, at a most critical time. During the seventh crusade, Louis IX, the king of France known as Saint Louis, was captured and imprisoned in Mansourah, Egypt. It is under her reign that he was freed, after compensating Egypt for the devastation his troops had caused. Information about Shagarat al-Durr was scattered and incomplete, although her fabulous life had been romanticized, and inspired many fictions. However, no full-length study had ever been devoted to her, except for a 1961 monograph in German by Götz Schregle, which has never been translated.

My fourth book, *Immeubles Heikal* (2013), took a different approach to revive cosmopolitan Alexandria. My family owned several apartment buildings whose units were occupied by people of different national origins. Many among them were neighbors who left the country during the Nasser era to start a new life abroad. They were close friends with whom we, the Heikal children, shared precious childhood memories, and maintained relationships over the years. It occurred to me to invite a few of them to write about their experiences growing up in our cosmopolitan city; they heeded my call enthusiastically; thus, the book was born.

My publications have been praised and favorably reviewed. Apparently, they have responded to the needs of readers eager to learn about the history and culture of Alexandria and Egypt from a credible and trusted source. I have been invited to speak about my books before academic audiences and civic groups throughout Egypt, Canada, France, Switzerland, and the US. It was a great satisfaction to interact with the guests, listen to their comments, and answer their questions. However, the meetings that touched me the most were those with the students of underprivileged schools in poor neighborhoods in Cairo. The youngsters were proud to see their villages, costumes, trades, musical instruments, even coffee shops mirrored by artistic giants in high-quality books. They were just as excited to learn about Shagarat al-Durr, and to admire her depiction in thirteenth-century Arabic drawings. These visits alerted me to the dire need for revising school curriculums.

The difficult task of improving instruction in Egypt's impoverished urban and rural schools is currently undertaken by May Zeid, Samir Chacour, and Jeanne-Paule Maury with many brave volunteers. Among them, there were some of my motivated Arabic students who took it upon themselves to go to Egypt and teach in its public schools, while being immersed in their target language and culture. Their accomplishments have been recognized by many, especially Hisham El Tawil. By establishing a formal program of French teaching assistants in Egyptian schools, France could actively combat illiteracy in Egypt. It would be promoting interest in its language and culture while broadening the views of young Frenchmen and those of millions of young Egyptian citizens. This program could parallel the one it currently offers to international university students who spend a year as teaching assistants of their native languages in French schools.

My recent experiences in the Cairo public schools prompted me to consider cooperating with educational leaders, in order to propose highly needed reforms and innovations. If my efforts in such an undertaking could lead to improving the lot of new generations of Egyptians, and making them more enlightened citizens, I would have achieved one of the most important missions of my life.

Paris, September 2015

Notes

[1] I would like to express sincere gratitude to Magda El-Nokaly, Jean Gordon, Ioanna Mavrides, Mona Risk, and Samia Spencer for their careful translation of the present chapter from French into English.

FINDING A PLACE FOR CONTEMPORARY EGYPTIAN DESIGN

HEDAYAT ISLAM

Clarice, the glorious city, has a tormented history. Several times it decayed, then burgeoned again, always keeping the first Clarice as an unparalleled model of every splendor, compared to which the city's present state can only cause more sighs at every fading of the stars.

Italo Calvino[1]

I lived most of my life in Egypt, growing up in a family that embraced the country's history, and reveled in the beauty of its past with a keen eye to its future. Every week, my mother used to take my sister and me on visits to different historical sites. Pharaonic, Coptic, and Islamic spaces and motifs were engrained in my mind, and I had a strong desire to revive them. I was intrigued when people spoke of Egypt's "bygone era," it seemed they were always wistful for a past that I would never experience.

My two grandmothers played a very prominent role in my life. My maternal grandmother, Doria Shafik (1908-1975) was a feminist, poet, and editor who dedicated her life to the women's liberation movement in the middle of the twentieth century. At 16, she was the youngest Egyptian to earn the French Baccalaureate degree, and went on to receive a PhD from the Sorbonne in Paris. In 1945, she was offered the position of Editor-in-Chief of *La Femme Nouvelle*, a popular women's magazine in French founded by Egyptian Princess Cevikar. She then established *Bint El Nil* (Daughter of the Nile), a magazine in Arabic, covering fashion, cookery, and current events, with extensive coverage of women-led initiatives. It was followed by the Bint El Nil Union which aimed at eradicating illiteracy and female unemployment, most importantly targeting the notion that Egyptian women had to have a voice in their country's policies. In 1956, she and her Union were instrumental in obtaining the constitutional right to vote for Egyptian women.

Sadly, she passed away when I was just two-years old but her legacy and work lived on through her two daughters, my mother and my aunt.

They both were brought up in a liberal home where trust was instrumental in their leading a healthy balanced life. My mother spent most of her teenage years at the pool of the Gezira Club, under guidance of her swimming coach, Monsieur Alex. She quickly rose to fame as Egypt's top swimmer and held international records for years. My aunt breezed her way through university and became the first student to be awarded the President Cup and crowned Miss AUC. Both came out to be highly accomplished professors in the field of science. They taught us the importance of finding one's calling, and pursuing it with hard work.

My paternal grandmother dedicated her life to us. She spent all her time lovingly recounting stories about the splendors of the past, the city, the fashion, and, most of all, the people. All these influences culminated in my yearning to create. I wanted to study, incorporate, and revive our rich ornamental past, and the vocabulary that appeared to have been somewhat lost under many layers of dust and nostalgia.

And so my Cairo, the city in which I lived for most of my life, remains my muse. Walking down the streets, whether through the much worn downtown or the leafy streets of Zamalek, I was always intrigued and stimulated. The eroded architectural adornment, neon oversized signage, and spotty grey compressors sticking out of windows did not repel me as much as propelled me to think. In my mind, I was always peeling away these layers, trying to envisage the Cairo of which my grandmother very often fondly spoke. The fact that I was surrounded by so much that either needed fixing, or promised revelation, empowered me. I hoped that change could be brought about.

The natural progression of such thought should have seen me gravitate to the world of architecture, where an education in that subject might have enabled me to be more effective. However, due to entering the American University in Cairo at a very young age, I chose to major in Political Science and minor in Art. During college years my academic learning was at university, but the practical exposure that would lead me to find my passion was through daily walks across the different craft areas of Cairo. I came to love the smell of fresh wood shavings in carpenters workshops, and watching seasoned craftsmen carefully sewing their patchwork in the tent makers' area, Khaymeyya. I relished observing metal forgers bend and manipulate the material like clay, and producing the most delicate wrought iron shapes. Upholsterers, carpenters, and skilled craftsmen started to occupy much of my thought. Eventually I realized that studying Interior Design would enable me to work with these people, and channel their incredible skills to fuel my ideas. When I graduated, I felt a little lost with regard to my career. Politics did not attract me in the least, even though I was grateful for the well-rounded liberal arts education I had received. After many conversations with my father, which culminated in him advising me to follow my heart, I decided to apply for a degree in Interior Design. I went to New York to study both the theory and practice at the New York School of Interior Design. I learned much at school, but I also found, much to my dismay, that Egypt was looked upon as a treasure trove of the past. No one seemed interested, or even aware that contemporary Cairo had so much to offer. It defied comprehension how insignificant we had become on the global design map.

Upon completing my degree, I returned to Cairo and started freelancing as an interior designer. At that point, awareness of the need for designed environments was growing and young designers were springing up. I was elated to be working within that atmosphere and with talented craftsmen I had come to love, and with whom I interacted on a daily basis. Nothing was more gratifying than seeing a two dimensional sketch turn into a living piece. I loved mixing materials and experimenting with them. I thoroughly enjoyed coming up with contemporary pieces, such as functional desks and shelving units, handmade by local craftsmen using up-cycled materials. It was not just about the energy of working with the various artisans; it was also about the new ideas and businesses that were bubbling in people's minds in Cairo in the late 1990s. There was an infectious mood among the new start-ups of whom many were aiming to revive the belle époque of Egypt. Nothing matched the thrill or challenge when the clients, owners of these ideas, asked me to translate concepts into spaces and objects.

While I was engrossed in creating interiors and furnishings that were to reflect their innovative owners, I did not want to forget about my initial inspiration, the city of Cairo. In 1998, I decided to pursue a Master's degree in Islamic Art and Architecture at AUC. I was blessed with the most stimulating professors and access to the awe-inspiring Creswell Rare Books Library. I lost my heart to Fatimid woodcarvings, Mamluk metal wares, and Ottoman textiles. Walking tours of much of old Cairo were a strong component of the program, which allowed me to explore the city further. All came together: my work and my passion for Cairo's history. I had never felt so fulfilled or excited about my endeavor and the future! I hired 'Am Fathy ('Am, an Arabic word meaning uncle, is a respectful way to address an older person), the son of our longtime cook who grew up in my paternal grandmother's house, to assist me in my freelance work and product development. He was a very proud Nubian, highly knowledgeable of his heritage, and just as eager as I was to embrace the past and come up with new ideas and pieces. Hiring him was very much a symptom of life in

Cairo, where the personal often spilled into the professional. He roamed the markets tirelessly to help me find talented artisans and develop products. He was to be our guardian angel, and very much an integral part of Eklego Design until his untimely death in the summer of 2013.

In 1999, my father passed away, and it was a huge blow. I seemed to lose my appetite for work, and found it difficult to reignite my passion. I retreated from my work in an attempt to deal with my loss. At that point, I met an architect who had just moved back to Cairo from Canada. We started talking about architecture, interior design, and potentially taking on a project together. Without much over thinking, we started working together as a team. We took on our first project and set up shop in the dining room of my grandmother's old flat in Zamalek where my little cousin Nadia was living. What could have been more inspiring than working in an atmosphere where grandma Doria's books were still as she left them, beautifully bound on the light-stained oak shelves. Dina El Khachab and I started taking on projects and thrived on applying the thoughts, skills and ideas we had acquired separately over the years. We worked indefatigably with no employees except for 'Am Fathy. We did it all on our own: drafting, marketing, accounting, and sourcing.

In late 2000, we decided to rent a small office, and officially register our company by the name of Eklego Design, derived from the Greek source of the word eclectic, which means to "choose or pick out." We loved applying that notion to our selection of concepts, ideas and pieces, where they would come together to create a new whole. What was interesting, too, was how different we were in our approaches, yet we managed to work harmoniously together. What united us was our passion for what we were doing, and our belief that together we could build a solid Egyptian brand. Our little office in the heart of Zamalek started attracting big clients such as Sony Music, Orascom, and many others who commissioned us to design spaces and furniture for their projects. One of our clients humorously called us "Ek" and "Lego." We worked day and night, and took on one new employee.

Between 2001 and 2005, Eklego Design grew to encompass 15 employees, including Dina and me. The capital of the company was basically the money from the projects being re-injected into the business with us taking a basic salary. We were both still living with our families and could afford to take a small salary, which enabled the company to grow faster. It was challenging to start managing employees and requiring of them certain drawing and creative standards. It was difficult to comprehend that we needed to dedicate time to train our designers, as much as we needed to spend on our projects. After all, things were fine when it was just Dina and me, but we wanted to grow. Proving to be even more difficult was attempting to maintain a consistently good quality of workmanship from the suppliers. Often pieces would have to be returned and made all over again. What we did not realize is that we were building the foundations for a great team, and coaching the artisans about consistency and quality. And it all paid off as we went on to grow into an award winning Egyptian design firm and furniture brand.

In 2005, two new babies were born: my first baby girl, Jehane, and Eklego's first venture into retail with its showroom in Zamalek. The delicate game of balance started in my personal life: juggling my first-born and my work. The challenge for Eklego laid in dividing time between projects and retail—a struggle that extends to this day. We rented another apartment in Belle Époque-style building, and decided to turn it into a space to showcase our furniture designs, stemming from our projects and surroundings. Our eclectic ideals and passion for the contemporary furniture industry helped us to come up with a unique collection that attracted local as well as international attention. Innovation met tradition in our widely popular Bukhara table, consisting of a hand embroidered *Suzanni*— a colorful needlework embroidered textile made in Central Asian countries—encapsulated and melted within two sheets of Perspex.

Bukhara table, Eklego Design, Cairo, 2008

Another piece was the *Depet*—barge in pharaonic—sofa inspired by the fine lines of Egyptian fishing boats. We gradually garnered an excellent reputation for furniture design and supply, and dabbed a little in importing pieces from Argentina and beyond, but quickly realized that our strength was in our own design and creation. Our quality and punctuality stood out in a market where client trust was difficult to maintain.

The company continued to grow. We acquired a new office, and took on board two new partners: Hala Said, who had already been working with us on marketing and vision, and Heba El Gabaly, a long time friend and Harvard Business School graduate. We were on top of the world with an amazing company, a harmonious team managing it, and a growing number of passionate supportive designers. Large residential and commercial projects started rolling in, and investors started to express interest. We raised money by selling part of the company, and opened our first large flagship store on the outskirts of Cairo. At that point, we had bitten more than we could chew, and started realizing that we needed to pace our growth. Quickly, we started to rectify our sudden overexpansion. By 2011, things had fallen into place again, but they were not to remain so. The January Revolution came and took over our lives. Projects were put on hold or altogether cancelled, but it had given us hope that a new Egypt would be born and the momentary loss of work or slowing down seemed nothing but a small price to pay for the way that was being paved forward.

The Eklego partners, from L to R: Hedayat, Heba El Gabaly, Hala Said, and Dina El Khachab, Cairo, 2012

Award winning "Modern Islamic" show apartment, Cairo, 2012

On the political side, we had yet to see how these events would unfold and be retold in history. As things normalized across Egypt, projects picked up and Eklego continued on its growth path. I loved working with my partners because ours was a relationship of mutual learning and growth. We were fortunate to evolve our design portfolio with innovative designers, and gifted craftsmen for whom Egypt's historical heritage was hardwired into their DNA. Together, we created products and spaces that celebrated our environment. We were a company founded and run by women in a society where people questioned how we managed to do it. From day one we faced no obstacles in that respect, craftsmen, employees and the trade were respectful, professional, and very collaborative. Our success was brought on by hard work and perseverance, and thankfully no gender related obstacles. Eklego Design continues to grow and gain recognition and we are proud to have built an Egyptian furniture brand, which honors our city as well as its artisans. In 2010, we were awarded the Arabian Property Award in the Interior Design Category, and by 2015 we had been bestowed with four international awards, published in three design books, and mentioned in several local and international publications. The awards constituted a much appreciated recognition of our efforts, and fueled our company to gain further international commissions. [2] More importantly, it cemented our relationship as a managing team and fueled us to keep on growing as a company.

In 2013, my husband and I relocated with our three daughters to the UK.   It was very difficult for me to extract myself from Eklego and all I had built with my partners. I continued to work on projects that I had committed to complete, but realized that it was now my opportunity to showcase the contemporary talent coming out of Egypt. At first, I wanted to create a Pop Up exhibit concept where I would highlight several design companies at a time, with Eklego Design at the forefront. As I took in my surroundings, I decided that some risks in life had to be taken. As an extension of our partnership, my husband and I bought a lease on a well-positioned showroom in the heart of Chelsea. The bureaucracy involved in setting up the company and the retail concept was grueling. Thankfully, my husband was extremely supportive, and helped with both setting up the business and taking care of our daughters. I almost gave up several times, but finally all our efforts came to fruition and we launched Jam Space in November 2014. The name JAM itself is composed of the initials of our three daughters, Jehane, Alia and Maissa, who inspired me with their observations about their surroundings. The launch was met with much celebration from both pedestrians and press.

Elle Décor labeled us "Modern Egyptology," and *Country and Town House* featured me as designer of the month. People expressed amazement at all the creativity that had come out of "turbulent" Egypt. The explosion of art and design that was born out of the Revolution had been completely missed by the international community. A few months later, I launched my first fabric and wallpaper collection entitled "Ornamental Stories," inspired by Ancient Egyptian ornament and decoration, and by 'Am Fathy's endless stories about Nubia. I felt pride as people admired the collection and exclaimed with relief that finally something was challenging the monotony of trends found in most brands. Jam Space went on to launch an interior design consultancy service by the name of Design Clinic, and another wallpaper collection entitled "From Cairo to London" celebrating facets of the Cairo scape such as the colorful shutters dotting mid-century buildings and hand poured century-old encaustic tiles. Jam Space is soon to launch its first e-commerce website representing different brands, but most importantly, bringing Egyptian contemporary design to the World Wide Web.

THE ROAD
TO CAIRO

*New to the London design scene, Hedayat Islam Taymour
is bringing an Egyptian flavour to interiors*

Words JACKY PARKER

gypt may not be the first place you think of as a hotbed of modern design, but interior designer, Hedayat Islam Taymour is on a quest to change that perception. A recent arrival to the capital, she splits her time between her design studio, Jam Space, in Chelsea and her international architecture and interior company, Eklego Design, based in Cairo. Set up with business partner, Dina El Khachab in 2000, Eklego has over 180 projects to its name including Sony Music offices and the award-winning Forty West apartments on the outskirts of Cairo. 'The contemporary Egyptian design scene is thriving,' says Hedayat. 'Young minds, innovative materials and skilled artisans have led to a vibrant scene. It gets dwarfed by political events, but should be celebrated as I believe the future and impetus for any progress is innovation and experimentation.'

Eager to highlight this, Hedayat has created Jam Space, to be part design clinic for interior projects and part retail space, offering a hand-picked selection of furniture, lighting and home accessories, with much of it sourced and made in the region. Her criteria when sourcing a piece is that it has a strong design element or interesting story behind it.

'I like it when I know the story behind something and value even more the idea of being able to customise it,' says Hedayat. 'When I moved here with my family in 2014 and began furnishing my own home, I found it was a choice between buying mass-produced furniture or paying a fortune to commission bespoke pieces. I wanted to provide beautifully-crafted furnishings within reach budget-wise. Most of the pieces at Jam Space have contemporary forms and materials, but are infused by an element that relates to a story or ornament.'

Whether they want to refurbish their entire home, update a room or buy a new dining table, customers can expect to find unique pieces inspired by local geography and traditions. There's the stylish Weave sideboard, which takes its reference from Egyptian reed baskets and the striking hand-blown Rain Drop

> *Egyptian design should
> be celebrated. I believe
> the impetus for any
> progress is innovation*

The Resident Magazine, London, 2016

Creating a retail or design concept in London is no easy feat, with many challenges lying ahead. Robert Frost said that "to be a poet is a condition, not a profession" and this is exactly how I feel about design. As much as it is a showcase for contemporary design, Jam Space is a vehicle for personal enrichment and a tool to engage in a dynamic design scene much imbued with tradition and history. I realize that I was naive to think that I could automatically build on Eklego Design and continue things as they were with no hiccups, but slowly I am coming to realize and admit that I am no longer in my Cairo. I am in a new city with new dynamics and challenges; I am looking forward to the path ahead, and hoping that I will be able to merge both successfully. Most importantly, I am enjoying the learning process and look forward to wherever this new experience may lead me.

In concluding this chapter, I would like to quote a poem written by my grandmother Doria Shafik that encapsulates the deep affection my family and I have for Egypt and our gratefulness for all it has engrained in us:

Thanksgiving
I render thanks
unto God
to have been born
in the land of mysteries,
to have grown up
in the shadow
of the palms
to have lived
within the arms
of the desert
guardian of secrets ...
to have seen
the brilliance
of the solar disk
and to have drunk
as a child
from the Nile
sacred river.

Doria Shafik, *Larmes d'Isis*[3]

London, February 2016

Notes

[1] *Invisible Cities* (London: Vintage, 1997), 4
[2] See www.eklegodesign.com
[3] *Les Larmes d'Isis* (Périgueux: Éditions Pierre Fanlac, 1979)

COMING HOME:
ART, BUSINESS, AND WINE ALONG THE NILE

FATENN MOSTAFA KANAFANI

If I feel in my heart that I am wrong, I must stand in fear even though my opponent is the least formidable of men. But if my own heart tells me that I am right, I shall go forward, even against thousands and tens of thousands.

Confucius, *The Book of Changes*

These words have been my motto in life for as far back as I can remember. The daughter of Egyptian diplomats, I was privileged to grow up in two different worlds until the age of 25. Physically, I lived in Brussels, Paris, Istanbul, and Vienna. Spiritually, I was neither of Europe nor of Egypt, and yet I belonged to both. That privilege morphed into a lifelong dichotomy of being torn between the warmth of my faraway Arab home and the immense liberty provided by this "other" Western world. My late father compounded this sense of hybridity by instilling the values of independence and equality between men and women, while at the same time imposing certain traditional rules. Unfulfilled by being codified as an Egyptian Muslim in Europe or a Westernized woman in Egypt, I relentlessly worked on carving a space in between these two fixed cultural identities until it was no longer possible to say with certainty where the Egyptian ends and the non-Egyptian begins.

To help me find the center of my world, my longitude zero, I resorted to reading. The French school system introduced me to philosophy and literature. I dived into Baudelaire, Duras, Pascal, Sartre, and Voltaire. My parents, on the other hand, introduced me to our multilayered roots: Arab, Egyptian, Muslim, Coptic, and Pharaonic. I researched Egypt's complex past and sought to understand its volatile present. Taha Hussein and Nawal el Saadawi became my companions. As I went to French schools and to an American university in Europe, I taught myself how to read and write classical Arabic by copying newspapers articles, and read the Quran in English and French.

Achieving personal excellence was my driving principle for proving my existentialist worth as a "different" individual. I recall how in 1975, at the age of 6, my older sister and I appeared odd to the girls at the Sacré-Cœur school in Brussels on our first day of class. Surrounding us on the playground as if we were caged animals in a zoo, the Belgian girls kept demanding why we had dark curly hair, where we were from, and why we could not speak their language. I also remember going hungry on the days when pork was served in the school cafeteria. In one of my assignments, this time at the Lycée Saint-James in Paris and age 12, I was singled out and given a condescending lesson on the concept of secularism in front of the entire class, as I wrote "There is no God but Allah and Mohammed is his Prophet" on top of the paper. As a response to these prejudiced acts, I quickly mastered the French language and soon established myself as an outstanding pupil, at times far superior than native peers. I earned the French baccalaureate in 1986 with the highest grades, and was interviewed by Egyptian national TV that summer for giving an honorable image of Egyptian students abroad. In the final four-hour philosophy exam, mandatory in the French baccalaureate, I scored an exceptional 18 out of 20. The subject, which had an uncanny significance in my own life, was to elaborate on Rimbaud's confession "Je est un autre" (I is someone else).

When my parents were posted to Istanbul in 1986, they decided their teenage daughters were better off going to a university in Europe, even if that meant sending them to live on their own. Many in our Egyptian entourage saw this decision as insane, as back then it was unheard of for Egyptian girls to live alone abroad. The consensus fell on Vienna because of its safety, and proximity to Istanbul. While studying for my Bachelor's degree in Economics at Webster University in Vienna, I decided to take on part-time jobs to increase my monthly allowance, and learn a thing or two. I gave English lessons to Austrian children, and taught belly dancing on Saturday mornings at the University. I was the Vice President of Webster's Student Union, and a member of the Organization for Arab Students. It felt good to be elected, and have a meaningful role in the life of a student body hailing from all corners of the world. After graduating with multiple awards in 1989 at the tender age of 21, I pulled all possible strings to remain in Vienna. By then, Egypt had merely become a summer destination, and my sense of belonging was fading away. I had chosen liberty with controversy over peace with shackles.

Seeking a job, I sent my CV to dozens of multinationals and to the United Nations office. The International Atomic Energy Agency, an organization that promotes the peaceful use of nuclear energy is headquartered in Vienna, offered me a position as financial staff in its

Operations Department. I took it for one year as the salary and perks were fantastic, but my aspirations were higher. Two incidents set me on a more ambitious path. All but one multinational, Procter & Gamble (P&G), had replied with an apology letter. P&G, however, requested an interview. My mind was blown away: after all, this was the world's largest consumer products manufacturer, and the marketing school *par excellence*! After five grueling interviews and one written test, the General Manager sent me an offer for an entry position in the Marketing Department stating that "[my] energy impressed [them], and [my] achievement-oriented personality was an excellent fit." However, the offer was contingent upon the company securing a work permit; its lawyer would have to prove to the Austrian authorities that I, a foreigner, had "indispensable" skills. The second incident was as significant as that first one. One evening, Kurt Waldheim, the then-President of Austria and former Secretary General of the UN, was giving a speech at the Marriott Hotel. I decided to attend, my diplomat father having nurtured my interest in the politics that impacted our region. For reasons of which I was unaware at the time, I approached Waldheim, a tall and imposing man, once he finished the Q&A session. His bodyguards immediately tried to block my way, but Waldheim was courteous, and shook my hand. I introduced myself, chatted about the Palestinian cause and, with an unusual courage, asked him if he could help me get an Austrian passport. I will never forget his facial reaction. Unexpectedly, he pulled his business card out of his jacket, asked his assistant for a pen and wrote down the name of a lawyer. The rest is history, as the saying goes. In 1990, I joined P&G and climbed the corporate ladder during eight years; and in 1994, I swore to the Austrian authorities that I would be loyal to the country and respect its Constitution.

As soon as I joined P&G, I was entrusted with the management of various brands. To succeed in such a cutthroat corporate environment, you quickly understand its "give and take culture." They train and groom you in a pampered environment, with five-star hotels and business-class flights, but in return they expect to extract the most out of you with unreasonably high standards. I learned then that what matters are the "alls": "giving it all," "knowing it all," and "solving it all"—in other words, be passionately curious and determined, know your business inside out, and think outside the box. An extreme and funny example is how I managed to convince Management to launch a complex and irrelevant pyramid shape packaging for toothpaste, in reference to my Egyptian heritage! I also learned that success has no gender, religion or age. In fact, claiming my differences and turning them into symbolic capital became a competitive advantage. The more I proved myself as the only Arab in the organization, the more I felt I was seen to speak on behalf of all people of my ethnic and religious background, and act as living proof of the existence of a peaceful mainstream. The Pan Am flight explosion of 1988 with two Webster students among the victims, Salman Rushdie's *Satanic Verses* the same year, and Iraq's invasion of Kuwait in 1990 had played out in an orientalist discourse, and reinforced our image as the less civilized peripheries.

Vienna was teaching me far more though, and paving my way for a later career in the world of fine arts. During my first weekend at Webster University, a group of students had decided to go to the Belvedere Museum. I was shocked by the choice of outing, for it did not fit my concept of teenagers' socializing. How many Arab families nurture their children's appreciation for the arts? Nevertheless, I went along seeking to make new friends. There, in that wintry room in Austria's great museum was a most beautiful painting: *The Kiss,* a 1908 large work by Austrian symbolist painter Gustav Klimt. Overwhelmed, I set my mind to understand a world that was alien to the environment in which I was raised. And so, parallel to my studies and later to my work with P&G, I attended free art lectures at the Viennese state university, and bought art history books with my hard-earned money.

As the years went by and I continued to live alone in Austria, the pressure began rising for my return to Egypt. After all, my parents' intention was to provide the best education they could afford, and had fulfilled that mission. But the decision to go back to Cairo, if ever made, would be on my own terms. My parents came to accept my choice, and today I am grateful to both my father and my mother for enduring the long distance, and giving me the opportunity to learn the meaning of responsibility at an early age, and shape my own future. Eventually, the appeal of returning to Egypt came the moment I was offered to replace an expatriate in P&G's Cairo subsidiary as Marketing Manager for detergents—its most important revenue-generating category. This was my chance to "test" Egypt: should I not feel at home, I would ask to be reassigned within P&G's international network. I was 25, accepted the relocation offer, moved out of my apartment on Rennweg in Vienna's third district, and never asked for reassignment.

In the span of a couple of years, I made a name for myself in the business community. It started when, soon after my return, I watched a popular prime-time TV show, *Words of Gold*, airing during the holy month of Ramadan, on which a celebrity presenter distributed gold Egyptian coins during "on-the-street" interviews with the masses. The disparity revealed in the poverty within Egypt's dual society was simply too painful to see. I convinced P&G's Regional President to kick off a national marketing campaign, linked to the TV program, and to give away gold coins—worth $ 250 at that time—to randomly selected consumers if they collected empty bags of P&G's flagship Ariel detergent.[1] I remember the day we went to Tanta, in the Gharbiya governorate, to knock on random homes in an underprivileged area, and how we were welcomed, if not sequestrated, by hundreds of people, so we could see the Ariel bags collected by different families. The success of the campaign far surpassed anyone's expectations, and translated into a two-fold sales volume growth achieved during my tenure between 1994 and 1996, for which Egypt received the 1996 Worldwide P&G Trial and Loyalty Award. It was also the subject of a case study at the American University in Cairo in 2011. Ariel became the brand of the people, distributing thousands of gold coins, refurbishing run-down schools, and donating incubators to various hospitals nationwide. The campaign underscored the power of TV to raise awareness on struggling social classes, and challenged other corporations to share responsibility. Naturally, any success attracts criticism, particularly from those who sit idle, and this massive campaign put forth a side of Egypt many had chosen to ignore.

After eight years with P&G, I was headhunted by PepsiCo International, a joint venture in which I worked as Marketing Director for one year, only to be headhunted again by Al Ahram Beverages Company (ABC), the legendary sole manufacturer of alcoholic beer in Egypt, founded in 1897. Having been nationalized by the Government of Gamal Abdel Nasser in 1963, and become a state-owned company, ABC was re-privatized in 1997, and sold to an anchor investor, the Luxor Group, headed by an Egyptian-American. The business challenge of turning a failing public-sector monopoly into an Egyptian beverage powerhouse lured me in to prove that local high caliber talents could lead such transformation, and that privatization was the right way forward for Egypt. I felt that the government priorities should be solely geared toward education and health, and should not be allowed to derail its resources into managing non-strategic businesses. But more importantly, I saw in the Stella beer brand a powerful tool for communicating Egypt's modern and secular identity, and a defense of individual freedoms. For the record, in 1927, there were 36 brewing companies in Egypt, and until the early 1980s, beer was widely seen as acceptable. Stella, whose century-old history paralleled that of modern Egypt, was also emblematic of Egypt—glorious and culturally dynamic in its past, but inefficient, inconsistent and contested in its present.

Headed by the company's business savvy Chairman, Ahmed Zayat, an eight-person Executive Committee was formed—seven men and myself, all Egyptian with the exception of one—and together we led the transformation of the enterprise. With the Chairman and his chief of staff, I would regularly travel to present to current investors and convince prospective ones to buy into our aggressive business plan, during four-day marathon roadshows across continents. While the amount of private and institutional wealth that sought investment opportunities was stunning, so was the number of publicly traded companies competing to grab a share of this wealth to fund their growth.

Stella beer print advertisement published in widely circulating popular magazines in Egypt (1998)

Thanks to my international experience at P&G and PepsiCo, I had mastered the art of marketing consumer goods. But neither had prepared me for marketing alcoholic beverages in a predominantly Muslim country. With only 10% of the Egyptian population claiming to be drinkers, I was constantly treading a fine line between pushing the limits of what was socially acceptable, and what might offend mainstream consumers. I pushed the envelope further by placing print ads on the back covers of weekly magazines, which had stopped for more than two decades, playing on the historical tolerance and familiarity with Stella in old Egyptian movies. We opened dry governorates with predominantly Coptic populations, and segmented the market with more affordable packaging and new brands. Sadly, it may be impossible to repeat some of these ideas today as conservative thinking is on the rise.

Fatenn, CEO and member of the Board of Gianaclis Vineyards for Beverages (2000)

I won over the best employees from the public sector, many of whom saw me as an alien "kid," and upgraded their skills to complement the large marketing department I had created with fresh graduates. After succeeding in putting the Stella brand back on track, I was promoted to

Chief Executive Officer, and member of the Board of Directors of Gianaclis Vineyards for Beverages—the sole wine producer in Egypt, founded in 1882, and acquired in 1999 by ABC from the government. At the age of 32, I had become the youngest Egyptian CEO of a non-family-run company, with over 200 employees, featured on the cover of *Business Today*, under the title "Coming Home". The challenges were more complex as the entire organization now fell on my shoulders, but also the

Fatenn on the cover of *Business Today* (June 2001)

general perception was that wines are more "sinful" than beer given their higher alcoholic content. Needless to say, wine making originated in ancient Egypt as a royal industry ca. 3000 BC, and poets Hafez and Omar Khayyam lauded the joys of love and wine, centuries after the advent of Islam. To wipe out the nicknames "Château Vinaigre" (Château Vinegar) and "Château Migraine" (Château Headache) associated with the Gianaclis and Omar Khayyam brands, we signed a technical know-how agreement with a reputable winemaker in Bordeaux to supervise all stages of the winemaking process. Further, I founded a Wine Academy, with training sessions in Bordeaux, to train and gain the endorsement of key players in the Egyptian hospitality industry.

As the fundamentals were addressed, sales quadrupled and profits tripled, I felt it was time to contribute to the community. Given the high price point and the aura of cosmopolitanism surrounding the product, the idea needed to be tailored more toward the upper classes than the masses. Perhaps partly for selfish reasons, I decided to link wine with contemporary Egyptian art. This way, we would not only educate the right target group about an important cultural aspect of present-day Egypt, but also promote struggling Egyptian artists. It was also a calculated and defiant move to marry wine and art, two controversial subjects in Islam because, for the ultraconservative, figurative art is forbidden. We rebranded Obelisk as "Egypt's Modern Vine Arts," by incorporating, bi-annually, pictures of artworks onto the labels of its three wine bottles,[2] acquiring the artworks, and advertising the new bottles in widely circulating magazines. Today, more than a decade later, the labels continue to change, and ABC owns a valuable corporate art collection. The selection of the works was done through a committee that included artists and gallery owners. This novel idea finally allowed me access to the art world from its back door.

Unlike Vienna where researching art felt accessible, the Egyptian arts scene appeared to be conceited, secluded and opaque, with outdated research material. Museum visits were awkward. The School of Fine Arts was chaotic. Browsing the few existing galleries was at times demeaning, as the owner or manager would not bother with an "art illiterate," or someone who seemed unlikely to be a potential buyer. From the day I returned to Cairo, I had decided to understand and collect Egyptian art by allocating part of my monthly salary to acquisitions. Without genuine guidance and little knowledge, I fell into the trap of acquiring important works by non-important artists, or non-important works by important artists. The most expensive work I acquired in the late 1990s was *Al Quds* (Jerusalem, 1978), by Egyptian pioneer painter Tahia Halim. My friends thought I was ridiculous, and I was afraid to tell my parents the exhorbitant price I had paid. I also remember being talked out of acquiring the second version of the iconic painting *Unemployment* by Hamed Owais, the pioneer of social realism; instead, I bought my first car. Today, the car is gone, and the painting is worth over quarter of a million dollars. My encounter with an Egyptian-Palestinian man, Hakam Kanafani, who later became my husband and lifelong soul mate, brought out the pan-Arab woman inside of me, and gradually I began to broaden my research and acquisitions with art created by Middle Eastern artists.[3]

By that time, I was leading three parallel lives— as a workaholic CEO, an avid art collector and historian, and, finally, being courted. At the peak of my corporate career, I had to make choices. To me, marriage was an unsuitable institution, synonymous with losing my independence. It took a brilliant and confident man to prove me wrong. When we met, Hakam, who had studied in the US and worked at NASA, was working in the occupied territories in Ramallah, Palestine. An established CEO himself in the telecommunications field, he risked his life, day in and day out, to contribute to the betterment of the lives of Palestinians. With a similar outlook on life, he enabled rather than inhibited my growth.

On the professional level, what triggered my resignation from ABC was our intention, as an Executive Committee, to sell ABC; our mission had been accomplished. ABC was now the undisputed model of privatization, and the subject of PhDs and case studies at Ivy League universities. It was also time to reap the fruits of our labor. Major negotiations with several potential buyers kicked off, and in 2003, Heineken International, the giant Dutch brewing company, bought ABC at the whopping price of $ 287 million—four times the privatization price. Being part of this history-making economic nationalism was a humble way of giving back to my country, as it could prove that it is possible to lure in foreign investment to Egypt's struggling economy. As I look around today, many of the fresh graduates I trained at P&G and ABC are now successful top executives around the world or have founded private companies in Egypt.

Walking away from my pride and joy at the top of my game was difficult yet liberating. The thrill of the corporate race was gone, and the excitement to start something new on my own and contribute to the quest of our national identity was born. I was convinced that to shape our collective future and identity at this juncture, Egyptians needed an intellectual paradigm shift, that of understanding our past and present through the eyes of socially engaged artists, one in which art would have a special role to play. I thought of different ways to make art history and appreciation accessible to a wider audience, with the ultimate objective to reinvent the great tradition of art patronage, and empower young artists.

By organizing lectures with renowned international and local cultural practitioners in the homes of prominent Egyptian art collectors, I introduced a new side of the arts to art lovers, in an informal yet informed setting. The unanimous acceptance of the few prominent collectors I called on to host the lectures—a majority of whom I personally did not know—took me off guard. Here were these heavyweight Egyptian families allowing up to seventy strangers access to their private and valuable art possessions. I salute each of them for their generosity. Requests to attend further events piled up and indicated that Egypt, on the larger scale, would benefit from nurturing aesthetic appreciation and rebuilding a culture of arts patronage. I expanded the concept and gave monthly lectures spanning various art movements, sensing then that I was creating a new era.[4] However, events during the 2011 Revolution put all further plans on hold. At 2 am, well past the curfew hour on the night

Fatenn making a presentation on the history of modern Egyptian art at the ArtTalks|Egypt Gallery in Cairo, 2013

of February 1, our family suffered a major tragedy. As violence intensified, runaway thugs hit my 71-year old father while he bravely participated in our neighborhood patrol to support the protesting youth. On April 25, 2011, he succumbed to his injuries, passing away as a hero, and taking a part of me with him. The inconceivable ordeal we faced to save his life was also a wake-up call to the scandalous health system in Egypt, plagued by inexcusable incompetence, greed, and unprofessionalism. Eighteen months after his tragic death, I opened a full-fledged commercial art gallery, ArtTalks|Egypt, with an inaugural show entitled *Long Live Free Art* to honor the life of my father.[5] Five years later, by providing superior knowledge and the highest in business practices, we have established ourselves as a trusted search engine and an authority in building valuable art collections. More importantly, we aim to send a message that liberation from any form of confinement our society suffers—whether religion, social taboos, patriarchal systems, oppressive governments—is the way forward for Egypt. Since there is no rehearsal to life, I have always believed that you must embrace liberty, take advantage of all the possibilities to carve your own identity, and cease to let fear whether of the "other," the unknown, or the weaker self control you. Become the version of yourself that you chose, and you shall go forward. As for me, I have chosen to be Egyptian, passionately Egyptian.

Cairo, October 2015

Notes

[1] Ahmed Tolba, "Ariel Egypt - From Market Penetration to Fierce Competition", *E-Marketing: Concepts, Methodologies, Tools, and Applications* (Hershey, PA: Information Resources Management Association [IRMA], 2012), 1: 514. https://books.google.com.eg/books?id=ZPWs1xbB4ysC&pg=PA515&lpg=PA515&dq=Ariel+detergent+Egypt+Words+of+Gold+sponsor&source=bl&ots=OBLaG8JnD5&sig=_DpjV8xFO8QTp8rBcl9DVwPYRaA&hl=en&sa=X&redir_esc=y#v=onepage&q=Ariel%20detergent%20Egypt%20Words%20of%20Gold%20sponsor&f=false, 19 November 2015.
[2] Al Ahram Beverages Company website: Obelisk, Egypt's Modern Vine Arts, 19 November 2015 http://www.alahrambeverages.com/Default.aspx?uc=Product/ProductList&SubCategoryID=14&seo=Wine-Obelisk, 19 November, 2015.
[3] Fatenn Mostafa, "A Diaspora Collection," *This Week in Palestine* 160 (August 2011): 34-36. http://archive.thisweekinpalestine.com/details.php?id=3480&ed=197&edid=197, 19 November 2015.
[4] Sara Elkamel, "ArtTalks Pays Tribute to the Masters of Modern Egyptian Art," *Al Ahram Online*, 14 November 2013 http://english.ahram.org.eg/News/86360.aspx. 19 November 2015.
[5] Ann Shaw, "Egypt's Art World Rallies to Defend Freedom of Expression," *Art Newspaper*, online, 24 January 2013 http://artsfreedom.org/?p=4975, 19 November 2015.

MY COUNTRY AND ME

SEHEIR KANSOUH

To my children Mahmoud Nour and Rasha Habib:
may you forgive me for long hours of absence

Prologue

It was summer 2015 when I was about to start drafting this chapter. I was 75, and had just arrived in Mykonos for a week-long retreat. This Greek island is renowned for its glamorous non-stop party atmosphere, but I was looking for calm and serenity. I found them by the Aegean Sea, amidst pomegranate and olive trees swayed by the Meltemi winds. On the way to my self-imposed seclusion, I observed youth. They were crowding in minimal attire, some on roaring motorcycles, others with a small bottle of mineral water in one hand and struggling to keep a cell phone in equilibrium while pulling a carry-on bag with the other hand. All appeared to be rushing to enjoy every minute of a well-deserved vacation in more upbeat quarters than my own. These young people are more conscious about food, comfort, health, and well-being than older generations, and they also favor revised concepts of marriage, parenthood, work, recreation, freedom, and independence. To use a metaphor, dawn and sunset both show a shining glow on the horizon, yet they carry opposite meanings: one ushers the rise of the day, the other its decline. In-between, there are life stories, each molded by time and place. Mine follows the historical backdrop below.

Life in Context

The 1940s

World War II (WWII) erupted in Europe on September 1, 1939. I was born two weeks later. When it ended in September 1945, I was only five and could not remember much of what happened. During the raids on Alexandria, I am told that my mother would carry me to the basement of our building in Glymenopoulo, an elegant and distinguished neighborhood that has since lost its luster due to continuous rural migration. Egypt's population has since swelled from under 20 million to 90+ today.[1] WWII caused massive deaths of civilians, and fear prevailed in all households.[2] It undoubtedly affected the child I was, and may explain why I remain a staunch peace advocate.

The 1950s

The most profound change in modern Egypt occurred after the 1952 Revolution, a military coup by the self-proclaimed "Free Officers" who overthrew the monarchy. Ousting King Farouk put an end to the Mohamed Ali dynasty in power since 1805; the last thirty years of which included an imperfect but functioning democratic system of government (1922-1952). The Revolution signaled the beginning of military rule in Egypt, enforced by a nationalist, socialist, and police regime. It was headed by President Gamal Abdel Nasser who sought to unite Egypt with Syria in 1958.[3] This marked the change of our identity. Until then, our country was simply Egypt, and its people were proud Egyptians. From then on, our rulers decided that we would be Arabs, and new generations were taught to be proud Arabs. *Misr* (Egypt) became the United Arab Republic; our flag, national anthem, culture were changed, and school curricula were re-written with a twisted view of history.

Prior to the establishment of the Gulf States and the expansion of their oil industry, Egypt was the leader among Arab countries and their benefactor. Although our Constitution was built on Sharia Law, Egypt was a liberal nation, socially, politically, and economically. The Muslim Brotherhood, founded in 1928 by Hassan El Banna, was an underground fringe association. The US agreed conditionally to supply Egypt with the armament it requested and the World Bank would finance the construction of the Aswan High dam, provided we accept demands that would also jeopardize Nasser's image as the leader of Arab nationalism. As a consequence, he turned for support to a more willing Soviet Union, and strengthened the ties with the Eastern bloc, while relationships with the US and the West soured. Communism, however, was never an option for Egypt.

The 1960s

Egypt being fundamentally an agrarian society, Egyptians are attached to their land. Losing the Sinai Peninsula to Israel after the 1967 Six-Day

War—known as *al-naksah* (the setback)—was thus terribly humiliating. Our country's earlier military support to the civil war in Yemen is believed to have been detrimental to the army's performance in the 1967 war.[4] Israel's territorial gains included not only the Gaza Strip and the Sinai Peninsula from Egypt, but also the West Bank from Jordan, and the Golan Heights from Syria.[5] All Egyptians were marked by this defeat: losing a war, losing land, and losing face. The 1967 war rekindled the everlasting Palestinian problem that continues to haunt the world to this day.

In our country, the nationalization process, land reform, and free education initiated by Nasser since his access to power, aiming in theory at achieving social equity, did not lead to the success he had anticipated. Analyzing the many causes and effects of the failure of the socialist regime are beyond the scope of this story. For me, one of the saddest results was to see many friends leave the country: some because they were Jewish or of foreign descent, some because their wealth was sequestrated or their property nationalized, and others because they could not live under a repressive regime. Regrettably, the ensuing brain-drain and massive exodus of workforce deprived the country of much of its promising youth and leading entrepreneurs.

The 1970s—1990s

Egypt's sense of pride was restored after the 1973 Yom Kippur October War. Following a surprise attack against Israel masterminded by President Anwar Sadat, Nasser's successor, Egypt was able to recover the Sinai and regained control of the Suez Canal. These changes paved the way for the 1978 Camp David Accords between Egypt and Israel. To date, however, the normalization of relationships between the two countries (*el tatbee'e*) has not gained popular approval. Dissatisfied with Sadat's peace initiative, the Arab countries expelled Egypt from the Arab League and moved its headquarters from Cairo where it had been founded in 1945 to Tunisia.[6]

On the home front, Sadat accomplished a major shift in the economic system. He established an "Open Door" policy (*infitah*) that reversed Nasser's socialist regime, ended the longstanding alliance with the Soviet Union, and renewed the ties with the US. An unprecedented era of private investment, import, fast food, and consumerism followed, bringing to an end the state domination of the economy—albeit inconsistently. During that time, I was Program Officer at the Cairo Office of the United Nations Development Programme (UNDP). Priorities had to be realigned with the new directions and alliances. It was crucial to understand how politics would affect development work. There were often hidden forces and agendas that contributed to water down the efforts or kill the dream. The assassination of President Sadat by a jihadist on October 6, 1981, during the annual parade celebrating the recovery of the Sinai following the 1973 war, should have warned us of the rise of religious fanatics operating in the dark.[7] Sadat's successor, President Hosni Mubarak, maintained the free-market economy and let it grow uncontrollably. His 30-year rule was marked by sharp divides between the haves and the have-nots, corruption, mounting poverty, unchecked population growth, and further decline in the education and service sectors.

The Twenty-First Century

In the new millennium, Egypt continued to face major socio-economic problems, most of which arising from decades of irrational political decisions, erroneous policies, and reprehensible practices. These issues escalated to the point of causing the Egyptian "Arab Spring," in quest for equity, freedom, and dignity. The historical uprising of January 25, 2011, expected to lead to democracy, was hijacked by the Muslim Brotherhood. Their candidate, Dr. Mohamed Morsi, was raised to power after an allegedly democratic election. Like President Hosni Mubarak two years earlier, he was ousted by popular demand on June 30, 2013. So far, the majority of Egyptians support current President Abdel Fattah El Sissi, a military man who leads a civilian government. However, continuous geopolitical, ideological, and armed conflicts in the region, as well as retrograde elements from within, are making it difficult for Egypt to regain its better self. To maintain security, authorities are constantly in violent confrontation with destructive elements of organized crime, and terrorist groups. Such policing, though necessary, affects personal freedoms. In the broader context, rapid technological advances in the sciences, and progress in the information and communication sectors are unsettling the business-as-usual practice.

My Life Story

Having sketched the historical background that affected Egypt during my lifetime, I will now focus on my own story. I am unapologetically nostalgic about the Alexandria where I grew up. Many among us, her inhabitants, were at least second generation Greeks, Italians, Turkish, or Syro-Lebanese; personally, I am of Turkish-Circassian descent. We were not clustered in separate communities, we lived together in a cosmopolitan society and considered ourselves Egyptians from Alexandria. We were Muslims, Christians, and Jews, who had mosques, churches, and synagogues, where prayers were held Friday, Saturday, and Sunday. That was the Alexandria in which I was fortunate to have been raised at a time when Egypt was a monarchy, prior to the 1952 military coup that wrecked the urbane social mix enjoyed by Alexandrians since time immemorial. Having lived in that Alexandria cannot be compared to any other experience. Even those who left the country, by choice or by force, continue to hold Alexandria in their hearts.

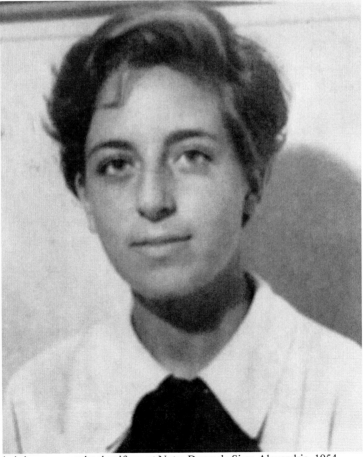

Seheir in summer school uniform at Notre Dame de Sion, Alexandria, 1954

At Notre Dame de Sion (NDS), an elite French Catholic school, I received an excellent education. Because religion is now an important issue in public discourse, I like to recall a time when it was never a subject of discussion at home or school, although part of the school uniform required that Christians wear a cross, and both Jews and Muslims wear a star. I cannot even recall whether it was a five-pointed or six-pointed Star of David, nobody cared. Jews and Muslims used to attend "*leçons de morale*," while Christians were taking "*leçons de catéchisme*." Each class was assigned a poor household to support throughout our school years. We provided them with food supplies and clothes, while our parents subsidized the children's education. We learned that there were people less privileged than ourselves, and that we had a responsibility toward them. Later, I understood that socialism failed its promise to provide a better life for all, while capitalism catered to the powerful few, with no regard for the masses.

My father's austerity, and my years at NDS made me a shy little girl who hid her determination, and did not cross any red line. The nightly "*examen de conscience*" (self-appraisal) that we had to perform for school continues to be a regular routine that I practice to this day. On the religious level, I remain a Muslim out of conviction, because I know that Islam preaches tolerance, not violence, while criminals distort its teachings by killing, looting, and raping in its name.

When I moved to Cairo in 1957, I was seventeen, getting ready to be married. At that time, it was not considered a child marriage as it is today. I divorced at age 22, remained a single mother for seven years, remarried at 29, and had a second child at 35. My father, an engineering fellow of the University of Liverpool and an imposing landowner, passed away when I was thirteen. Had he been alive, he would have insisted I graduate from college before being married. When I realized that a solid academic foundation was essential for continuous professional learning, I resumed studies in Political Science at the American University in Cairo (AUC). It was followed by a one-year internship as Research Fellow at Ohio State University, during which I was elected Vice President of the Inter-University Consortium for International Social Development, for a three-year term.[8]

Development Talk

With time, as a field UNDP official, I came to understand that international organizations—even though I do appreciate many of their achievements—can also contribute to a maze of confusion and ineffectiveness, because each agency advocates for its own agenda. Therefore, it may pull resources to achieve non-priority items in the nation it serves. Up until the 1990s, there was seldom coordination between the various UN agencies. I was well placed to know it, being at center stage regarding inter-agency coordination within the UN system

Seheir with husband Tarek Habib, and children Mahmoud Nour and Rasha Habib, Cairo, c.1979

and aid donors to Egypt. In the meantime, the word "donors" was modified to become "Development Assistance Group," and "Partners in Development." The purpose was meant to imply that "aid" was not charity from one group of countries to another, but rather an action of mutual benefit. In 2005, a new concept emerged, "Delivering as one," aiming at enhancing coordination among all UN agencies.

In my work, I also observed that global priorities do not necessarily respond to national needs. The Millennium Development Goals (MDGs) illustrate the discrepancies between international calls for action and situations at home.[9] For example, in Egypt, as in many countries with poor sanitation, viral hepatitis is an endemic deadly disease. However, the MDG main health target was to combat HIV AIDS, which causes many fewer casualties than hepatitis in those countries. The lack of sensitivity to local needs was one of the major reasons that hindered the achievement of

MDGs by the target year of 2015. Instead, another slogan, "Sustainable Development Post 2015," was coined.[10]

Speaking about public issues in my personal story is compulsive, as work for me was never a 9 to 5 job, but a mission and a passion. My late husband and life companion for 43 years, prominent media pundit Tarek Habib, used to reprimand me gently, and sometimes not so gently, when he would become irritated that I devoted too much time to work, and too little to homemaking—actually, I had domestic help for that. "Are you going to reform the world?" he would ask me. Social reform was no doubt my unspoken quest; and my profession as an agent for development allowed me to pursue that dream.

Leaving a Mark

My career with UNDP started in 1967; ten years prior to my retirement in 1999, I had become Head of the Policy Team of the UN Resident Coordinator System. It is difficult to determine how much credit to claim for my achievements, because there are always other players and external factors that affect development progress. I believe in sharing vision and knowledge among team members for the mutual enrichment of all, irrespective of hierarchy.

My flagship was to have introduced and internalized the concept of human development in Egypt, and turned it into concrete policies and programs. This was at a time when failure of the socialist paradigm pushed countries toward a market economy, believing that a trickle-down effect would achieve equity. However, renowned thinkers, such as Amartya Sen and Mahbub Ul Haq, introduced a series of indicators and constructed the now famous Human Development Index (HDI) to prove the shortcomings of this theory. They argued that income alone could not achieve human development—the ultimate goal of progress—and that other socio-political factors were necessary to attain that end. The approach I used was strategic, participatory, and result-oriented. I triggered a momentous geographical disaggregation of the HDI, also by gender. For the first time in Egypt, the governors of the country's 26 administrative divisions would meet in roundtables to discuss the significant inter-governorate human development discrepancies and gender disparities that HDI revealed. The special measures prompted by my initiative to achieve geographical and gender equity were considered a model of a human development country strategy by UNDP at large, and presented as Best Practice at the 1995 World Social Summit in Copenhagen. Three times, I was honored with Lifetime Awards for Contribution to Human Development, most recently in 2014—fifteen years after my retirement.[11] For me, the real reward was to have placed vulnerable groups and neglected rural populations of Upper Egypt as a high priority item on the national agenda. In concrete terms, it meant that many deprived households started to have access to sanitation and other services.

Seheir receiving a Lifetime Award for Contribution to Human Development from Minister of Planning Ashraf El Araby (R), in the presence of UN Resident Coordinator Anita Nirody (L), Cairo, 2014

In the early 1990s, an Economic Reform and Structural Adjustment Program (ERSAP) was launched in Egypt. It followed the prescriptions made by International Financial Institutions (IFIs) for a necessary process toward privatization, globalization, and a more liberal economy. I did not believe that the Social Fund for Development (SFD) that IFIs prescribed to mitigate the negative impact of structural adjustment on vulnerable groups was sufficient to overcome institutional shortcomings. Thus, I directed my thoughts to the social sector, which had not received the attention it deserved, and triggered the formulation of the first National Strategy for Social Development. It aimed at paving the way for a full-fledged necessary reform of the social sector, to complement the economic reform underway. Although social reform was not fully implemented, social development gained unprecedented priority on the national agenda, and those of development agencies. The snowball effect of this initiative continues to unfold to this day.

Regarding women's issues, I was instrumental in building the first national women's machinery, established by presidential decree to support a three-pronged process aiming at the social, economic, and political empowerment of women. I also contributed to establish the first women's ombudsman in Egypt, and learned along the way that patriarchy was difficult to dislodge, and that harmful practices deeply rooted in traditions take time to eliminate: female genital mutilation (FGM) is a case in point. The environment had also become another area of interest for me. As early as 1982, I promoted the use of clean energy by spearheading the development of the first National Strategy for New and Renewable Energy, with a map of all the resources and possible applications. Concern for these issues remained dormant until climate change and the looming water and energy crises renewed the wakeup call.

As a UNDP field officer, I was entrusted with the regional portfolio of the Arab States and across regions, and had to deal with extremely delicate situations. One of these was the decision of the Arab League—angry at Sadat's peace treaty with Israel—to withdraw its sponsorship of the Alexandria-based Arab Academy for Science, Technology & Maritime Transport, a flagship of institutional success and inter-country cooperation. Diplomatically and using political astuteness, I was able to maintain that support.

As a staunch advocate for cooperation between the Nile riparian countries, I stood behind a project named UNDUGU (brotherhood in Swahili), led by then-Minister of State for Foreign Affairs, Dr. Boutros Boutros Ghali. I also managed the formulation of a Master Plan for Water Resources Development and Use, long before that resource became a major global concern. At a time when development assistance was restricted to governments, I was instrumental in forming partnerships between UNDP and NGOs, and instigated conceptual linkages between development and human rights, as well as supporting inclusive processes through small grant programs.

Seheir (R) with UN Resident Coordinator Pedro Mercader (C) receiving UN Secretary General Boutros Boutros Ghali (L) at UNDP, Cairo, c. 1994

Beyond was not only the title of a public policy quarterly that I founded in 2002, and kept running for years, it was also the symbol of my life after retiring from formal employment.[12] While my strong interest in social issues remains unflinching, I am increasingly concerned about the menacing forces that threaten world peace.

Loyalty

Throughout my professional life, I worked with extraordinary colleagues without whom I could not have achieved as much as I did, and who went on to pursue distinguished careers on their own. I am indebted for their unfailing support, and treasure the testimonies of our relationships that they expressed in articles, public letters, or personal notes.

Fatemah Farag left UNDP to work in journalism. As founder and CEO of the youth media service *Welad El Balad* (country folks), she was selected by the Nieman Foundation for Journalism at Harvard University as a 2016 Knight Visiting Fellow. In an article published in *Al-Ahram Weekly*, she described me as: "Bewitched, bothered, sometimes bewildered, but never without a cause. I remember her as the elegantly dressed whirlwind that would sweep into the office at an ungodly early morning hour... She thinks ... that the collective goals can only be attained if we pass on our tools to others ... She had quietly taken it upon herself to underline the importance of sustainable development long before the bandwagon was built, let alone rolling."[13]

Maya Morsy interrupted her successful career with the UN at a young age, when she was elected President of the National Council for Women, a position previously held by Egypt's then-First Lady, and a seasoned ambassador. She saw me as: "An Egyptian woman leader, enabler, connector and mentor to a large number of young women leaders. A woman with vision and clear strategic orientation... She supported the establishment of the first National Women's Machinery in Egypt, adding a lot to the women's empowerment agenda ... Her advocacy and lobbying efforts engendered policies that enhanced delivery of services to poor and marginalized women."

Katharina Ammitzboel, Senior Peacebuilding Advisor, and candidate for the 2015 Danish Parliament, whose internship at UNDP I supervised in the 1990s, recalls me as "visionary and analytical ... dedicated to improve the lives of those in need ... unique and remarkable ... She is a role model for many as she has been to me, and I still recall and use a lot of the learning that I gained from her."

Reem Abdel Hamid Gazzaz specializes in social identity and sustainable charitable work. She has been hailed for her human rights activism; and she practices as private philanthropy advisor in Saudi Arabia. She wrote: "SK has always been one step ahead in all aspects of her life ... She single-handedly put UNDP Cairo on the global map with her innovative approaches, professional accuracy, and her commitment and dedication to human development ... She paved the way for generations to come ... a passionate humanitarian who taught me to stand up for my belief, gave me a sense of value, and the tools to take my ideas forward. ... She showed me integrity in practice."

Last but not least, I am greatly indebted to Professor Emeritus Saad Z. Nagi of Ohio State University for his teachings in pursuit of social development. To all these friends, I hereby express heartfelt thanks.

Conclusion

Since the beginning of time, man has dared nature with inventions that changed the world incrementally. In the present era, the speed of technology advances is playing havoc with all that we believed to be constant, with variables easy to predict and manage. Defying negative vibrations of high-velocity winds of change is the biggest challenge of our interconnected world. Two issues are currently pressing: the first is climate change, which has finally received world consensus for action; and the second is dealing with terrorism. With these daunting tasks on the global agenda, there has been a shift in priorities and the allocation of resources to important issues, namely to combat poverty and social polarization. In Egypt, spending on health, education, and family planning—three crucial areas requiring major intervention—is likely to be reduced, while scientific research may be considered a luxury. Today, women's rights are greatly threatened by retrograde thinking, and the need for policing as a security measure is hampering freedom of association and expression. Brain-drain continues to afflict Egypt.

In concluding my story, I remain deeply concerned that life on earth is increasingly endangered by irrational and dogmatic behavior, and unpredictable power struggles. Continuous alertness to detect problems and address them before they become difficult to control is a must. On the other hand, infinite possibilities and potentials spurred by technological advancement are waiting to be grasped.

Epilogue

My journey may have not taken me to where I would have liked to land: a better world for the Egyptian people and all of humanity. Back to my roots, I find solace in the inspiring verse of Alexandria-born poet Constantine Cavafi (1863-1933) in his eternal *Ithaca* (1911):

Have Ithaka always in your mind.
Your arrival there is what you are destined for.
But don't in the least hurry the journey.
Better it last for years,
So that when you reach the island you are old,
Rich with all you have gained on the way,
Not expecting Ithaka to give you wealth.
Ithaka gave you a splendid journey.
Without her you would not have set out.
She hasn't anything else to give you.

I wish my readers a splendid journey, with a rewarding Ithaca.

Cairo, April 2016

Notes

[1] When Italy invaded British-controlled Egypt from Italian-occupied Libya in 1940, special war-related security and safety measures were triggered in Egyptian territories.

[2] WWII death toll is estimated to be between 50-85 million, including the Holocaust and the atomic explosions of Hiroshima and Nagasaki.

[3] President Gamal Abdel Nasser, a charismatic leader, ruled Egypt from 1954 until his death on September 28, 1970.

[4] Nasser had reportedly committed 70 000 troops to the civil war in Yemen (1962-1970), but withdrew the Egyptian military in 1967.

[5] It is estimated that 300 000 Palestinians fled the West Bank, and about 100 000 Syrians left the Golan Heights as refugees. Across the Arab world, Jewish minorities were either expelled or departed voluntarily, seeking asylum in Israel, Europe, and the Americas.

[6] In 1989, after the Arab League endorsed the Palestine Liberation Organization (PLO) plan for a negotiated settlement with Israel, Egypt was reinstated, and Cairo once again became its headquarters in 1990.

[7] The Muslim Brotherhood, however, remained under control until January 25, 2011, when it hijacked the Egyptian version of the Arab Spring. They remained in power until the second major popular uprising in two years, namely on June 30, 2013, when the people overthrew the so-called first democratically elected president, Dr. Mohamed Morsi, although the validity of elections was seriously contested.

[8] The Inter-university Consortium for International Social Development (IUCISD), now called International Consortium for Social Development (ICSD) recognized me with an Award for Excellence in Program Planning of International Symposia for Social Work (1998).

[9] The Millennium Development Goals (MDGs) were the world's time-bound eight goals and quantified targets to be achieved by 2015 for addressing extreme poverty in its many dimensions: income poverty, hunger, disease, lack of adequate shelter, and exclusion, while promoting gender equality, education and environmental sustainability.

[10] At the 2015 UN Sustainable Development Summit, World Leaders adopted the 2030 Agenda to Sustainable Development, which includes a set of 17 Sustainable Development Goals (SDGs) to protect the planet, and ensure prosperity for all by 2030. The new SDGs, and the broader sustainable agenda, go much further than the MDGs, addressing the root causes of poverty and the universal need for development that works for all people.

[11] Awards for Lifetime Contribution to Human Development were granted by the UN Resident Coordinator and the Government of Egypt in 2014; by the same bodies though under different management for Programming Human Development Concepts in Egypt in 2008; by the United Nations Information Centre for Lifetime Achievement in Development in 2004; and for the advancement of women by the American University in Cairo (AUC) in 2006, and for protection of the river Nile (2010).

[12] Due to logistical reasons, publication of the public policy quarterly *Beyond* in cooperation with *Ahram Weekly* ended in 2010. The 2011 Egyptian Arab Spring inspired me to collect the policy views and solutions relating to Egypt's problems in the first decade of the new millennium, made by distinguished experts in the quarterly. They were included in a widely-acclaimed book entitled *Daring to Care: Reflections on Egypt before the Revolution and the Way Forward* that I edited, and which was published in 2011 by the Association of Former International Civil Servants in Egypt (AFICS-Egypt). I founded that Association in 2002 and chaired it for seven years. I remained active as senior advisor to a number of cabinet ministers and councils for a few years, and now serve as free-lance consultant on development and gender, in addition to my voluntary activities.

[13] http://www.masress.com/en/ahramweekly/22663 (2002)

CHANCES I FOUND
AND CHANCES I TOOK IN LIFE

MADIHA EL MEHELMY KOTB

I have never been much of a planner, even when it came to my own life. So, I often wonder what I would have done differently had I planned it myself. Looking back at the different twists and turns that my life took, I am at peace with the fact that I could not have imagined or planned the way it turned out, not even in my wildest dreams. The best part is that I really liked what happened, especially that I was blessed with a loving family, great friends, and a successful and fulfilling career. People often wondered if there was a secret to my success, or how I managed to achieve it. Honestly, if I had a magic recipe, I would have shared it with everyone, especially with those I love. What I know for a fact is what worked for me: hard work and perseverance, coupled with the willingness to take advantage of the chances and opportunities that came my way.

Taking chances implies taking risks, as you may often embark on initiatives for which you are not fully prepared. In fact, had I done only those for which I was ready, or waited until I was 100 percent guaranteed success, I would have accomplished only a fraction of what I did. Each one of us gets different chances and opportunities at various stages of life, they do not always come at a time of our choosing, and if we let them slip by there is no guarantee they will present themselves again. Learning never to say I think I am not ready, or I don't know if I am up to it, is probably what helped me to achieve success in my professional career. Born in Giza in 1953, I always considered myself a child of the 1952 Revolution. Those two factors of time and space had a great impact on my life. Giza is more than just the suburb of Cairo that most people associate with the Great Pyramids—the majestic structures that withstood the test of time, and continue to challenge archeologists, scientists, and engineers, even in our 21st century. Likewise, the Revolution brought with it an aspiration to change our world; it left its mark on me.

I was the youngest of four siblings, three girls and one boy, who all went to the Lycée Français in Zamalek, the neighborhood where we lived.

I started school a year younger than the usual age. The story goes that when my sisters and my brother went to school I used to cry for being left alone at home; not knowing better, I probably thought that school was as much fun as the club. Apparently, my dad worked out a deal with the school by committing to keep me an extra year in *Jardin d'enfants*. After the Suez crisis war broke out in late 1956, the school administration changed, as did its name which became Lycée la Liberté, and my dad felt free from his commitment. I loved my school and my teachers; however, I believe that a simple comment in my math test report in fifth grade had a huge influence on my life and my education. It simply stated "*douée en mathématiques*," gifted in math. This remark is engraved in my mind to this day. I loved math and performed well in it without much effort, but the comment made me look at the subject in a different way; it was no longer a subject matter, it became like an art that I was cultivating. It strengthened my passion until I reached more complex levels of algebra and geometry, and had to work harder at it.

Several international events, including the space program, marked my teenage years. I was especially fascinated by the Russian cosmonaut dog Laika—the first animal to make it into space—and the Soviet Union-American race to conquer outer space. I was following with awe the possibility that man could reach the moon. So, you can imagine my excitement when on July 20, 1969, Neil Armstrong took his first steps on the moon on my 16th birthday. My fascination with the space program only kept growing, and the challenges of the space program with its misses and successes made me believe that the sky was no longer the limit, and that with determination, training, hard work, and perseverance mankind could accomplish what was once considered impossible. To quote Nasa flight Director Gene Kranz who managed the Apollo 13 mission: "To recognize that the greatest error is not to have tried and failed, but that in trying, we did not give it our best effort," and that "failure is not an option." As a result of his careful thoughts, a major catastrophe was averted and human lives were saved.

When time came for me to start college, opting for Engineering was not a difficult decision to make. Fortunately, in my family there was never a question whether a career choice was fit for a man or a woman. In fact, my father actually empowered us children and allowed us to make our own choices. That said, he strongly believed in the importance of education, more so for girls than for boys. He used to say that a girl's education is even more important than that of a boy, because it would allow her not to stay in a situation where she was not happy. My father was a civil engineer, and a major partner in a construction company. As a child, I was fascinated by engineering, not even knowing what engineers do, except that my father used to say that engineers may not be able to solve all of life's problems, but they are trained to find solutions to every problem. For me, it was not a question that "father knows best," but that engineers know best.

My mother married before finishing school, later she was home-schooled and finished middle and high school about the same time as my oldest sister. She continued her education and went to college, graduating a few years later with a Bachelor of Arts in French literature. Everyone knew that she was not going to start a career, but her education though symbolic was a strong message to us on the importance of education, an enabler that builds character and allows us to tackle life's challenges. One of my father's famous quotes was that "doing one's job properly is what matters, regardless of the actual title or position one holds." In other words, it is important to thrive for excellence in everything we do. Engineering was also one of the most respected professions, to the extent that calling someone *"bashmohandess"* (an Arabic word for Mister Engineer), was a tittle of great respect. Engineering was also a well-paid profession, so it was naturally attractive for those who were competitive, and had good grades in school.

My oldest sister chose to study civil engineering and was the first woman engineer in my immediate circle. Her choice probably made mine easier. In the late 1960s, the American University in Cairo (AUC) started a new engineering program with only one specialization in Materials Engineering. After taking the national high school exam in 1970, I applied to university for admission. Although competition for medical and engineering schools was not as tough in those days as it is now—Egypt's population was 30 million, not 90 million—my grades were not high enough to get into the Faculty of Engineering at Cairo University or Ein Shams University, both public institutions with a reputation equivalent to that of the "Ivy League." Nonetheless, they were high enough to get me a scholarship at AUC. There was only one problem, though, my English was not good enough, so I was allowed to take only a light course load of science and mathematics, and had to enroll full-time in its English Language Institute. Once I reached the required proficiency level, I was allowed to start full-time studies in Engineering. It was cool to be an "AUCian," not only for the educational part, but especially for being part of an exclusive group. The AUC campus and exciting student life were quite different from those of other universities.

The first chance I found and could not let slip by was one of many twists and turns that occurred in my life in 1970. My sweetheart Ehab

(Bob) Kotb, a civil engineer, was toying with the idea of leaving Egypt in search of a more promising future in Canada. Bob had strong family connections and a good position with one of the largest engineering firms in Egypt, and I did not think he would consider emigrating. So when he started talking seriously about going to Canada, I was not sure what I wanted to do. On the one hand, I wanted to follow him; and on the other, I could not bear the thought of leaving my family, and definitely not before getting my degree. We got engaged in March 1974, and he left for Canada on August 15 of the same year.

Less than a month later, life played a bad trick on me when my father passed away September 11, and I was in a state of turmoil. The logical choice was to join Bob in Canada, although there were some major caveats: I had not completed my degree and we needed to get married before I could leave, yet we were oceans apart. So, on December 1, 1974 we were married by proxy. Back then, communication was not as simple as it is today; actually, overseas phone calls had to be planned and reserved ahead of time with the national telephone company, with no guarantee they would go through. So you can imagine Bob's surprise when I woke him up in the middle of the night to announce that we had become husband and wife. Well, it was not a total surprise since he had an idea that it was about to happen. From then on, things moved quickly, and as soon as I received my landing papers I booked my flight and headed for Canada two weeks later.

Preparing for this abrupt move, I had interrupted my studies in the middle of fall semester, and applied to both McGill University and Sir George Williams University in Montreal. To my great surprise, I was invited to meet with the Dean of Engineering at Loyola of Montreal. There was only one problem, and a major one: I had no idea what this was all about, since I did not know this school even existed, had not applied to it, and was bewildered how they ever found out about me. Later, I was informed that Concordia University was in the process of being founded by the merger of Sir Georges Williams University and Loyola of Montreal; thus, my application was transferred to Loyola. I was offered admission to the Faculty of Mechanical Engineering, which had a total class of three male students. You can imagine the impact I had not only on this student population, but on the women students in general. My classmates were already in their third year together, so I was not sure if they were going to accept me. However, after looking at me as a creature from outer space that landed upon them from a flying carpet, or rather after riding a camel all the way from Egypt, they embraced me as one of theirs. In fact, I became their "protégée," and found myself surrounded by more than classmates; they were like three new brothers I had found. This was yet another chance given to me that I took and tried to make the best out of it, not really knowing where it would lead me. It occurred at a tense time of my life, when I made many decisions without having the time or luxury to analyze them.

Madiha at graduation from Concordia University, Montreal, 1976

I graduated in 1976 and sat through a number of on-campus interviews, trying relentlessly to find a job, in vain. Back then, being a woman mechanical engineer was unusual, and many potential employers shrugged at the idea of hiring one. Furthermore, Canada was going through a recession, and my husband would soon become unemployed as the project on which he was working was coming to a halt. Our options were limited, as there were hardly any jobs available for either of us in Canada. So, we took what seemed to be an attractive offer that Bob's company made him, and moved to the small town of Sapele, in Nigeria, where he worked on the construction of a thermal power plant. Our commitment was for two years, and I hoped to find an engineering job there, but had no luck there either. Although our stay in Nigeria was a great experience, it was not quite what we had anticipated for our life, so we decided to return to Canada in 1978.

Bob changed jobs a few months after we were back in Montreal, and I was still figuring out what to do with my life. I did not feel confident enough to look for work or even attempt job interviews, as the only thing I could show for my last two years after graduation was a life of travelling, socializing, playing badminton, and talking to my dog Gaston. Then again, just when I least expected it, one of our friends who had just received his PhD in Mechanical Engineering from Concordia University suggested I consider going back to school for a Master's in Mechanical Vibration. Canada was developing a model of a high speed magnetically levitated train (MAGLEV), and research funds were available. So, one more time, I took a chance and got a National Science and Engineering Research Council Grant, and started to work as a teaching assistant while studying and doing research for my Master's.

Two years later, as I was finishing the degree, I became pregnant with our first child who was due December 21. Toward the last trimester of my pregnancy, I developed a serious case of pre-eclampsia, yet I was feeling full of energy and kept ignoring my doctor's recommendation for rest. I was in a race against time, since our friend was moving to Saudi Arabia, and I wanted to make sure I finished my thesis before he left. Considering that I was a high-risk patient and my due date was close to Christmas, I was admitted to the hospital earlier to be under medical supervision. Over the weekend my husband came to visit, and brought me the local newspaper. In the employment section, he had circled an ad from the Quebec provincial government, which was looking for mechanical engineers in different technical positions in the Public Works Department, and the Department of Labor. I cut the clip, and decided to take a chance and apply. A few weeks later, I was called for an interview and offered a position, just when I had become a new mom not quite ready to work. They accepted to wait for me, and on June 15, 1981, I assumed my responsibilities as technical support engineer in the Department of Labor, Pressure Vessels Division. Along with my colleagues, we had oversight over the Regulation, Codes and Standards, and the Inspection Program for the Province.

A few months later, I received a call from the Dean of Mechanical Engineering, the Co-Director of my Master's thesis. He was congratulating me, because two research papers we had submitted for publication in the *Journal of Mechanical Vibration* of the American Society of Mechanical Engineers (ASME) had been accepted, and I was invited to join him to an ASME technical conference to present my papers. It was my first encounter with ASME. I was still learning about my job, and had not yet realized that our Provincial Regulation for Boilers and Pressure Vessels was based on the ASME Boiler and Pressure Vessel Code (BPVC). In 1985 and the following years, major organizational changes occurred in our Department resulting in my being given more responsibilities. In 1989, I became the Chief Boiler Inspector for the Province, and the member representing Quebec on the ASME BPVC Conference Committee and the National Board. In 1991, I was elected to the Board of Trustees of the National Board, the first female ever to serve as a Trustee. Women were not only a minority in Mechanical Engineering, but even more so in the Boiler and Pressure Vessel industry. This was my first leadership position. I served my two-year term, and later decided that I wanted to get more involved with ASME committees.

The National Board and ASME always held a joint annual meeting, and encouraged members to attend and actively participate in ASME committees. Serving on ASME committees for a young woman engineer was rather intimidating, but also very challenging. I asked to be considered for appointment on ASME committees, and these meetings provided me access to many technical experts of my field. For more than two decades thereafter, I benefited from financial support from the Board, and for the time to serve from my employer. Evidently, I must have made a good case for myself, since I was also granted the time needed to travel and attend meetings. Often on those trips, I felt lonely with no other woman around, and was somewhat offended when people referred to me as a gentleman, or as Mr. Kotb. Before long I was voted "honorary gentleman," and started to be amused rather than offended. I also developed many friendships among these male colleagues, even some shopping buddies.

Madiha with ASME US and Canada National Board Members, seated between Albert Justin, ASME Executive Director (to her R), and Donald Tanner, ASME Chairman of the Board of Trustees (to her L), Anaheim, California, 1998

For the most part, my participation in ASME committees was technical work that could be justified as relating to my professional responsibilities. Then in 1993, came along the opportunity to serve at the ASME Board level, which was a step up toward a higher leadership position, with much more exposure than just my technical field. It was an offer I could not refuse; yet, I did not dare or even attempt to explain it to both my employer and the National Board, or to ask for their support. The Associate Executive Director of ASME, who had believed in me for years and whom I considered to be my mentor, was very upset to see my hesitation. To this day, I clearly remember him telling me: "Is it going to kill you if you ask and get 'No' for an answer? Just do it, and if they turn down your request, let me know and we will figure out something." Reluctantly once again I made a good case for myself and to my greatest surprise and pleasure, I received the needed support. It made me realize that, as individuals, we often create for ourselves obstacles that do not exist.

I continued to move up, and became ASME Vice President for Conformity Assessment in 2003; then further up again, serving on the Board of Governors from 2008 until 2011. Afterward, I attempted a shot at the Presidency, but was not successful the first time; I thought it was the end for me. My supporters, though, would not let go, and pressed me to give it another try. I was successful the second time; thus, in June 2012, I became the 132nd President of ASME, the fourth female President, and the first ever to reside outside the US. My presidential term, which ran from

June 2013 to June 2014, was definitely the highlight and epic of my career. That year saw me travelling around the world to meet the leaders of our profession in Brazil, China, India, Singapore, South Africa, Botswana, France, UK, UAE ... even in Canada and Egypt. There were also numerous opportunities to inspire students and early-career engineers, and show them that they too would have a chance to advance and reach the top.

Madiha, 132nd ASME President, receiving ASME seal, gavel, president badge and pin from Marc Goldsmith, 131st ASME President, at the President's Dinner, Indianapolis, 2013

Through the years and the course of my career, I was fortunate to meet people who believed in me, and gave me the chances they thought I deserved. I was not always convinced that I did, and was sometimes hesitant to take them, but I did take most of them. Those same people were also very generous with me, helping me to learn, and transferring their knowledge and expertise. That was invaluable, and in return I vowed to do likewise, always giving others a helping hand, and opportunities they deserve, in order to pursue their aspirations and reach their goals. Looking back, I must admit that Engineering was not just a profession, it was an integral part of my life. It is true that I was always drawn to engineering, but the more I think about it, the more I realize that I did not choose Mechanical Engineering, but that Mechanical Engineering rather chose me.

My life has not always been an easy ride, at time it felt as if I was on a rollercoaster. In retrospect, it was a great ride as I loved the way it turned out. You could say that I followed my destiny, seized opportunities, and took the chances that came my way. I led a balanced life, enjoyed both its professional and personal sides, and cherished my colleagues as much as I did my family and friends. I had the opportunity to visit and live in different places, and met and connected with great people whom I consider to be my real wealth and fortune. I often wonder if I could turn the clock back, what would I do differently? Honestly, I am sure I would not change a thing, although sometimes I regret that neither of my daughters Dahlia and Nora chose Engineering for their careers. Then again, life is all about choices, and they chose their own paths different from mine. Now, I get it: maybe they felt there were already too many engineers in our household, and no need for more. Looking at my two grandchildren, Noam and Samira, I wonder what the future holds for them. I only wish that they too find and take their chances in life, just like I did. It also occurs to me that maybe we just skipped a generation of engineers, perhaps someday they will follow in the footsteps of their grandmother: it definitely worked for me.

Montreal, December 2015

BREAKING NEW GROUNDS ON THE WAY TO THE TAEKWONDO HALL OF FAME

CAROLINE AMASIS MAHER

In the patriarchal and conservative society in which I was brought up, women often failed to achieve their full potential because they lacked self-confidence or did not acknowledge their talents. I was fortunate to be born into a supportive family that had high expectations for me, and encouraged me to reach for the stars. Unlike some of my friends, I never felt that I was treated differently from my two brothers. Early on, I had great ambitions, lofty goals, and a tremendous desire to succeed and make a difference. I wanted to be the best in anything I undertook, and knew that it would require full commitment and hard work. Positive reinforcement for a job well-done generally added to my self-confidence, prompted me to try harder, and ascertained my potential before my harshest critic: my own self.

At a young age, I discovered that I had a passion for physical activity and sports. When I was nowhere to be found, my parents would say: "Look for her on the court, any court." They were right. Once they realized the extent of my passion, they encouraged me to train and succeed. However, I never became too serious about any particular sport until age 10, when it was obvious that Taekwondo—a combative sport that crosses both gender and cultural boundaries—was my favorite. No matter how often I would come home beaten up and bruised, my mother supported me unfailingly. At that time, I had but one goal: to be good enough to beat the best player on the team, a girl who was threatened by "the rookie" I was, and whose hostility would lead her to kick me with unwarranted aggressiveness. After training for a few months, I was invited to accompany the little league of my club to Germany where I participated in an international championship. My very first trip out of the country brought me my very first silver medal. It was then that I realized I had a second passion beside Taekwondo: I loved to travel. Furthermore, the exhilaration of winning was a strong incentive that kept me going, I was eager to achieve more victories and earn more medals.

My performance at such a high level at this very young age caught the attention of coaches who were anxious to prepare me for other competitions. At that point, I had no idea how far I could go in that sport, although I was willing to sacrifice time on other sports to concentrate on Taekwondo. By age 12, having won a few additional medals, I was invited to train with the senior national team where the minimum age was 18: it was a dream come true. I also realized that in order to maintain my place at the top, I would have to invest thousands of hours in training, face multiple injuries, and go through severe diets for years, to remain within a specific weight category. Despite my busy schedule with Taekwondo, I started to develop an interest in soccer, and joined the school team. We won First Place in the ISSAC Soccer Tournament, in which all the international schools in our region participated. Then came the time to choose between the two; sadly, I gave up soccer to be able to concentrate exclusively on Taekwondo.

At age 14, I felt absolutely terrified when I had to participate in championships with the professionals of the senior national team who were 18 and older. Nevertheless, I was determined to embark on this new venture, cognizant that it would be a formidable undertaking, but also a process of self-discovery. Continuing to compete and win, I started to have Olympic dreams, and set a new goal for myself: becoming an Olympic champion. In the process, the training became more and more demanding, exceeding anything I could have ever imagined. It brought out in me endurance I did not know I had. Every step seemed to carry me closer to my goal, and I learned not to let fear hold me back from achieving greatness. To dissipate the anxiety, I worked even harder, and focused on one day at a time, in order to accomplish more. Fortunately, I had confident and supportive coaches who had faith in me. Over time, my travels took me to more distant places to compete and earn more medals. With each recognition, my passion intensified, my resolve doubled, firmly convinced that I was well placed to reach my destination. I also set higher standards for myself, believing that it would take every ounce of energy, focus, and determination to reach the superlative results I had in mind.

At age 15, I placed 5th in the Women's World Taekwondo Championship; and at 16, I earned a silver medal in the Francophone World Games, competing against professionals in their 20s and 30s. For my outstanding achievements, the Egyptian Ministry of Youth and Sports recognized me among the best 10 athletes in the country, for three consecutive years. I was the only female Taekwondo player on the Egyptian Olympic Program preparing for the 2004 Athens Games. The taxing routine required that I take several days off from school, in order to travel to distant camps where I trained three times a day. I knew that the inflexibility of the school system, the inadequate training facilities, and the lack of support for this sport would make it an uphill battle for me in an elite international competition, but I never flinched, and never considered backing out. Despite the many obstacles, I managed to maintain a straight A in my studies while continuing to train and advancing in my sport. Taekwondo was my reason to live, and I was not about to let anything come between me and my dream.

With increased pressure on my time, I had to drop from school for one semester, in order to give all I could to the Olympic preparation program. It included daily training of up to seven hours, at camps in other countries, requiring months of absence away from home. Perhaps the most excruciating part was the rigorous diet, especially for a growing teenager of my age. To maintain my weight, I was allowed to eat only an egg for breakfast, a salad for lunch, and an apple for dinner; and for two weeks or up to a month before a championship, an apple was all I could eat all day. Despite the ordeal, I was determined to do whatever it was going to take to stay fit and achieve my dream. Suddenly, three months prior to the 2004 games, came the devastating and heartbreaking news: another player was going to replace me on the team. That person lacked my training and track record, but had powerful connections. Evidently for the decision makers, Egypt's chance of winning and I did not matter.

For a month, I neither watched nor played Taekwondo and wanted to quit, but I just could not bring myself to do it. The better part of me advised that I should not leave the dream behind and must try again for the next games, in four years. I also remembered the maxim: "What does not break you makes you stronger!" I returned to training with even stronger determination, intent on earning a medal at the 2008 Beijing Games. By then, it was time for graduation from high school. In recognition of my record, the administration honored me with an "Outstanding Academic & Athletic Performance Award."

Shortly thereafter, I entered the American University in Cairo (AUC), as the recipient of an Honor Scholarship for Sports Achievement. The challenges were even greater now, with a hectic schedule requiring intensive Taekwondo training, increased academic assignments, strict deadlines, and class attendance. Trying to excel on two separate fronts—curricular and extra-curricular activities—taught me to be extremely organized and disciplined, and to use my time effectively. Again, I had to drop from school for a semester and make up for the credits later, in order to move forward toward the achievement of my dream. Training harder and more vigorously, I was proving to myself, more than I did for anyone else, that I was capable of doing much more than I ever thought possible. I was getting stronger, fitter, faster, even lighter, with every passing day. There were times of doubt, but my loving parents were always by my side. I could open up to them and share my insecurities; they supported me and taught me to accept and appreciate who I was, despite the insecurities.

To be a competitive athlete fully dedicated to my sport required an implacable lifestyle, and an excruciating exercise program to hone my skills. On the way to reaching my goal, I was driven to have unhealthy eating habits and exercise in an obsessive manner, in order to keep my weight down, and ensure that I would participate in the 2008 Beijing Olympic Games. I was willing to do anything, even purposely starve myself, to make sure I would not gain a single ounce. Some days, I cried myself to sleep out of hunger, and could not even speak due to extreme exhaustion.

Once again in 2008, I was not selected on the Olympic Team. For the second time, knavery and bribery killed my dream. I lost faith in the system, and had to recognize that quality of performance was not the basis of selection; corruption, dishonesty, and favoritism reigned within the Egyptian Taekwondo Federation. I bitterly felt that four more years of hard work were for naught, and once again, I was about to quit. Yet, realizing that I had already sacrificed much, and having nothing to lose, I should try one last time for the 2012 London Olympic Games. I wanted never to have any regrets. Thus, picking myself up and gathering more courage, I started to train again, with the full support of my family and my coaches, and put behind me all the negative thoughts. Instead, I focused on the gold medal, expecting London to be one of the greatest moments of my life, and hoping that my achievements would inspire other Egyptian women to pursue their dreams.

In 2009, I ranked 3rd worldwide in Taekwondo, which stimulated my determination to continue the fight for my dream. That year, I also received the Bachelor degree in Integrated Marketing Communication with High Honors, and was second runner-up for the Parental Association Cup Award, presented to a graduating senior demonstrating outstanding academic and extracurricular achievements. Throughout my four years at AUC, I had managed to be on the Dean's Honors List, earning several accolades, including among others, the Award for Excellence for Best Positioning for my graduation project, presented by the JWT Agency; and the Award for Excellence for the Best Overall Presentation on a Campaign for Girls' Education. Additionally, I received seven gold medals in the annual Universities Championship, the Best Player Award for four consecutive years, as well as the title of 2009 Best Athlete. I also participated in the University Olympics, gaining 8th place in the World University Taekwondo Championship. Best of all, seven days after graduation, I was offered a position at Allianz, where I was fortunate to have as Manager Rasha Reda, the Head of Human Resources, who remains my role model to this day. She was caring and supporting, and thanks to her understanding, I was able to train two or three times daily while maintaining my full-time job. Once again, it was extremely challenging; but, for me, challenges are a way of life.

In 2010, recognizing that I was growing older, and constantly pushing myself beyond my limits, I started to be concerned about my health. I consulted my coaches about changing the weight category with which I had stuck for nearly10 years, in order to enhance my performance. That year, I succeeded in maintaining my ranking as 6th worldwide. However, in 2011, I faced the greatest and most unexpected challenge of my life. By sheer coincidence, having never been notified, I found out that I had been suspended by the World Taekwondo Federation (WTF) for allegedly testing positive for steroids. Needless to say, it was emotionally and mentally devastating to learn that, after the formidable efforts and the years I had invested in that sport, my reputation would be tarnished. I was not about to accept this damning accusation, and now had to fight for my name.

Together with my mom, we identified Paul Greene, an outstanding sports attorney who accepted to take my case. His fees not only drained my entire savings, but forced me to borrow from my parents and get a bank loan. My case was pleaded before the Court Arbitration of Sports (CAS) in Lausanne, Switzerland: the sample containing the steroids was not mine. After seven agonizing months, the CAS finally ruled in my favor, ordering the highest compensation in the history of sports for my legal fees, and I became the first athlete in history to win a case against the powerful WTF at the CAS. Apparently, they did not expect a woman from a developing country to stand up to that organization, but they did not know who I was. After what I had gone through over the years to make a name for myself as one of the world's finest Taekwondo athletes, I was not about to lose it for a serious error of mixed-up sample on the part of the World Federation.

Surprisingly or perhaps unsurprisingly, the Egyptian Taekwondo Federation refused to let me participate in the Olympic Qualifications; I was unable to be in 2012 London Games. It was vexing to realize that my dream as an Olympic champion was over, that I would never be part of the Olympics. There were no regrets, though, for there was nothing else I could have done. In 2015, I retired from professional participation in

Taekwondo, and established a new set of goals. I must admit, however, that it was one of the most difficult decisions I have ever had to make, and the period of transition into life without professional sport most unsettling.

Caroline at home surrounded by her 130 medals and trophies, Cairo, 2015

Caroline (R) with her mom, Rosana Mourad, at the ceremony of her induction into the Taekwondo Hall of Fame, Las Vegas, 2013.

As I look back at my 17 years in sports, I have to say that I will always value what they brought me: unparalleled learning opportunities, and a chance to travel the world over, discovering amazing places and fascinating cultures. While the obstacles were great, the rewards were even greater. During those years, I represented my country among the finest players, and earned 130 trophies in 39 countries, for various national, regional, international, Arab, African, and Francophone championships. I also became a 5th Dan International Black Belt Holder, and a Certified Senior Coach and International Referee.[1] In 2013, I was the first African woman to be inducted into the Taekwondo Hall of Fame, the most prestigious title that any athlete could be awarded; and, in 2014, I was recognized in the United Nations Global Campaign "Women of Achievement," a series of portraits spotlighting remarkable women who reached the top in their respective fields, by overcoming barriers and beating the odds to reach their goals. Additionally, I became a well-known role model for young women, and was invited as guest speaker in several Arab countries to represent Outstanding Arab Women. This year, I had the opportunity to add my own TED Talk at TEDx Women, and last but not least, I was the first person in Egypt to propose a Para-Taekwondo National Team to the Egyptian Taekwondo Federation.

Caroline beside her name among the Women of Achievement recognized by the United Nations, UN Headquarters, Cairo, 2014.

Participation in sports at the highest high level has been stimulating and enriching, but the life of an athlete is not as much fun as it may appear from the outside, for there are significant hardships to overcome before one becomes a decorated athlete. Living for a dream, focusing on sports, and dedicating all of one's time and effort to succeed also means becoming socially and emotionally isolated. It requires exacting sacrifices that make you feel different, and appreciate those closest to you, family and friends who understand how special you are. As athletes, we are overstressed, always focused on numbers as we try to excel and stay at the top.

I am currently employed as Human Resource Manager at Peugeot Egypt, the youngest manager on board. I believe that one of the main reasons for my professional success at my age is the support of my inspiring boss, Nevine Ellabban, the Chair and Chief Executive Officer, who has an unsurpassed ability to deliver results, and whose positive attitude and great personality motivate me, as well as the other managers. I am also a HR Manager and Consultant for "Helm," a nonprofit NGO that seeks to promote employment and integration of Egypt's 15-17 million people with disabilities (PWD) into all aspects of life. My work with "Helm" has taught me two important lessons: first, each person can make an impact; second, you must surround yourself with positive energy.

To my great surprise, I was recently selected among the five best women referees in Africa to attend the 2015 International Taekwondo Referee Camp, where those who will serve in the Rio de Janeiro Games will be chosen. Perhaps another plan is in the making for me, a different way to be part of the Olympics and achieve my dream. Furthermore, this year, I completed my MBA in Human Resource Management at Victoria University of Switzerland, ranking 1st in my class. I was also selected among 16 amazing women to participate in the 2015 Global Sports Mentorship Program (GSMP)—an initiative to improve women's empowerment through sports, sponsored by the US State Department, and administrated by the Center for Sports, Peace and Society at the University of Tennessee. This program has been a life changing experience, for it made me realize that women face similar challenges all over the world. Two professors in that program, Dr. Sarah Hillyer and Dr. Ashleigh Huffman, have been a source of great inspiration that contributed to honing my leadership skills. I believe that each of us has a mission on earth, mine may very well be to help PWD to unlock their potential and achieve their dreams. I have always enjoyed inspiring others, and hope to use my skills to empower others and improve their lives through sports.

Two unexpected surprises occurred as I was putting the final touches to the present chapter. In late 2015, I was notified of my selection among 25 female athletes to participate in a global mentoring program designed by the Ernst & Young (EY) Athletes Business Network, and the International Women's Forum (IWF), to harness the untapped leadership potential of female athletes after their retirement from sport. However, the most exciting and most overwhelming piece of news occurred on New Year's Eve 2015, when I learned of my appointment as Senator—the youngest appointed member ever to serve in the Senate! According to the Constitution, the President has the right to name 28 Senators, in other words 5% of the Senate. I am thrilled to have the opportunity to serve my country in that capacity, and to work with the 87 women Senators out of the total of 596—another historic record for women.

To put things in perspective, as I look back on events of the past few years, I must say that not being supported by the Egyptian Taekwondo Federation for the Olympics has been more than compensated by numerous other rewards. To my family that sacrificed a great deal to accompany me on my unusual journey, I want to let them know that it is thanks to them that I am who I am today. If I was able to go through many sleepless nights, time constraints, stress and breakdowns, it is because of their presence by my side. Life is a journey not a destination, we learn along the way; we grow when we struggle, and we celebrate our victories when we succeed. This is not the end of my journey, it is only the beginning since I am still in my 20s. I intend to continue to work hard, and juggle career, social work and sports; all of which are demanding tasks, but my determination, self-confidence, and strength are inexhaustible.

Cairo, January 2016

Notes

[1] The Dan ranking system is used by many Asian organizations to indicate the level of one's ability or expertise in a given field. The Chinese character for Dan literally means step or stage, and generally refers to one's ranking or grade.

ONCE A REBEL ALWAYS A REBEL

MONA MAKRAM EBEID

The Early Years

From the day I was born, and even before as mother often recounted, I had given her no peace. I caused her such labor pains during three days that I had to be pulled out with forceps by the nimble hands of the most illustrious gynecologist of the time, Naguib Pasha Mahfouz. As a child I had been an *enfant terrible* as my natural instinct was toward rebellion, which compelled my mother to place me in the famous Pensionnat Notre Dame de Sion, a French Catholic school, as she and her mother had attended a similar institution in Cairo, the Pensionnat du Sacré Cœur. In her view, only a Catholic education would tame my rebellious nature and I became a boarder, as my nanny, an Austrian *Fraulein* who took care of both my brother and me, threatened to leave otherwise.

Ironically, these were the happiest days of my turbulent childhood life, although punishments for my disobedience and disrespect for authority were plenty. Three years after my enrollment in the school, I was expelled in the midst of the year for having distributed to my classmates a song by famous French singer Edith Piaf called *"Hymne à l'amour,"* where she says *"Je renierai Dieu pour toi!"* [I will deny God for your sake]. This was too much for the good sisters who insisted that I had written it at 9-years old—a proof that I was devilish. I must say, however, that it is my French education that gave me the solid intellectual baggage that I carried all along my life, although my rebellion against parental and school discipline shaped and dominated my whole childhood and adolescence, confirming the fact that one does not become a rebel by chance. Next it was the English Girls' College in Alexandria, the famous and elitist EGC, where you needed to be highly sponsored to be accepted. So my father asked Prince Saïd Toussoun, his close school friend and a member of the school's board, to sponsor me which he did. These were blissful years where my whole personality blossomed, as I had broken free from my father's authoritarian yoke—although I revered him—by being once more a boarder.

By that time, the 1952 Egyptian Revolution had taken place, but a residue remained of the cosmopolitan mosaic of languages and nationalities that had characterized Egypt during the *ancien régime*, particularly Alexandria. So the girls in school just as our family's milieu were Egyptian, Lebanese, Italians, Greeks, Armenians, British, French, Muslims, Christians and Jews who intermingled in a world that bore a remarkable resemblance to Laurence Durrell's Alexandria Quartet. The very language we spoke reflected this cosmopolitanism. Like the old Russian aristocracy, the Egyptian upper class was polyglot and particularly prone to lapsing into French or English, though French was considered "our" language.

It is in this liberal upbringing, whether at school or in my family, that I grew up. The variety of extracurricular activities that a prestigious British school offers definitely marked me forever. Sports of all sorts figured prominently in our daily schedule: from hockey, to tennis and handball, to swimming and swimming ballet, all were part and parcel of our education. And when I became games captain of my class, this honor compensated my very poor record in mathematics. Another activity that definitely left its mark on my future life was being member of the Dramatic Society, which meant acting in the annual theater performance presented by the school. So from "Pride and Prejudice" to "Macbeth" and "Iphigenia in Tauris," I revelled in acting which served me well later on when I had to face enormous audiences, whether at the university or during my political campaigns. On the other hand, this liberal upbringing instilled in me a sense of volunteerism, as we were asked to donate from our own pocket money what was called "hospital money."

From there, I attended the American University in Cairo (AUC), graduating in Political Sociology and was so enamored with academe that I never left it for 24 years, and became a teaching and research assistant, then a Post Master's Fellow. I had excellent teachers, but the one who really had an impact on me was Dr. Saad Eddin Ibrahim, world-renowned Egyptian sociologist and leading intellectual, my real mentor to whom I owe much of what I had become. His incisive mind, added to his encyclopedic knowledge, definitely left their mark on me. His instinct for collaboration propelled me to join him in many of his numerous activities: first at the Ahram Center for Strategic Studies, followed by a new independent political organization modeled after the British Fabian Society, then the Arab Thought Forum in Jordan where I eventually became an Executive Board Member, and as a Founding Member of the Ibn Khaldun Center, which advocated for democracy and free civil society. He had made a lifelong mission of championing the rights of women and minorities, and the spirit that he symbolized and instilled in us was a harbinger of things to come.

As for my years at AUC, I was greatly gratified by two appreciative moments: one, when I was asked to become the main speaker at the Commencement of the graduating class of 1995; the other when I was awarded the Distinguished Alumni Award by our beloved AUC President the late John Gerhard. Meanwhile, thanks to a Fulbright scholarship which I had obtained due to the recommendation of the AUC Dean of Students, I was enrolled at the Harvard Kennedy School of Government. My two years there have certainly been a turning point both in my life and my career. The extensive use of the case study method, unfamiliar to me up until then, enabled me to expose new analytical frameworks and the latest research within a context of real world executive decision-making. From the enriching curriculum and distinguished faculty, to the peer learning and lifelong networks, it provided me with the richest learning experience of my life. It is there also that I met many world renowned personalities in politics, academe, and others, such as Crown Prince Hassan of Jordan, with whom I have kept a solid friendship until this day, Israeli Minister Aba Ebban, Lebanese President Amin Al Jumayel, US Senator Ted Kennedy, and Benino Aquino before his assassination. Most dignitaries who came to the US paid a visit to Harvard.[1]

Returning Home

Upon returning to Egypt, I decided to embark on a political career, as Harvard had instilled in me an openness to different perspectives and an instinct for collaboration. It prompted me to join the newly established Wafd Party under the leadership of Fouad Sarag El Din, an opposition party "loyal" to a certain extent to the ruling regime. From a very early age, I was bitten by politics and a passion for history. In fact, most of my favorite readings were concentrated on the lives of world leaders, famous women, and war heroes, which fostered an argumentative spirit that became inherent. I could have easily worked with the government rather than join the opposition, but my family background and the pattern of rebellion against authority that began when I was still a child impelled me to the New Wafd. I chose opposition, rather than accommodation, and this stance was maintained for an appreciable period of my life, up until the Revolution of 30 June 2013. My family background had a great deal to do with my choice. My father had been a Wafdist parliamentarian prior to the1952 Revolution, but the major influence on my early life was my uncle, the patriarch of the Makram Ebeid family.[2] He was one of the prominsnt leaders of the 1919 Revolution,, who had been exiled by the British to the Seychelles with Saad Zaghloul, and who knew the Quran almost by heart—a rarity for any Egyptian let alone for a Coptic Christian.

Mona as a child, in the arms of family patriarch Makram Ebeid

It is his aura that surrounded me since I was a child, as I lived with him more than I did with my own parents. When they used to complain to him that they were unable to curb my willfulness, he would reply: "Let her be, she has a personality of her own," often adding "heyya el waheeda elly talaaly" (she is the only one taking after me). The occasional indications he gave of his pride in me would make my heart swell with joy, and made a lasting impression on me. He catapulted the family name into national politics by being a key figure in the Egyptian national movement of 1919.

Among the reasons that impelled me to join the New Wafd was that I firmly believed in securing intergenerational continuity in the family's legacy. I wanted to become their standard bearer in the political arena, moved by my desire to perpetuate its national political prominence.

My entrance into politics was far from smooth. I had to struggle against considerable odds mainly from my family. As staunch Upper-Egyptian male chauvinists—although all had studied at the best universities abroad—they refused the idea of a woman in politics. As long as it was in academe, it was acceptable, even honorable, but active politics was "a man's business." Once again, my rebellious character against patriarchal authority drove me to defy them. As a result: I was ostracized for a long period, but greatly energized by the strong backing of Makram-Ebeid's widow, an 85-year old aunt/grandmother who saw in me the seeds of a future political leader, and who put all her weight behind me. In fact, when I first ran for Parliament, she called on some of her husband's old supporters, those who were still alive, to help and support me—a fact that says a great deal about women, no matter how old they are.

Once a member of the New Wafd, politics was nothing short of an obsession, it governed every aspect of my life, from the most banal incident or conversation to the most important issues. I became Rapporteur of the Committee on Foreign Relations under the leadership of one of the most the famous constitutional lawyers in the Arab region, Dr. Waheed Raafat, from whom I learned a great deal. I also chose to teach civic education, and became the intellectual mentor of many young Wafdist of the time, who still remember me. The crowd attending my twice-a-week lectures included a real mixture, from carpenters and plumbers, to newly entrants in the media, mainly journalists and TV employees. Once the Party established a newspaper, I became a regular weekly columnist who contributed a great deal to its public prominence, particularly since my articles did not always toe the line of the Party's more conservative stance.[3]

On the whole, and to this day, both politics and my academic profession have been central to my life, which helps to account for my small family size: only one child. In 1987, I ran for parliamentary elections on the Wafd ticket, under a system of party lists. During two months, with my colleagues on the list, all men, we paid daily visits to the different areas of the north district of Cairo, which included extremely populous areas, such as Shobra, El Sahel, Zawya El Hamra, and Rod El Farag. It was an absolutely fascinating experience as I was treated as an "honorary gentleman," meaning that I could enter cafés and even play backgammon with the clients, and go to places traditionally not frequented by women. Once in the public arena, I was told there were no restrictions on my campaign. I was given the opportunity to visit with families in their homes, something men could not do according to local customs. This allowed me as a sociologist to have a hands-on experience of the different strata of society, learn about their harsh daily lives, their frustrations, and their aspirations for their children.

In 1990, my Party decided to boycott the upcoming elections, a decision I staunchly opposed. In the meantime, I was chosen by the US National Democratic Institute (NDI) to be an observer of the elections in Pakistan—a first for an Arab woman. There, I asked Benazir Bhutto who was campaigning in her constituency while harassed by daily accusations, if she had ever thought of boycotting the elections. Her reply was: "Never! Any representation is better than no representation." Empowered by this statement, I had it published upon my return in one of the main newspapers as a clear message to my Party about my position.

Later that year, I was appointed to the Parliament by President Hosni Mubarak. It was almost a first, as hardly ever was an opposition member "appointed"; therefore, it was expected of him/her to join the ruling National Democratic Party (NDP). I chose to remain Independent, as I was asked by my Party to resign upon acceptance of the appointment; but little did I know that the position of Independent did not exist in our political culture. You are either "with us or against us," and extra-parliamentary authorities expected compliance from a Presidential appointee. So it was, within this atmosphere and hemmed in by these constraints, that I had to function, never losing my enthusiasm for the game of democracy. Linguistic assets, family background, education, and personal drive were valuable tools in entering Parliament. However, even more than privileged birth, education was the hallmark of success, and I must acknowledge the fact that I would not have achieved as much as I did in politics without the excellent educational foundation provided by my parents, despite the fact that my major childhood trauma was the death of my father.

My professional expertise, as well as my linguistic fluency in French, English, Arabic, and Italian, served my frequent inclusion in Parliamentary delegations travelling overseas, in particular the International Parliamentary Union, Parliamentarians for Global Action, as well as the Union of French-Speaking Countries. I was awarded the prestigious title of *Commandeur de la Pléiade* by the Board of the *Association Internationale des Parlementaires de Langue Française*, and knighted *Chevalier de la Légion d'Honneur* by President François Mitterrand, and later promoted *Officier de la Légion d'Honneur* by President Nicolas Sarkozy. Furthermore, party work and contacts have enabled me to make a substantive contribution to debates and discussions on the making of laws, and to represent Egypt abroad.

Being a member of the opposition has often been dangerous, but satisfying to the soul, and it enabled me to circumvent the bias against women in politics and earn a place in Egypt's political landscape. I was looked upon as an ambiguous role model for women, one that stimulated discomfort as well as emulation, for I chose to participate not as a leader of women, but as a woman leader. I was always convinced of the close, positive, and reciprocal link between national development and progress for women, because I considered that education was more important for girls than for boys, and that the development of Egypt and progress for its women went hand-in-hand. In 1995, that conviction drove me to found the Association for the Advancement of Education (AAE) that I led for thirteen years, and for which I obtained an observer status at the UN. Apart from dealing with hundreds of schools in the most deprived areas, with support from the Swiss-Egyptian Fund, the goal was to try to change the conventional notions of behavior regarding a wide range of issues through civic education and awareness.

In most of my interventions in Parliament, I focused on the importance of civil society and against the limitations on NGOs due to the restricting law of 1964 that authorized the government to interfere with their work. I was heckled by opponents of the proposal, mainly the ruling government party, and had almost no support except from leftist intellectuals, such as Lotfy El Khouly, Philip Gallab, and Khaled Mohei El Din. The exposure to competing ideas and belief systems that I had acquired at Harvard nurtured an ability to reconcile ideologies and their component ideas that are, to many, fundamentally contradictory and hence irreconcilable. This ability accounts for the fact that, regardless of my position in the opposition and personal changes in the regime, I remained in close contact with powerful individuals, including, among others, Drs. Osama El Baz and Mostafa El Fikky, two prominent advisors to Mubarak. Also and interestingly, as a scion of the ancien régime by family background, and not a Nasserist though an admirer of Nasser, I was able to survive politically in the Sadat and Mubarak eras, despite being in the opposition.

While in Parliament, my professional expertise and my instinct for collaboration have propelled me in a series of roles, including the following: Member of the World Bank Advisory Team for the Middle East North Africa Region; Member of the UNDP Capacity 21 Initiative and Regional Specialist for the Arab States 2001-2003; Founding Member of the Egyptian Council for International Affairs; the Arab Organization for

Mona with Nelson Mandela, in Stellenbosch, South Africa, 1994

Child Development; the Center of Strategic Studies in Washington; the Anti-Corruption and Transparency Committee of the Ministry of Local Administration; Advisor to the Minister of Labor, Immigration and Manpower for issues pertaining to Egyptians Abroad; and Advisor to the Supreme Council of the Armed Forces (SCAF) following the 2011 Revolution.

In 2010, at the behest of my supporters and my Party, I ran for elections in Shubra El Khema (north of Cairo). Although I am no fan of the quota system recently introduced for women, I accepted to be a Wafd candidate for the women's seat. As I had done previously, I conducted a vigorous campaign focusing on my work as Board Member of the Amal (Hope) Organization, an NGO whose main task was to give loans to needy people, especially women, to start small-scale enterprises, modeled after the Grameen Bank of Muhammad Yunis. It allowed me to stress community service, and show public spiritedness and the ability to get things done, apart from achieving a distinctive political credibility.

Although declared a winner at the end of the election, and results announced on television the same evening, my name was eliminated the next day on the false pretense that my NDP rival who had 700 votes less than me had won the seat. Clearly, my vocal criticism of the regime, particularly the dynastic succession plan of the President's son, worked against me. The 2010 elections were to be one of the main sparks of the 2011 Revolution. They have proven to be the worst elections the nation has ever seen, in terms of flagrant vote buying, rigging, thuggery, and manipulated voter lists.

Mona with Hilary Clinton at Menesterly Palace, Cairo, 1995

A New Dawn

On January 25, 2011, Egypt found itself in the throes of a Revolution. Joining the country's young women and men, I found myself engulfed during 18 days in Tahrir Square chanting with the demonstrators "Bread.

Dignity. Social Justice." Among the many amazing signs that a "New Egypt" was born, sexual harassment disappeared from a site where massive crowds of hundreds of thousands of women and men were literally crushed together. Overnight, we as Egyptians had ceased to be objects, and became responsible citizens taking charge of our own security after disappearance of the police.

Another remarkable feature of this unique popular Revolution was the conviviality and solidarity between Muslims and Christians. A spirit of tolerance and brotherhood saw the Crescent embracing the Cross on hundreds of banners, with Copts standing guard around Muslims performing their prayers and Muslims hoisting the Bible along with the Quran: absolutely amazing. Among the many challenges the youth movement faced, the most significant was the fact that it was essentially a leaderless Revolution. I remember asking one of my student protestors: "Who is your leader?" to be told with great self-assurance: "When you are in a boat, you all row together, you do not need anyone to guide you." Although the most crucial of the Revolution's demands remain unfulfilled, history will remember the immeasurable courage and self-sacrifice of these young people.

Following the 2011 Revolution, I was appointed to the Advisory Committee of the Supreme Council of the Armed Forces; and in 2013, I entered the Shura Council (Senate) as one of 4 Coptic appointed members recommended by newly seated Coptic Pope Tawadros. This was quite an experience, as the Senate was entirely dominated by members of the Muslim Brotherhood and the Salafis. However, we, the non-Islamists, managed to form an opposition bloc of seventy members who were active in the process of resistance to government encroachment on the main institutions. One of my main battles in the Senate was to resist the retrogressive change that the new leadership of 2012 wanted to impose, and to pressure instead for progressive change. We often found ourselves in the crosswinds of a fierce maelstrom of political jockeying and had to weather a barrage of attacks, but the majority was unable to secure our compliance. We offered our resignation and joined the historic upheaval of June 30, 2013, that a cross-section of millions of Egyptians were setting in motion in rejection of the theocratic system in the making.[4]

Conclusion

As I think back about my experiences, my first reading assignment at AUC comes to mind. It was an essay by C. Wright Mills entitled "On Intellectual Craftsmanship" that offered a number of ideas that have served

Mona with Field Marshall Abdel Fattah El-Sisi, then-Minister of Defense, Cairo, January 2014

me well over the years. I learned these principles of craftsmanship during my studies at AUC, then later applied them at Harvard, and have since drawn on them many times in my career. They played a particularly important role in my decision to join Parliament. When I first entered AUC, I had no political ambition whatsoever; my goal was to become a university professor. Yet, when the multi-party system was consolidated, my decision to pursue a seat in Parliament was based on three considerations. First, I felt a strong obligation to participate in the decision-making process in my country, rather than simply sit on the sideline and offer criticism. Second, I had a desire to apply my academic training to the many problems that Egypt confronts. I was trained as a sociologist at AUC, where I acquired the skills for objective, dispassionate analysis of society and its problems, particularly in the areas of education and foreign policy. Thirdly, I believed that women must overcome the cultural barriers that prevent them from participating fully in public life. In 2011, I was appointed to the Supreme Council of the Arrmed Forces (SCAF), and had the opportunity to meet Field Marshall Abdel Fattah El-Sisi, then-Minister of Defense, whom I later supported as President of Egypt. I am convinced that public service has made me, if not a better

Egyptian, perhaps a more grateful Egyptian—realizing what a privileged country Egypt is, and what creative, friendly, and tolerant people Egyptians are. We have every reason to be proud of our past history and accomplishments, and have confidence in our ability to meet successfully the challenges ahead: building a civil society and a democratic system, and strengthening civility and tolerance in our Nation as a whole.

Cairo, November 2015

Notes

[1] Between contacts made at Harvard University, and subsequently as a Member of Parliament, I had the opportunity to meet personally with many world leaders, and have photos with most of them. They include, among others, Nelson Mandela; Madeleine Albright; Hillary Clinton; Queen Sylvia of Sweden through my work fighting drug addiction; Sheikha Lobna Al Kassimi, the first female minister in the UAE, with whom I shared a panel in New York on Arab businesswomen; President Jimmy Carter; Greek President George Papandreou; President Bill Clinton; French Prime Minister Alain Juppé; French President Nicolas Sarkozy; Queen Rania of Jordan; Sheikha Moza of Qatar; Yasser Arafat; Itamar Rabinovich, Israel's Ambassador to the US, with whom I shared membership in the group Search for Common Ground; and Emma Bonino, Italian Minister of Foreign Affairs, longtime friend, and fellow parliamentarian.

[2] In 2015, on the occasion of the centennial of my uncle's birth, I published a book entitled *Kalimat wa mawakef* (Words and Situations), to memorialize his long and distinguished career in public life. The book has been reviewed in the daily *El Masry el Yom*, http://today.almasryalyoum.com/article2.aspx?ArticleID=479495&IssueID=3736. November 15, 2015.

[3] While at Harvard, I published my first piece of journalism in *The Christian Science Monitor* entitled "Mubarak is His Own Man," in 1981.

[4] As a result, in 2013, I was offered the *Prix du Combat Politique*, the famous annual award given to a public figure by the Moroccan Amadeus Institute, under the patronage of King Muhammad VI of Morocco.

LIVING INTENTIONALLY ACROSS "BOUNDARIES": THE CHALLENGES OF PROFESSIONAL REINVENTION

HELENE MOUSSA

Formative Years

Living across national and socio-cultural boundaries has been my way of life since birth. My father was a product of the 1920s Egyptian Revolution against British occupation. The rallying banner of the party he supported, Al Wafd, was "Religion belongs to God and the Nation to all. Long live the Crescent and the Cross." Despite his modest family background, he managed to receive a Bachelor's degree in Law from Cairo University, and eventually a PhD in International Law from the University of Leeds in the UK. He was among the pioneer Egyptian diplomats of the period. Stationed in Washington, DC (1924–1927), he met my mother, an American and a Roman Catholic. A marriage like theirs may not seem unique in today's world, but in the 1920s it was rather radical for an American woman to marry an "African," let alone for her family, one who was not a Roman Catholic. One of the most important values upheld and modelled by my parents, albeit in different ways, was acceptance of the "other" in a very deep and personal way, irrespective of creed, class, cultural origin, or race.

After Washington, my father was posted in Berlin, where my older brother Michel was born; Ethiopia, where my brother Farag and I were born; then Italy, and Spain. While we lived briefly in Egypt in-between these diplomatic missions, it was not until 1939 that we settled in Egypt. That same year, my father had to leave the diplomatic service because of a law barring Egyptian diplomats from being married to foreigners, and was transferred to the government's legal administration as Deputy Royal Counselor at the State Council. To this day, Ethiopia has had a very special place personally and professionally in our family. My father's seven year diplomatic mission in Ethiopia and relationship with the Emperor Haile Selassie I in particular continued long after our departure in 1935. My brother, Farag, published a book on our father's diplomatic career, in which the longest chapter is on Ethiopia: *Egyptien et diplomate*, *Farag Moussa* (Paris: Riveneuve, 2014; English translation forthcoming). Because of my father's close relation with the emperor, I was honored to have Empress Menen as my godmother—a bond that extended beyond the baptismal ritual. The following pages will indicate how I continued these family ties in my professional career.

A second important value my brothers and I learned from my father's professional career, and one which he impressed upon us, was that "education was a privilege to be put at the service of society and the Nation." That principle was reinforced when I attended the American University in Cairo, particularly by Visiting Professor Aida Guindi, on sabbatical leave from her position at the UN Social Development Department in New York, and a role model who taught me more concrete ways how to serve the social development of my country. Significantly, while my MA at the University of Washington was in Sociology, I also took courses in Social Work, as I wanted to have a hands-on practical approach to my studies and future career. Other role models for me were Huda Sha'arawi, nationalist and founder of the Egyptian Feminist Movement in the 1920s; Doria Shafik, one of the main leaders of Egypt's Women's Liberation Movement in the mid-1940s, whose efforts resulted in the Egyptian women being constitutionally allowed to vote; and Marie Assaad, who also tells her story in the present volume. My father, Aida, and others—as different as their backgrounds were—served as sources of inspiration to sustain me in the professional challenges I faced as an adult, and enabled me to reinvent myself professionally in the various countries where I resided.

Education for Change

In 1957, my mother and I left Egypt for Ethiopia, my father having passed away eleven years earlier. Initially, I worked in the In-Service Department of the Ministry of Education, which provided me with a good introduction to the social and educational needs of the country. Within a year, I was asked to become Co-Director of the Medical Social Work Program in the Ministry of Public Health. Started by Anna-Ma Toll, a UNICEF consultant from Sweden, it was to become the first School of Social Work in Ethiopia offering a diploma at the University College at

Addis Ababa and, a few years later, an undergraduate BA degree at Haile Selassie I University.

Eventually, I became the Dean of that School, with a mandate that students be trained in a generic approach to social work, strongly geared to the social development of their country. The curriculum had to be different from traditional programs in the Western world, with an emphasis on community development and organization. Student placements in the field were literally creating social and community services as part of their practical training requirements. The faculty, including myself, taught specific courses, and were involved in various advisory capacities in new and ongoing social agencies, while being responsible for fieldwork supervision. Thus, integrating and interrelating theory and practice was not an abstract concept but a lived experience. As educators, we had to adapt and recreate available literature to the reality of Ethiopia. Our key questions were if and, if so, how we were making a difference to the lives of the people and the institutions we served. This was my first professional experience of plunging into a situation in which I had to cross various academic boundaries, never knowing what would come out at the other end of the process. I was fortunate to have a dedicated and capable staff committed to this form of education, and especially students willing to engage with the teaching-learning approach of the curriculum.

In 1976, the school was closed because of the Marxist Revolution that took over the country; social work was now considered "bourgeois." Over the years, I learned to let go when I moved on, and to accept the fact that those who would take over after me would have their own imprint. I also realized that the needs of a country change over time, and therefore what I had attempted to do at that point would necessarily look very different than when I first started a job. Interestingly, in 2002, a decade after the 1991 Marxist government's fall, and thirty-four years after leaving Ethiopia, I was invited as a consultant by one of the services our student field placement had created, to assist in developing short- and long-range planning strategies, in the context of present social conditions and recent history.

In 1964, my husband was transferred to New York, and our family, including my mother and my daughter Jacqueline—also born in Ethiopia—left the country. For a newcomer in New York, job searching presented a whole new process and way of thinking. For one, I had to learn that the concept of working to serve one's country, which was by then a deep-seated norm for me, had to be reconceptualized. An opportunity emerged when, out of nowhere, Margaret Bender, an American whom I had met at a UN conference in Ghana, invited me to her office. She was retiring, and her job was to be divided into two positions. She offered me the position of Executive Secretary for Development Education, and Training with the Women's Division of the United Methodist Church Board. She thought that my experience in Africa and my approach to education in Ethiopia would contribute to the vision of the new program the Church wanted to initiate. Furthermore, she believed that the ethics of "service for a greater good" would be consistent with my own principles. At that time, I had never considered working in a church organization, let alone that a church called the United Methodist even existed. It was to become one of the most meaningful "spaces" in more than twenty years of work with church organizations.

My particular position was located in the United Methodist Office for the United Nations (UMOUN), right across from the UN Headquarters. It involved coordinating, planning, organizing, and facilitating seminars on issues of world development for lay women, community and church leaders, and volunteers and educators from across the US. Every month, one or two groups of ten to fifteen people each came to New York for ten days of intensive education on world development issues on the agenda of the UN, with a social action/social justice strategy—another new concept for me. Participants were expected to return to their hometowns and organize similar workshops, called "spin-offs." We provided them with the needed resources, which led to a publication I edited, titled *World Development: An Introductory Reader Raising Basic Questions of Social Justice and Challenging Common Myths* (NY: Macmillan, 1971). As participants spread this information, the number of women and men exposed to the issues discussed at the UMOUN seminars was multiplied to several thousands. This program also included a six-month international training course for six women leaders from Australia, Chile, Ethiopia, Pakistan, Switzerland, and the US, who in turn organized sessions for the groups they represented.

Although my experience in Ethiopia was certainly relevant, I was challenged, once again, to create and experiment with a model of learning for adults to take action at the local level. While we invited guest speakers from the UN and other institutions, the approach used in the seminars came to be called "participatory education." Participants developed an analysis of the 1960s relevant social issues on the global and US agenda: racism/apartheid, women's rights, and economic and social development in the process of decolonization, among others. Much of the learning exposure deeply challenged participants at the personal level, as they were expected to reflect on their own assumptions, and often faced with unlearning what they had come to believe. Coupled with this social analysis, a faith-based and biblical/theological perspective was offered, to explain why Christians were called upon to become involved in issues of social injustice. It was both awe-inspiring and humbling to observe the ripple effect of these training seminars across the country.

In 1970, our family immigrated to Canada—a country I knew next to nothing about—and settled in Toronto. I did not know where to start my search for meaningful employment. In the first four years, I managed to teach a few courses at York University and the University of Toronto. Then, once again out of the blue, I met a former colleague, Murray McInnis, who had worked in the same building as the UMOUN. He encouraged me to apply for a job at the Center for Christian Studies (CCS), an academic institution sponsored by the Anglican and United Churches. They envisioned a new experimental curriculum, but had not been able to find the right person to develop and implement what was called the "Core Group." Murray felt that my experience in Ethiopia and New York provided the appropriate background for the position. I went ahead and applied, even though I doubted that they would appoint me, but they did.

The theoretical foundation for the Core Group concept was the seminal work of Brazilian educator Paulo Freire, described in his *Pedagogy of the Oppressed* (NY: Herder & Herder, 1970). In contrast, however, it was going to be applied in an academic setting, with the objective of training church educators who came largely from middle-class, Anglo-Saxon/Canadian backgrounds, to prepare them for lay and diaconal/educational ministries in their respective churches. This teaching-learning approach was unique in that I did not come into the classroom with a preconceived lecture plan. The small groups of students worked with me in teams to design, organize, and sometimes even lead their sessions. The first-year Core Group addressed the range of educational and pastoral ministries of the church; in the second year, it focused entirely on its social justice mission of the church. While there were reading assignments, they also wrote reflections about what they had learned each week, challenges they faced, and new insights about education and themselves as future church educators. Integrated with the Core Group were more traditional field placements in social and community services and ministries, including inter-church social justice coalitions and academic courses at the University of Toronto.

Almost daily I felt that I was crossing boundaries into a new "territory," not only because I came from different Christian, national and cultural traditions, but also because I was facilitating a concept of education where learning required asking difficult questions at the personal, spiritual, and political levels. By implication, the application of the curriculum was continually changing, and the program was very intensive and demanding. Looking back, I am amazed at how my past experiences in Ethiopia and New York were consolidated, and yet took on new directions.

After fourteen years at the CCS, I took a sabbatical leave to go back to school. I enrolled in the doctoral program of the Ontario Institute for Studies in Education (OISE), in the Department of Sociology at the University of Toronto, not knowing that this would, once again, become a turning point in my professional career.

Refugees: Crossing National Boundaries

At OISE I learned about feminist theory and practice, which was at its zenith in 1988. The choice of my thesis topic was significant, and paved the way for new career directions. I decided to focus on the journey of Ethiopian and Eritrean refugee women who were beginning to arrive in Canada. The catalyst for this focus was the lack of understanding in the Canadian refugee system about either country's history or culture. Moreover, the world had just awakened to the plight of refugee women, en route and in camps, particularly the fact that 80% of refugees were women and their children. At a very personal level, I wanted to do something useful at a time when Ethiopia was undergoing drastic changes under the Marxist government, and I was unable to respond meaningfully to the incredible violence that people I had come to love and admire were experiencing. My thesis, *Storm and Sanctuary: The Life Journey of Ethiopian and Eritrean Refugee Women*, was published in Toronto by Artemis in 1993; it was the first book on refugee women. A major focus of my research—learned from the refugee women I interviewed—was that even though they had faced death, literally and figuratively, the survival skills they had learned as women even before becoming refugees were a source of empowerment and determination as they set about rebuilding their lives. They clearly did not see themselves as refugees *only* or *forever*. They may, indeed, have been victims of violence, but in perceiving them as helpless and dependent, we prolonged their victimization. This had to change: instead, their resilience and courage had to be recognized.

This research was the impetus to leave my teaching position at the CCS and become a consultant on refugee-related concerns. While I published a number of papers on these issues, most humbling was when my research was used at the policy level in Canada. For instance, the background paper on refugee women that I was asked to write for a major study by the Canadian Panel on Violence against Women was used in the panel's advocacy for the Canadian Government to establish Gender Persecution Guidelines—the first such guidelines in the world. A project with refugee women at the grassroots level led to the development of a book titled *Challenging Myths and Claiming Power: A Handbook to Set Up and Assess Support Groups for and with Immigrant and Refugee Women* (Toronto: Education Wife Assault, 1994), which was translated into several languages.

In 1994, once again my professional life took a leap into the unknown, this time across national boundaries. With the encouragement of family and friends, I applied and was accepted for the position of Executive Secretary for Uprooted People—refugees, internally displaced persons, and migrants— at the World Council of Churches (WCC) in Geneva. My responsibilities included facilitating and supporting ongoing ecumenical regional and inter-regional programs, including training workshops, and advocacy at the international level in Geneva. One of the most significant tasks was coordinating, together with one of my WCC colleagues, the development of global policy and advocacy with the regional ecumenical councils of the three hundred WCC member churches. This policy was the outcome of countless consultations and workshops at the local, national, and regional levels with member churches and, most importantly, with uprooted people. The outcome was a WCC policy statement titled *A Moment to Choose: Risking to be with Uprooted People* (1995). A comprehensive resource book with the same title accompanied the policy statement, which articulated a new paradigm of church responsibility in the changing global social, political and economic situation of the forced movement of people. This two-year process culminated in the coordination of the *Ecumenical Year in Solidarity with Uprooted People* (Geneva: World Council of Churches, 1997), which disseminated the policy statement back to the churches with a mandate to put it into practice. During that time, I had the privilege of working and being inspired by forcibly displaced people who further reinforced my thesis findings. Sadly, the response to refugees and migrants in the summer of 2015 appears to be déjà vu, the only difference being that social media brings immediate attention to the horrors of wars and human rights violations in their countries, and their dreadful flight experiences.

When it was time for me to retire, "legally," I felt I had to do something different to make the voices of uprooted people heard in a different way. I asked those in the global WCC network to send me poems, lyrics, photos of artwork I had heard or seen on many of my trips. I received several volumes' worth of submissions from around the world, but in the end published only 90 contributions in a 174-page book titled *Stormy Seas We Brave: Creative Expressions by Uprooted People* (Geneva: World Council of Churches, 1998). It celebrated not only their courage and resilience, but also their creativity, as they expressed their own understanding of their experiences, their fears, and their hopes for peace with justice. More significantly, the book reminded readers to look beyond public statements, media images, and even policies that purport to act on the refugees' behalf.

Celebrating and Sharing Coptic Cultural Heritage

Shortly after my return to Canada, I discovered that the St. Mark's Coptic Orthodox Church in Toronto had a museum, the creation of Father Marcos A. Marcos, the first Coptic priest to be commissioned to North America in 1964. The Museum was blessed and inaugurated by H.H. Pope Shenouda III in 1996, and opened to the public in 2000. At that time, I volunteered to serve as a guide, and gradually this activity has become a full-time professional occupation as the "volunteer curator." I had been a museum-goer since the age of sixteen, and the study of culture and identity was not only one of my favorite courses to teach as a sociologist, but also pertinent in my work with refugees. While my research skills were useful, the responsibility of curating a museum demanded more. I had to take a graduate certificate in Museology and attend Coptic Studies conferences to learn about this growing academic discipline. These two sources of professional development have allowed me to keep on top of the care, conservation, research, and interpretation of an ever-growing, very diverse collection. The Museum's motto is "Coptic Art as a Living Tradition," and its artefacts date from as early as 1331 BC. Spanning the centuries to the present day, the collection also showcases contemporary artists and their works (www.copticmuseum-canada.org).

Museums as cultural institutions also have the responsibility to educate and transmit legacy and history to future generations. Thus, the mandate of our Museum is to research the collection and communicate Coptic cultural heritage not only to Copts, but also to the wider Canadian society. These goals are achieved through workshops for teachers and students from public and private schools, church groups in the ecumenical community, tourists, as well as internships for university students. Training volunteers is also an integral part of managing and operating the Museum.

Changing "My" World?

"Living Intentionally across Boundaries" is a metaphor for what has become a way of living purposefully, whether the boundaries are social, religious, cultural, racial, physical, or geographic. Each phase of my professional life has provided greater insight on the past, and required that I reinvent myself so as to meet new challenges, and the opportunities to make a difference in the present. I may have changed "my" world in a particular place, at a particular moment in history; I can only hope that I have made as much difference as all those I have had the privilege of serving, working with, and learning from. The journey continues …

Toronto, September 2015

REFLECTIONS ON MY LIFE:
FULL CIRCLE FROM EGYPT
TO THE US AND BACK

NAGLA NADOURI NIAZY

Throughout my personal and professional life, I have often reflected on what I was doing, what I had accomplished, and where I was headed. When I was invited to participate in this book project, I hesitated to consider the proposal because I thought my non-scientific writing skills in English would make it difficult. However, I accepted the challenge, as I always do. Now, as I look back at the three distinct parts of my life and my career, I see that they were almost equal in duration, but different in circumstances, aspirations and experiences, all have contributed to craft my present identity.

I was born in Alexandria to an upper-middle class family of five children. My parents believed that girls deserved a special kind of education, one that would emphasize their fluency in French and build their character. Therefore, the three girls in the family attended an elite French school, Notre Dame De Sion, run by Catholic nuns. During those early years, I received an education that profoundly impacted my personal and intellectual development. At school, the student body was made up of Moslem, Christian and Jewish girls of different national origin: Egyptian, Syrian, Lebanese, Greek, Italian, and Armenian. All of us learned to live together in an environment of tolerance and mutual respect, and were introduced to the practice of self-examination, a rule that I try to follow to this day. Every morning, each student was asked to stand in front of her class, and state, according to her view, which of the following ratings she deserved for her conduct and academic performance the previous day: "honorable," "average," or "poor." I was fortunate to have had some outstanding teachers who provided a wealth of knowledge in both the sciences and the humanities. The school hymn said it all in the verse: "Beloved home where we learn to live, work, think, and decide."

My parents never guided me in my studies nor helped with school work, but they always took pride in my good grades. They had full confidence in the school and the teachers, and entrusted my education entirely to them. Now that I think about it, it seems strange that no one in my family circle ever discussed career plans with me. Likewise, no advice on the matter was offered at school. This was probably the case with most young women of my generation, they were expected to marry soon after graduating from high school.

I received a French Baccalaureate clearly reflecting my gift for the sciences. For the first and only time in his life, my father tried to influence my choice of college: he would have liked for me to be an MD. At that point, medical school meant having to dissect frogs and cockroaches—an idea I categorically rejected. Later, I realized the importance of career counseling in high school, and thought that with proper guidance I could have been a successful physician. I was admitted to the Faculty of Science at Alexandria University where I developed a passion for chemistry and an eagerness to pursue an academic career in that discipline. This is when my parents started to take a real interest in my plans and supported my goals. My husband-to-be, Saïd Niazy, whom I had met during a summer internship at Shell Oil Co, was proud of my academic achievements and shared my dreams for the future. I graduated at the top of my class in a "Special Chemistry" program, and was appointed Teaching Assistant in the Department of Chemistry, a post leading to Assistant Professor and tenure, once I complete the PhD. Soon thereafter, I embarked on a new life as a graduate student and a married woman, each with its own demands and responsibilities.

One day, fate headed my way. While assisting one of my professors, Dr. Ashraf El Bayoumi, in an undergraduate lab, he inquired about the progress of my Master's thesis, and casually asked if I would consider getting the PhD from a university in the US; in which case, he would support my application with a letter of recommendation. Dr. El Bayoumi had returned from the US, and taught my undergraduate course in Quantum Chemistry—a subject totally unknown to us at that time. He transported his students into an abstract world of probabilities and uncertainties with an amazingly vivacious teaching style. He would often recall his learning experiences in the US with just as much enthusiasm, and would describe nature in that continent as "God's paradise on earth." That day, I went home to my husband fairly excited. For two weeks, we discussed this unexpected opportunity and decided that it would be a great chance for both of us to travel, see the US, get my degree, and add to his professional experience.

With advice from Dr. El Bayoumi, I started to correspond with American professors who were working in Electrochemistry, my area of interest. The first to respond was at the University of Pennsylvania, and with strong endorsement from Dr. El Bayoumi, he offered me a research fellowship. Now, the idea of leaving Egypt and starting a new life far away, on another continent, was beginning to take shape and become a reality, although it was still a hard decision to make for both of us. We thought it would only be for about five years, at the end of which we would come back home. Saïd applied for a leave of absence from his management position at Shell Oil to accompany me, and seemed confident in our plans. However, during family gatherings when my brothers would tease him about having to wash dishes or work in a gas station in the US before finding a suitable position, I could feel his anxiety. It is only much later that I realized the extent of the sacrifice he made, jeopardizing his 15-year professional career, in order to be with me and support my academic career plans. I had never given much thought to the possibility of life away from home and family. In fact, I remembered one of my friends who had come to say goodbye to my father before she emigrated to Canada. My father was emotionally shaken at the idea that he may not see her again, and I wondered how she could have caused such pain to her family and acquaintances, thinking this would never happen to me. Little did I know that a day would come when I would have to do what I thought I never would. It took much courage for my husband and me to leave behind a happy and secure life with parents, brothers, sisters, extended family, childhood friends, to face the unknown, alone.

On March 21, 1968, the second phase of my life was to start. We flew to New York City, and, prior to heading for Philadelphia, we spent a week at my cousin's beautiful American home, in an upper-middle class suburban neighborhood. Our first encounter with the Penn campus in West Philadelphia was very disappointing. It did not resemble any of the modern houses and the manicured lawns I had seen in Hollywood movies. The old gothic-style university buildings were scattered in a neighborhood of run-down residential dwellings. It brought to mind a conversation I had had prior to leaving Egypt with one of my professors, a Princeton graduate. His words were ringing in my ears: "My friend, the first week, you will feel as if a pit had been dug and you were thrown in it." He was right: it was exactly how I felt our first night in a shabby campus hotel where we had been sent. I cried my heart out. Fortunately, my husband was by my side to cheer me up. Years later, I came to appreciate and admire the beauty and majesty of Houston Hall, College Hall, and Irvine Auditorium, and realized that they were national historic landmarks.

In two months, we had moved to an apartment on campus, I had already passed the prerequisite French reading exam, enrolled in a German course, and started on my thesis research. Summer 1968 was a depressing time, indeed. Two great national figures Martin Luther King and Robert Kennedy were assassinated, and the mood in the country was somber. I worked eight hours a day in the lab, and studied for my courses in the evenings. Saïd took night shifts in a large chemical company, a job far beneath his experience and position level in Egypt, yet he never complained. We were both homesick, and longed for our happy summer days at the beach in Alexandria, with family and friends. The next academic year, a research assistantship allowed me to fulfill my course requirements without having any teaching responsibilities, yet I had to spend 14 hours each day in classes, the library, and study time.

During our second summer in Philadelphia, we moved to a very pleasant garden apartment in the suburbs, and I resumed my eight-hour schedule in the lab to work on my thesis. By then, my husband had moved to a subsidiary of his original company as chief chemist, and we made a small circle of friends. With only a ten-dollar down-payment, we bought a brand new Volkswagen Beetle, and started to explore Philadelphia and vicinity on the weekends: museums, shores, music festivals, barbecue on the river side. In other words, life in the US was beginning to take on much brighter colors, except at work. On many occasions, the graduate students in my group, mostly foreign nationals, would refer to our advising professor as the "slave driver." At first, I did not pay much attention to their conversations, but gradually I came to be aware of serious problems between him and several graduate students at various stages of their work. They were bitter about their predicament, yet seemingly unable to do anything about it. Although my research was progressing relatively well, I started to feel tremendous pressure by the professor: he was closely monitoring my arrival and departure times, my whereabouts, and my lunch breaks. Being at the very early stage of my thesis work, it seemed wise not to remain trapped in a perturbing situation. I had come to the US primarily to complete my doctorate degree, and I wanted it to be a satisfying experience.

I decided to meet with the department chair, let him know of my desire to change thesis advisor, and inquire about the possibility of a teaching assistantship. He was well aware of the difficulties in our research group and was willing to help me, but he did not want to be a party in the decision. I had to make it entirely on my own: resign from the group, submit a new application for an assistantship, and wait for a response, which could be positive or negative. Once again, my husband was by my side, ready to support me as long as necessary, until a new financial package would materialize. Now, I fully understood the reasons for the anger and frustration of the foreign graduate students who, unlike me, had no means to finance their studies in case they lost their research fellowships. Fortunately, it was not long before I received a teaching assistantship, selected a different advisor, Dr. Philip George, and plunged full force into a new research project. The environment in this group was healthy and stimulating, and my responsibilities as a teaching assistant for undergraduate students were a great opportunity to prepare for my future academic career.

A year later, I had to face another major challenge. After the tragic loss of his son in a mugging incident, Dr. George decided to take a sabbatical leave overseas. His other two graduate students managed to defend their theses before his departure, while I was left to work completely on my own for one and a half years. During that time, I communicated with him by fax—long before email and the internet—to update him on my research, and receive much-needed advice and suggestions. This was a very difficult time, but I was determined to carry on and put the odds on my side with self-reliance and hard work. The department chair would sometimes stop at my door, raise his thumb, and say: "So, you are making it after all!" My perseverance finally paid off: two years after my advisor's return, I successfully defended my dissertation, earning the title of Dr. Niazy.

I accepted a two-year post-doctoral research position in the Biomedical Engineering and Science Program at Drexel University. I worked with a great educator, Dr. Richard Beard, who always provided the financial travel support I needed to present my work at national and international meetings. These experiences contributed to my professional growth and development. At that point, Alexandria University summoned me officially to return to Egypt as a tenured Assistant Professor of Chemistry. In the meantime, while I was still working on my degree, my husband had to resign his position with Shell Oil in Alexandria, after his request for an additional extension of his leave of absence was denied. By then, we had become US citizens, bought our first house, and Saïd was Vice President in the international division of his company. We had learned to enjoy and appreciate all aspects of our US life, Philadelphia felt like home: we decided to remain in the "City of Brotherly Love."

Since my undergraduate days in Egypt, my career goal had been focused solely on an academic career. In the US, I realized that there were many different opportunities. Being married to an industrial chemist, I was attracted by the challenges of the chemical industry and its financial rewards, and had to choose between two different paths: academe or industry. After considerable thought, I opted for the former. The search for a tenure-track position in the greater Philadelphia area was unsuccessful; therefore, I accepted two consecutive non-tenure posts at the University of Pennsylvania, and Drexel University. Teaching freshmen courses at these institutions was a fulfilling experience, while the challenges were many. Early on, I had to learn to deal with cultural differences. In one of the first lab meetings, two students were hugging and kissing. Shocked and embarrassed, I looked at them and said: "What are you doing?" They looked back at me, just as shocked as I was, but not at all embarrassed, and answered: "Doing what?" I swallowed my retort, and decided not to make any comment when students facing me would put their feet up or wear earphones. Such attitudes showing lack of respect would not be tolerated in Egypt, I would have asked the students to leave the classroom. Teaching at the college level in the US did not require any prior training, nor were instructors provided with any pedagogical guidance. I had to find my own way by trial and error. I learned how to give effective presentations for the students to grasp scientific principles, and get them excited about chemistry by showing them its intimate relation to their everyday life. In lecture demonstrations, I always tried to relate abstract concepts to their physical manifestations. As an educator, my responsibilities involved other tasks as well. I had to address a range of academic deficiencies, and help those who brought their emotional problems to the classroom. Long office hours were spent counseling students, and with patience, encouragement and steady monitoring, many achieved good results. Nothing was more rewarding than to meet them as they prepared to graduate, and observe that they had developed into fulfilled and confident individuals.

However satisfying it was to teach at two prestigious institutions, I decided to venture into industry and joined an international semiconductor manufacturing company, Thomson CSF, since my academic positions were non-tenure track. Now, I was leaving the secure world of academe and stepping into the "real" world—a dramatic and stressful transition from an environment where I was the teacher, to one where I had to become the learner. In the new setting of fast growing technology, my focus had to be directed at commercial demands and economic value for the company. It required major adjustment, not the least of which was to develop the necessary humility and modesty in my interactions with plant superintendents. Due to my ability to learn and adapt, and my effectiveness in solving technical problems, I soon acquired the needed knowledge and expertise, and won the respect of my coworkers.

Years of experience in chemicals used in the manufacture of semiconductors led to my next industrial appointment as Senior Research and Development Scientist for Microelectronic Chemicals at J. T. Baker, Inc., a subsidiary of a multinational company, Proctor & Gamble. I was part of a group in charge of formulation and application of these chemicals, hence the necessity to interact with the marketing staff, and respond to consumer demands. During that time in industry, I enjoyed learning new skills: business awareness, teamwork, effective communication, and time management, all crucial for achieving company commitments and goals. Succeeding in fully understanding and adapting to the industrial environment resulted not only in tremendous personal excitement, but also in significant rewards in performance appraisals, salary increases, and added responsibilities. By then, I had spent 23 years of my life in the US—years of struggles, hard work, learning, success, rewards, and, more importantly, happy and fulfilling personal time with my husband, whose presence remained unfaltering, and his support unflinching. Unfortunately, after 26 years of genuine partnership, I lost him.

A year after his passing, I decided to go back to my roots, and spend the final stage of my life in Egypt, close to my extended family and friends. Since I was still passionate and enthusiastic about teaching chemistry, I accepted an offer from the American University in Cairo. Equipped with years of experience in guiding and motivating students in the US, I was glad to have the opportunity to contribute, finally, to the education of young Egyptians—a mission for which I had started to prepare myself years earlier.

Wishing to invest in my community the extensive technical knowledge I had acquired, and contribute to improving the poor environmental conditions in my hometown, I volunteered in a recently formed NGO "Friends of the Environment Association in Alexandria." In a short time, under the able leadership of the late Dr. Adel Abou Zahra, one of its founders and its Secretary General, the Association was successful on many fronts: finding the needed human resources, receiving grants, raising public awareness, gaining national recognition, and winning court battles in favor of environmental protection. I organized various workshops for groups in the media, education and industry, to enlighten them on the sources and problems related to pollution, and to alert them to their impact on the health of workers and citizens. As a chemist, I ran technical seminars to introduce the latest technologies to assist industrial establishments in complying with new environmental regulations for treating wastewater before discharging it. Today, the Association maintains its growth, continues to attract additional volunteers, and embarks on more projects. However, it is only with the effective actions and support of the city government that the huge challenges ahead could be addressed.

Looking back at my life while drafting the present chapter, I have realized that my greatest rewards derived mainly from finding personal fulfillment and pride in every project I undertook, from receiving accolades and appreciation for my work, and from achieving a healthy balance between my personal and professional life. It has now been 24 years since I lost my husband. The overwhelming grief and sorrow that I felt at his death lingered for many years; today, they appear like distant memories except when something triggers the pain and heartache. This happened in the course of writing this text. I was constantly thinking about the one person who was no longer with me, and from whom I drew courage, guidance, and unconditional love. Yet, I felt his presence with me more than ever. To his memory, I dedicate these reflections.

Alexandria, September 2015

SAVING THE WORLD HERITAGE AT UNESCO

SONIA ABADIR RAMZI

Was I really the first and only Egyptian woman to head the promotion of the World Heritage at UNESCO? That was the headlines of an article about me by a well-known journalist in the Egyptian daily *Al Ahram*.

The elder daughter of a loving family, I grew up in Cairo surrounded by my father, a renowned engineer; my mother, an amazing lady endowed with a special talent for painting; and my loving brother and sister. When I was born, my grandmother feared that my father would be disappointed to have had a daughter instead of a son, but to her surprise and that of everyone else around, he took me in his arms, and danced and laughed with joy. What a great start in life it was for me!

In my early years, I received an excellent education at a private French school for girls, the Mère de Dieu, which left a strong impact on me. Although it was a Catholic institution, all religious holidays were celebrated, Christian, Muslim and Jewish. I was impish and liked to play pranks and make jokes, especially during the Arabic language class, much to the chagrin of the teacher. One of the most exciting events to take place at the school would occur on the students' wedding days—a tradition followed by the Christian girls accompanied by their friends, regardless of their faith. On that day, the young woman would return to the school chapel with her friends, and place a bouquet of flowers under the picture of the Holy Virgin. On my wedding day, I was delighted when the mother superior told my husband: "Take care of our daughter Sonia, because you now have forty mothers-in-law!"

I went to Ain-Shams University, graduating with a B.A. in French. Because of my sentimental attachment to my school, I accepted to replace a teacher who had been hired but changed her mind at the last minute. My position was supposed to be temporary until a permanent person would be recruited, but I knew that the principal was not looking very hard. To my surprise, I discovered that I actually liked teaching, especially the thirteen-year olds, and the classroom experience served me well in later years. A major turning point in my life occurred when my husband, Maher Ramzi, a civil engineer, accepted an offer in Algeria. A descendant of the pharaohs deeply rooted in Egypt, I did not wish to leave my family and my country, but I had to accompany Maher.

While living in Algeria, I developed courses at the University of Algiers, including one on women in Arab literature, and another on the novels of Naguib Mahfouz (1911-2006)—the only Arab author to receive the Nobel Prize in Literature. As an instructor, I continued to enjoy the enthusiasm of the students I taught and motivated, and, in the process, I learned to explain ideas very carefully, making sure that my audience would fully understand the meaning of what I tried to convey. That habit that I acquired and practiced turned out to be very useful in my work at UNESCO. At the University of Algiers, I was fortunate to encounter the renowned author Assia Djebbar (1936-2015), who chaired the Department of French, and was later elected to the French Academy—the only woman from the Maghreb to be part of that august body, and a contender for the Nobel Prize in Literature. Simultaneously, I conducted research for my doctoral dissertation at the Sorbonne in Paris, on the subject of "Arab Women in the Maghreb and the Mashrek: Reality and Fiction." It was successfully completed in 1982, and later published in Algiers.[1]

In the 1960s, a monumental project was underway in Egypt: the building the Aswan High Dam. It galvanized the attention of all Egyptians as well as that of the political leadership, because its financing created tremendous tension between Egypt and the West. When the World Bank turned down our request for funding, the Soviet Union stepped in, ready to assist. Construction was imminent, although the resulting flood would cause the submergence of the majestic temple of Abu Simbel. The consequences of the project were often discussed in our family, as my father headed the engineering department of the company under contract to erect the dam. Like all Egyptians, we were deeply concerned about the future of these illustrious relics of our glorious history. Eventually, we were greatly relieved when the international community came to the rescue with a worldwide fundraising campaign launched by UNESCO. The concept of a common heritage for humanity was born, its purpose being the protection of historical sites and monuments whose destruction would be a loss for humankind. This was one of the twentieth-century strongest and most unifying notions linking all people and their cultures. Little did I know back then that, some day, I would play a major role in that kind of activity.

Sonia speaking at a UN Conference on World Heritage, New York, 2001

During the reception celebrating the successful completion of my doctoral thesis, the Director of the Women's Program at UNESCO suggested that I consider working in her department. I put my name down, was appointed, and served as Consultant for seven years. When the position of Program Director came open, I applied and was shortlisted; however, a candidate from Scandinavia was selected because her region was at the forefront as champion for women's rights. Deeply disappointed, I requested a meeting with the newly elected Director General of UNESCO, Frederico Mayor. Armed with a load of documents and publications I had produced, I went to see him. "Mr. Director General, you have taken away my position!" He was surprised by my statement, and asked for an explanation. I showed him my contributions to women's issues during the previous seven years, proving that I had the needed skills and experience for the position. Among others, I had implemented a literacy project for women in rural areas, and another on structuring the development of women in informal sectors. Evidently, he must have realized that I had been unfairly treated, because he offered me a position as Program Specialist in that division. Feeling hurt and indignant, and without thinking, I immediately refused; yet, I needed a job.

I was later offered a position in the Culture and Cultural Heritage Program. This time, I controlled myself and did not launch into a tirade about my skills and experience. Hence, my international career as a UNESCO professional took off in a direction quite different from what I had originally anticipated. However, over the years, I came to realize that not getting the job in the Women's Program was actually a blessing in disguise, because in the new division where I started to work I was able to do a lot more than focus only on women's issues. While safeguarding the precious cultural achievements of humanity, I also promoted and improved the status of women. Discovering and preserving the world's creative genius of humans was fascinating and challenging: it did not consist only of protecting and conserving ancient stones and buildings, more importantly, it meant saving populations who lived nearby, or made a living from the endangered sites. Each day brought to my attention interesting cases, requiring new ideas, and intense efforts. Invigorated and energized by the variety of situations, I developed a passion for my work, and continued to advocate for women in the projects I undertook.

The responsibilities were overwhelming. For example, one day, I would have to address the problem of Mauritania's ancient cities struggling against encroaching sands, and the socio-economic survival of the region's population, especially its women. The next day, I would be taking a trip to Asia, to consult with a group of experts on the Imperial City of Hué in Vietnam. Upon returning, I would be looking at saving historic monuments in Istanbul and Goreme in Turkey, or the island of Goree in Senegal. We would then cover Venice, Haiti, and so on and so forth. My colleagues and I worked together as a team, in a spirit of collegiality and solidarity, all passionately engaged in our task. We never counted the days or the hours, which often extended over weekends and holidays, occasionally ending with a glass of champagne. Our missions included meetings with ambassadors, government officials and country experts, and generally mobilized a large number of youth, women, civil servants, university students, and the media. Despite our best efforts, our team alone could not respond to all the needs, and had to be assisted by forty outstanding interns of various nationalities. Today, many among them hold important positions around the world, for example, at the Getty Museum, in the US administration, or at the European Investment Bank, to mention but a few. Among those we trained, some left an indelible mark; one of them was Monique Medalia, an American who volunteered for a year but ended up staying three years, and became instrumental in the development of several major projects.

Until 1997, the extra-budgetary financing of projects was covered by member states, UN agencies, or intergovernmental organizations. That year, however, I dared to establish the first partnership between UNESCO and the private sector. In an effort to seek additional resources for the restoration of monuments and sites, an important question crossed my mind: which sector of the economy is likely to benefit the most from the preservation of the world's cultural heritage? Tourism was the obvious answer. I went to ITB Berlin—the world's largest travel convention —to launch my campaign "Without cultural and natural heritage, there is no tourism." I asked major tourism enterprises to partner with UNESCO, diffuse our message through their communication channels, and contribute to our funding efforts. I pleaded that UNESCO had raised awareness about the importance of safeguarding the world heritage, and thus greatly benefited their industry. I ended my remarks by reminding them that it was thanks to UNESCO that their business continued to flourish and grow. At first, they seemed unimpressed, and I went to bed that evening thinking the campaign had failed. However, the next morning, an article strongly supportive of my initiative appeared in the ITB journal, it cleared the way for its approval.

My efforts were backed by the Director General of UNESCO, and his successors maintained a strong presence at the ITB Berlin conventions. He was also able to overcome internal criticism from conservative colleagues who feared the private sector would misuse UNESCO's name for commercial gains. Over time, significant partnerships were developed with some of the world's largest and most prestigious tourist organizations, including, among others, International Hotel and Restaurant Association, EF Tours in the US, Radisson SAS Hotels, ACCOR group in France, TUI in Germamy, as well as the European Commission. As a result, we collaborated on many projects in different parts of the globe, extending from Angkor in Cambodia, to Petra in Jordan, and Robben Island in South Africa.

Working with universities and institutions of higher learning was also a mission close to my heart, and I wanted to create a network for those concerned with the tangible and intangible cultural heritage of humanity. Two days after meeting a young woman from Spain who became involved in a project to mobilize universities, I received an invitation from the President of Valencia Polytechnic Institute (VPI) to present my initiative to create a university network. A first meeting with several deans and professors was held in the President's office; then, feasibility was discussed with instructors in the Master's Program in Heritage, and a report on the matter was due by the end of the day. I outlined my proposal clearly and convincingly before them, in order to assist them in completing their work. In the car, on the way back from lunch, the Director of the Master's program said: "Madam, I did not wish to mention

this in the meeting, but I do not believe this project will go through."
Responding diplomatically, I said: "Sir, the final decision rests with you."
Following the afternoon session, the Director himself presented the report
and recommended adoption of the proposal. The next day, the VPI
President made a public announcement about the initiative, and offered to
fund an international conference to launch the university network in
collaboration with UNESCO.

In 1996, Forum UNESCO-University and Heritage was created,
followed by seminars in Quebec, Canada; Melbourne, Australia; Fez,
Morocco; Buenos Aires, Argentina; Salvador de Bahia, Brazil; Lund,
Sweden; Paris, France, as well as other cities. Today, the Forum connects
450 colleges and universities, and successfully links privileged and less
endowed institutions. Although the US was not a member of UNESCO at
that time, a number of American universities joined the group, including
the Savannah College of Art and Design, Harvard University, Columbia
University, and Villanova University. Museums such as Getty and the
Smithsonian also cooperated, as well as a few NGOs. Remarkable
cooperation was established with the American Association of Retired
Persons (AARP), which took part in roundtable discussions and various
activities. A series of meetings were held at AARP headquarters in
Washington, DC, then at the UN in New York, and finally in Paris.

Sonia with rectors and deans from member institutions of "Forum UNESCO-
University and Heritage," at Deaken University in Melbourne, Australia, 1998

The 60 missions conducted under the aegis of this global initiative presented innumerable difficulties, not only in communication due to time differences, but also for travel to distant and remote places, various housing conditions, and unusual work habits. However, these problems were more than compensated by amazing cultural enrichment and professional contacts with exceptional individuals who later became personal friends. I will always remember a jamboree in a UN village in Chile, where I stayed in a small tent, and could not sleep all night because of the loud music played by young scouts. There were also many memorable moments, surprises and events: amazing decorations in Canada, China and Brazil; gorgeous flowers in Australia and Germany; an unexpected invitation to Savannah, Georgia, with the visit ending with violin music to celebrate the completion of a joint project with Cuba; a chance encounter with the President of Argentina at a book fair where, at the dismay of his guards, I convinced him to visit the UNESCO exhibit on World Heritage. "Sonia has kidnapped the President," cried some of my colleagues jokingly.

Calls for alerts and urgent action were endless: the head of the Sphinx needs restoration; Dubrovnik is burning; the bridge at Mostar is destroyed; the Museum in Bagdad is looted; the Buddhas of Bamiyan have been dynamited. The March 2001 demolition of these monumental statues of Afghanistan, carved into the side of a cliff in the sixth century AD, was devastating for the entire world. It was an example of extreme religious intolerance; they marked the beginning of a campaign of "sacred obligation" by terrorists to bring down temples, monuments, and museums, as part of their barbaric war. It called into question whether we had failed to raise awareness about safeguarding a cultural heritage that belongs to future generations. As I sought to promote its protection, I believed it was urgent to alert the world to the gravity of the situation, and to develop a concrete global response. We organized roundtable discussions with various UN agencies, and decided that the UN was in the best place to launch a planetary campaign of awareness, and mobilize the masses in favor of the preservation of the rich heritage of humanity. A UN Year for Cultural Heritage would demonstrate the political will and engagement at all levels, and considerably strengthen UNESCO's efforts.

UNESCO-35ème session de la conférence générale - Paris 2009 - © Ph.Sayah Msadek
www.parisphot-presse.fr

Sonia with Koichiro Matsura, UNESCO Director General, Paris, 2009

Galvanized by the tragic destruction of the Buddhas of Bamiyan and wishing to take advantage of the momentum it created, and after consultation with various UN departments in New York and Paris, my team developed a strategy. Our objective was for the 2001 UN General Assembly to declare a UN Year for Cultural Heritage. In a memorandum to the Director General, I outlined the broad lines of my plan, and received the green light. Then, I asked Egypt's Ambassador to the UN to present the Resolution to the 58-Member UNESCO Executive Board. It was co-sponsored by fourteen countries, and passed in time to be presented at the General Assembly in New York. The initiative required non-stop effort: agreement of UN delegations on a special technical document; coordination for inclusion on the agenda of the meeting of November 21, 2001; and discussion with various country representatives. These activities and the sustained cooperation between UNESCO and the UN would not have been possible had it not been for the strong support and active involvement of UN Secretary General Boutros Boutros Ghali. He was the first at the helm of the world organization to place culture among development priorities. I arrived in New York exactly five days prior to the General Assembly, having already met with numerous delegates. Although the US was not a member of UNESCO, I was able to secure the support of their UN mission, and they became the 37th co-sponsor of the Resolution. Needless to say, I was overjoyed and proud of my accomplishment.

Sonia with former UN Secretary General Boutros Boutros Ghali and his wife Lea, Paris, 2014

That year, South Korea presided over the General Assembly, and it was important to seek their early endorsement and co-sponsorship of the Resolution, in order to avoid blockage and accelerate the process. On the day of its presentation at the General Assembly, I was seated on the right side of the hall, in the special section reserved for UNESCO. My heart was pounding as I heard the President of the General Assembly announce the agenda item, and the Egyptian Ambassador to the UN, Ahmad Abou El Gheit, make his presentation, which I had helped to draft. He explained the purpose and objectives of the UN Year for Cultural Heritage, and cited the names of the country co-sponsoring the Resolution. As the hall applauded, and the Ambassador descended the podium, he smiled at me and said: "Are you happy for UNESCO?" At that moment, I was laughing and crying at the same time, and could not stop saying: "Thank you God, thank you God!" This was one of the greatest and most intense moments of happiness in my life. Incidentally, two years later, Ambassador Abou El Gheit became Egypt's foreign minister.

There is no doubt in my mind that with determination, tenacity, hard work, commitment, and passion women have indeed changed the world, and will continue to do so for generations to come!!

Paris, February 2016

Notes

[1] See, Sonia Ramzi, *La femme arabe au Maghreb et au Mashrek: fiction et réalité* (Alger: Entreprise nationale du livre, 1986).

FROM CHEMISTRY IN THE LAB
TO CHEMISTRY BETWEEN PEOPLE

MONA RISK

The French boarding school Notre Dame de Sion (NDS) in Alexandria has educated thousands of girls since the early twentieth century. Hidden behind an eight-foot high wall and a massive wrought-iron door, an alley of palm trees led to the impressive three-story building. In addition, the school ground, an eight-acre property, harbored several smaller houses, an open-air gym, a water-lily basin, and tennis and basketball courts. For twelve happy years, my classmates and I dwelt in this peaceful institution where forty nuns and a staff of lay teachers taught us French, Arabic, and English as well as math, social studies, religion; and in the upper classes, literature, philosophy, physics, and chemistry. We also forged friendships that would last a lifetime in spite of the miles and oceans separating us. Unbeknownst to us, more subtle lessons were instilled in the pupils. We learned to set goals and achieve them. We learned to fight obstacles and never give up. We learned that with discipline and hard work we could conquer the world. And many of us did—or at least we managed to make an impact on the societies in which we lived.

Fulfilling my parents' lofty expectations, I passed the Franco-Egyptian baccalaureate and was the highest ranking graduate in my city. My sheltered youth ended as I joined the Faculty of Pharmacy at Alexandria University. On the first day, the huge amphitheater was already crowded half an hour before the lecture began. With a sigh, I squeezed into a back row, hardly able to see the professor or hear him through the defective loudspeakers. My positive spirit plummeted. How was I going to listen to my classes under these conditions? Soon, the Dean surprised us with a visit. After surveying the nervous audience of fifty female students crammed in among three hundred males, he scowled and declared the women should be given priority of seats. From then on until the day we graduate, the first five rows would be reserved for the ladies. The male students grumbled but the girls smiled ear-to-ear. A sigh of relief escaped me. Now, I would be able to sit in a front row and follow the lectures without problems.

My five years in Pharmacy remain etched in my memory as a wonderful time. Thanks to hard work and determination, phase two of my life ended on a good note as I graduated with honors and prepared to marry my fiancé, Samir F. Risk, a young engineer from Cairo and a friend of my cousins. Three weeks later, I fulfilled two dreams on the same day: marriage and career. On the very morning of my wedding, Swisspharma Corporation—a joint venture between three Swiss pharmaceutical companies, Ciba, Sandoz and La Roche, and the Egyptian Government—granted me an interview at its Cairo headquarters. Instead of getting ready for the ceremony, I spent several hours at the company premises talking with various executives. Finally at 4 pm, I returned home and rushed to the hairdresser who chided me for being late but combed my hair into a fabulous twist. My mother and aunts helped me get dressed in record time while the groom's brother and sister were waiting in the living room to escort me to the church, as was the custom in Egypt at that time.

After the ceremony and the reception at my grandparents' house, my new husband and I left for a honeymoon in Marsah Matrouh, a beach resort west of Alexandria. Three days later my father called to inform me that Swisspharma wanted me to take an exam. I spent the last two days of my honeymoon studying for the unexpected test that I passed with flying colors. The company hired me as a pharmaceutical chemist and we settled in Cairo. My contract letter stipulated that I would start working on Wednesday, September 1st. Meanwhile my father, George Zayed, a professor at Alexandria University, was invited to Boston College in the US to set up the doctoral program in the Department of French. Papa had a signed letter from the President of Egypt congratulating him on the honor brought to his country. My parents were scheduled to leave Cairo on Friday, September 3, and I badly wanted to spend the last two days with them. I asked my employer if I could start working on Saturday, September 4, but my irascible new boss refused. I had to swallow my resentment and go to work on the assigned date.

For almost a year, I analyzed the active ingredients of pharmaceutical products. In spite of my husband's loving attention, I had trouble adjusting to my new life. I missed my parents and wrote to them daily. No one had ever taught me to cook, and we would have lived on sandwiches if my grandmother had not provided us with a maid who cleaned our apartment and cooked our meals. Things got more complicated when I discovered I was expecting. In spite of our relatively good salaries for beginners, we could never raise a child comfortably on our income. We decided to emigrate to the US. After months of horrendous difficulties and an incredible amount of formalities, we received an entry visa for the US and left Cairo. While the plane soared into the cloudless sky, I could not utter a word. My throat clogged with repressed tears at the thought I was abandoning my country, the land where my ancestors had built a stable life.

A week after we landed in Boston, my husband found a job and enrolled in a Master's program in Engineering. With my first baby on the way, I stayed home and tried to get used to the cold weather. Since we did not have medical insurance, we lived with my parents and saved every penny to pay for the hospital and the doctor fees. My baby brought joy to the whole family and brightened the difficult beginnings. Six months later, Samir obtained a good position with an international company, we moved to our own two-bedroom apartment, and bought our first car. Full of nostalgia for my homeland, I framed my kitchen cabinets with postcards of Alexandria.

It was time to think again about my professional future; unfortunately, my enquiry at the Massachusetts College of Pharmacy brought a big disappointment. The Dean informed me that the Egyptian Bachelor of Pharmacy was not recognized in the US as it consisted of a different curriculum. To practice as a pharmacist, I would have to register in an accredited American college of Pharmacy, and take the missing required courses and training, before passing the Board of Pharmacy. After a thorough evaluation of my transcript, he advised me to prepare a Master's of Science in Chemistry. Determined to obtain a US degree, I followed his advice and applied for the graduate program in Chemistry at Northeastern University. My parents agreed to babysit their grandson while I went to school three evenings a week. Life fell into a routine: cooking and caring for our little boy by day, going to school and studying by night. I had always been a motivated student and managed to pass all my courses with good grades. Actually, I took my last exam two weeks prior to delivering my second child, a little girl.

After dedicating several years to raising my children, I prepared my résumé and sent it to various pharmaceutical companies. Half the negative responses mentioned that I was under-qualified for a chemist's position because of my lack of US experience. The other half claimed that I was overqualified as a technician because of my Master's degree. Quite desperate to find a job, I volunteered at the pharmacy of Newton-Wellesley Hospital. A month later a position opened up, and I started my career as a technician earning $3.50 per hour: it hardly paid for the babysitter.

Since I did not plan to remain a technician for long, I kept sending résumés right and left. Millipore, a company manufacturing filters, hired me in their new Marketing Laboratory. My supervisor put me on a rotational program in various labs until I learned to use and troubleshoot different pieces of equipment. Meanwhile a colleague made my life so miserable I could not wait to leave that place. By then, I had learned a valuable lesson: to succeed in life I should toughen up and not let anyone step on my toes.

Soon New England Nuclear (NEN), a radiopharmaceutical company specializing in the preparation of radionuclide drugs used for cancer diagnosis and treatment, invited me to come in for an interview. For my bad luck, a horrible snowstorm engulfed the whole area the night before the meeting. I left the house at 5 am driving at ten miles an hour on treacherous highways and slippery roads while praying the Lord to let me arrive safely. I finally made it, parked the car in a deserted parking lot at 7 am, entered the building, and sat in the parlor, patiently waiting. The hiring manager arrived at 9 am.

A month later the blessed call came: "We would like to make you a job offer!" On my first day at NEN, my supervisor and colleagues did their best to make me feel welcome. The drugs we analyzed could save thousands of patients affected by cancer, but we had to protect ourselves from radiation by wearing a lead apron before entering the "hot" labs and handling radioactive substances. I enjoyed three successful years at NEN until the day my husband was promoted to an executive position in the Cincinnati office of his company—a great opportunity for him, but a heartbreak for me. I hated to leave Massachusetts, my parents, my friends, my job, and move to the Midwest. Eventually, I accepted the inevitable and flew to Cincinnati, Ohio, to buy a house and look for another job.

Our new neighbor hired me as a development chemist in the small company he directed. Somehow I survived for seven months in a poorly ventilated two-room laboratory situated in the basement of an old building, reeking of solvent. After inhaling for hours the pungent vapors wafting around me in the confined space, I fainted and was carried outside to the open air. Needless to say, this alarming episode prompted me to resign and move to a different company. The big pharmaceutical complex, Merrell-Dow, boasted new buildings, modern laboratories, and state-of-the-art equipment. The ceramic floors were so clean one could eat off of them—a dream-come-true facility where chemists competed like fighting tigers. I did not mind the hard work. The experience I gained in this place proved invaluable.

One day, I woke up with an excruciating pain in my back and left leg.

Unable to walk, I crawled into my car and rushed to the emergency room of the nearest hospital. The x-rays and CT-scan showed a slipped disc in my vertebral column. Painkillers did not help. After a three-month bed rest, I had to wear a special brace around my lower back. The company granted me a six-month sick leave. "No more standing on your feet in a lab. Change career," my doctor ordered. As soon as I could walk without pain, I applied for the PhD program in Analytical Chemistry at the University of Cincinnati (UC), with Samir's support of my decision. By then, our children were thirteen and eight-years old, both quite independent and doing well in school. Convinced that I could succeed if I worked hard, I presented my resignation to Merrell-Dow and threw myself wholeheartedly in the student life again. Dressed in blue jeans and t-shirt, I multitasked, driving the children to after-school activities and waiting for them with a book in my hand. Before the first exam, I swallowed two aspirins to soothe my frazzled nerves, and aced it.

After much thought and consideration, I chose the Chair of the Chemistry Department as my thesis director. His students specialized in advanced Analytical Spectroscopy and worked on sophisticated instruments. Our group included another young woman from Thailand and ten male students. At the end of my first year at UC, we drove together to Philadelphia to attend a conference and give a presentation. I shook like a leaf in the wind before giving my first talk, which was well received; it was followed by many more over the years, in New Orleans, San Diego, Boston, among others.

Four arduous years, numerous exams, and several published papers finally led to graduation. My parents flew in from Boston. Unfortunately, the night before the big ceremony, my father had a stroke and remained in bed. The Chair had selected me to carry the flag of the Graduate School. Wearing the red gown of the doctorate recipients and the black cap with the blue tassel of Chemistry, I raised the flag high to lead the procession of faculty and graduate students. Sitting in one of the front rows with our children, my husband snapped hundreds of pictures of that momentous day; then we rushed home to be with Papa.

A few weeks before graduation, while still on campus, I had received a phone call from a recruiter who wanted to interview graduating PhD students for a managerial position in the analytical laboratory of Environmental Chemical Corporation (ECC). He insisted I should meet with the CEO. The one-story old building did not impress me. It comprised only two offices, a shiny lab, and a huge warehouse in the back, but the CEO of the company, a charismatic and confident man, put me at ease right away. "Dr. Risk," he said, "you have a remarkably versatile experience, exactly what I am looking for. I want you to start this lab, buy the instruments you need, and hire the right staff. Show me what you can do. I will never clip your wings." Delighted with the man's attitude, I accepted the offer right away and, with a staff of four chemists, I started to work on two contracts from the Environmental Protection Agency (EPA). From day one, I decided to be firm and never let anyone derail me from my goal: to make this laboratory productive and successful.

Mona Risk, PhD Graduation, Cincinnati, 1985

While supervising the lab operations, I wrote many proposals and won several contracts with the US Army Corps of Engineers. To accommodate the expensive equipment I had ordered, I convinced the CEO to build six new labs in the empty warehouse and I interviewed many chemists and technicians, and carefully explained the pressure of laboratory life, but I offered the employees a good salary, health insurance coverage, and flexible time. To their credit, my chemists rarely complained about the long hours spent to analyze samples of hazardous water and soil waste materials. They did an excellent job, and the good reputation of the ECC lab soon spread around. We received contracts from different government agencies, and applied for several state certifications.

Growing at the same quick pace, ECC Corporate Office expanded its responsibilities. The company president moved his headquarters to San Francisco and promoted me to Director of the Analytical Division in

Cincinnati. Incidentally, I was the only woman among the executive staff of ten friendly and supportive members. Every quarter, I traveled to San Francisco and presented my report to the corporate office. To free myself from the daily supervision of lab operations, I hired a manager and promoted three chemists to supervise the staff of fifty chemists and technicians, and dedicated my time to submitting proposals to government agencies and networking with professionals who could help ECC's growth.

Mona Risk with Vice President Al Gore, Washington, DC, 1994

To expand our work, I studied the Department of Defense section of international projects and wrote a winning proposal. The company was awarded a contract to refurbish a military laboratory in Belarus. ECC President called to congratulate me and informed me that I should go to Washington, DC to sign the new contract. Pride and anxiety warred in my heart when I learned that I would also be attending a fundraising dinner hosted by Vice President Al Gore. My picture with the VP is framed on my bookcase, and the ECC President keeps a copy on his own credenza.

My first trip to Minsk, the capital of Belarus, occurred at the end of October 1994. A decorated colonel welcomed our delegation. My first night at the hotel, I literally froze in the unheated drafty room. The next day, our group acquired several electric heaters and I bought myself a cute mink hat called "chapka." During our meetings, I continuously asked for a cup of hot tea, but was often offered vodka instead. Between 1994 and 1997, my staff and I traveled to Minsk more than fifteen times to install new equipment and train Belarusian chemists. Several key personalities attended the inauguration of the refurbished lab, including the Minister of the Environment, the Minister of Defense, and the American Ambassador. We were featured on the TV evening news. The Major General awarded me a medal for services rendered to Belarus.

Mona Risk receiving a medal from Major General of Belarus, 1996

More international contracts took me to Kiev and Uman in Ukraine; to Almati and Stepnogorsk in Kazakhstan; to Moscow, St. Petersburg and Sergei Possad in Russia. Each new project presented more challenges due to clash of cultures, different languages, and work habits. Soon I realized that I had reached the end of my rope. Working an average of fourteen hours a day for sixteen years, I had garnered more degrees than the average student, and reached as high as I could in my career. I had been honored by my employer and the executives with whom I collaborated, and was rewarded with a salary that many professionals would envy. It was time to take an early retirement and fulfill another dream: I wanted to write and publish romance novels.

On September 1st, 2000, I gathered the staff for a last meeting and informed them of my decision. During the farewell speech, I could not hold my tears and many of my chemists cried too. They had become my second family. ECC offered me a contract as a consultant and two years later flew me to Moscow with my husband to audit a refurbished lab. In 2010, the company invited me to participate in its 30th anniversary and awarded me a "Certificate of Recognition for Personal Leadership Demonstrated toward the Development, Advancement, Recognition, and History of Women within ECC and our Industry." I gave the keynote address to three hundred attendees.

Turning the page, I concentrated on my new goal. English was my third language after French and Arabic. To write novels and compete in the publishing industry, I bought grammar and writing books, and once again I started at the bottom of the ladder. I sent an email to my favorite romance author who advised me to join the Romance Writers of America (RWA). At the monthly meetings of the RWA local chapter, I met published authors and beginners. We formed critique groups and helped each other, until I gathered the courage to submit excerpts of my writing to various publishers. After receiving my share of rejection letters for five years, one finally offered me a contract.

Through my first novel *To Love a Hero* (aka *Her Russian Hero*) released in 2008, I practically relived my fantastic trips to Belarus. Many of the adventures I experienced in Minsk are related in my book, such as my fall on the broken escalator of the airport. But my lucky heroine fell straight into the arms of the Major General, a gorgeous hero, and enjoyed a lovely romance. Several more books followed, set in the fascinating places I had visited during my business or vacation travel. In 2011, I tried my hand at self-publishing and was stunned by the amazing number of ebooks I sold on Amazon, and the enthusiastic reviews of my fans. But my biggest reward came from bedridden readers who said my novels brought joy to their lives and took them on an armchair trip around the world.

Babies in the Bargain won Best Contemporary Romance of the year at Editors & Preditors, and Amazon translated the book in German (*Babies Inklusive*) and in French (*Des bébés en prime*). *No More Lies* won Best Novel at Readers Favorite. After publishing twenty books and contributing to more than ten anthologies, I earned the top honor for a published author: the enviable status of "*USA Today* Bestselling Author," and "*New York*

Times Bestselling Author."

My legacy to my daughter, granddaughters, and the Daughters of Egypt is the following: set your goals high and work hard to follow your dream. You *can* make a difference. You *can* improve the world around you.

Fort Lauderdale, Florida, September 2015

CROSSING BORDERS
IN THE SHADOW OF GIANTS

FAIZA WAHBY SHEREEN

The first discussion my parents had about me took place before I was born. Their three children were grown up. I was neither planned nor expected. To be welcomed into the world against all odds was perhaps a prologue to a life of unexpected turns and serendipitous successes. Though my mother was in her forties and my father almost sixty when I was born, they were both powerful figures in my early childhood and adolescence. I am grateful for the courage and openness my mother always displayed and the discipline and commitment to moral positions that I learned by observing my father in various contexts. My sister, twenty years my senior, assumed more or less, the responsibility of my upbringing. When I was two, she took me to the Homecraft House pre-school, after which I was to be sent the English Girls' College (EGC), the "best school in the country," as she told my parents in her attempts to convince them.

The choice was one she had to justify to my parents, for the girls in the family had always received a French education. But she was determined that my education should be in English, the "international" language of the future. The EGC was modeled after the English public schools and students sat for the Oxford and Cambridge ordinary and advanced examinations. The school was physically beautiful, and I believe that this aesthetic quality had an impact on our eagerness, every morning, to go to school. The classroom was a space of mental activities where we were encouraged to think critically—to question, to reflect, and to examine knowledge. We formed lasting relationships in the school; many of us have remained friends despite geographical separation and the passage of time.

I excelled in the sciences but in the senior year, I surprised everyone by choosing to focus on the arts. I remember distinctly the day when I was summoned to the headmistress's office soon after I had signed up for the arts. My math, biology, chemistry, and physics teachers were all there to advise me to reconsider my choice and follow the science track. But, my mind was made up. I had had Kate Noone as my language and literature teacher, and the kinds of questions she taught us to ask intrigued me even more than algebra. I graduated from the EGC at the Oxford and Cambridge O level (GCE), and received the cup for highest achievement in English, presented to me at graduation by the Egyptian Minister of Education

Graduation Day at the EGC. Faiza receiving the cup for English Literature from Alexandria Governor, Hamdi Ashour, and Egypt's Minister of Education, Sayyed Youssef, Alexandria, 1964

Then, I joined the English Department of Alexandria University. We had some of the finest British-educated Egyptian professors as well as a group of young teachers from the UK. The old colonial British types of my early childhood had long since disappeared from the social fabric. These young teachers, products of a post-British empire European culture, were dynamic educators with new ideas. They exposed us to habits of thought that were alien to the Egyptian ethos, an approach that shunned the dramatic or the sentimental and cultivated a special humor and a sense of irony—so very British. The four years passed quickly. Upon graduation, I looked for job opportunities where I could use my languages. I had English, Arabic and French at native or near-native levels, and had studied German for six years, at the EGC and later at the Goethe Institute. A call from the Chair of the English Department at the University offering me an instructor position, however, ended my search and determined my future. I later thought how absolutely inevitable it was that I would end up in an academic career. If I had not received the call that day, something else would have steered me in this direction eventually.

I got married at that time. My husband, Ahmed Shereen, was a mechanical engineer, and within a year of our marriage, he received an internship with Fiat in Italy. This was the first of many times in my life when, having to choose between career and family, I chose the latter. I accompanied my husband to Torino, with every intention of resuming my career as soon as possible. My time in Italy was divided between learning Italian and reading the modernist writers. Isolated from my Alexandria commitments, I had the time to indulge in the pleasure of avid reading. I was absolutely transported by the rhythm and cadence of Woolf's poetic prose, by the sheer power of Joyce's intoxicating words, and by the hundreds of tiny glimmers that together recreate life in Proust. That year I also discovered the heterogeneity of cultural "reality" and the incomparable, multiple pleasures of living in a new environment—an experience that fostered interests later manifested in my professional choices.

Upon our return to Egypt, I had to face another dilemma in my position at Alexandria University. At that time, graduate work in English literature in Egypt was a real challenge. I gave up a scholarship in England because my husband, and by now our baby girl, could not have joined me on the terms of this option. The solution to my dilemma was proposed by my brother who had completed his studies at Columbia University and was now living in Dayton, Ohio. He suggested I pursue graduate work in the US, where my husband could work and build an international base of experience. We would have to leave Egypt as emigrants. To me, the very idea of emigration was particularly painful. I suffered a great deal of anguish during this period of life-transforming decisions.

Following my brother's advice, I applied to three universities in Ohio, in and around Dayton where he lived. I was pleasantly surprised when, almost immediately, I was offered a scholarship and an assistantship by the University of Dayton (UD). Naturally, I accepted the offer, and within days, I received a second and a third from the other two universities. I wrote back to the University of Cincinnati (UC), asking them to keep my file on record as, though I had accepted the UD assistantship for the MA, I would reapply a year later for the PhD at Cincinnati.

Just as we were ready to purchase our airline tickets, the 1973 war broke out, and the airports were closed. One day, my husband called me from Cairo and said: "Pack everything and bring Laila to Cairo. The airport is open. We leave in two days." If I had prepared myself emotionally to leave my country, I had not expected it to happen so suddenly. What was reasonable when considered theoretically became alarming when grasped as an imminent reality. I packed all night. There was a hand mirror, beautifully encased in silver with my grandmother's initials engraved, that always lay on my mother's dressing-table. She would hold it up to see her back in the wall mirror. I asked her if I could take it with me. "No," she said, "I'll give it to you when you return." At dawn the next day, mother came into my room with the silver mirror and quietly put it in my luggage. I value this memento of home profoundly.

Faiza's last Egyptian Passport picture, 1973

The English Department at UD was welcoming, and I quickly overcame my apprehensions about learning a new way of doing things or teaching English to native speakers. I brought a cosmopolitan perspective to a very local culture, and I think that was valued by my colleagues and teachers. What I learned quickly about the American way of doing things is that there is always a structure and a predictability that make it easy to perform. In a little over a year, I had completed the MA requirements, including a thesis on early 20th century British literature. The next fall, I entered the PhD program at UC with a teaching assistantship that was the first of several scholastic honors, including two Taft Fellowships.

During those years I formed one of several relationships that I cherish and that influenced my choices in crossing frontiers. I met Edward Said, Palestinian-American intellectual and literary theoretician, and Professor of English and Comparative Literature at Columbia University. I shared more with him than professional interests. Of Palestinian origin, Said grew up and went to school in Alexandria where he attended Victoria College— the EGC equivalent for boys—and, despite the difference in our age, we had known a similar Egypt. Said's description of his relationship to the languages with which he grew up reflects a reality at the heart of my own identity. He says: "Arabic, my native language, and English, my school language, were inextricably mixed: I have never known which was my first language, and have felt fully at home in both and in neither."[1]

I was nine months pregnant with my second child when I took my comprehensive and oral examinations. The period following this threshold represented a lull in my career as my husband's job required us to move every other year. It is during this time that I had three more children, the youngest of whom was born in California. With five children now, and the upheaval of frequent moving, my career seemed doomed. Wherever we went, there were a number of boxes marked "Faiza's dissertation." "You will never get back to it!" was what I kept hearing from friends and family. But I knew I would. My commitment was absolute, but I had come to the realization that in my life there would always be two competing allegiances: my family and my career. The first I could never sacrifice; the second was my own passion. Neither could replace the other; the two combined constituted my self-fulfillment. I received the PhD on the day of my oldest daughter's graduation from high school. To determine the scope of my job search, I drew a circle of thirty miles around our home, in Cincinnati now, and applied for academic jobs within this circumference. I was appointed in a tenure-track position at the University of Dayton.

Faiza's PhD hooding ceremony (UC) followed her oldest daughter Laila's high school graduation, Cincinnati, 1988

My PhD advisor at UC, novelist and critic Austin Wright, had a huge impact on the direction I took as an academic. My apprenticeship to Wright's incisive and unrelenting critical inquiry led me to go beyond literary appreciation to theoretical speculation. Art and literary theory provided the bases for my research and were the source of new areas of interest, such as Postcolonial literature and culture. He introduced me to Wayne Booth, one of the leading American critics whose work was seminal in my dissertation; I went to Chicago to meet him. The interview morphed into an impassioned discussion of contemporary European theorists, and we went from his office to a lunch that lasted three hours. On the way home, I was dizzy with ideas. Our relationship continued over the years in conversations carried on by mail, and in person when we met at various professional conferences, and when he came to Dayton as a guest speaker and did me the honor of co-teaching one of my theory classes. Austin Wright passed away in 2003 and Wayne Booth in 2005. Their deaths made me feel intellectually orphaned. Now, it was no longer a time of learning only, but a time of contributing to knowledge, and the task was daunting.

I believe that at critical moments of transition, a fortunate stroke of serendipity has sometimes put me on a course that helped me to fulfill my destiny. Middle-Eastern fatalism? Perhaps. The year I received tenure at

UD, one of my colleagues walked into my office and put a Fulbright catalogue on my desk. "You would be a good fit for this sort of thing," he declared. But I put the catalogue away, thinking I could not go anywhere and leave my family. However, the more I thought about it, the more it seemed like an attractive possibility. At that point, my husband was trying to start a business in Southern California, where we had always wanted to return. This situation meant that his job did not tie us to Cincinnati anymore. It was a period of flux, a great opportunity for me to travel. I applied for a Senior Scholar grant in Morocco to research postcolonial Francophone literature. How was literature written in French by writers of an Arabic Islamic culture to be understood? What "language," what "codes" functioned in the creative process of this binary identity?

I fell in love with Morocco from the start. Perhaps with nostalgic empathy, I delighted in the familiar lines of Islamic architecture. I was impressed by the culture's preserved identity, in contrast to the condition in Egypt, where much of the local color was either erased or only found in the old and neglected neighborhoods. The climate was gentle and temperate by comparison with the American Midwest. The landscapes were remarkably varied, reflecting the vastly different subcultures: the blue Mediterranean towns, the Atlas mountains, the Atlantic coast, and the red sand dunes of the south were as different as the Berbers of the Rif are from the Touaregs of the south. I traveled throughout the country, and became intimately familiar with the culture. One of my most memorable experiences was a trip to the deep south to interview an oral story teller.

The oral tradition being one of the local threads of Moroccan Francophone literature, I was anxious to meet an authentic story teller. When another American Fulbrighter told me of an "ancient" story teller he had met in the South, I decided to visit him. I took the road from Rabat to Fez, through the Atlas mountains and down to the desert—a magnificent trip. In the village of Erfoud, my fellow Fulbrighter met me and introduced me to the driver who would take me the next morning to the story teller's abode in the sand dunes.

I felt no apprehension or anxiety until we left the main road and drove into the sand. Gradually all landmarks disappeared, and my guide drove the car through the sand like a ship at sea. I could not fathom how he navigated, guided only by an occasional bush and the direction of our shadows. A small structure finally appeared on the horizon. We had indeed arrived at the storyteller's home. He welcomed us in the one long and narrow room, where a number of pillows were arranged around a very low table. Over the traditional very sweet mint tea, he talked. I taped two hours' worth of tales and myths threaded into some very accurate accounts of the region's history. Just as I was ready to say goodbye, his young daughter walked in with a magnificent dish of couscous. The notorious hospitality was just as much a question of honor in this remote and solitary home as it was in the well-equipped villas in the city. He smiled and stroked his long white beard, and beckoned to his shy daughter to join us. This was one of my most memorable meals.

My first year in Morocco was unforgettable in many ways, but the opportunity it afforded me to develop lasting friendships was invaluable. I got to know many writers who lived in Morocco at the time. From the American legend Paul Bowles, to the famous feminist sociologist and novelist Fatima Mernissi, I had the privilege of engaging with active, contemporary thinkers. But most particularly, I value the relationship I developed with the late Abdelkebir Khatibi. In 1994, when I first met him, he had received the *Grand Prix de l'Académie Française*. I translated some of his work, and we started a long and productive professional friendship.

I attended a conference in Rabat where Khatibi was speaking on a panel with Jacques Derrida, the French philosopher whose colossal contributions transformed the world's leading ideologies and defined postmodernism. After the conference, Khatibi brought Derrida down to introduce us, and we went out to dinner to continue the inquiry started in the discussions. We maintained a steady correspondence and, a couple of years later, I received an invitation from Derrida to participate in a closed seminar in Paris at the *École des Hautes Études en Sciences Sociales,* with a number of renowned scholars, including Hélène Cixous, whose work had always intrigued me.

Faiza at the international conference, The Idea of the University, with Dr. Lahcen Haddad, Morocco's Minister of Tourism, Rabat, Morocco, 1997

Khatibi and Derrida read my play, *The Country Within*, and both urged me to publish it. The play introduces two couples and a single man from very different backgrounds who arrive in New York as Egyptian immigrants in the late 1960s. In Egypt, their paths would have never crossed; in New York, they become friends and their relationships develop. The action, punctuated by a number of narratives, extends across two generations and examines the dual perspectives of people who straddle cultures and cross boundaries. It was written at the request of a group of Egyptian-Americans in Los Angeles who asked me to write a play that could be produced by the Egyptian-American Organization. At first, I laughed at the image of myself as playwright, but the seed was planted, and I found myself imagining scenes as I drove to the library to work on my dissertation. The play premiered in Cincinnati at the St Joseph Theater, and was performed a number of times, most recently at the Irvine Barclay Theater in 2012. In addition to these performances, the play was the subject of a couple of doctoral theses and scholarly articles.[2]

My first year in Morocco did not only shape the direction of my research, it had another important effect on my life. I watched my children's imaginative scopes expand as a result of their immersion in a different culture; I saw them develop what I call a "double vision," the ability to see things both as an insider and an outsider. In my case, this quality is the privilege gained from the circumstances of my youth in a barely "post" colonial culture and the result of being uprooted from one place and migrating to regrow in another. I also watched exchange students in Morocco from various American universities adding a study abroad component to their education, and I wanted to create such possibilities for our students. The opening of the first university with English as the language of instruction during my Fulbright year encouraged me to dream of possibilities. I called our Provost and proposed an exchange agreement with the new university. That was the beginning of a shift in my career from scholar/teacher to administrator, and I spent the next fifteen years building international programs that took students around the world. When I was asked to direct the Center for International Programs at UD, I hesitated briefly—reluctant to give up my literary interests—but I accepted, for the passion of my conviction about the value of international education dominated my professional aspirations.[3]

My love affair with Morocco continued. While I investigated possibilities and designed programs in many places around the world, I continued to foster my relations in Morocco and focused my scholarly research on the literature of North Africa. After my first Fulbright, I returned to Morocco thirty-two times, often as a guest speaker or program director, but two more times I was there for extended periods on research grants, the last of which was a second Fulbright. I got to know the country more intimately than most Moroccans, and feel at home there in a very special way.

In 2002, the great library of Alexandria was reborn as the *Bibliotheca Alexandrina*. I was privileged to be invited among a group of Egyptian Americans being honored during the events of the inauguration. Among others, I read a poem I had written entitled "Alexandria." In the first row, Dr. Azza Kararah, one of my professors at Alexandria University, was sitting with her husband, Dr. Moustapha El Abbadi, a leader in the Library project. She looked at me with tears in her eyes as I read my lines. This was a moment laden with emotion that I shall always keep in my mental store of cherished memories.

The following year, I organized an international conference at the *Bibliotheca Alexandrina* entitled "Of Lighthouses and Libraries: History ReLit," under the auspices of the African Literature Association. The conference was scheduled for March 2003. Unfortunately, beginning in January, the alarming expectation that the US would invade Iraq concerned registered participants, and the large number who had planned to attend dwindled as we approached the date. We considered cancelling; the lingering effects of the postcolonial reality seemed to continue to shape our world, but Edward Said, who was the keynote speaker, insisted that we go ahead as planned. The conference opened on March 19, the same day the Iraq War started. The success of our event despite the political challenges was immensely gratifying.[4]

My children were growing up and going to college, and I thought I had settled down to a stable routine when I was recruited to run the International Center at the California State Polytechnic University, Pomona (CSU). My husband and I had always dreamed of returning to California after our first three years there in the 1980s. The opportunity was too tempting, and my husband encouraged me to take the position. "It's your turn now," he said.

In my new position as Senior International Officer at CSU, I traveled around the world, putting in place programs for our American students, and creating opportunities for foreign students to study in the US. The first few years were very productive, as we successfully moved International Education to a more central position in the academic division. However, the economic crisis of 2008 seriously impacted International Programs, and I went back to teaching. In 2013, however, I returned, once more, to the administration of international education as Resident Director of the California State University System in France. Our programs being in Paris and Aix-en-Provence, I divided my time between the two locations. In Paris, I relived in my memory the intellectual adventures of the year when I had the good fortune of being admitted in a circle of intellectual giants.

Two important events in my life occurred in 2015. My first and my last daughters graduated two weeks apart, the oldest with a PhD in Media Arts, and the youngest with a PhD in Mathematics. Both have unique histories with multiple degrees across the disciplines. My oldest son completed his PhD in Physics some years ago, and my youngest is in medical school. My middle daughter, an anthropologist, has given me two wonderful grandchildren, a boy/girl pair of twins. To my amazement, my oldest also had a pair of twins—two adorable sisters for my first grandchild, Amel. I am absolutely delighted that my children's work sounds incomprehensible to me!

It is a long time since that day I left Alexandria with my baby. I journeyed to many places, mentally and emotionally, and crossed boundaries, both real and conceptual. The usual mix of gain and loss brings me to this moment. But Egypt has always been with me. I can always trace the Nile in any map of my experiences. What remains now is necessarily much less than what has passed. But I have always believed that the meaning of one's life is determined by the contributions one makes, and I still have a great deal to give.

Los Angeles, California, November 2015

Notes

[1] "Between Worlds," *Reflections on Exile, and Other Essays*, Cambridge, MA: Harvard University Press, 2000. 556–57.

[2] Theses and articles about *The Country Within* include the following, among others: Amira Nowaira. "Negotiating Self in Diaspora: Historicizing Faiza Shereen's Play, *The Country Within*, *Studies in the Humanities* 30.1 (2004): 131-39; Luther Gibson, "*The Country Within*—Universal," *The Cincinnati Herald*, 23 November 1991: 2; Dalia Bassiony, *The Country Within*, dissertation, Department of Theater, City University of New York (CUMY), [YEAR]; and Latifa Halim, *The Country Within*, dissertation, Department of Arabic Language & Literature, University Cadi Ayyad, Morocco 2000. It was also taught by A. Amin, Theater Department, Georgetown University, 2004; and by M. Hayward, "Diaspora Literature," Ocean County College, 2004.

[3] My interest in International Affairs led me to serve as President of the Arab Arts Society in Cincinnati, and as Member of the Board of Directors of the Dayton Council on World Affairs. In California, I served once more on the Board of the Egyptian-American Organization. In these capacities, my goals were always to bring better understanding between my two cultures.

[4] In the following decade, I continued to work on North African literature, to write, and be active in the community. In 2004, my novella, *Gifts of Time*, published in *Women Writing Africa* (Vol. 4, *The Northern Region*, NY: The Feminist Press, 2009) was awarded the RAWI Prize for Creative Writing—Fiction. [RAWI, the Radius of Arab-American Writers, is a non-profit literary organization dedicated to disseminating creative and scholarly writing by Arab-Americans]. In 2009, I received the Outstanding Achievement Award from the Egyptian-American Organization. In August 2015, I was honored among "Women of Value" by the National Alliance of Free Women.

CROSSING CULTURES TWICE: FROM ALEXANDRIA TO ZÜRICH THEN OTTAWA

ABLA SHERIF

I was born at home in Cairo, the second of four children. My father was an engineer and my mother a homemaker; a traditional upper-middle class family indulging in the comforts of an easy-going life. My parents gave their children a good education, and the opportunity to be part of a refined and polished society. During my early years, we moved several times back and forth between Cairo and Alexandria, following my father's professional career. My most vivid memories, however, are mainly of Alexandria where I eventually went to university. It was a time when Alexandria was one of the Middle East's most vibrant multicultural cities, where several languages were spoken by a diverse multinational population. I was fortunate to benefit from that rich environment, in addition to being educated in an excellent English school, sponsored by the British Council. I spoke both English and Arabic fluently, and French haltingly. My family was conservative, and I was expected to abide by accepted social norms. Despite my traditional upbringing, life took me on an unconventional path. Along the way, I found that my choices and decisions were greatly influenced by my mother's personality.

For several years, my father worked as a senior executive in Egypt's largest textile company in Mehalla Al Kobra, a town in the Nile Delta. We lived with my mother in Alexandria where the best schools were located, and my dad would come home on the weekend. A loving and powerful woman, my mother was a firm disciplinarian who managed the family business in the absence of my father. I am convinced that my own determination and strength developed as I witnessed hers in action. She was self-assured, believing there was nothing she could not do. Like her, and despite the Middle-Eastern limitations on our gender, I too, grew up knowing that I could accomplish and excel in anything I set out to undertake. The characteristics I took after my mother served me well in the years to follow, especially after I left home and had to face many personal and professional challenges.

Upon graduating from Alexandria University with a Bachelor's degree in English Literature, I resisted pressure from my parents who wanted me to stay in Alexandria. They would have liked me to indulge in a leisurely life, attending social functions and meeting interesting people, until I found the right partner and settled in marital bliss close to the family. Instead, I went to Cairo where I lived in my grandfather's house, and worked as a translator at the High Council for the Arts and Literature—a government administration headed by my uncle who was a member of Nasser's cabinet. In my job, I had the opportunity to participate in several international conferences held in Cairo under the auspices of the Afro-Asian Council, another organization directed by my uncle. Working in this exciting environment was an eye-opener. Far from the protected and privileged environment of home, the experience was both demanding and stressful, but it was also rewarding as it added to my knowledge and my exposure to various cultures and the world of politics.

One particular experience stands out in my mind. One evening, a few months after arriving in Cairo, I received a phone call from my uncle who asked me to accompany him to the presidential palace, to be a translator from Arabic into English with a visiting delegation that had unexpectedly arrived in Cairo to meet with President Gamal Abdel Nasser. This late in the day, the palace was unable to locate the official translator, hence the need for me to fill in. I accompanied my uncle to Kubbah Palace, where the meeting was held in one of the largest parlors. Members of the delegation stood in a semicircle facing the President, and I was next to him, translating his words into English as he paused. It was a privilege to meet President Nasser in person, the most popular and venerated Arab leader the Middle East, the one who instilled pride in his people after years of British occupation. He impressed me with his confidence, imposing stature, and piercing eyes that commanded attention. In subsequent years, however, there were many occasions when I disagreed with his policies, and felt crushing disappointment at the turn of events under his leadership. But I must also admit that he was a patriotic leader who enjoyed unparalleled popularity and respect, whose standing and charisma few Middle-Eastern figures would ever match.

After a year in Cairo, I got married. Mohamed Ali Sherif who became my husband was no stranger; ours was not the typical arranged marriage. Mohamed Ali was the only son of our family doctor; his parents and mine were friends, and we had known each other for years. We shared similar social and intellectual backgrounds, and deeply cherished democracy, freedom, and the rights of the individual. He was mature beyond his years and fiercely independent. Our values conflicted with those prevailing in the social and political climate of Egypt in the 1960s and 1970s; thus, we decided to leave and pursue graduate studies in Switzerland.

The move to Zürich was a culture shock for me. In this new country, I missed the emotional security and financial comfort of my family, as well as the social network that included many high-ranking dignitaries, among which were a cabinet member, a titled *Pasha* and a member of President Nasser's inner circle. In Switzerland, I was an ordinary foreign student who needed to prove herself by adapting to the cultural and social norms of a different society. Not only did I have to learn a new language, German, I also had to change some of my "old" ways, and adapt to the Swiss way. The Swiss people may respect and appreciate international visitors and tourists who add to their economic prosperity, but they are unwilling to make any concession to foreign students or workers. Being accepted depends entirely on your ability and willingness to conform. The more you behave like the Swiss, the better your chances of success. My life and studies required self-discipline, self-control, dogged determination, and a search for perfection, all highly prized in the Swiss culture. In exchange for the sacrifices I had to make, I was rewarded with a quality of education next to none.

My professors were outstanding scholars, with amazing knowledge of language, history, and the humanities. Switzerland allows only those who possess a nearly perfect command of their subject matter to rise to the rank of professor. Those who taught me demanded rigorous discipline and scholarship. For my doctorate, I had to take exams in Latin, as well as Old and Middle English before being allowed to start on the dissertation. There were also additional requirements. I chose Colonial History and Arabic Literature, thinking the latter would be easy for me, as it would be taught by a visiting Swiss professor from the University of Basel. I was wrong. The professor was much more versed in that subject than I could ever aspire to be. At the end of my studies in Zürich, I received a PhD with Highest Honors, and felt a great sense of pride having overcome many hurdles and obstacles along the way. This achievement was even more significant because I had just given birth to our first son a year and a half earlier. Taking care of the baby while trying to meet a demanding course of studies was arduous, to say the least, but it was a mission well accomplished. It was also useful practice that prepared me well for what was to follow, when I had to juggle family and career.

While in Zürich, my husband and I were keeping a close watch on events in Egypt, hoping the political situation would change from its drive toward socialism and communism, and its close ties to the Soviet Union. Unfortunately, the country's direction continued to run counter to our basic principles and values. Then came the time to make a decision: we would either have to go back to our homeland and comply with a regime unacceptable to us, or start a new life in another country. We chose the latter option, and emigrated to Canada.

I always tell people that moving from Zürich to Montreal was like returning halfway home to Alexandria, for Montreal was a city after my own heart: diverse, multicultural, and more international than any European city. In that environment, there was no obligation to adapt to any particular norm, or to fit into a defined mold. This was a truly unprejudiced society celebrating differences and embracing diverse cultures. I was welcome the way I was because I added value to this rich and alive society. English and French were the official languages, but many other tongues were spoken and no one seemed surprised or disapproving. What a change! How could I not fall in love with this beloved country! I felt right at home. According to the 2015 Legatum Institute Prosperity Index, Canada ranks 1st in the world for personal freedom and social tolerance. It comforts me to know that we made the right decision in 1968 when we opted to set up roots in Canada.

I started my career as a teacher at Dawson College, the first English language Community College in Montreal. It was a time of excitement and innovation, as I interacted with young and dynamic minds, exploring literary masterpieces and their relevance to contemporary world problems. The students were different from those I encountered in Zürich. Whereas the Swiss system instilled discipline and conformity, the North American educational philosophy encouraged inquisitiveness and free discussion. In the late 1960s and 1970s, Montreal was a hot-bed of free ideas, non-conformity and creativity. The young minds with which I came in contact might have been a challenge to authority, but they were creative and dynamic. My work as a teacher was to capture the interest of my students, and give them free reign to question issues and decisions. I helped them to express their thoughts and organize them cogently—a challenging and stimulating endeavor.

During our second year in Canada, Mohamed Ali accepted an offer as a senior executive in the Federal Government in Ottawa. The family moved to the capital at the beginning of the academic year, but I decided to continue to work in Montreal until the end of the year. The two-hour commute morning and evening, four days a week, was exhausting. That particular winter happened to be one of the worst in many years, with record snow falls. During one of these trips, the train was stuck on the tracks for seven hours, unable to move due to the enormous amount of snow. Food and drinks had to be supplied to the train by helicopter. At the end of the day, we returned to Ottawa never having reached Montreal.

The following year I started to work in Ottawa as a Professor of English Literature at Algonquin College, the second largest Community College in Ontario. Shortly thereafter, I became the Dean of the Faculty of Media and Design. Canada has one of the world's most successful models of community colleges, which offer a multitude of programs based on a mix of broad-based educational courses, as well as strong vocational hands-on training, including field placement within industry. In general, the employment rate of their graduates in their chosen fields of study is around 90%, far exceeding the placement of university graduates.

Developing programs for a community college is exciting, as it aims to merge academic studies with skills identified by industry. It requires constant contact with professional partners, in order to respond promptly to their needs, and serves as a perfect bridge between academe and practical life. My position at Algonquin College made me intimately involved in the Ottawa community. The success of the programs that I helped to put together eventually led me to assume new responsibilities. This time, the assignment was to offer similar opportunities for students overseas, by developing international partnerships with educational institutions in other countries. In collaboration with them, Algonquin would offer its programs at their particular locations. The endeavor required curricular transfer, teacher training, and implementation of quality evaluation to ensure that students achieved the required outcomes. Upon completing their studies, international students received the credentials offered by the Ontario Ministry of Colleges and Universities. These programs were offered in various countries throughout the world, including Africa, India, China, and Europe. I was privileged to visit the partners in these nations, and work with their educational providers. Witnessing young people thousands of miles away receive Canadian education and professional qualifications was especially rewarding. As students graduated, they became goodwill ambassadors for Canada all over the world.

One particular enterprise that left a lasting impression on me resulted from a 3 million dollar project sponsored by the Canadian International Development Agency (CIDA). It partnered three Canadian community colleges from across the country with three community colleges in South Africa. The purpose was to help the South African partners improve their educational delivery, which was lagging from isolation during Apartheid. I was selected to coordinate the project, and took my first fact-finding trip to

South Africa in 1993, when the legendary leader, Nelson Mandela, had just been released after years in jail. It was a journey of discovery

South Africa dazzled me with its scenic beauty, its oceans, mountains, vineyards, villages and moderate climate. Most of my work was in Cape Town where the majority of people are a mix of Europeans and Africans. My counterparts were talented and highly educated, yet they had been subjected to racial prejudice. 1993 heralded change, and the country was bouncing with anticipation and excitement. For the next five years, I continued to visit South Africa regularly to supervise the progress of the partnership until the project was completed. With every trip, I could notice remarkable social, economic and cultural growth and development, as a new generation of leaders assumed charge of the country. It was a distinct privilege for me to witness history in the making. The friendships and bonds between the Canadian and South African participants in this program have remained strong and lasted to this day.

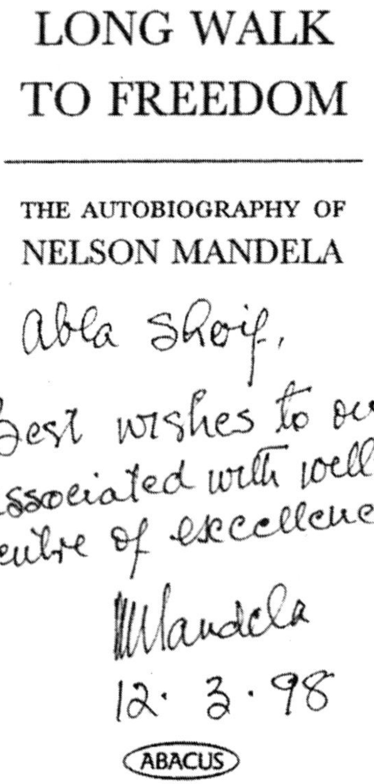

LONG WALK
TO FREEDOM

THE AUTOBIOGRAPHY OF
NELSON MANDELA

To Abla Sherif,

Best wishes to our associated with well-known centre of excellence.

Mandela

12· 3·98

(ABACUS)

Nelson Mandela's dedication of his biography to Abla

There were other interesting projects in emerging countries, including India and China. The first trip I took to China occurred shortly after concluding an assignment in India. Because the two were so close, I was struck by the similarities and differences between the two countries. Both were rising economic powers, with a population base that spurred growth, and governing regimes that embraced economic development. What impressed me most was the marked difference in the philosophy governing social interactions. My first trip to India started in Delhi where I landed in the early morning, the time when most flights from Europe arrive. The limousine picked me up from the airport and took me to the Taj Mahal Hotel where I was staying. Two hostesses in saris were waiting for me on the steps, they escorted me directly to my room and registered me as a guest, so I did not have to stand at the reception desk. An arrangement of beautiful fresh flowers brightened my room, a tasteful sign of welcome. This was only a sample of the way the rest of the visit proceeded, with all the plans made with a touch of old-world hospitality. The different individuals with whom I worked came from different social and religious backgrounds, reflecting the diversity of the country, although their manners exhibited the same formal and charming graciousness that I encountered everywhere. At the same time, they were intelligent and shrewd business people determined to get the best deal in all interactions. A visit to the old bazaar in Delhi was pure delight. Most of the goods were handcrafted, exhibiting skills handed down through generations. Silverware and jewelry items were splendid prized possessions for those who could afford them. Delhi impressed me as a city that kept its traditions while transitioning to the modern era.

My visit to Shanghai was quite different. Here was a modern metropolis with high rises everywhere, and more cranes and new construction than I have ever seen anywhere. They were only outnumbered by car dealership lots. Shanghai is a business center with hustle and bustle similar to that of any North American city; it is replete with fancy shopping centers brimming with designer stores and expensive goods. Somehow, I found it difficult to reconcile these obvious signs of capitalism in a country where the communist regime is still quite powerful. There was, however, ample evidence of economic prosperity and success. The colleagues with whom I collaborated were efficient and practical, polite and hospitable. Delhi may have captured my heart with its old-world charm, but Shanghai filled my mind with hope for the future of its people.

While living and working in Ottawa, I made a point of participating in volunteer work to pay back to the community some of the debt I owed for its gift of an unparalleled quality of life. I served on the boards of the Ottawa Hospital, the Royal Ottawa Health Care Group, and the Community Foundation of Ottawa, to name but a few. To satisfy my interest in literature and culture, I also sat on the boards of the International Writers' Festival, the Ottawa Chapter of the Canadian Federation of University Women; and I currently serve on the Board of the Canadian Institute for Mediterranean Studies. In other words, I can truly say that I am a full participant in the Ottawa community.

My journey from Egypt to Zürich was one I never imagined or anticipated while growing up in Alexandria. I had exchanged a world of security and complacency for a world of adventure and self-actualization. I did not do it alone, I have a supportive husband and three wonderful sons who respect their mother's strength and look up to her achievements. I was also blessed to have gone through one of the world's most reputable educational institutions, the University of Zürich; however, my greatest good fortune was to have chosen Canada as an adopted country.

I will always be Egyptian at heart. Egypt is the land of my childhood memories, my loving family, and the warm and generous people that I cherish. Egypt is home to one of the world's most brilliant ancient civilizations, an integral part of the temperament of its inhabitants. Today, after years of colonization and corrupt rulers, it is attempting to develop and spread its wing, while making every effort to improve the quality of life for its citizens. Kindness, hospitality and sharing are essential parts of the Egyptian psyche; as an Egyptian woman, I feel that these are part of my nature, and I tried to instill them in my children who were raised in Canada. As Egyptian as I am, I am also a devoted Canadian, proud to be part of an independent democratic country that welcomed me as one of its own children, allowed me to be who I was, and added me to the rich fabric of its culture. Canada is the nation that gave me amazing opportunities to grow professionally and achieve goals I never dreamed I would have. Thank you, Canada, for taking me in and making me part of your democracy.

Ottawa, December 2015

MY JOURNEY INTO MOSAICS: TURNING A CHILDHOOD FANTASY INTO FINE ARTISTIC WORKS

SUZANNE SPAHI

I make my living from mosaics and this work enables me to travel around the world. It has been a challenging journey, but I have always managed thanks to my utter determination, passion, and deep interest in the mosaic world. My success has been a long process of hard work, as it did not come without effort and sacrifice.

It is true that your early years are what shapes you. My parents have Turkish, Syrian, and Tunisian roots, but were born in Egypt. My grandfather founded the largest privately owned textile factory in Egypt, so textiles are in my veins. As an only child, I was often on my own, playing on an oriental rug in the living room. I loved the patterns and shapes on the rug, and would choose the particular one on which to play. When I became a teenager, I watched a lot of television, and longed to do something other than be passively fed the images. Then as a student in my twenties, I often went to the movies, and was introduced to independent films. They nourished my fantasies and helped me to dream of the many possibilities in life. Two films stand out in particular. The first I saw when I was about 5 years old. I do not recall its name, but what I do remember is a scene of two children sitting on a flying carpet traveling above a city. I was thinking how lucky they were to travel in that manner. The other was, surprisingly, a James Bond film, *For Your Eyes Only*. The breathtaking scene that had a strong impact on me was when Bond and the Bond girl dived into the Mediterranean off Greece, and came upon a huge mosaic floor on the bottom of the sea. I watched the movie several times, and wondered if I could live surrounded by such beauty, what would be the emotions it would trigger.

I was not particularly good in school and never really knew what to do with my life. After graduating from high school in the US, I went to university in Montreal and received a degree in French Literature and Translation. On the side, I studied Italian and Art History, having been attracted to Italy ever since I first visited that country when I was 18. In 1993, looking through a home decorating and cooking magazine, I came upon an article about Picassiette mosaics, and was struck with the possibility of making fine art work with tiny broken pieces of crockery. The magazine gave a how-to lesson: mosaics became my hobby.

During my final years in university I got married. Unable to find work in Montreal upon graduation, my husband accepted a job in Dubai, in the UAE. I, too, found employment there, teaching French in a primary school. Sometimes I used to talk with a colleague about my mosaic hobby, she would encourage me to start giving workshops. It was a great suggestion. I followed it, and it turned out to be a hit. Through word of mouth I was invited to teach in private homes. Then, my husband accepted a more challenging job, and another friend advised me to apply for work at the Dubai International Art Center where I started to teach on a regular basis, and was soon invited to the homes of expatriates. Eventually, I was also asked to teach continuing education art courses at the university.

It was somewhat strange to be considered a mosaic specialist while I was just learning from trial and error, and through books. To pursue my own education, I decided to explore the mosaic world on the internet; this is when I came upon the hands-on classes and international travel opportunities offered by renowned mosaicist Martin Cheek whose book I had already read. Discovering that he spent his life traveling and teaching his art made me feel as if he was living my dream. I have since followed the evolution of his career via the internet, along with that of other celebrities in that art, such as Sonia King, Emma Biggs, and Elaine Goodwin, who have published extensively on mosaics. I also discovered Luciana Notturni's Mosaic School of Ravenna, Italy, where I decided to take a week-long class with a friend. The experience changed my life, as well as my view of mosaics. I realized that this art does not simply consist of putting together broken pieces of crockery; there are rules to follow and a challenging technique to be applied. From that moment on, I knew what I wanted to do with my life.

I kept on with my mosaic work, but never created anything that would define me as an artist, although one style and one subject matter began to reoccur, all having an exotic oriental feel. I attempted to challenge myself by trying to create oriental rugs in mosaics, and tried with the basic details. The next step was an interpretation of a Persian rug I wanted to buy, entitled "51 Camels." To this day I regret not buying the original. When my Persian friend Neli who did watercolors was looking for a subject that would sell, I encouraged her to try oriental rugs in watercolors, and lent her my books. Her paintings were magnificent, and I dreamed of doing the same thing in miniature mosaics, although I was not sure it would work with tiny pieces.

When my husband and I returned to Montreal, I quickly researched the world of mosaics in that city. In a local newspaper, I saw an advertisement by a company called Mosaika that was offering mosaic classes, and I went to visit them. Upon entering the studio, I was both intimidated and struck by the quality and size of the mosaics they were creating, and the infinite array of vibrant colors they were using. A tall, beautiful blonde lady greeted me and explained what they did. I told her that I had just returned from Dubai where I had lived for five years, and was looking to teach mosaics. We connected immediately as she had family living there. They were a very small company whose goal was to interpret original works of well-known artists in large scale mosaics for public installations. I suggested they promote their work at a design show in Dubai. Saskia and her partner Kori agreed, although in the end the trip had to be cancelled because of the September 11 events.

At that time Mosaika was still a new business. They were offering classes on the side, and I quickly became part of their team, teaching at their studio. As time went by, they gave me carte blanche to do whatever I liked in the workshop programs. Mosaika never stopped wanting to do a mosaic show in Dubai, and in 2002, the project materialized. We put on a show that won a contract to do a large scale mural for the Dubai municipality. I was proud to have helped promote the company, and realized that helping other artists was very close to my heart. I continued to work for Mosaika for a couple of years, until they were awarded important commissions for the New York City subway. At that point, they needed the teaching space I was occupying, and decided to let me fly with my own wings. With their support, I founded Mosaikashop, a business of my own, independent from theirs, where I launched a mosaic school. I had a little store front, and eventually a small gallery where I sold mosaic supplies and gave classes. It was a subject of curiosity that added charm to the neighborhood. Although it was interesting work, after a while I felt the need to change, as the routine became somewhat monotonous, and I sought new challenges.

In 2007 my marriage ended in what our friends called "the most civilized divorce." I was now living on my own, and started to work on a miniature copy of an oriental rug. The task was quite overwhelming, as the pieces measured between 3 mm and 5 mm, and the total size of the work was 30 cm x 42 cm. Seven months later, I had completed the piece, but was then faced with the daunting task of installing the piece. This is when I used the installation technique developed by Mosaika. I called it the

"Mosaika Method." It consists of working on a sticky film and then transferring all the tiny glass pieces onto a permanent surface. The process is demanding, extremely delicate, very challenging, and risky. But I did it, and have since worked on refining the technique.

After finishing the piece, I felt a sense of void, and found myself starting another mosaic rug, then a third and a fourth, but somehow I always stopped short of installing them, finding the task too complicated. Finally, as a New Year's resolution, I decided that I had to mount all my finished mosaics permanently onto a firm backing material. I did it, and it took me five years to master the installation technique. Once I felt comfortable with it, I decided to teach it, and also started to consider participation in exhibitions, greatly encouraged by my Vancouver artist friend, Lilian Broca, whom I had met through Mosaika. She told me about the International Festival of Contemporary Mosaic in Ravenna, Italy, and insisted I apply. Unfortunately the deadline had passed, but I decided to write the organizers anyway, and charm them into accepting me at that late date. I sent pictures of my creations, hoping it would help. Surprisingly, it worked; they approved my request. I was awestruck seeing my pieces displayed among those of some of the biggest names in the field.

From then on, I made it a habit to apply to all the mosaic events where my work would be suitable. I also started to research how entrepreneurial artists have succeeded, and applied their techniques to my promotional efforts. The most important rule I learned is not to take rejection personally but constructively, for behind each rejection there may lie another opportunity. In between reading and promotional work, and putting my heart into Mosaikashop, I continued to work on my mosaic rugs. Although it was getting logistically more complicated, I learned to be disciplined and make good use of my time, and accumulated a good body of work, but it felt as if it was going effortlessly. In the meantime in 2013, I had the opportunity to collaborate on a collective mosaic mural in Rome, an event that turned out to be something of a turning point, as by then mosaics were becoming a near addiction for me.

Following a newspaper article on my work, the Montreal Oriental Rug Society contacted me. Its director, Giusepe di Leo, was intrigued with my creations, and invited me to become a member and attend their conferences. Gradually, I became more knowledgeable about rugs, and started to meet prominent collectors and authors. Di Leo planned to exhibit my art alongside antique rugs, and encouraged me to give a talk about my works and the history of mosaic rugs. Meanwhile, in order to give more visibility to my products, I set up a small gallery space in my school, and launched a solo exhibition. It was a hit, which led me to organize more exhibitions and more viewings.

In one of the conferences of the Montreal Oriental Rug Society, I was fascinated by a most entertaining presentation by Stefano Ionescu, based on a book he had authored about a famous Romanian rug forger named Teodore Tuduc. I bought the volume, and decided to interpret one of the rugs shown into a mosaic, named it "Tuduc or not Tuduc," and dedicated it to him. By now, the network of contacts I developed in the field continued to expand and bring many opportunities for travel and exhibitions around the world. My friend Maureen O'Kane, a mosaic artist whom I met in a class in Italy, invited me to conduct a Christmas ornament mosaic workshop in Argentina. During my last days in Buenos Aires, I received an email from Stefano Ionsecu asking me to join him in a textile-themed trip to Uzbekistan that he was organizing. It was another opportunity to enlarge my circle, and meet interesting rug collectors. He also invited me to co-organize with him a trip to Italy focused on the theme of oriental rugs and mosaics, which materialized the following year.

Stefano also informed me about an annual antique rug fair in Sartirana, Italy, and put me in touch with famed rug collector and gallery owner Alberto Boralevi who accepted my pieces, and offered me free exhibit space. About that same time, I started a series of Moroccan mosaic rugs, and came across Austrian collector Gebhart Blazek. A couple of his rugs struck me as being perfectly adaptable in mosaic; however, before copying them, I thought of asking the owner's permission. He was thrilled with the idea, and surprised me by sending one of his originals to be displayed next to my reproductions at the Sartirana Antique Rug Fair. Beside feeling proud to see some of my students at that event, the highlight actually followed the exhibition. Alberto Boralevi took us to his gallery in Florence where he had prepared a surprise for me: there was a special display of my mosaic rugs along his own, with the "Tuduc or not Tuduc" as the centerpiece.

There was yet another surprise during that trip to Italy. I found out that I had won Third Place in a mosaic competition in Gaziantep, Turkey. In addition to a cash prize, I received an all-expenses paid trip, and my mosaic rug entitled "SouthWest Anatolian Kilim" was acquired for the collection of the future Contemporary Mosaic Art Museum in Zeugma, Turkey. Having just returned from Italy, I had to prepare to leave again within a couple of weeks for a most memorable trip to Turkey. I was asked to give a ten-minute speech about my work, and was graciously encouraged and coached by famous mosaicist Martin Cheek. The event was another opportunity for me to have access to prominent mosaic artists, including Giulio Menossi, the First Place winner of the competition. He was the first artist I met in Istanbul, and we immediately developed a warm friendship. Later, he opened important doors for me in Italy.

Suzanne with Alberto Boralevi in his gallery, in Florence, Italy, with the "Tuduc or not Tuduc" mosaic rug in the background, 2013

In 2014, as a member of the Italian-based International Association of Contemporary Mosaicists, I was invited to speak and exhibit my works in Austria where I connected with some of the artists whose careers I had been following for years through their publications, such as Elaine Goodwin and Lillian Sizemore. It was also very pleasant to reconnect with others I had met on previous occasions. Furthermore, Pamela Irving, an artist from Australia who was organizing the 2015 conference of the Mosaic Association of Australia and New Zealand (MAANZ), asked me to speak at that event, and organized an opportunity for me to teach five classes over a three-week period. Naturally, I was thrilled to accept this fabulous offer, and to discover a distant part of the globe I had never thought I would reach.

The mosaic chair, "Venetian Fantasy or Don't Take Without Giving," that won Second Place in the MusiVarium Festival, in Clauiano, Italy, 2015

My mosaic career has continued to flourish, allowing me to invite renowned international instructors to teach at my school in Montreal. These events were very successful, although the logistics became complicated, as I had to manage the workshop, allow time for promoting my personal creations, tend to the daily obligations of Mosaikashop, and teach in schools, museums, and beyond. All the while invitations kept coming at an even faster rate. The frenzied pace is continuing, with 2015 being the peak of my professional life. There were several return trips to Italy, including one to Clauiano, where I was Canada's delegate among ten nations representing a prominent chair manufacturer. The competition required participants to cover a chair with mosaics in ten days. I worked uninterruptedly from 9 am to 5 pm on my project; fortunately, my efforts did not go unrewarded as I won Second Place. A lady who saw my chair was moved to tears when I told her that it embodied my fascination for Venice and my love for textiles, the sea, and especially oriental rugs.

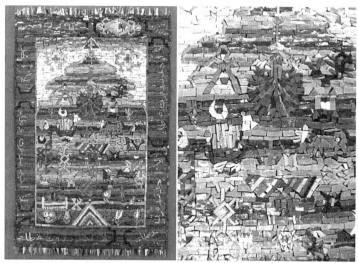

Venetian Rug, a composition of mine based on a variety of motifs from both rugs and personal jewelry, Warren G. Flowers Art Gallery, Dawson College, Montreal, 2009

During my final days in Clauiano, I learned that I had been selected to participate in the Fourth International Festival of Contemporary Mosaic, in Ravenna. In conjunction with that event, I was also invited by Luciana Notturni, the former teacher with whom I took my first mosaic class. She was organizing an exhibition entitled "Schools of the World," a tribute to her former students who had opened mosaic schools outside Italy. The year 2016 promises to be an even bigger one for me, with several plans and challenges ahead.

I like to share these stories with my parents, especially my father who takes immense pleasure in hearing about my travels, the people I meet, and the recognition I receive. As I look back at my life so far, I am gratified that, beside being fulfilling, my mosaic work has also offered ample opportunity to share my passion with outstanding artists, realize my dream to travel and discover the world, and be honored and recognized by my peers while surrounded by beauty. Somehow, the two movie scenes that so impressed my early years are now combined into my reality. This brings me to conclude that everything is possible with determination, hard work, and especially absolute passion. And lest we forget, Omar Khayyam reminds us that "Life passes like a mysterious caravan. Take from it its moments of joy."

Montreal, January 2016

FROM COSMOPOLITAN ALEXANDRIA TO THE "LOVELIEST VILLAGE" IN ALABAMA

SAMIA I. SPENCER

Peace, calm, serenity, stability are the first words that come to mind as I look back on my early years in Alexandria. Life in my upper-middle class family was simple, and daily routine flowed gently, unperturbed. There were few people and cars in the streets, no loudspeakers, only the human voice of vendors and calls to prayer. Courtesy was the rule, and crime and random violence rare. Until age 14, I walked to my nearby small French Catholic school where discipline, respect, and civility were ingrained in us. Then, it was the Lycée Français where classes were larger, mixed-gender, and more diverse. During the first year there, my classmates were multinational; gradually most non-Egyptians left, those who remained were largely of Middle-Eastern descent. During those critical years, lifelong friendships were made among students based on personal affinities and interests, not national origin or religious preference. Following the 1956 war by England, France and Israel, in retaliation for President Nasser's nationalization of the Suez Canal, the government stressed national identity and sentiment; the all-French curriculum was modified to include light military training and social science courses in Arabic.

Life at home was comfortable and carefree thanks to my mother, Solange Khalil. She skillfully managed the household, and made sure the frequent guests were warmly and graciously welcomed. Leisure times were easygoing: movies and radio were the main source of entertainment, and the Alexandria Sporting Club the favorite place to meet friends. It is with a bit of nostalgia that I remember some of the cherished places and activities that are forever etched in my memory, and contributed to the development of my identity: Sunday morning with my parents at the elegant tearoom Athineos to enjoy live classical music; afternoon coffee at Baudrot, another fashionable institution; and frequent visits with my friend Safinaz Awad Magour to a small bookstore where we rented the latest French publications for a few piasters. In the summer, daily routine consisted of mornings at the beach cabin, and evenings at the open-air cinema San Stefano where three

American movies were shown starting at sundown—a regimen of nine films weekly. Today, in the age of the internet, video games, cell phones, Facebook and Twitter, those wholesome pastimes and quaint places of yesteryear seem to belong to a different world. And indeed, they do. Most of the cabins along the Alexandria coast have been leveled, and few if any Egyptians swim at the city beaches; Athineos is a crowded and noisy eatery; Baudrot no longer exists; the bookstore has become a clothing shop; and the charming San Stefano hotel and adjacent movie theater have been replaced by an unsightly gargantuan building that houses a multilevel shopping center, a five-star hotel, a multiplex theater, and luxury apartments. The stability of those early years has no doubt impacted the adult I have become. According to a colleague, I was described as "unflappable" by a professor who interviewed me for a position at Auburn University; it has since remained associated with my name.

Samia and her dog Nancy, in the garden of her parents' villa in Zizinia, Alexandria, c. 1963

My father, Dr. Samuel Iskander, a renowned physician who owned a private practice in a popular part of town, was my idol. I admired his unequivocal dedication to his patients, and enjoyed the stories he would tell us about the unusual cases he treated. On many occasions, I urged him to write his memoirs, but he never took the time to pen them. Patients of all walks of life, from bedouins and villagers to aristocrats and members of the royal family, used to come to our home to express gratitude and offer gifts of various kinds; live poultry and sheep, art work and precious gems were not unusual. Over the years, many patients became family friends. One of the most unusual presents was from a lady we nick-named "Madame petits-fours." After my father succeeded in curing her where several doctors had failed, she pledged to send us regularly her delicious homemade cookies; so, week after week, a large box of goodies would be delivered.

Naturally, I wanted to follow in my father's footsteps, although I had a problem dealing with blood. My parents believed that medicine was unsuitable for women, and encouraged me to study French literature instead. They considered university education a means to make me an accomplished person, not a way to prepare for a career because I would never have to work. Yet, when time came for my brother to choose between engineering and medicine, he was strongly urged to go to medical school. However, within a few years, mentalities changed, and three of my younger female cousins became doctors. By the time I graduated from Alexandria University, as a result of the societal changes under Nasser's socialist regime, most households needed the added income that women would bring. My classmates accepted positions as teachers or bank employees, while it took me several months to find employment. I was eager to travel and explore the world, and wanted to work in an international environment that would allow me to expand my horizons and realize my dream. I completed an internship in an airline office that offered travel benefits, but no vacancies were available. I ended up accepting a dull job in a law practice.

A few months later, an unexpected event occurred, one of several that would fortuitously change the course of my life, or add a broader dimension to it. A position became open in the English Teaching Program of the Thomas Jefferson Library—the American Cultural Center—sponsored by the US Information Agency. The young woman who had been appointed was engaged to a naval officer; when the authorities found out, they advised him against the employment of his bride by a foreign government, she had to resign. One of my father's friends recommended I apply. Reluctantly, I did, convinced that I would not have a chance since I did not graduate from an English school, and was not fluent in English. In French schools, we were mainly taught to read English, not to speak it, but I had acquired some speaking ability through movies and radio. During the interview with the American director of the program, I put forth my best efforts. To my amazement, she offered me the job.

For the next two years, I worked with students enrolled in the English language classes offered at the Library, and the American teachers who taught them. Nearly all the instructors were married to Egyptian men who had studied in the US. They would talk endlessly about their country and its people, and urge me to visit their homeland. Through them, my curiosity for American culture grew, and I fantasized about the places where they invited me to go. This was all in the realm of dreams, because the Nasser regime had severely restricted foreign travel and access to currency. Visas were difficult to obtain, only emigrants or scholarship recipients, mostly in the hard sciences, were allowed to leave the country. My degree was in French, not in English, and a scholarship to study in the US was clearly out of the question. During leisure times, however, I used to leaf through the *Lovejoy* list of colleges and universities, and, surprisingly, I discovered that many US institutions offered graduate degrees in French. Casually, I sent a few applications, thinking I was throwing a bottle in the sea.

Suddenly, on June 5, 1967, I woke up to the news that the Six-Day War had started, and the Library had been burnt. I was heartbroken because of the damage to the majestic building where I worked, and more importantly for the end of the successful educational programs that were offered to Egyptians. Once again, I was unemployed. The experience at the American Cultural Center opened the door to a temporary position with a project sponsored by the World Food Program (WFP), followed by another at the Alexandria regional office of the World Health Organization (WHO). A few weeks later, the mail brought two important letters. The first was the offer of an assistantship from the University of California Santa Barbara beginning in September 1967; the second from the University of Illinois suggesting I could start in spring semester if fall were too close—that was the clincher. In February 1968, I was off to Champaign-Urbana where a new chapter of my life was to begin, in the midst of a snowy season and political unrest.

The Land of Lincoln was no Hollywood, and an academic career was not necessarily my goal, yet somehow I found myself unwittingly thrown into it. The French program at the U of I was one of the largest and best in the country, with teaching assistants from every part of the globe. Graduate courses followed a traditional sequence, divided by centuries. The nineteenth was taught by a Swiss novelist who gave interdisciplinary lectures combining literature, history, and the arts; I chose him as my thesis director. Months later, it became clear that he had no interest in my work, although he had suggested the topic. Eventually, I had to change advisors, and focused instead on the eighteenth century. It was a blessing in disguise as I became passionate about the Enlightenment where I found an echo to values and principles I held dear, and discovered the foundation of contemporary institutions. In the meantime, I had spent my first US summer in New York working at the United Nations Development Program (UNDP) and teaching French to UN employees. It was a dream come true, an experience that could have been extended, but it was too late to apply for PhD studies in the Big Apple. I returned to the U of I in the fall.

Since I had not trained as a teacher having never considered teaching as a profession, I felt at a loss entering my first classroom without proper instruction. I asked to observe an experienced colleague prior to meeting my students. For an entire semester, I attended his class daily before teaching my own. In the elementary and intermediate courses I taught, the reading materials were boring and irrelevant. After several days discussing excerpts of a French novel, an exasperated student exclaimed that he could not wait for the main character to die! Having come from a different background, I was not wedded to the archaic system, and pleaded for more pertinent alternatives. Following considerable discussions with my supervisors, I convinced them to offer not one but several reading options among which students would choose according to their personal interests and academic majors. I also developed a grading system that rewarded those who excelled throughout the semester, and exempted them from taking the final exam—an effective way to promote excellence that I have continued to use throughout my career. Although the four years in Champaign-Urbana were a good introduction to academic life, they were also difficult for many reasons, not the least of them was the rugged climate.

When time came for my husband, William A. Spencer, to look for a faculty position, I applied on his behalf while he was in Bolivia completing PhD research. I did not respond to job announcements in states where I did not wish to live: Montana, North Dakota, Idaho, Alaska, Alabama, among others. Unfortunately, none of the many inquiries I sent resulted in a positive response. Toward the end of the academic year, Bill returned to Illinois and attended a conference where he encountered a department head from Auburn University (AU) in Alabama who was looking specifically for a candidate with a PhD in Education from the U of I. Bill had the perfect profile: he was promptly invited to campus, and offered a position almost immediately. It was reason to celebrate but not wholeheartedly, as I did not relish moving to the ill-famed Southern state. During the interview, Bill was asked about his wife, and it was recommended I apply for a position in French. Today, asking a candidate about marital status in a formal interview is illegal. In fall 1971, Bill went to Auburn while I remained in Illinois to work on my PhD. A year later, I joined him, having been appointed in the Department of Foreign Languages & Literatures.

The first few years in Alabama were undoubtedly the worst in my life, away from everyone and everything I cherished. "The loveliest village on the Plains," as Auburn was known, was simply a campus town in the midst of a rural area—a wasteland. Although people were generally amiable and friendly, no meaningful relationships could be established with most of them, for intellectually, culturally, and politically we were worlds apart. The first neighborhood party we attended is impressed in my mind as if it happened only yesterday. The husbands were sitting in the living room discussing American football and gardening, while the wives were gathered in the kitchen preparing food, and speaking about babies and diapers. As the only working woman, with no children at the time and no interest in sports, I could not relate to either group nor participate in their conversations.

The political unrest and demonstrations against the Vietnam war on large campuses in the Midwest and on the two Coasts had no echo in a Deep South still immersed in Civil War memories, prejudice, and segregation. The new neighborhood where we bought our first house was starting to develop, then, overnight all the "For Sale" signs were switched to "Sold." Later, we found out that the manager of the Sears department store had purchased a house across the street, and the African-American assistant manager was interested in one of the new homes that suddenly became unavailable.

The land-grant institution of Alabama, AU was renowned for Agriculture and Engineering, but most importantly for its American football team.[1] There were few women on the faculty, and no African-Americans. It was a real event when the first female assistant professor was appointed in the History Department where she did not last long. When a black professor arrived on campus, he was more comfortable living in nearby Tuskegee—a majority African-American town and institution. Two decades later, in the 1990s, under pressure from federal authorities that threatened to sue AU, increasing the number of "minorities" in the nearly all-white campus became a priority. Departments were given the opportunity to "buy one get one free," as the commercial goes. In other words, appointment of an African-American faculty member would generate an extra position. Furthermore, in light of the scarcity of qualified African-American candidates and the market-approach in US academic institutions, those who were recruited had to be paid more than senior professors. Needless to say, the practice did not make for congenial relationships among colleagues, and was short-lived.

In the mid/late 1970s, AU sought to increase enrollment, strengthen its academic offerings, and enhance its reputation. Faculty recruitment became more formalized and more professional, while departments were allowed to grow. The French program established a Master's degree and expanded its offerings. At the same time, another unexpected occurrence changed the focus of my academic interests. I received a textbook entitled *Women in France* that provided information on the history, status and accomplishments of French women through the ages—a fascinating new field that had never been introduced in graduate school. Before long, I developed a course using the book, and combined my interest in the eighteenth century with my new passion for women and interdisciplinary studies in an anthology titled *French Women and the Age of Enlightenment* (Indiana University Press, 1984, 1993). French women of that era were studied from various disciplinary perspectives, and through the lens of other European cultures—a first of its kind. Although well received, favorably reviewed, and re-edited in paper edition, the book was belittled by some male colleagues as being "outside" my field.[2]

Growing up in a cosmopolitan society where French culture was alive and vibrant influenced my approach to teaching. In my view, the ultimate purpose of French studies was to embolden student curiosity beyond their limited environment and Southern culture. When a Master's degree student deplored that she was unable to read a French newspaper—not for lack of skills, but for unawareness of current events—I offered courses on the French press, and assigned papers comparing coverage of same-day events in France and the US. The exercise sharpened the students' analytical skills, and their understanding of both cultures. Over the years, I added to my repertoire courses on French film, women, fashion, and gastronomy, in order to make the study of French more relevant and more exciting.

As Advisor of the French Honor Society, and Director of the French Graduate Program, I invited business executives to inform students about employment opportunities in multinational companies; arranged student internships with a French vacation club and a French hotel chain, and an exchange program with a French institution; brought to campus French artists and performers; and started a French film series in a town where foreign films were never shown. A national conference I organized resulted in the publication of *Foreign Languages and International Trade: A Global Perspective* (The University of Georgia Press, 1987). I directed study-abroad programs in France and Quebec; and, in collaboration with the Paris Chamber of Commerce and Industry, I developed a unique program combining the study of the French language and the fashion industry. It included formal tours of renowned Parisian designer houses, and an internship in one of their boutiques. These practical venues benefitted the students and offered them exceptional experiences and employment opportunities. Many among the alumni of these programs became personal friends and were later invited to campus as guest speakers, to share their success stories, and inspire younger cohorts.

In the process, the activities I created for students enriched my own knowledge, broadened my horizons, and allowed me to discover the intricacies of various French institutions and industries. They also extended my professional network beyond scholarly associations. There were many memorable experiences: checking on a student-intern at Gravelines, France's largest nuclear facility; interviewing UN Secretary General Boutros Boutros Ghali in his office on the 38th floor of the UN building in New York; making arrangements for the French Olympic SwimmingTeam to train on the AU campus prior to the 1996 Atlanta Games; visiting Françoise Giroud, the first cabinet member in charge of Women's Status in the Giscard d'Estaing government; in her Paris home; reporting on the Francophone Summit in New Brunswick, Canada;[3] and greeting French President Jacques Chirac to whom I handed his photo with my one of my students. These were some of the shining moments that brightened the academic journey.

Sometimes, a simple idea can have unanticipated results. That was the case in the early 1980s, when I invited the Quebec Government Delegate in Atlanta to give the keynote address at the French award ceremony. During our discussions, he suggested I take a tour of the French immersion programs in his province. It was an offer I could not refuse because I knew absolutely nothing about Canada or Quebec. Discovering *la Belle Province* and its people added yet another invaluable dimension to my personal and academic life. In Montreal, I was generously welcomed by Quebeckers, and inspired by a multicultural and multilingual society reminiscent of Alexandria of yesteryear—one for which I yearned and longed. Many among the people I encountered and interviewed during the numerous research trips that followed became personal friends and associates, whom I involved in academic panels and conferences I organized on campus and beyond. The ensuing visits to Quebec resulted in greater appreciation for its history and culture, which led in turn to additional funding opportunities, stimulating research projects, and publications breaking new grounds in a field that had not yet been fully explored: women and politics. This work culminated in two major undertakings. In 2002, a conference titled "Women and Politics: A Global Perspective" brought to AU high-ranking female leaders from Canada, the Democratic Republic of the Congo, El Salvador, France, South Africa and the US, to assess the status of women in public life, and the means to overcome the obstacles they encounter. It was followed in 2004 by a week-long residential program, "The Women Leadership Institute," in which exceptional university students were recruited nationwide to sharpen their leadership skills.

My academic path was unlike that of most of my peers who focused on a single topic or a specific area. Mine was a winding road, along which I continued to learn and explore new fields of research that linked personal and professional interests, and provided immense fulfillment on both fronts. The findings were shared with students and colleagues on campus and beyond. Although neither being a university professor nor living in Alabama were my initial goals, I did not waste time deploring my fate. Instead, I used effectively the opportunities and resources at hand, in order to make the dream come true.

At AU, I will always be grateful to many enlightened officials who supported my efforts to enhance the visibility and reputation of the institution, and granted me generous research and travel funds to undertake projects, and disseminate my knowledge throughout the US,

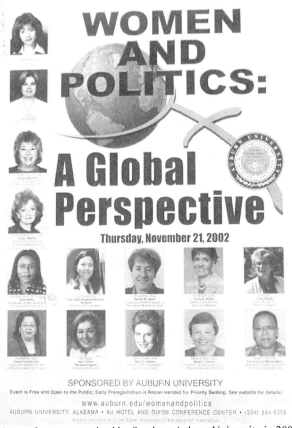

Poster of the conference organized by Samia at Auburn University in 2002

Canada, Europe, and as far away as India. They also recognized my achievements with some of the highest rewards, including titled professorships, and a Lifelong Achievement Award. On the other hand, academe, like other professional milieus, is not devoid of rancor and hostility. Ill-intentioned individuals thought that by undermining my work and destroying programs I had strived to build and grow, they would disable me and obstruct the progress of my career. What they did not know is that their actions only reinforced my "thick skin"—the ability I had to develop to protect myself, disregard their deeds, not to look behind, and continue to move forward. Along the way, I also learned that people are rarely jealous of those beneath them.

Representatives of the Governments of France and Quebec, whose assistance I sought while pursuing my projects, appreciated the efforts I put forth to promote the language and culture I cherished. In addition to bestowing upon me the coveted title of *Chevalier dans l'Ordre des Palmes Académiques* and promoting me to the rank of *Officier*, the Government of France appointed me Honorary Consul of France in Alabama, a responsibility rarely attributed to non-French nationals. Upon completion of that mandate, I was knighted in the *Ordre National du Mérite*. Likewise, my

Samia receiving the French National Order of Merit, with Consul General of France, Denis Barbet, Auburn, Alabama, 2015

work on behalf of the province of Quebec and its culture did not go unnoticed. In 2010, I was inducted into the exclusive *Ordre des Francophones d'Amérique,* in which only one non-Canadian citizen from North and South America is enlisted each year.[4]

Samia inducted into the *Ordre des francophones d'Amérique,* in the Salon Rouge of the Quebec National Assembly, Quebec City, 2010, with husband Bill (R) and son Mark (L). Not pictured is son Sam

Going over my life for the purpose of this chapter has been both challenging and enlightening. It has given me the opportunity to delve into my heart and soul, in order to understand where I started and where life has taken me. The thoughts kindled both happy and sad sentiments. During my adult life, it has been heartbreaking to witness the decline and devastating growth of my birth place, and the wrecking of its charming landmarks. On the other hand, the "wasteland" where I arrived more than 40 years ago has turned into one of the most livable cities in the region. AU has become one of the highest-rated public institutions in the US. Tim Cook, famed Steve Jobs's successor at Apple, Inc., and Jimmy D. Wales, Co-founder of Wikipedia, are only a few among thousands of outstanding graduates.

In the process, I have also come to appreciate, more than words could ever tell, the principles and values that my parents and my Alexandria environment have instilled in me. My father communicated to me his love of people and his passion for his work. My mother had a strong personality, and was endowed with an innate sense of aesthetics, elegance, refinement, and discretion. The more I think about it, the more I feel fortunate to have come to life where and when I was born and raised.

Auburn, Alabama, February 2016

Notes

[1] Land-grant universities are US institutions of higher education that resulted from the Morill Land-Grant Acts of 1862, in response to the Industrial Revolution. Each State was granted federally controlled land to develop an institution dedicated to the teaching of agriculture, science, military science, and engineering.

[2] Although I worked on many other topics, I continued to focus on the eighteenth century, its culture, and its women. I contributed and served as co-editor of *The Feminist Encyclopedia of French Literature* (Westport, CT: Greenwood Press, 1999), and as editor of the two-volume *Dictionary of Literary Biography: The French Enlightenment* (Farmington, MI: Thomson-Gale, 2005). With the support of the Southeastern American Society for Eighteenth-Century Studies, I founded a journal, *XVIII New Perspectives on the Eighteenth Century*, and became its General Editor for more than a dozen years (2004-17).

[3] The Francophone Summit is a biennial meeting of the Heads of States of the *Organisation Internationale de la Francophonie*. The OIF is made up of more than 50 nations or regions where French is an official or customary language, or that have a notable affiliation with French culture.

[4] I would be remiss if I did not acknowledge many cherished friends who strongly supported me through the years, and nominated me for these honors: René-Serge Marty, Consul General of France in Atlanta (2001-05); Denis Barbet, Consul General of France in Atlanta (2012-16); and Ginette Chenard, Quebec Government Delegate in Atlanta (2006-11). Although it is not possible to thank all those who have been instrumental in the achievement of my projects, I would like to recognize two who have become close personal friends, and remained by my side for more than a quarter of a century: Yvette Roudy, Minister of Women's Rights in the first Mitterrand Government (1981-86); and Céline Hervieux-Payette, Member of the Senate of Canada (1995-2016).

THE POWER OF FLOWERS

MALAK TAHER

Beginnings

Although my journey into the flower business started some 30 years ago, the passion for flowers has been engraved in my heart and soul since childhood. Some of my most cherished memories go back to the days spent with my parents at our farm in Mansoureya, a rural area on the outskirts of Cairo. These were my favorite outings because I loved playing with the animals and running around the gorgeous mango trees. My love affair with flowers began when I was a young girl who enjoyed the land and thought that everything touched by nature was simply magical.

Upon graduating from high school, I knew that I wanted to study at the Faculty of Agriculture, but my mother opposed the idea of her daughter becoming a farmer. Instead, she persuaded me to go to the American University in Cairo, where I majored in Economics; however, before completing the degree, I got married and went to Canada where I spent the next five years. In Montreal, I applied to Concordia University where I continued my education and received a Bachelor's Degree in Economics. When I returned to Egypt, I was pregnant with my first child, Sherif, and did not wish to work, although I felt the need to find something to stay active. This is when I met Salwa Fadel, an extraordinary lady who had spent a few years in Japan, and upon returning to Egypt, she started to offer courses in *Ikhabana*—the Japanese art of flower arrangement. With her encouragement, I was able to master that traditional art based on straight lines and a modern-minimalistic approach to floral design. The first course opened my eyes to the many wonderful possibilities; it was a critical step toward starting my career, and establishing my future flower business.

Shortly thereafter, I was blessed with a second child, my daughter was born. My love for flowers was growing, and must have influenced the name we chose for her, Yasmine (jasmine in Arabic). Over the next few years, I was busy raising two children, and my floral design ambitions were limited. They remained on the back burner until 1986, when I had the opportunity to turn my hobby into a lifetime passion and business. Actually, the turning point occurred when my brother opened a small flower shop in Cairo, and asked me to manage it because he had no time to run it. I was hesitant at first, but then decided to give it a try; little did I know that the decision to give him a hand would be a life changing experience.

When I took over, there were only two people working with me: a florist and an assistant. It was a simple operation, and a new learning experience. In the morning, it was a pleasure to wake up, go to work, receive fresh flowers, clean them, and prepare daily arrangements. At the beginning, the shop was virtually unknown because it was located in the basement of an apartment building; the flowers did not sell well. Gradually, my sense of entrepreneurship was building up, and I thought of different ways to turn my hobby into a successful business. In order to publicize what I was capable of doing and gain more clients, I started to make nice bouquets and offer them to friends.

The early years were difficult but also quite interesting. Most of my time was spent to learn about the different types of flowers and ways to extend their life, and study the various schools of floral design. After a couple of years, I managed to buy a small van that I used to drive around Cairo to deliver the orders. One day, while waiting for my assistant to deliver a bouquet to a customer in a residential building, I spotted a lady I knew; my immediate reaction was to hide. I automatically threw myself on the floor of the van and waited until she passed by and could no longer see me. Today, it is fun to remember those early days when I did everything myself: arranging, decorating, and driving. My company, *Flower Power*, started as a baby that I was carrying; then, I enjoyed watching it as it came to life, and blossomed into a fabulous business.

From a Flower Shop to a Floral Boutique

Between 1986 and 1998, the reputation of our small store was growing; now, it had a small base of loyal clients. I decided the time had come to expand, and opened a second store in a more strategic location, easily accessible and more visible. My dream was to create a *salon de fleurs* where people would be warmly welcomed, feel comfortable, and find all the flowers, decorations, and accessories they may want, including vases, containers, and cards; in other words, it would be a one-stop shop for all their needs. The concept behind *Flower Power* was born: it was the first place of its kind in Egypt. Soon, it built a broader client base, and acquired a sterling reputation in the market.

While my hobby was developing into a more serious enterprise, my best and loyal friend Mona El Deeb-Marie decided to join me in *Flower Power*. She became an integral part of the company, not only a friend and confidant, but also a true partner without whom I would have never been able to run a successful business. While Mona managed the finances, logistics and technical details, I focused on the creative and artistic side. We complemented each other in many ways, and together we were a winning team. Prior to working with Mona, I was not a savvy financial negotiator, did not have a good sense for business, and was generally shy with clients. Mona taught me to be more confident and more direct with those we served. During the next ten years, we made it a point to meet together with clients, and go through the details of every event jointly. I believe that was the secret to our success.

Malak and Mona to her left, with members of the *Flower Power* team, at the opening of the second Cairo shop, 1998

The Team

By 2000, after many years of hard work and perseverance, *Flower Power* had become a reputable and respected name, and good fortune was on our side. I signed my first contract with one of the world's leading hotel chains, and was gradually able to build a large team of employees to meet the increasing demands for our services. By then, the small store had grown into a full-fledged floral design company. Instead of three employees, *Flower Power* now had over 100 employees, including 40 dedicated floral designers and assistants who were amazingly devoted to our artistic business.

Today, *Flower Power* is definitely a one-stop shop for all our clients' floral and decoration needs. We strive to provide the best quality flowers, as well as tasteful and aesthetic floral creations. My staff is committed to meet and exceed our clients' highest expectations, and is continuously motivated to innovate and create floral magic. The company was started by me, but it was built by the hardworking women and men who make up the team, many of whom joined our staff without any prior knowledge of flowers or floral design. In fact, several came from Beni Suef, a rural town in the Nile Delta. These brilliant young women and men moved to the big city in search of opportunities, and a better life. I discovered in them artists and creators that needed to blossom. Their talent, imagination, and creativity continue to inspire and impress me, and I am grateful for their dedication and loyalty. They are the backbone and the solid support of our flourishing business. Needless to add that without them I would never be where I am today: in other words, we are one big close family.

Creating a successful company and building a great team have not been easy. I faced a number of challenges, mainly from competitors who sought to entice some of my employees by offering them higher salaries. I am thankful that most resisted, and remained loyal to Flower Power. I also did face problems with former workers who took pictures of our arrangements, and tried to imitate them; perhaps, this is to be expected when a business is expanding and successful. Actually, I am proud that my employees are highly regarded in the floral design field, and are sought after; it means that we are doing our job well since, as the saying goes, imitation is the highest form of flattery. I believe competition is healthy, it has prompted me to be more creative, and to challenge myself to design more attractive arrangements and reach higher standards.

The Clients

One of the main reasons for my success as a florist and event planner is my ability to listen to my clients' needs, and try to connect them to my own vision as an artist and designer. By working closely with them, I have

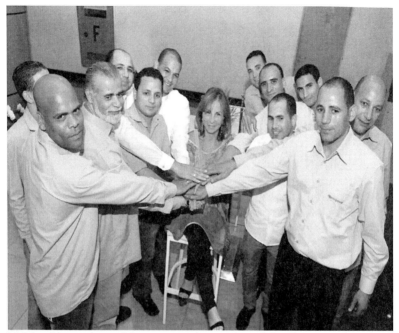

Malak with members of her team at the opening of the Kattameya branch of *Flower Power*, 2013

gained tremendous experience, not only about flowers, but also about planning and creating a holistic vision for important life events, mostly weddings. Meeting with brides is a daunting and time-consuming task, especially when they tend to be nervous and excited about the forthcoming ceremony. As we get closer to the wedding date, I can sense the stress they go through. While planning for a wedding, there are times when I act more like a therapist than a florist. My job is not only to design and plan the floral arrangements, but also to make the women feel secure and happy about the big day ahead. Conversations with them require a great deal of diplomacy, encouragement and calm, to make sure they are happy with the final result. To be successful in this business, I had to be patient and flexible, in order to ensure that the professional services we provide please everyone in the party.

Turning down business opportunities is hard in my line of work. Fortunately, I have never been tempted to accept proposals that did not resonate well with me, and would not lead to a floral event to my liking. I have always been careful and protective of the image and brand of

Flower Power. On a few occasions, I received strange requests that I had to advise the client against, or in extreme cases flat out refuse. For example, a lady insisted on hanging bird cages with live birds all over the ballroom where the wedding would be celebrated. I tried to convince her that it would not work, and explained that the birds would be very disturbed by the loud music, the bright lights, and the guest noise; but she would not listen to me, and insisted on pursuing the idea. In the end, I had no option but to decline what could have been a profitable contract. Another client wanted to create a beach theme inside the ballroom; she suggested bringing large quantities of sand to fill the ballroom. Mona, who attended the meeting with me, was as surprised as I was. She did not hesitate to tell the lady that if she wanted a beach wedding, she should have it at the beach, not in a five-star hotel. Eventually, we suggested a different theme, and convinced her to go through with an elegant fairytale motif, using white with accents of gold, beautiful chandeliers, and gorgeous lighting.

Composition and Execution

Floral arrangements require more than an artistic touch, they must follow basic principles of floral design. As in all art compositions, there are lines, forms, textures, colors and balance to be taken into consideration. In my floral designs, I tend to embrace fundamental rules; however, while these are important in guiding our design, sometimes it is necessary break them, in order to create a unique and magical piece. I enjoy working in a free flowing manner, even being bold and audacious. This may involve blending two seemingly mismatched colors, or using oversized flowers with smaller ones in an asymmetrical way. Working with colors resonates with me, and gives me a sense of celebration. In my leisure time, I like to experiment with new forms and elements, to emphasize the most striking traits of a flower, be it the stem, color, or shape. Flowers are naturally beautiful, so it is important to respect each one, and to treat it with utmost love and care. Flowers and plants have the capacity to touch all our senses; it is the reason I remain passionate about them. For large installations, I work closely with clients; nothing beats the creative process of handling flowers to produce a unique piece that is both impressive and soundly designed. Then, I dive into the project and make it happen, reflecting a fine balance between passion and hard work.

At this point in my life, I have been working with flowers for over 30 years. With time, I have become more confident, and my approach as a floral artist has become bolder. Today, I feel ready to tackle the most difficult projects head-on. In the early years, I used to make basic floral designs and retail arrangements; now, I create what some may call floral sculptures. Working with partner hotels like the Four Seasons chain has been an amazing learning experience, and has given me the freedom and flexibility to design and create on a grand scale. My artistic floral creations are highly prized and have now become a trademark of that hotel. Such opportunities have allowed me to venture out of my comfort zone, and strive to achieve far more advanced technical and artistic experience. For example, Christmas is always a special time at the Four Seasons. I can create large scale projects using a variety of structures and a broad range of materials, such as glass, fiber, and plexiglas, complemented by crystal balls, candles, and beautiful vases. The objective is to inspire and impress the hotel guests, and make them feel as if they entered a magical world of beauty and refinement. Every step and every detail in the creative process, starting with the original themed concept to the final product, is a collaborative effort with my team. It is both a stressful and exciting endeavor to produce flower arrangements and decorative pieces on a grand scale, but these fabulous pieces have made our reputation as an enterprise capable of transforming large spaces into breathtakingly beautiful and strikingly dazzling havens.

Planning Memorable Events

Inspiration can come any time any place, slowly or quickly; sometimes it may not come at all, especially when it is needed most. Once the business took off, I realized that becoming a world-class florist and earning a reputation in the market required a lot more than passion and creativity. Over the years, the hobby turned into a business involving planning, creating, and organizing major events that delight and enchant the guests. In order to succeed, the element of surprise was crucial; therefore, I never repeated the same theme twice. First impressions in any event are critical, and must leave indelible memories. As they enter a space I have arranged, my clients must feel and breathe beauty, romance, and elegance. The ambiance is enhanced by flowers, lighting, and decorations, all blending together harmoniously. The ritual in a pleasing and successful event also involves food, drink, music, laughter, candlelight and dancing, but the decorations and flowers are the main elements in creating a dream-like atmosphere.

Christmas decorations at the Four Seasons First Residence, Cairo, 2015

Table decoration is an art in itself. Flowers on guest tables must be elegantly displayed but not dominating, striking but not distracting; they must inspire people to muse as they communicate with each other. In other words, flowers are the crown jewel on the table, each of them deserving its own unique attention. It takes real skill to place everything in its right space without crowding a table. While all aspects of an event should match and flow to create harmony,—style, colors, flowers and lights—to create harmony, adding contrast to produce a surprising element is also useful, but must be done gently, so as not to disrupt the total effect.

Wedding reception at the Four Seasons Nile Plaza, Cairo, 2012

Outdoor Events

When planning an outdoor event, I always check the weather forecast because a perfect setup can be ruined by rain or storm. Fortunately, Egypt is blessed with clement weather most of the year. For outdoor events, my job is not only to transform a space and create magic, it is also to make sure everything goes according to plan, with attention to the smallest detail. It is also important to play it safe, and prepare plan B, in case plan A does not develop as anticipated, which happens sometimes. Since outdoor venues are limited in Cairo, it occurred to me to create a space on our farm in Mansoureya, which I called *The Garden*, and make it available for weddings and special events. This was another baby born out of my involvement in *Flower Power*. My daughter Yasmine's wedding was celebrated there, and it was out of this world!

The Garden was relatively successful until the 2011 Revolution; however, the instability in recent years has made people cautious about having weddings outside the city limits. Today, the majority of outdoor weddings are either "destination weddings" held in exotic locations, such as Luxor or Gouna on the Red Sea, or in downtown Cairo hotels. Once the situation stabilizes, I hope that *The Garden* could be revitalized, to resume the celebration of special occasions. Since 2011, when "destination weddings" became popular, we have done many in venues located far from Cairo. These require more elaborate planning, and the logistics are much more complicated as everything must be carried from Cairo. We need to make sure that every detail is anticipated because most of these distant locations do not have the facilities needed for grand scale events.

Expanding Beyond Egypt

In recent years, I had the chance to work in the region and beyond. For example, in 2006, I was invited to create the Christmas decorations at the Ritz Carlton in Bahrain. It was an interesting opportunity that took me out of my comfort zone, and away from the people with whom I am used to collaborate. Despite the challenge, it was an enriching experience, during which I was exposed to a different culture, met new people, and displayed my creations in an unusual setting. It was also an honor to be invited to the Maldives, to work on Christmas decorations at the One and Only hotel chain. Going to that island republic was an amazing experience, and a real tribute to our arrangements to be exhibited in such an exotic destination.

Not long ago, I was also approached by a sheikh from Dubai who offered me a business opportunity. I graciously turned it down, because I could not envision myself working away from family and friends. All the money in the world could not move me from the land I call home. Egypt is where I grew up, where I began my journey, and where it will end. *Flower Power* has been successful because I have been surrounded by people I love, and with whom I work; I could not imagine going anywhere else or doing anything else.

The Passion Lives

Today, what began as a hobby and passion is a flourishing business. Although, I am proud of our achievements and success, sometimes I miss the good old days when I had time to experiment leisurely with flowers, and did not have to worry about the commercial side of the enterprise, or the responsibility of caring for the many households it supports. My purpose in writing this chapter has been to share my passion for flowers. I believe that people should not only enjoy flowers on special occasions, they need to make them a regular part of their daily life, for their therapeutic impact on body and soul. Furthermore, flower scents ignite our senses and improve our mood. Working with flowers, I feel as though I am a painter, placing each one like the stroke of a brush, with care and attention; it is a way to express myself while anticipating the pleasure of those who will enjoy them. It could also be compared to the art of a poet arranging words to create an exquisite reflection of life. Flowers have the power to transform our space and connect us with nature at its best. Even after 30 years in this business, I continue to feel the passion and excitement. Flowers remain my driving force and my muse.

Cairo, February 2016

PASSIONATE PURSUITS: READERS, WRITERS, AND THE REVIVAL OF CULTURE ON THE NILE

HIND WASSEF AND NADIA WASSEF

When I was a child, when I was an adolescent, books saved me from despair: that convinced me that culture was the highest of values.

Simone de Beauvoir, *The Woman Destroyed*[1]

Sowing the Seeds

As two girls born to older parents, we had access to a different set of experiences of childhood and adolescence. Our father was ruthless in his quest for perfection, and could not accept anything but hard work and the most meticulous attention to any detail. Our mother took us to every single museum, theater, or opera she came across at home or on annual summer holidays abroad—a habit we continue with our own children. We became avid readers, worshippers of culture, and lovers of an Egypt that had once existed. We wanted to create a new relationship with our country: this was a time of hope and change. We were embarking on a new phase—our country and us.

At the end of the twentieth century, Egypt looked to be a place of tremendous promise: the economy was growing, young Egyptians educated abroad were returning home with visions of putting their mark on their beloved country, and there was a general mood of optimism. During the 1990s we had both worked in NGOs in the field of social development, and by the end of that decade each of us had come away with her own qualms. We were ready to embark on a second career. As often happens with life changing moments, this one unfolded accidentally and in a very light hearted setting. We were having dinner with some family friends when the conversation turned to the hypothetical question: "If you could do anything, what would you choose to do?" Both of us, answered without hesitation: "Open a bookstore!" With the proviso that it wouldn't be just any kind of bookstore, its shelves would be curated. It suddenly dawned on us that bookstores should pay homage to all forms of cultural output, and while the concept of retail was starting to take off in Egypt, this did not apply to the fields of culture and publishing.

In 2001 there were a few bookstores that were either affiliated to universities or served as extensions to existing publishing houses. They were united by unattractive interiors, a disregard for customers, and often located in inaccessible areas. In the same spirit as African entrepreneur Bethlehem Tilahun, founder of Sole Rebels, we decided that our bookstore would be born, "into this world, and against it." We set out to research what already existed; but, more importantly, what the elements were of the space where we would like to spend a lot of time. Our exploration led us to interview writers and journalists who stared in bewilderment at these two young women—we were 30- and 27-years old at the time—armed with their Master's degrees in literature, eyes that saw differently, and a great deal of passion. The outward skepticism about our endeavor, which matched our passion, fueled our determination further. It became clear that readers had stopped reading, writers were writing for their coterie of authors, and all the stakeholders had lost interest.

Sisters Are Doin' It For Themselves[2]

At the start of 2002 the scene was as follows: two sisters with no experience of business or retail sinking their money into a bookstore in a prime location, in a stunning Art Deco building, on an island with colonial architecture, in the middle of the Nile.[3] The first branch of Diwan Bookstore opened its doors on 8 March 2002—coincidentally, International Women's Day. At that time, we were three women taking on all the challenges—Nihal Schawky, one of the shareholders, took on a major stake in running the business with us. For the next decade we worked, fought, laughed, cried, and learned side by side. We remain chosen sisters in spite of all the challenges and disagreements that ensued.

We had finally articulated our vision: Diwan was passionate about the production and consumption of culture. We decided to retail in the same space children and adult books in English, Arabic, French, and German; multimedia; and stationery—bringing together cross-cultural experiences. We aspired to make buying a book a unique consumer experience by emphasizing customer service and ambiance. And in the middle of this oasis, we placed our café with its intimate tearoom feel. We consciously created a space to pay homage to books. We poured all our love and dedication into every detail with the utmost sincerity.

People felt it. The reaction to the first Diwan was unexpected: it was an incredible success. People arrived on opening night to admire the stylish interiors that had been slowly taking shape months before.   Diwan's spectacular logo had attracted the attention of passersby on Zamalek's busy main road. True to Diwan's identity it merged beautiful Arabic calligraphy with English letters on a highly textured background that signified the layers of history and culture. Nermine Hammam's[4] designs for Diwan paved the way for a new style of visual hybridity. Out of not knowing better, we spared no expense in the creation of beautiful store bags in which people could take away their purchases. The bags became a badge of honor the cultured wore to signify to others their membership in the club of culture-lovers. They eventually became a means by which we communicated with our customers: designing new bags with the opening of a new shop, or the celebration of an anniversary, or even to commemorate an event.

Diwan's store bag

Mark Twain once said: "All you need in this life is ignorance and confidence; then success is sure"—and we were armed with those, as well as good luck! The same year we opened, a rather obscure dentist named Alaa Al Aswany published a novel entitled *The Yacoubian Building.*

Finally, an Egyptian bestseller was born that engaged a broad spectrum of readers across boundaries of age, sex, class, and gender. That novel was pivotal in signaling a shift in the production and consumption of books. Authors were no longer professional writers of an older generation, but younger men and women who had different occupations and took to writing on the side. They fiercely vied for the attention of the growing market of readers through any channels available to them. The rise and spread of social media cemented this relationship further.

Interior of the first Zamalek Diwan

We continued to add innovations to the existing book market in Cairo: book launches celebrating the birth of new titles, and bringing together readers and writers became a regular weekly occurrence. We courted our customers, asking them to tell us what they wanted more of—in an age that preceded collaborative filtering, we were doing it manually. Our customers informed our buying decisions and helped us introduce new categories to Diwan's carefully curated shelves. And because we listened well, we were able to implement quickly. Diwan's bestseller lists, entirely fuelled by its customers' purchases, would regularly go up on its walls for the different categories we sold. Future writers would talk about how their goals were to find their names on Diwan's walls. Our staff wore uniforms and nametags displaying a pride in selling books—something that had not existed before.

The Art of Not Knowing Better

After even a short walk through Cairo's stifling heat and throat-clogging car fumes, the Diwan Bookstore, with its quiet café and histories of the pharaohs, is a welcome oasis. But the shop is much, much more than just that…. Diwan was founded by an unlikely pair of entrepreneurs: sisters Hind and Nadia Wassef.

Time Magazine, 22 August 2011

The assumption remained that the challenges facing us were because we were young women in business in a developing country. Indeed most press coverage about the women of Diwan discussed just that.[5] As we were probed about the home/work balance in our lives, we realized that it was extremely important to us to raise our children to witness their mothers working and toiling away at what they loved, even if it meant that that balance was slightly skewed. We were also asked about our measures for success, which we realized were extremely subjective. None of us expected to make a fortune out of Diwan, but we did want to share a vision that we believed would make a difference to our country's future. Reinserting culture into the mainstream, and commoditizing it to a certain extent in people's lives forces a reconnect. Over the centuries, we had lost touch with the role of women in society, the role of entrepreneurship, and history. Without a thorough knowledge of what once was, there can be no glimpse of what will be.

We know that many factors play a part in someone's success: education, hard work, luck, or simply being at the right place at the right time. Being women neither helped nor hindered. Our biggest challenge remained that no blue print existed for this type of business locally or regionally—which was also the reason for its success. We were faced with operational issues such as creating warehousing solutions for our stock; importing barcoding systems to facilitate in data collecting and reordering—at the time few publishers used ISBNs and no software could support Arabic and English characters—and simply dealing with the bureaucracy of our country. One humorous incident occurred when we received a letter from the censor's bureau notifying us that Jamie Oliver's recently released cookbook, *The Naked Chef*, would be banned. The matter was only resolved after a visit to the office explaining that the chef was fully clothed, and that this was a style of cooking!

The biggest challenge by far remains the staffing of any bookstore. If, as Mahatma Gandhi said: "A nation's culture resides in the hearts and souls of its people," then it is more so for a bookstore. One of the reasons for the first Diwan's staggering success was primarily that the souls of Hind, Nadia, and Nihal were so heavily intertwined with it. We not only ran the operation, but we were on the shop floor daily, talking to customers, sharing our favorite books with them, and welcoming them into our hearts. So when we were looking for a bookstore manager, or a customer service agent, or even someone to barcode the books that were coming in as part of our restock, we soon realized that none were readily available. From that point on, a decision was made that would impact staffing policies in Diwan for the rest of its life: we looked for attitude over skill set. We preferred hardworking, dedicated, passionate people to those who were actually specialized in the fields of library or customer service.

And so the steep learning curve began—for all of us. We taught our customer service staff the appropriate body language, the necessity of placing the book in the customer's hand to initiate that first point of contact, and hygiene. We made toiletry bags for our staff explaining to them the necessity of shaving daily, applying deodorant onto a bathed body, and not re-wearing unwashed clothes. We wrote up scenarios of how to approach customers; and every three months we updated manuals for staff training on the key titles in every section of the bookstore. The uphill battle proved to be against the socialist mindset that prioritized a government job where minimal effort was demanded in return for secure, but minimal wages. The private sector was seen as a gamble because an employee could be let go.

We learned that everything had a cost: how do we sustain a meticulous and costly operation on the very low margins of books? When we opened we had no money left for marketing because we had spent lavishly on our bags and other elements such as wrapping paper, stickers, and bookmarks that were dispensed with every purchase. As a result Diwan could not engage in above the line marketing—and that mistake became the cleverest marketing decision we ever made. We only appeared in magazines or newspapers offering book recommendations or our bestseller lists, otherwise we let our brand architecture spread our news. Our customers loved the intentional subtlety and the playfulness of the Diwan brand, and their loyalty only increased with time.

Reaping the Harvest

After five years of operating Egypt's premier boutique bookstore and learning lessons about ourselves, others, life, and success, we were faced with a decision. Due to Diwan's success, smaller bookstores appeared, mindlessly imitating our wooden and stainless steel interiors, and even sometimes our logo. We had to decide whether we should content ourselves with running this bookstore and perhaps one or two more and let others expand into the consumer markets that we had tapped into and developed, or do we? Naturally, we unanimously decided that we had to expand. We wanted to share our precious Diwan with as many people as possible, so that Diwan becomes not just an isolated idea, but a way of life punctuating an era signaling a new zeitgeist, spreading our love of reading, and our mindset across our beloved country. Once that decision was taken, we had to produce our first business plan—prior to that we never had a budget or a plan to operate from, everything was done instinctively.

The next decade was one of uplifting dreams and crushing disappointments. By 2010 we had ten shops, 170 employees, the joy of turning our dream into a reality, and the sadness that comes with realizing that some dreams should have stayed small. With every new branch of Diwan that opened, something of the original soulfulness was lost. To satisfy the greedy efficiency of a rollout plan, parts of the originality and serendipitous nature of the first branch was sacrificed. Some of our customers felt it, others who did not know the first one were quite happy with the replicas sprouting all over Egypt. We stopped doing the tasks that manifested our passion for our business and that also—it became clear—made the business successful. Instead, we were forced into roles that oversaw others ordering books, coming up with marketing ideas, and barcoding, among many others. Eventually, given the size that Diwan had reached, we took a decision to step back and let our first-born move into the next stage of life in the capable hands of new management. And herein lies another important lesson: the entrepreneur and founder is not necessarily the best manager and leader of a business at all its life-stages.

We look back upon the fifteen years of Diwan with gratitude: that we shared these wonderful experiences, and survived the harsher lessons that life had to offer. In countless interviews over the years we were asked to divulge the secrets of our entrepreneurial success. Simply put: hard work and perseverance. But then our parents had taught us that lesson from a very young age. Life showed us that our best teachers were often our mistakes; so we eventually became less scared of making them, and realized that a mistake was a wise investment provided we learned from it and did not repeat it. We also gained more by listening to our harshest critics, rather than our dearest friends.

Our father always said: "When you wake up every morning it is very important to remind yourself that you can always do better and be better." In short, the minute you think that you have succeeded and arrived at your destination, you have taken the first step toward failure. This remains a guiding sentiment in our lives. Even when we won the Veuve-Clicquot Initiative for Economic Development Award in 2011, the Best Woman Entrepreneur Award in 2013, or when one of us was on *Forbes'* List of the 200 Most Powerful Women in the Middle East in 2014, we still believed we could be and do a lot better.

Literature, music, and art that is genuine, into which the creator has poured his/her heart, is felt and understood by its recipients. The same applies to work. Diwan remains a labor of love that gave back to us even more than we put in. Ultimately its success rides on the fact that it was honest, sincere, and genuine in its aspirations. Just as our mother shared with us love and beauty through exposing us to as many manifestations of the arts as she could muster, we did the same for our children and for our country.

London, October 2015

Other Publications on Diwan Include the Following:

"Nadia Wassef: The Reader," *Cairo West Magazine* 54 (October 2014): 20.

Nafeesa Syeed & Rahilla Zafar, "Nadia Wassef: Opening a New Chapter for Arabic Booksellers," *Arab Women Rising: 35 Entrepreneurs Making a Difference in the Arab World*. Ebook published by Knowledge@Wharton, February 2014.

Jack Shencker,"Egypt: Future Makers," *Monocle Magazine* 48 (October 2011): 75-80.

Michael Schuman, "Seeking the Growth after the Arab Spring," *Time Magazine* (22 August 2011): 39-42.

Elmira Bayrasli, "Where Silicon Valley Meets Emerging Market Entrepreneurs," *Forbes Magazine Blog* (27 June 2011). http://www.forbes.com/sites/elmirabayrasli/2011/06/27/where-silicon-valley-meets-emerging-market-entrepreneurs. 2 November 2015.

Sam Bayoumi, "Little Black Book: Nadia Wassef, One of the Founders and Co-Owners of Diwan Bookstore Divulges her Favourite Local Haunts," *Gulf Life Magazine* (September 2009): 24.

"Path to the Top: Five of the Country's Most Prominent Businesswomen Reflect on their Success," *Business Today Egypt* (March 2010): 80-83.

Graeme Neill, "Profile: Carving Out Culture in Cairo," *The Bookseller: London Book Fair Daily* (16 April 2008): 14.

"Diwan Opens its Doors in Heliopolis," *Daily News Egypt* (14 December 2007): 10.

"In Depth: A Manuscript for Success," *Business Monthly* (September 2007): 47.

"Diwan: The Union of Culture and Delight," *Diva Magazine* (May 2007): 36.

"The Women of Diwan," *Ahram Weekly* (8-14 March 2007).

Rania Al-Malky, "The Little Bookshop Around the Corner Turns Five," *Daily News Egypt* (19 March 2007).

Hanan Edrees, "Career Profiler: Nadia Wassef," *What Women Want* (Fall/winter 2006): 71-72.

Notes

[1] Simone de Beauvoir, *The Woman Destroyed* (London: Harper Perennial, 2006), 23.

[2] "Sisters Are Doin' It for Themselves" is a 1985 song recorded as a duet by the British pop duo Eurythmics and American soul/R&B singer Aretha Franklin. It is considered to be a modern feminist anthem, and was written by Eurythmics' Annie Lennox and Dave Stewart.

[3] This is the suburb of Zamalek in the capital city of Cairo.

[4] http://www.nerminehammam.com

[5] Suzanne Fenton, "An Open Book," *Forbes Woman Middle East* 3 (October-December 2014): 56-58.

A Message from
A Top Communication Expert

Loula Abou Seif Zaklama

The Early Years

In 2015, I celebrated 60 years of marriage and business career. Although it is a challenge to put down decades of life in a few pages, I will give it my best. Born and raised in Assiut, a conservative town in Upper Egypt, I was the youngest of four children, two boys and two girls. As such, I was spoiled by my father, and could get away with anything I wanted. Suddenly, at age 10, my whole world crumbled when my father died of a heart attack, he was only 48. It was a catastrophe in every aspect; yet from hard times come strength and inspiration. A widow at 35, my mother was my inspiration and role model. She was able to move on, and bring up the four children the way she and my father had planned. It was a monumental task in an extremely conservative environment that did not believe in the rights and independence of women. Mother fought, and managed to get all of us successfully through high school or college. My older brother became a doctor, the younger a prominent businessman, and my sister married a banker. As for me, you will find out in the next few pages.

Given the very strict rules applied in raising children in Assiut, especially girls, my only way out was through marriage. In 1955, I was barely 17 when I met Ramzi Zaklama and got engaged to him. At that age, it was exciting to have a fiancé, go out to fancy places, show off my engagement ring, and get away from under the yoke of my mother and brothers. Little did I know how difficult it would be for an adolescent to marry and assume responsibility. My mother insisted, however, that I complete high school at the American College for Girls before getting married. Mine was a long and difficult engagement during which I had to manage my studies as well as the elaborate preparations for the wedding.

The first years of marriage were hard, they might have been less so had I been more mature, and ready to cope. Before reaching age 20, I became the mother of two wonderful daughters, Sherine and Dina, and I was in charge of raising them. Daily household duties were not burdensome, as we lived in a large "family house" governed by my mother-in-law, where we were treated almost like guests. At that time, it was customary for some families in Egypt to include all siblings with spouses, children, maids and dogs, in the same home. I did not particularly appreciate the arrangement, finding the environment loud, hectic, and crowded. A few years later, a second catastrophe of even greater proportions was to occur, one that was more devastating for me than the passing of my father: the arrest and imprisonment of my husband for false political reasons. The event added to my role as mother of two daughters that of a working woman in the arcane world of business—one heretofore alien to me.

A Time of Crisis

When I married in 1955, it was barely three years after the 1952 Revolution, when King Farouk was dethroned by a group of young officers headed by Gamal Abdel Nasser. From a kingdom dominated by powerful landowners and a rich business and industrial elite of various national and religious origins, Egypt became a Republic governed by the military. As President, Nasser imposed a socialist regime, introduced agricultural reform that limited land ownership, and gave individual peasants small farms to cultivate. Furthermore, he nationalized banks, industries, and the Suez Canal, and confiscated properties of the wealthy. Seeing the handwriting on the wall, many among those who were affected, whether Egyptians or foreigners, left the country; only those who could not depart remained in Egypt. Although we were dispossessed of much of what we owned, we decided to stay. Nasser was hailed throughout the region as a great Arab leader, but he was less popular within the country due, in large part, to the aggressive intelligence system he had set in place. Anyone who did not agree with the regime could be taken into custody, without any reason or explanation.

In the fall of 1961, on September 28 to be exact, my whole life collapsed. At 6 am, the doorbell rang, two men showed up and asked Ramzi to leave with them. I had no idea where they were going. At that time, Ramzi was advertising and public relations manager at Misr Air, Egypt's national airline—the former name of EgyptAir. My first thought was that there must have been an accident or a crisis requiring his presence at the office at that early hour. Later, his secretary called to inquire why he had not come to work. Days and nights went by, there was no word about Ramzi's whereabouts. I lost track of the time I spent on the balcony, hoping he would appear on the horizon. My siblings, relatives, and friends tried to help; they checked all the hospitals and police stations, but there was no sign of him whatsoever. Approximately ten days later, a well-connected acquaintance told me in confidence that Ramzi had been detained in an undisclosed location. No explanation was given for his arrest, no reason for his detention, no charges against him, no information either about the length of time he would be kept. Anyone who knew Ramzi could tell that he was a peaceful and private man, and a real scholar. His arrest as troublemaker simply made no sense, but nothing made sense in those days. My first reaction was to hire a lawyer, but I was reminded that there was nothing to defend in the absence of a charge. Then, why was Ramzi imprisoned? No reply.

Here I was at age 24, with no money, no university degree, not having worked a single day in my life, not knowing if or when my husband would come home, or if he would get his job back; yet, I had two children and a mother-in-law to look after. What could I do to pay for the girls' schooling and for groceries? Stay home, cry and lament my bad fortune? Beg my brothers for help? Or react and take charge of my life? I remembered the courage of my mother, a young widow who suddenly lost her husband, and had to bring up four children. She was my inspiration. Like her, I pulled myself together, and with faith and the grace of God, I ventured into the unknown.

Becoming a Businesswoman

A few months prior to his arrest, Ramzi, together with two of his friends, founded Radar Advertising Agency, a small company to supplement his income. At that time, advertising was a monopoly of the public sector, run by the government. After Ramzi's arrest, fearing for his life, one of the partners fled to Switzerland, while the other remained in Egypt. Radar had a couple of clients who were nervous about doing business with a company in dire straits: one of its owners was in jail, another in Europe. The remaining partner insisted that I go to the office, for he believed that my physical presence would reassure the customers, and confirm that business was still going on as usual. This is when I gave up my maiden name, Hoda Abou Seif, and used the nickname "Loula" that my husband had given me, to which I added his last name, Zaklama. Clients came to know me as Loula Zaklama.

I started to attend the meetings with the two clients. First, I did not say much; instead, I carefully observed my experienced partner because I needed to understand what advertising was about, and how the process worked. It would start with a client's brief, the development of a strategy and an advertising message, the creative process, the shooting of the ads— in which, incidentally, my daughters were often featured—and finally, the finished product on television. It was a fascinating learning experience, during which I succeeded in establishing meaningful personal relationships with clients, and earning their trust. Gradually, I took a more active role, and my reputation started to grow as a young woman who was daring to compete with the public sector, and ably breaking into the advertising world.

Competitors approached my clients, blackmailed them, and forced them to move to the public sector, or else the Egyptian market would be closed to their products. My customers had no choice but to terminate their business relationship with my company. It was an uphill battle to keep on, but I was not about to give up. Within a few years, Radar Advertising gained an excellent reputation as one of the most professional agencies in Egypt and beyond, renowned for its care for clients, its attentiveness for their needs, and its effective and successful campaigns. By the 1970s, the tiny enterprise of three increased its staff size ten fold to 30 employees, and grew its client list to 12, including prestigious multinationals, such as Proctor & Gamble, British American Tobacco, Yardley Cosmetics, among others. When Ramzi finally came out of prison, he was proud of what I had achieved during his absence, and insisted that I continue to run the company. Leaving Radar entirely to me, he created a travel and tourism company named "Mediterranean Tours & Travel."

Rada Research and Public Relations

In the 1980s, having operated an advertising agency for nearly 20 years, fighting to keep it going in a closed economy, and watching it grow, mature and succeed, I thought the time had come for a new chapter of my life. Once again, my decision was determined by the political climate. Following Nasser's death in 1970, his successor, President Anwar Sadat, led the country in a different direction, promoting a vision of "open door" economic policies. The market opened up, and endless opportunities became possible. I realized that there was an urgent need for marketing research and public relations in Egypt, and I wanted to be a pioneer in those fields. Up until then, these concepts were misunderstood by many for whom they were limited to the image of a pretty girl carrying a bouquet of flowers, welcoming guests, and helping them to make hotel reservations. I knew better. I decided to liquidate Radar Advertising, and to establish a company that would provide the desperately needed marketing research that was still unnavailable for the multinationals flocking into the country. However, before taking this major step, I believed that I needed to update my knowledge and sharpen my skills. Thus, I headed to Cincinnati, Ohio, where I signed up for seminars on Communication and Research Methods at the Burke Institute.

Upon returning from the US equipped with newly-gained expertise, I established my present company, Rada Research & Public Relations. The first part of the word Radar was maintained, while the final letter "R" was moved to the next word, Research. Once again, I started from scratch, with only five employees: a research manager, a public relations executive, a secretary, an office helper, and myself. This time, the challenges were different. In my previous experience, I fought the monopoly of the public sector while trying to convince the clients that a young woman could successfully run a privately-owned company. Now, I was introducing two new disciplines, and attempting to promote the concept of marketing research as a way to design effective communication strategies. People were uncooperative, they did not understand how the new disciplines could help them, and preferred to stick to the old ways. Sometimes, fear of the unknown intervened and put people on the defensive. Furthermore, authorities would not grant me the permits I needed to work, and most of all, there were no qualified employees, as these disciplines were not taught in Egyptian business schools.

I had to work on two fronts simultaneously: training my employees, and using a scientific definition of public relations to change its image in my country. Meanwhile, the company gradually became a model for young entrepreneurs. Today, Rada is recognized as a world leader in its field. My work gave meaning to the famous words of Benjamin Franklin: "Vision without action is a dream. Action without vision is a nightmare." I had both a vision and a dream, and was ready to put them to work. I felt doubly privileged: first, because I was born and raised in Egypt, and had always worked in my country, which gave me a deep understanding of consumer habits, culture, and mentalities. On the other hand, I had also acquired extensive international experience and know-how, through my collaboration with multinationals and my training in the US. Now, I was ready to approach the market from a new perspective; all I needed was to recruit bright young people, and train them to perform at the level I expected.

One of my first challenging missions occurred when I was approached by an international company to create a campaign for a most sensitive product related to women's hygiene. How could we deal with this assignment on a subject that was still taboo in our country? It had to be handled cautiously and required careful planning. I designed a dual-pronged project focused on education and health. The first step consisted of developing a program to inform girls, especially adolescents, about the natural biological changes occurring in their bodies during puberty. It was endorsed by both the Ministry of Health and the Ministry of Education. Simultaneously, a media campaign was ongoing to communicate a message that menstruation was not a taboo subject. The key was to spread the medical and health benefits of proper hygiene. Gradually, menstruation became a subject that could be discussed openly in the media from as a health issue. Eventually, restrictions and censorship on advertising sanitary towels were relaxed. The school program that started in Cairo was a great success; it was later extended to other cities. Ultimately, it led to the lifting of the ban on advertising sanitary napkins. I was proud to have succeeded on two fronts: my campaign had helped to change some outdated ideas about women's health; and it promoted a needed product marketed by the company that had approached me.

Another challenge that I was able to turn into an opportunity concerned the more ordinary practice of laundry. Egyptians have some entrenched habits that are difficult to change. Thirty years ago, Proctor & Gamble introduced the first detergent in Egypt. People had no idea what to do with it, having never seen it or used it. In order to start changing the century-old process, we conducted extensive research in both Upper and Lower Egypt, in urban and rural areas. We learned that laundry was a real pain, it occupied most of the day, up to seven or eight hours, and consisted of several steps: sorting white and colored items, soaking them, washing them slightly by hand first, rinsing them, then boiling them, and finally bluing them to brighten the whites. In the process, the housewife needed several products: a block of hard soap for the first stage, crushed soap for the boiling part, and a bluing agent last. The detergent was to replace three products with only one. Having studied the process, P&G suggested that we emphasize the time-saving factor. Laundry could now be done in one hour instead of seven or eight. However, when we positioned the product for its time-saving benefit, it was not perceived as an advantage, and did not catch on. For the housewife, laundry was a fact of life, a tradition that had been passed on through the generations, from her grandmother to her mother and to herself. To hang proudly the clean clothes that her neighbors would envy was simply a lengthy process that needed time to be well done. Period.

How could we convince her to change her habits? Since the concept of saving time did not work, we had to find another benefit. We decided to focus on money, instead of time. It worked like magic! To achieve the cleanest clothes and whitest linens: the housewife only had to buy one product, instead of three, and she could save the rest of her money. Saving time did not work, but saving money did. Lesson learned, habits are difficult to change. Through the years, my achievements have been recognized and rewarded. Among others, I was recently elected President of the North Africa Public Relations Association (2014); identified among the 200 Leading Arab Businesswomen in the Middle East by *Forbes Magazine Middle East* (2014); received the International Advertising Association Champion Award from the International Advertising Association in London (2013); as well as the International ATLAS Lifetime Achievement Award of the Public Relations Society of America (2007).[1]

Loula Zaklama receiving the International ATLAS Lifetime Achievement Award of the Public Relations Society of America, Philadelphia, 2007.

While it has been gratifying to be honored by my peers, I must admit that my greatest fulfillment has been to witness the involvement of three generations of Zaklamas in the company I created: my two daughters and their husbands, and my three grandchildren. The younger partners are pumping in new technologies and state of the art innovations, and moving Rada's leadership forward.

Having earned the nickname "Iron Lady of Egypt," I acknowledge that balancing home and career has been rough and came at a high price; but, if I were to do it again, I would not hesitate to walk the same path. In the end, despite the bumps along the way, Rada kept the family together, and made all of us proud to have enhanced Egypt's reputation, and contributed to the development of its economy.

Seated is Ramzi Zaklama. Right behind him is wife, Loula. To her left is daughter Sherine, and to her right are granddaughters, Farida Barsoum and Ingie Saleeb. Second row (L to R) are daughter Dina, her husband Sami Barsoum and their son Medhat Barsoum; next to him is Sherine's husband, Diaa Saleeb; to his left is Salah Ghobrial, husband of granddaughter Nada, next to him.

This chapter is dedicated to my late husband Ramzi Zaklama who left us for a better place in 2015, and to my loving daughters Sherine and Dina, from whom I continue to derive strength and support.

Cairo, November 2015

Notes

[1] Additional honors I received include the following: World President, International Public Relations Association (IPRA, 2006); recognition among the 50 Leading Businesswomen in the Middle East by *Forbes Magazine Middle East* (2006); Special Achievement Award of the American Chamber of Commerce in Egypt (2004); one of 50 Leading Women Entrepreneurs of the World by the Star Group, (IBM, and *Fortune Magazine*); the Samir Fares Award at the International Advertising Association Congress for Outstanding Contributions to IAA (1998); and a Medal of Merit from the International Advertising Association (1986).

MY JOURNEY AS EGYPT'S AMBASSADOR TO SWITZERLAND

NIHAD BALIGH ZIKRY

Sipping my morning tea and looking onto the vast campus of the German University in Cairo (GUC) from my third-floor office window, I could not help but think of my late parents and wonder what they would have thought of the path my life has taken. It is with great pride that I look back on the critical decisions they made, which shaped my life and career. As Director of International Policy Planning at GUC, I rarely have a dull moment. The day is filled with interactions with students, faculty, staff, and other academic institutions, at both the local and international levels. Whether drafting an international exchange agreement, or welcoming a foreign delegation, I seek to break down barriers, and strengthen Egypt's position within the global educational community. In a way, I find it at once starkly different and yet surprisingly similar to my previous position as Ambassador of Egypt, or working at the Ministry of Foreign Affairs. In my current academic setting, the focus is on the welfare of students, the quality of education they receive, and the networks I can establish for them. In the foreign service, I was also promoting the interests of my country, and developing its relationships with the outer world. In both cases, I was linking different people and organizations, and creating new partnerships.

Actually, there is no single event or decision in my life that could be hailed as the turning point that led to where I am today. Rather, this is the result of a series of decisions and turning points, most of which I could trace back to my childhood in Giza where I grew up. My parents, Dr. Baligh Zikry, a chemist, and Gulsoheir Abou Hadid, a stay-at-home mom, were staunch believers in the power of education, at a time when it was not necessarily a high priority in a family of three girls, and a mother who never had the opportunity to complete her education. Perhaps, this was precisely the reason my mom insisted on sending the three of us to the renowned German School of Cairo. It was hard to get in, and even more difficult to keep up because neither of our parents spoke German, although they had an unfaltering drive to instill in us the virtue of hard work and perseverance. The academic programs at the German School were tough, by any standard. In addition to the rigorous curriculum, there was a great deal of emphasis on discipline, and the value of time. The deeply rooted principles instilled in me at a young age, both at home and school, built the foundation for the adult I became. Furthermore, under my mother's watchful eyes, we girls learned to speak German, French and English, in addition to our native Arabic. When time came to apply for college, I was admitted to the Faculty of Economics and Political Science at Cairo University, while my sisters went to medical school. My studies paved the way for my entry into the foreign service upon graduation in 1975, when I began my career as a diplomatic attaché.

In my first assignment, I was placed in the cabinet of the Minister of Foreign Affairs. In this much coveted post, I had the opportunity to get an insight into the current political situation from within the government, was trained by seasoned diplomats, attended important meetings, and met prominent national and international personalities. It was an exciting and exhilarating job, a dream come true. It was there that I met my husband, Mohamed Assem, who worked in the office of the Assistant Minister of Foreign Affairs. An open-minded and enlightened diplomat, he fully understood my ambition to pursue my own diplomatic career, and committed to support me in every way he could, in order to succeed in my career—a promise he kept throughout our life together. We both agreed to help each other professionally, so we could both achieve our goals.

A year after our marriage, Assem was up for his first posting abroad, in Ottawa, a wonderful capital where we started our family. Mine was the age-old decision that married women face as they try to find a balance between personal responsibilities and professional ambitions. At that point, I took a leave of absence from my job at the Ministry of Foreign Affairs, and joined my husband in Canada. It was in this great multicultural city with extremely friendly people that we were blessed with our two children, Ibrahim and Yasmine—the main source of joy in our lives. With their arrival, the balancing act of work/life/kids became even more difficult, in view of my determination to pursue my diplomatic career. I had to prepare myself mentally and professionally to go back to work after a four-year leave of absence, in order to pick up where I left off and move forward.

Upon returning to Cairo and settling the family, I quickly resumed my duties at the Ministry, in the Department of International Organizations, headed by a prominent and ambitious diplomat, Amr Moussa, who would later become Minister of Foreign Affairs, then Secretary General of the Arab

Nihad with husband Assem, and daughter Yasmine, celebrating son Ibrahim's birthday at Dr. Mahassen Ghobrial's cottage in Gatineau, Quebec, c. 1991

League. For the following two years, with the support of my family, my boss, and my loyal colleagues, I continued to prove myself as a dedicated diplomat eager to learn and serve her country. Proudly, I represented Egypt at several national and international forums, including one on the Status of Women in Vienna, and another on the International Red Cross in

Manila.

Sadly, at that time, I lost my beloved mother at the young age of 46. Her sudden passing had a strong and long-lasting impact on the entire family, especially me, as she had always been my mentor and my source of inspiration. It was especially during the years when I was wrestling with decisions regarding my children's schooling and education that I missed her most, and appreciated even more the choices she had made for me. A larger than life person, and a generous, affectionate and loving woman, she cared deeply for those around her, and for others in general. The vivid memories of her that lived on in my heart and my mind continued to provide acumen and strength.

Just as life had settled into a quiet routine, my husband was assigned to the post of Counselor at our Embassy in Canberra, Australia. A four-year mandate requiring another extended leave of absence for me, because spouses of diplomats were not allowed to work within the same embassy. Although staying behind in Cairo and pursuing my career was a possibility, I opted to join Assem, preferring to preserve the unity of the family, and the best interest of our children. So, off we went on a wonderful adventure and a whole new perspective on the world. The four years in Canberra are fondly remembered as an opportunity to establish precious friendships, enjoy world-class performances at the Sydney Opera House, and explore a beautiful and rich country/continent with our children. Travelling around the coastal line of Australia, especially Batemans Bay in the south and Queensland in the north, was fascinating and provided unique opportunities to admire the majestic landscape. Meeting the Aborigines, visiting their homes and learning about their habits added to the memorable experiences. Australia's close ties to Asia gave us an insight into the intriguing cultures of the Orient, heretofore unbeknownst to the family.

Unable to work at the Embassy and in search of options to grow professionally, I decided to pursue a degree at the Australian National University (ANU), and received a Bachelor of Letters in Political Science. This was one of the proudest moments in my life, made even more so as I witnessed my children's excitement watching their mom at the graduation ceremony. This was yet another milestone in my development as a diplomat, and clear evidence that I was determined to keep my career on track. I was proud to be the first Egyptian student to be admitted to the graduate program in Political Science at ANU. My thesis was about the negotiation process that led to the Camp David Peace Accords.

The years flew by and before we knew it, once again, it was time to pack and head back to Egypt for another chapter of our lives. Upon returning to Cairo, I rejoined the Department of International Organizations and resumed my duties seamlessly. The ANU degree helped to bolster my credentials and smoothed the transition back to the working life. I was fortunate that my senior colleagues enabled me to update and enhance my knowledge. Most of the work in my Department focused on activities related to various organizations and specialized agencies of the United Nations.

Less than two years later, my husband was transferred to New York, one of the liveliest and most vibrant cities in the world. From the Metropolitan Museum to the Guggenheim and the Lincoln Center, from the UN Headquarters to Columbia University and the Broadway theaters, New York was a whole world to discover. The more we lived in it, the more I realized it would take a lifetime to know it inside out. I was absolutely thrilled to walk into the UN headquarters, having worked on many of its dossiers. When I first entered the building, and saw the various halls and lounges where the world's leaders gather for the annual meetings of the General Assembly, I felt as if it were a dream.

Once again, I had to figure out how to keep professionally active during another four-year leave of absence. I lobbied hard for an opportunity to work at the UN in some capacity, even offering to help as a volunteer, fearing that the issue of pay would hinder my request and keep me out. Fortunately, the Head of the Egyptian Mission at the UN—one of my former bosses—approved my appointment. Thus, for the first time since we were married, I was allowed to be employed officially abroad, while my husband was on assignment overseas. In four years in New York, I represented my country on the UN Third Committee on International, Social and Economic Affairs, and was able to work on some of the most interesting questions in my career, dealing with issues similar to those I had handled at the Ministry in Cairo. Among others, these included fighting poverty, ensuring that women and children receive the rights and care they deserve, and the dire living conditions of Palestinian refugees. Racial prejudice and ethnic discrimination, as well as violence against women were items that regularly appeared on the agenda of the Committee. Taking part in the discussion of these matters and the decisions that ensued was enlightening and stimulating.

Assem's support during those years was essential, given the unconventional nature of my employment. My children's understanding, too, was crucial because of my long hours away from home, even though by then, they were old enough to manage their schoolwork independently. Because of the fast-paced tempo of New York life, its rich multicultural social fabric, and its bustling entertainment scene, I did not feel the four years go by.

When I returned to the headquarters of the Ministry of Foreign Affairs in Cairo, I was promoted to the rank of Counselor—a clear sign that my hard work during the leave of absence had paid off. I was appointed Deputy Director of the Minister's Cabinet, the first woman to hold that tough and politically sensitive post. Needless to say, I took my responsibilities very seriously, and spared no effort to live up to the Minister's expectations. Undoubtedly, it was the most challenging job I had ever had due to the demands and responsibilities of the position, which I held for nearly 12 years, five of which on assignment to the Secretariat of Egypt's President. This was yet again another rich and sensitive experience that expanded my knowledge and horizons. I accompanied the President and the First Lady on many trips, and was able to take a look at the world from the top, in China, France, Italy, Poland, and Spain. In the US, I was received at the White House with the presidential couple, and met President George W. Bush and First Lady Laura Bush.

Meanwhile my husband served as Ambassador in Ethiopia, Kenya, Sudan, and finally in Israel. During those years, however, the children stayed with me in Cairo, because they needed stability during their high school and college years. I was constantly going back and forth between those countries and Egypt, to spend some time with my husband and some time with the children. Ethiopia and Kenya were particularly interesting, their cultures, landscape and wildlife, especially their tea and coffee plantations, were fascinating. In Kenya, we went on several safaris, and the visits to Massaymara and Naivasha and their breathtaking sceneries were among the best times our family spent together. Living conditions in Sudan were harsh, the weather unbearably hot, the roads unpaved and hard to access, and the restaurants and social activities minimal. As a distinguished diplomat with an excellent reputation in the Ministry, Assem held critical national security posts for Egypt abroad. It was tough for the family to be separated during that time, but we made the best out of these difficult conditions, and reunited as often as possible. In the meantime, Ibrahim and Yasmine were going about their studies responsibly in Cairo, and growing up to be thriving adults. Their cultural exposure and living experience throughout the globe added depth and wisdom to their well-rounded personalities. Both graduated with honors from the American University in Cairo with degrees in Business Administration.

In 2004, while my husband was Ambassador to Sudan, I was appointed Ambassador to Switzerland—a coveted assignment that I welcomed with pride and excitement. As the first Egyptian woman ambassador to serve in that country, I felt added pressure to perform well, in order to meet or exceed the high expectations. It was my first posting overseas, and despite my long years of experience at the Ministry, I felt as if I were embarking on a whole new career. I was thrilled at the opportunity to dust off my German, and pleasantly surprised at the number of professional opportunities that my language skills created, and the lifetime friendships they enabled me to forge. One of the highlights of my time in Bern was attending the World Economic Forum in Davos together with Egypt's Prime Minister. It was fascinating to mingle with the planet's leading economists, businessmen, and heads of states who come together to debate global issues and challenges. Bern holds a special place in my heart, as it allowed me to fulfill a lifelong ambition. Our solid and friendly relationship with Switzerland was reflected in nearly all venues. The Swiss government and the Swiss people were extremely hospitable and courteous.

Nihad at her ambassador's desk in Bern, Switzerland, 2008

My husband and my children visited as often as they could, and for the first time, Ibrahim and Yasmine had the opportunity to see their mom—not their dad—in the limelight. Actually, Yasmine was making the trip from the Boston where she was an MBA student at Harvard

University, while Ibrahim was much closer. After receiving the MBA from the Stern Business School of New York University, he was working in Paris at that time. Living in the beautiful ambassador's residence in Bern, I often wondered about my life journey. One of the most vivid memories of those years was of a discussion in fluent German with Swiss President Joseph Deiss. It brought to mind my mother who never had a chance to finish high school, yet insisted that her daughters never be denied a chance at education, and sent them to an excellent German school. I only wish she would have lived long enough to see the fruit of her foresight.

Upon returning to the headquarters in Cairo, I was promoted to Assistant Minister of Foreign Affairs for Cultural and Scientific Affairs, an assignment that gave me a different perspective on the tourism industry and the educational system, as I dealt with issues related to national and international agreements in those areas. The experience I gained during that time paved the way for my post–retirement position as Director of International Policy Planning at the German University in Cairo. Once again, my German language skills came in handy, and are a huge asset and a distinct advantage when I meet with our German counterparts.

Nihad at the Geneva International Fair where Egypt was honored, 2007

When I reflect upon my personal and professional journey, I feel blessed to have had the opportunity to see the world, thanks to my husband's postings in Canada, Australia, the US, Ethiopia, Kenya, Sudan and Israel, and also through my own experience as Egypt's representative in many conferences and events, and especially as Ambassador to Switzerland. Furthermore, I am a fulfilled mother, proud of her son's prominent position in a London investment firm, and her daughter's success as a small business owner in New York City. As a loving grandmother, I only wish my two wonderful grandchildren were closer to me, but I never miss a chance to go visit them in the Big Apple.

I hope my story as a daughter of the Nile will inspire others that they, too, can achieve their personal and professional dreams. It does not come easily, but it is well worth the hard work and sacrifice.

Cairo, February 2016

CONTRIBUTORS

HANNA ABOULGHAR
A Professor of Pediatrics and Clinical Nutrition at Cairo University, Dr. Aboulghar has worked for more than 15 years with various Egyptian NGOs caring for children at risk. She was instrumental in the establishment of Banati Foundation, the largest Egyptian NGO serving girls in street situations. In 2014, Banati was the recipient of the Stars Impact Award for Child Protection in the MENA region. Dr. Aboulghar also created Elbasma, the first and only health clinic for children at risk. After the 2011 Revolution, she was involved in the founding of the Egyptian Social Democratic Party where she remains very active. Dr. Aboulghar is the mother of two daughters currently studying at university in England.

TYSEER ABOULNASR
After completing her degree in Engineering at Cairo University, Dr. Aboulnasr received the MSc and PhD from Queen's University in Ottawa, Canada, where she spent most of her adult life. She concluded her academic career as Dean of Engineering at the University of Ottawa, and Dean of Applied Science at the University of British Columbia. She received many honors and awards, including the prestigious Order of Ontario (2012). Currently, Dr. Aboulnasr is spending considerable time in Egypt, engaged in an academic culture focused on goal setting, constructive citizenship, and innovations to serve society and the greater good of the Egyptian people.

FAWZIA AL ASHMAWI
A Professor of Arabic Language and Islamic Studies at the University of Geneva, Dr. Al Ashmawi has recently been elected to the Executive Committee of the Green Party, working for the promotion of biodiversity and the protection of nature and the environment. She is also involved in two new NGOs connected to the UN in Geneva: The Alliance on Global Concerns, a forum on spirituality and values; and The Geneva

Centre for Human Rights Advancement and Global Dialogue, which seeks to achieve prosperity for all humans.

RANIA A. AL-MASHAT

The recipient of a PhD in Economics from the University of Maryland, College Park, Dr. Al-Mashat started her career at the International Monetary Fund (IMF) in Washington, DC. Between 2005 and 2016, she was Sub-Governor for Monetary Policy at the Central Bank of Egypt (CBE), served as its liaison with IMF and rating agencies, and was recognized among the "50 Most Influential Women in the Egyptian Economy" (2016); the "Young Global Leaders" by the World Economic Forum (2014); and the "Economic Leaders for Tomorrow in Africa" by Institut Choiseul of France (2014 and 2015). In August 2016, she was scheduled to return as an Advisor to the IMF, in Washington, DC.

NAYERA AMIN

A banker for 40 years, 30 of which with Citibank Egypt and North Africa, Ms. Amin holds an MBA in International Business & Marketing from AUC. She has taught banking at AUC, Egyptian universities, the Egyptian Bankers' Association, and the Citibank Training Center. Currently, she is Executive Vice Chair of Piraeus Bank, Egypt (Ahli Bank of Kuwait, Egypt). A recipient of numerous honors and awards from *Forbes* and various business associations, she was recognized in 2016 among "The 50 Most Influential Women in the Egyptian Economy."

MARIE BASSILI ASSAAD

A social scientist and development specialist with 70 years of experience working with marginalized communities, Ms. Assaad dedicated her life to several worthy causes, empowering women and youth, and the garbage collectors' community of Cairo. She also occupied many prestigious posts, including Deputy Secretary General of the World Council of Churches (WCC) in Geneva, the first woman to serve at that level. At the forefront of mainstream policy-making, Ms. Assaad headed the FGM Task Force, and advised individuals and NGOs on development-related issues, even in her golden years. Currently, she continues to enjoy friends and family.

HODA BADRAN

The first Egyptian and the first Arab woman to receive a PhD in Social Welfare, Dr. Badran continued to break new grounds throughout her career. She was the first Chair of the International Committee on the Rights of the Child at the Center for Human Rights in Geneva, and the first Secretary General of the National Council for Childhood and Motherhood in Egypt. For her extensive work on behalf of women and children in her country and beyond, Dr. Badran has received several national and international awards. Additionally, she has authored many publications, both in Arabic and English.

MAYSAA BARAKAT

A professor of Educational Leadership and Research Methodology at Florida Atlantic University, Dr. Barakat has 15 years of experience as school administrator in Egypt and the US. Her research interests and publications include social justice, cultural competence, and educational leadership preparation. Most recently, she has also engaged in international education with a special focus on the Egyptian educational system.

MAGDA EL-NOKALY

Born and raised in cosmopolitan Alexandria, Dr. El-Nokaly (PhD Chemical Engineering) spent most of her career working for P&G in Cincinnati, in the US, and around the world. Her research resulted in numerous global patents and publications in the field of Consumer Goods. After retirement, she returned to live in Cairo tending peacefully her garden and cats: the circle is now complete.

HALA HELMY EL SAID

The Dean of the Faculty of Economics & Political Science, Dr. El Said is also Assistant to the President of Cairo University for Research & External Affairs, and Member of the Board of Directors of the Central Bank of Egypt. Previously, Dr. El Said served as Executive Director of the Egyptian Banking Institute. Additionally, Dr. El Said sits on the boards of several economic and financial research centers, and various NGOs and public service organizations. Dr. El Said is the author of many papers and articles, and is recognized as one the most successful women in Egypt and the region. In 2016, she was selected among the "50 Most Influential Women in the Egyptian Economy."

SAHAR MOHAMED EL SALLAB
Starting her career at Citibank in Cairo and Athens, Ms. El Sallab moved to Chase Manhattan, then to CIB as Vice Chair, Managing Director, and Board Member. Following her experience in the Egyptian government as Deputy Minister of Trade & Industry, she currently serves as Chair of HitekNofal, a family-owned investment company. The recipient of numerous honors and awards, including a 2008 accolade from *Forbes Arabia*, Ms. El Sallab has been consistently ranked among the most powerful and successful Arab businesswomen in the region. Most recently, she has been honored as one of the "50 Most Influential Women in the Egyptian Economy."

NEVEEN HAMDI EL TAHRI
An alumna of both Harvard University and the London Business School, Ms. El Tahri is widely recognized as one of the region's top businesswomen, most recently in 2016 among the "50 Most Influential Women in the Egyptian Economy." Starting her career at Chase Manhattan Bank, she then launched her entrepreneurial journey by establishing numerous financial companies. Ms. El Tahri was the first woman to sit on the board of the Egyptian Stock Exchange, as well as on those of many public and private sector enterprises. Among others, these include the Egyptian Financial Supervisory Board, Orange Mobile Operators, and the Suez Canal Development Zone.

AZZA FAHMY
Listed among Egypt's most influential women, and one of the Middle East most esteemed jewelry designers, Ms. Fahmy travels internationally as a cultural ambassador for her country, and has held more than 200 exhibitions throughout the world. In 2013, she partnered wtih the Alchimia Contemporary Design School in Florence to establish the Design Studio by Azza Fahmy, aiming at educating and equipping aspiring designers. Currently, Ms. Fahmy is a Board Member of the Dubai Design and Fashion Council, and she works with the Bahraini government on vocational training and know-how.

SAFAA ABDEL SAMIE FOUDA

A chemical engineer, Dr. Fouda spent most of her career as a research scientist with Natural Resources Canada, in the area of clean fuels. She is actively involved in cross cultural interfaith peace building, and community charitable work in her city of Ottawa, where she currently chairs the Christian Muslim Dialogue Group. Dr. Fouda's activities have earned her many honors and awards, including Queen Elizabeth Diamond Jubilee Medal (2012), and the Mayor City Builder Award (2015). She was recently invited as guest speaker at the 12th Doha Conference on Interfaith Dialogue, in Qatar (2016). Dr. Fouda is married, and has two daughters and four grandchildren.

MAHASSEN MALAK GHOBRIAL

A Fellow of the Royal College of Physicians and Surgeons of Canada, and a Diplomate of the American Board of Pediatrics, Dr. Ghobrial is a community pediatrician who has been in practice for 45 years. She is affiliated with both the Ottawa Hospital and the Children's Hospital of Eastern Ontario, and has been recognized by both institutions for her years of continued service. Dr. Ghobrial is also a volunteer doctor who participates in the international missions of Health Team International, and the Coptic Medical Association of North America.

NIMET SABA HABACHY

Born and raised in Cairo, Ms. Habachy spent her adult life in the US, where she is a New York based broadcaster with Classical WQXR Radio. She also lectures on opera, and has been a presence at the Metropolitan Opera, the Metropolitan Museum, and other venues. With her sister, Suzan, Ms. Habachy sells in New York the cottage industry products of the garbage sorters of Mokattam Hills in Cairo, the "zabbaleen."

FAYZA HAIKAL

In addition to her ongoing teaching and research at AUC, Dr. Haikal is a member of the Administrative Board of the Grand Egyptian Museum currently under construction in Cairo, and remains very active in Egyptological life. She travels extensively throughout the world to participate in professional congresses, most recently in the Shanghai International Archeological Forum. As a mother and grandmother, she also tries to spend as much time as possible with her children and grandchildren.

AWATEF HAMED

Born in Mansoura and growint up in the Nile Delta, Dr. Hamed is the first woman to head a Department of Aerospace Engineering in the US. Serving 12 years in that capacity, she earned competitive grants totaling more than $ 45 million. Her publications in the areas of gas turbine engines and aircraft propulsion systems include eight books and chapters, and more than 300 articles. In addition to her numerous honors and awards, Dr. Hamed has the unique distinction of being a Fellow of both the American Institute of Aeronautics and Astronautics (AIAA) and the American Society of Mechanical Engineers (ASME).

AZZA HEIKAL

Born and raised in Alexandria, Dr. Heikal was a professor of French literature at Alexandria University, and has taught Egyptian-Arabic language and culture at the Sorbonne and the Institut National des Langues et Civilisations Orientales in Paris. Her research and publications have focused on the cosmopolitan heritage of Alexandria, and she remains actively involved in strengthening Franco-Egyptian relations. She is often a guest speaker on these topics at public events throughout France, Europe, North America, and Egypt. Dr. Heikal and her husband Farouk Amoudi have two children and four grandchildren.

HEDAYAT ISLAM

Upon completing her studies at New York School of Interior Design, Ms. Islam returned to Cairo to work as an interior designer while undertaking a Master's in Islamic Art and Architecture at AUC. In 2000, she partnered with Dina El Khachab to establish Eklego Design. Together, they successfully completed more than 180 projects throughout Egypt and the region. Additionally, they designed and manufactured their own furniture collection, featured in various international publications. In 2015, Ms. Islam relocated to London and launched Jam Space, with its own line of fabrics and wallpapers, and an interior design consultancy service.

FATENN MOSTAFA KANAFANI

Born in Cairo and raised in Europe, Ms. Kanafani attended classes in Art History parallel to her graduate studies in Economics at Webster University in Vienna. She is the founder of ArtTalks|Egypt, a leading Cairo-based art space dedicated to the promotion of emerging local talent, and the management of selective estates of late Egyptian artists. During her 15 years of international corporate management experience, she served as Marketing Director at PepsiCo and P&G in Egypt and Austria, and as Senior Member of the Executive Committee of Al-Ahram Beverages Company. Together with her Egyptian-Palestinian husband, Hakam Kanafani, they have three children.

SEHEIR KANSOUH

International expert in strategic planning for development and gender, Ms. Kansouh studied French Literature at Cairo University, before shifting to Political Science for graduate studies at the American University in Cairo. As a Research Fellow at Ohio State University, she focused on the relationship between system and social dynamics. Ms. Kansouh spent most of her career at UNDP Cairo handling the regional portfolio, and became Policy Team Leader of the United Nations Resident Coordinator System. Her outstanding contribution to Human Development was presented by UNDP as Best Practice to the 1995 World Social Summit in Copenhagen, and earned her several national and international awards.

MADIHA EL MEHELMY KOTB

A mechanical engineer with degrees from Concordia University in Montreal, Ms. Kotb is a Fellow of the American Society of Mechanical Engineers (ASME), and the first non-US citizen to serve as its President (2013-14). During a 35-year career with the Government of Quebec, her responsibilities involved public safety, and development of regulations, codes, and standards. For her considerable role, she has received numerous certificates, awards, and peer recognitions. The most recent is the National Board Safety Medal (2016), which honors her distinguished career and notable contributions to public safety.

CAROLINE MAHER
An HR Manager at the Peugeot Company in Cairo, Ms. Maher is the youngest manager on board. Additionally, she is an international Taekwondo Referee, and an HR Consultant for HELM, a non-profit NGO for people with disabilities. In early 2016, she became the youngest member to be appointed to the Egyptian Parliament by President Abdel Fattah El Sisi. As she aspires to make the world a better place, and to serve as a role model for women of her generation, Ms. Maher tries to fulfill her many obligations responsibly and honorably.

MONA MAKRAM EBEID
A graduate of Harvard University who has taught at AUC and currently teaches at the Arab Academy for Science and Technology and Maritime Transportation, Dr. Makram Ebeid is preparing to offer an MA course at Abu Dhabi Sorbonne University, in UAE. As a former Parliamentarian and Senator who has traveled around the world and participated in innumerable conferences and political meetings, she enjoys sharing her experiences with students. The most recent of her many honors are the Woman of the Year Award from the Amadeus Organization of Morocco, and the Legion of Honor from the Government of France.

HELENE MOUSSA
The author of numerous articles and books in the areas of education, social work, international development, refugee women, and more recently Coptic Art and Icons, Dr. Moussa has taught at universities in Egypt, Canada, and Ethiopia where she was Dean of the School of Social Work. Additionally, she served at the World Council of Churches in Geneva, as Executive Secretary for Uprooted People in the Middle East, Asia, and the Pacific Islands. Currently, Dr. Moussa is the Curator of St. Mark's Coptic Museum in Scarborough, Ontario, Canada.

NAGLA NADOURI NIAZY
After receiving the PhD in Physical Chemistry from the University of Pennsylvania, Dr. Niazy held teaching and research positions in US universities and industrial companies. Upon returning to Egypt in the 1990s, she taught at AUC and consulted for industrial waste water treatment plants. As a member of the

Board of Directors of an NGO for environmental protection, she participates in projects dealing with environmental education and awareness training. Currently, she lives in Alexandria, and continues to be involved in efforts to find solutions to the environmental problems of her hometown.

SONIA ABADIR RAMZI

The recipient of a PhD from the University of Paris la Sorbonne, Dr. Ramzi is the first Egyptian and the first African with a key role at UNESCO, where she was instrumental in the promotion of the Women's Program, and the World Cultural Heritage. Currently, she consults with countries committed to preserving their natural and cultural heritage, and presides over the international association *Les amis des musées d'Egypte*. Her long list of accolades includes awards from Laval University (Canada) and the Valencia Polytechnic Institute (Spain), as well as the title of Ambassador of Peace bestowed upon her by China.

MONA RISK

After graduating with a Bachelor's degree in Pharmacy from Alexandria University, Dr. Risk received a PhD in Chemistry from the University of Cincinnati. As a new immigrant in the US, she worked hard to establish herself and become an environmental company executive. Exhausted by her hectic schedule, she took an early retirement to write romance novels. With more than twenty books published, she reached the enviable status of *New York Times* and *USA Today* Best Selling Author. A resident of Florida, Dr. Risk continues to write while traveling or babysitting her grandchildren.

FAIZA WAHBY SHEREEN

A Professor of English at California State University (Pomona), Dr. Shereen is actively engaged in international education. Currently, she is developing a research program about the Middle East and North Africa for a Fulbright-Hays grant. Dr. Shereen divides her time between her writing and her children and grandchildren. She and her husband Ahmed Shereen enjoy their home in California and travel frequently to meet up with friends and family around the world.

ABLA SHERIF

Born in Cairo but raised in Alexandria, Dr. Sherif graduated from the English Girls' College and Alexandria University. Upon receiving the PhD from the University of Zürich, she moved to Canada where she started her career in education. Most of her professional life was spent at Algonquin College in Ottawa where she advanced through the administrative ranks to become Chair of the English Department, then Dean of the School of Media and Design, and Director of the International Education Center. Dr. Sherif was instrumental in implementing partnership projects between Canada and South Africa, India, and China.

SUZANNE SPAHI

After studying French Literature and Translation at McGill University in Montreal, Ms. Spahi went on to develop her passion for mosaics, which had started as a hobby years earlier. She founded Mosaikashop in 2003, with support from Mosaika, a company renowned for large scale mosaics. Ms. Spahi exhibits regularly in Italy, in addition to traveling extensively around the world to teach her art and tell the stories behind her mosaic rugs, most recently in Australia, in 2015. Although she resides in Montreal, she is often on a plane to Italy.

SAMIA I. SPENCER

After a brief career in her native Alexandria, Dr. Spencer spent most of her professional life as Professor of French at Auburn University, in Alabama. Her multidisciplinary research and extensive publications have focused on the French Enlightenment, and women and politics in France and Quebec. The many awards she has received include knighting as *Officier dans l'Ordre des Palmes Académiques*, and being appointed as Honorary Consul of France in Alabama. In recognition of her efforts on behalf of Quebec culture, she was inducted in the exclusive *Ordre des Francophones d'Amérique*.

MALAK YOUSSEF TAHER

After completing the BA in Economics at Concordia University in Montreal, Ms. Taher returned to her native Cairo where she founded Flower Power, the first one-stop shop for all floral needs. As an artist passionate about flowers and deeply connected to nature, especially the beautiful Egyptian countryside, she remains the Creative Director and CEO of the chain of stores she has established. In her 30-year career, she has earned a notable reputation for planning special events, especially weddings, and for her large-scale artistic floral creations at Cairo's luxury hotels.

MELANNE VERVEER
Recognized for her leadership in advancing progress for women and girls around the world, Verveer was appointed by President Obama to be the first US Ambassador for Global Women's Issues. Prior to the State Department, she co-founded "Vital Voices Global Partnership," an international NGO that invests in emerging women leaders, where she served as Chair and Co-CEO. Earlier she was Assistant to the President and Chief of Staff in the first Clinton Administration. In all these positions, she has engaged with women in Egypt. Currently, she is Executive Director of Georgetown University's Institute for Women, Peace & Security. Verveer is co-author of *FAST FORWARD: How Women Can Achieve Power & Purpose* (NY: Houghton Mifflin Harcourt, 2015).

HIND WASSEF
With degrees in Political Science and English & Comparative Literature from AUC, Ms. Wassef worked in social research with an Egyptian women's NGO, and taught at AUC. Then, with sister Nadia, she co-authored *Daughters of the Nile* (AUC Press, 2001), a photo archive of the Egyptian feminist movement. A year later, they co-founded Diwan bookstores, where she continues to chair the Board of Directors.

NADIA WASSEF
In 2002, Nadia and her sister Hind co-founded Diwan, a small bookstore in Cairo. Over the following 14 years, it grew into Egypt's leading chain, currently with 10 branches. Ms. Wassef has been on *Forbes Magazine*'s "The 200 Most Powerful Women in the Middle East" for two years running. She holds two M.A. degrees, one in Social Anthropology from the School of Oriental and African Studies, University of London, and another in English & Comparative Literature from AUC. She is currently working on a third degree in Creative Writing at Birkbeck, University of London.

LOULA ABOUSEIF ZAKLAMA
Born and raised in Egypt, and trained in the US, Ms. Zaklama is a public relations and marketing expert with 50 years of experience in communication. Her clients include the Egyptian government, as well as national and multinational companies. She is the founder and CEO of Rada Research & PR Company, the only one in Egypt specializing in three disciplines: Marketing Research, Public Relations, and Training. Ms. Zaklama considers that "Reputation management" is one of the most important components for success or failure of any entity.

NIHAD BALIGH ZIKRY
Born in Cairo, and educated at the German School, Ambassador Zikry holds degrees in Economics and Political Science from Cairo University, and the Australian National University in Canberra. She served in many capacities at the Ministry of Foreign Affairs, and represented Egypt at numerous national and international conferences, with her last posting as Egypt's Ambassador to Switzerland. Currently, Ambassador Zikry is Director of International Policy Planning at the German University in Cairo.